TAIWAN STUDIES REVISITED

This book examines and reviews some of the key figures in Taiwan Studies to plot the development of the field by revisiting their earlier influential books and bodies of work.

Often autobiographical in detail, each chapter asks the author to discuss the origins of their research and how their engagement with the field has developed since. The contributors then discuss their methodologies, fieldwork and arguments, as well as how their work was received at the time. They also go on to reflect on their chosen methods and core findings, assessing whether they have stood the test of time. Reflecting the diversity of the Taiwan Studies field, subjects covered in this volume include sociology, musicology, linguistics, comparative politics, international relations and anthropology. As such, this comprehensive overview adopts a distinctly interdisciplinary approach to understanding Taiwan.

Painting a picture of the changing state of international Taiwan Studies through the work of leading scholars, this book will be invaluable to students and scholars of Taiwan Studies, Chinese Studies and Asian politics, culture and society.

Dafydd Fell is the Reader in Comparative Politics with special reference to Taiwan at the Department of Politics and International Studies of the School of Oriental and African Studies (SOAS), University of London. He is also the Director of the SOAS Centre of Taiwan Studies.

Hsin-Huang Michael Hsiao is the Adjunct Research Fellow of the Institute of Sociology, in Academia Sinica, Taiwan and Chair Professor of Hakka Studies, National Central University. He is also the chairman of both Taiwan-Asia Exchange Foundation (TAEF) and the Executive Committee of Center for Southeast Asian Studies (CSEAS), National Chengchi University.

ROUTLEDGE RESEARCH ON TAIWAN SERIES

The *Routledge Research on Taiwan Series* seeks to publish quality research on all aspects of Taiwan studies. Taking an interdisciplinary approach, the books will cover topics such as politics, economic development, culture, society, anthropology and history.

This new book series will include the best possible scholarship from the social sciences and the humanities and welcomes submissions from established authors in the field as well as from younger authors. In addition to research monographs and edited volumes general works or textbooks with a broader appeal will be considered.

The Series is advised by an international Editorial Board and edited by *Dafydd Fell* of the Centre of Taiwan Studies at the School of Oriental and African Studies.

Series Editor: Dafydd Fell, SOAS, UK

26. A New Era in Democratic Taiwan
Trajectories and Turning Points in Politics and Cross-Strait Relations
Edited by Jonathan Sullivan and Chun-yi Lee

27. Social Movements in Taiwan's Democratic Transition
Linking Activists to the Changing Political Environment
Yun Fan

28. Positioning Taiwan in a Global Context
Being and Becoming
Edited by Bi-yu Chang and Pei-yin Lin

30. Young Adults in Urban China and Taiwan
Aspirations, Expectations, and Life Choices
Désirée Remmert

31. Taiwan Studies Revisited
Edited by Dafydd Fell and Hsin-Huang Michael Hsiao

For more information about this series, please visit: https://www.routledge.com/asianstudies/series/RRTAIWAN

TAIWAN STUDIES REVISITED

Edited by Dafydd Fell and Hsin-Huang Michael Hsiao

First published 2020
by Routledge
2 Park Square, Milton Park, Abingdon, Oxon OX14 4RN

and by Routledge
52 Vanderbilt Avenue, New York, NY 10017

Routledge is an imprint of the Taylor & Francis Group, an informa business

© 2020 selection and editorial matter, Dafydd Fell and Hsin-Huang Michael Hsiao; individual chapters, the contributors

The right of Dafydd Fell and Hsin-Huang Michael Hsiao to be identified as the authors of the editorial material, and of the authors for their individual chapters, has been asserted in accordance with sections 77 and 78 of the Copyright, Designs and Patents Act 1988.

All rights reserved. No part of this book may be reprinted or reproduced or utilised in any form or by any electronic, mechanical, or other means, now known or hereafter invented, including photocopying and recording, or in any information storage or retrieval system, without permission in writing from the publishers.

Trademark notice: Product or corporate names may be trademarks or registered trademarks, and are used only for identification and explanation without intent to infringe.

British Library Cataloguing in Publication Data
A catalogue record for this book is available from the British Library

Library of Congress Cataloging-in-Publication Data
A catalog record has been requested for this book

ISBN: 978-0-367-20171-5 (hbk)
ISBN: 978-0-367-20172-2 (pbk)
ISBN: 978-0-429-25993-7 (ebk)

Typeset in Bembo
by Taylor & Francis Books
Printed by CPI Group (UK) Ltd, Croydon CR0 4YY

CONTENTS

List of figures	*vii*
List of contributors	*viii*
Acknowledgements	*xiii*

1 Taiwan Studies revisited	1
Dafydd Fell and Hsin-Huang Michael Hsiao	

PART I
1980s–early 1990s   **13**

2 My journey of social movements and civil society research revisited	15
Hsin-Huang Michael Hsiao	
3 *State and Society in the Taiwan Miracle* revisited	34
Thomas B. Gold	
4 Revisiting *Taiwan: China's Last Frontier*	48
Simon Long	

PART II
1990s   **61**

5 Revisiting *Taiwan and Chinese Nationalism: Identity and Status in International Society*	63
Christopher R. Hughes	

vi Contents

6 *Politics in Taiwan: Voting for Democracy* revisited 75
  Shelley Rigger

PART III
2000s towards a golden era 89

7 *In the Name of Harmony and Prosperity* and beyond: Gender and
  labour as a (renewed) research agenda 91
  Anru Lee

8 Tigers on the mountain: Assessing *Is Taiwan Chinese?* in 2018 112
  Melissa J. Brown

9 Healthy democracies and welfare politics in Taiwan: The
  arguments, refinements and limitations 141
  Joseph Wong

10 *Peking Opera and Politics in Taiwan* revisited 160
  Nancy Guy

11 *Party Politics in Taiwan* revisited 178
  Dafydd Fell

12 Writing Taiwanese: Then and now, how, why and who? 197
  Henning Klöter

13 Depoliticizing a structurally politicized society: The importance
  of responsible political agency 215
  Mikael Mattlin

Index *234*

FIGURES

10.1 Cover of the 1981 decree. Jiaoyubu (Ministry of Education). 1981. *Disanci zengding zhunyan guoju jumu* (The third revised and enlarged permitted national opera titles). Taipei: Jiaoyubu Yinfa. 163

10.2 The first seven of fourteen guidelines that preface the 1981 censorship decree. Jiaoyubu (Ministry of Education). 1981. *Disanci zengding zhunyan guoju jumu* (The third revised and enlarged permitted national opera titles). Taipei: Jiaoyubu Yinfa. 164

10.3 Master performer of the *xiaosheng* role type, Kao Hui-lan, in 1993 as Zhou Yu in *The Meeting of Many Heroes* (Qun ying hui). Photo by Lo Te-fen. 170

12.1 The entry 'Tiong-hoâ Bîn-kok' ('Republic of China') in the Holopedia 209

12.2 A Taiwanese campaign ad 211

CONTRIBUTORS

Melissa J. Brown is Managing Editor of the Harvard Journal of Asiatic Studies (HJAS), published by the Harvard-Yenching Institute. She was on the faculty at the University of Cincinnati (1997–2001) and Stanford University (2001–2011) before coming to the Radcliffe Institute for Advanced Studies at Harvard in 2011 and joining the HJAS staff in 2014. Brown's research examines identities and nationalism, marriage and kinship, footbinding, household economies and cosmopolitanism. Her publications include Is Taiwan Chinese? The Impact of Culture, Power, and Migration on Changing Identities (2004), Explaining Culture Scientifically (2008), 'Changing Authentic Identities: Evidence from Taiwan and China' (Journal of the Royal Anthropological Institute 16, 2010), 'Marriage Mobility and Footbinding in Pre-1949 Rural China' (Journal of Asian Studies 71.4, 2012), 'Collective Identities, Shifting Population Membership, and Niche Construction Theory: Implications from Taiwanese and Chinese Empirical Evidence' (in Population in the Human Sciences, Oxford University Press, 2015), 'Dutiful Help: Masking Rural Women's Economic Contributions' (in Transforming Patriarchy, University of Washington Press, 2016) and 'Economic Correlates of Footbinding: Implications for the Economic Importance of Chinese Daughters' (PLoS ONE 13.9, 2018).

Dafydd J. Fell is the Reader in Comparative Politics with special reference to Taiwan at the Department of Politics and International Studies of the School of Oriental and African Studies (SOAS), University of London. He is also the Director of the SOAS Centre of Taiwan Studies. In 2004 he helped establish the European Association of Taiwan Studies. He has published numerous articles on political parties and electioneering in Taiwan. His first book was Party Politics in Taiwan (Routledge, 2005), which analysed party change in the first 15 years of multi-party competition. His second book was Government and Politics in Taiwan

(Rouledge, 2011) and the second edition was published in early 2018. He co-edited Migration to and from Taiwan (Routledge, 2013) and his next edited volume, Social Movements in Taiwan under Ma Ying-jeou (Routledge) was published in 2017. He is also the book series editor for the Routledge Research on Taiwan Series.

Thomas B. Gold is Professor of Sociology at the University of California, Berkeley, where he has taught since 1981. He also served as Associate Dean of International and Area Studies and Chair of the Center for Chinese Studies at Berkeley. From 2000 to 2016 he was Executive Director of the Inter-University Program in Chinese Language Studies. Tom became interested in China as an undergraduate at Oberlin College. After graduating he taught English at Tunghai University in Taiwan. He then received a Masters in Regional Studies-East Asia and a PhD in Sociology, both from Harvard University. In February 1979, while at Harvard he was a member of the first group of American exchange students to study in China, spending a year at Fudan University in Shanghai. Professor Gold's research focuses on many aspects of the societies of East Asia, primarily Taiwan and mainland China. In the largest sense, he examines the process of the emergence of the increasingly empowered and autonomous individual and a private sphere in authoritarian societies. Specific topics include youth, civil society, guanxi, micro-scale private business, popular culture and identity. His book, State and Society in the Taiwan Miracle (1986) is a standard work in the field. He continues to research social change in Taiwan since the end of Martial Law in 1987.

Nancy Guy is an ethnomusicologist whose scholarly interests include the musics of Taiwan and China, varieties of opera (both European and Chinese), music and politics and the ecocritical study of music. Her first book, Peking Opera and Politics in Taiwan (University of Illinois Press, 2005) won the ASCAP Béla Bartók Award for Excellence in Ethnomusicology and was also named an 'Outstanding Academic Title for 2006' by Choice. Guy's second book, The Magic of Beverly Sills, focuses on the artistry and appeal of the beloved American coloratura soprano (University of Illinois Press, 2015). Her article, 'Flowing down Taiwan's Tamsui River: Towards an Ecomusicology of the Environmental Imagination', (Ethnomusicology, 2009) is a foundational text in the emergent field of ecomusicology and was awarded the 2010 Rulan Chao Pian Publication Prize. Guy is a Professor of Music at the University of California, San Diego.

Hsin-Huang Michael Hsiao is the Adjunct Research Fellow of the Institute of Sociology, in Academia Sinica and Chair Professor of Hakka Studies, National Central University. He is also the chairman of both Taiwan-Asia Exchange Foundation (TAEF) and the Executive Committee of Center for Southeast Asian Studies (CSEAS), National Chengchi University. He has served as a Senior Advisor to the President of Taiwan since 2016. His areas of specialisation include: middle class, civil society and democratisation in Asia; environmental movements, sustainability and risk society; and comparative Hakka studies in Taiwan and Southeast Asia. His most recent publications are: Middle Class, Civil Society and Democracy in Asia (ed., Routledge, 2019); China's Footprints in Southeast Asia (co-editor, National University of Singapore Press, 2018); Social Welfare Movements and Policy Impacts in Taiwan: 2000–2018 (in Chinese, co-editor, Chu-Liu Book Company, 2018); Urban Climate Issues and Governance in Taiwan (in Chinese, co-editor, National Taiwan University Press, 2017); Comparing the Hakka Ethnic Identity in Taiwan and Southeast Asia (in Chinese, editor, National Central University Press, 2017); Citizens, Civil Society and Heritage-Making in Asia (co-editor, ISEAS/ Academia Sinica / IIAS, 2017); Youth and Social Change in Taiwan and Hong Kong (in Chinese, co-editor, The Chinese Univ. of Hong Kong, 2016).

Christopher R. Hughes is Professor of International Relations at the London School of Economics and Political Science (LSE), where he also served as Director of the Asia Research Centre from 2002 to 2005. His PhD (from the LSE) was on the topic 'Taiwan and Chinese Nationalism: National Identity and Status in International Society' and was awarded the British International Studies Association best thesis of the year prize for 1995. He teaches specialist courses in the International Politics of the Asia Pacific, Chinese Foreign and Security Policy and Foreign Policy Analysis. His research focuses on the Asia-Pacific with special reference to Chinese foreign policy and politics, with monographs on Taiwan and Chinese Nationalism (Routledge 1997), China and the Internet: Politics of the Digital Leap Forward (edited with Gudrun Wacker, Routledge 2003) and Chinese Nationalism in the Global Era (Routledge 2006). He has various articles on Chinese politics and foreign policy, the international politics of the Asia Pacific, international relations theory and foreign policy in leading academic journals.

Henning Klöter is Professor of Modern Chinese Languages and Literatures at the Humboldt University of Berlin. He has previously held positions at the universities of Göttingen, Mainz, Bochum and National Taiwan Normal University. His major publications are Written Taiwanese (2005) and The Language of the Sangleys: A Chinese Vernacular in Missionary Documents of the Seventeenth Century (2011). His current research is concerned with the social meanings and the cultural manifestations of language variation and multilingualism in the sinophone world.

Anru Lee is a faculty member at the Anthropology Department, John Jay College of Criminal Justice, the City University of New York. She is the author of In the Name of Harmony and Prosperity: Labor and Gender Politics in Taiwan's Economic Restructuring (2004) and is co-editor of Women in the New Taiwan: Gender Roles and Gender Consciousness in a Changing Society (ME Sharpe, 2004). Her current project investigates urban public transit systems as related to issues of technology, governance and citizenship. Her most recent fieldwork looks at the Mass Rapid Transit (MRT) systems in Taipei and Kaohsiung, the two largest cities in Taiwan, in the context of the country's struggle for cultural and national identity. Her articles on this subject include: 'Subways as a Space of Cultural Intimacy', 'Place-Making, Mobility, and Identity: The Politics and Poetics of Urban Mass Rapid Systems in Taiwan' and 'Gender, Everyday Mobility, and Mass Transit in Urban Asia'.

Simon Long is a journalist at The Economist, where he has worked since 1995, as Asia editor, International editor, Finance and Economics editor, South-East Asia correspondent, South Asia bureau chief and author of 'Banyan''', a weekly column on Asian affairs. He is the author of 'Taiwan: China's Last Frontier' (1991) and of numerous articles, papers and chapters on Asian affairs. He spent nine years with the BBC, as an analyst on East Asian affairs based in London, as Beijing correspondent from 1989–1991, including during the Tiananmen protests and their suppression, and Hong Kong correspondent from 1993. In Beijing and Hong Kong, he was concurrently correspondent for the Guardian newspaper and writer for many other outlets. He was for a number of years the author of Economist Intelligence Unit country reports on China, Taiwan and Hong Kong. In an earlier seven-year career as an investment banker, with Morgan Grenfell, he worked in London and Singapore, rising to a position of responsibility for the banking division's Asian business.

Mikael Mattlin is a Professor in the University of Helsinki. He also holds a Collegium Researcher position at the Turku Institute for Advanced Studies (TIAS). Professor Mattlin is Associate Fellow in the European Research Centre for Contemporary Taiwan (ERCCT), University of Tübingen, as well as Non-resident Research Fellow at the China Policy Institute (CPI), Nottingham University. He also runs the Helsinki-based Foundation for Foreign Policy Research. Professor Mattlin's most recent book Politicized Society: Taiwan's Struggle with Its One-Party Past was published in April 2018. The book is a revised and expanded second edition of his acclaimed 2011 book. His peer-reviewed journal articles have appeared in The China Quarterly, Cooperation and Conflict, Journal of Contemporary China, Simulation & Gaming, Issues and Studies, Asia-Europe Journal, East Asia and China Perspectives.

Shelley Rigger is the Brown Professor of East Asian Politics and Chair of Chinese Studies at Davidson College. She has a PhD in Government from Harvard University and a BA in Public and International Affairs from Princeton University. She has been a visiting researcher at National Chengchi University in Taiwan (2005) and a visiting professor at Fudan University (2006) and Shanghai Jiaotong University (2013 & 2015). She is a non-resident fellow of the China Policy Institute at Nottingham University and a senior fellow of the Foreign Policy Research Institute (FPRI). She is also a director of The Taiwan Fund, a closed-end investment fund specialising in Taiwan-listed companies. Rigger is the author of two books on Taiwan's domestic politics, Politics in Taiwan: Voting for Democracy (Routledge xii List of contributors

1999) and From Opposition to Power: Taiwan's Democratic Progressive Party (2001). In 2011 she published Why Taiwan Matters: Small Island, Global Powerhouse, a book for general readers. She has published articles on Taiwan's domestic politics, the national identity issue in Taiwan–China relations and related topics. Her monograph, Taiwan's Rising Rationalism: Generations, Politics and 'Taiwan Nationalism', was published by the East West Center in Washington in November 2006. She is working on a study of Taiwan's contributions to the PRC's economic take-off and a study of Taiwanese youth.

Joseph Wong is the Ralph and Roz Halbert Professor of Innovation at the Munk School of Global Affairs and Public Policy, University of Toronto, where he is also Professor of Political Science. Wong held the Canada Research Chair in health, democracy and development for two full terms, ending in 2016. Professor Wong is the author of several books, including Healthy Democracies: Welfare Politics in Taiwan and South Korea and Betting on Biotech: Innovation and the Limits of Asia's Developmental State, both published by Cornell University Press. He is currently working on a book with Dan Slater on democracy and development in Asia. Professor Wong is also leading a large-scale project on poverty reduction in low and middle income countries. Professor Wong is the Associate Vice President and Vice Provost, International Student Experience, University of Toronto.

ACKNOWLEDGEMENTS

Putting together an edited volume is never easy and this was the most challenging such project we have managed so far. It led Fell to say more than once, 'I will never do another edited volume.' It took almost four years from the first panel presentations in 2015 to the submission of the final manuscript. At times we both wondered whether we would ever get this book published. But in the end we made it!

There are many people and organisations we need to thank for making it possible to finish this book project. First of all we need to thank our wonderful team of authors. Some of them submitted their chapters ready for review very early, and we are grateful that they remained patient with us as we struggled to get enough further chapters for a full book. We are also grateful to those authors who joined at a later stage and fully embraced our idea of revisiting their early works. We do apologise to you all for so many nagging emails over the last few years.

The book project started out with two panels at the Second World Congress of Taiwan Studies back in June 2015. This was a collaborative conference co-organised by the Secretariat of the World Congress of Taiwan Studies (WCTS) in Academia Sinica and the SOAS Centre of Taiwan Studies (CTS). The conference was partially supported as part of a CTS three-year Taiwan Studies research grant from Taiwan's Ministry of Foreign Affairs. We would like to thank our colleagues at the Taipei Representative Office in the United Kingdom for their support since the establishment of the SOAS Taiwan Programme back in 1999. We sincerely would like to thank the fantastic CTS colleagues Chang Bi-yu, Jewel Lo, Niki Alsford and the amazing team of student volunteers (class of 2014–2015) for making the conference such a success. The same warm appreciation goes to Ginger Chiang and Susana Wang of the Secretariat of the WCTS in Academia Sinica.

When it looked like the project would fail due to a shortage of chapters we were saved by creating the Taiwan Studies Revisited Lecture Series at SOAS, where authors gave standalone lectures and then revised these into book chapters. The lectures by Thomas Gold, Nancy Guy, Christopher Hughes, Anru Lee, Simon Long and Shelley Rigger have been some of the most popular events at the SOAS Centre of Taiwan Studies in recent years.

Apart from Chang Bi-yu and Jewel Lo, we would like to thank the organisational support of colleagues Laura Ritchie-Roberts and Huang Chia-yuan in this lecture series. Fell was especially heartened when on asking Laura on her last day at SOAS about her favourite event, she chose Simon Long's lecture in the revisited series. Another individual we would like to thank is the SOAS undergraduate student Rhitik Jassar who worked on transcribing Rigger's lecture. A number of these lectures were videoed by Ms Jewel Lo and can be viewed on the SOAS Taiwan Studies YouTube channel.

1

TAIWAN STUDIES REVISITED

Dafydd Fell and Hsin-Huang Michael Hsiao

A number of developments suggest that we are now witnessing a golden age of international Taiwan Studies (Fell 2017, Schubert 2017, Rawnsley 2017) in both Taiwan and in the world. This stands in stark contrast to the situation when we began studying Taiwan. At that time there was not yet really a sense of Taiwan Studies as a field, but instead Taiwan was often regarded as a marginal topic on the edge of Chinese Studies. While Fell (2008, 5) described Europe as a 'Taiwan Studies desert' in the late 1990s, there has been a remarkable transformation of the field over the last two decades. There has been a rapid expansion in the numbers of active Taiwan Studies programmes in overseas universities. There has also been a proliferation of Taiwan focused courses at European and American universities, with University of Texas at Austin and SOAS University of London standing out with their Taiwan Studies degree programmes (Chang and Fell 2019). Another important development has been the institutionalisation of conference organisations such as the North American Association of Taiwan Studies, the European Association of Taiwan Studies and the Japanese Association for Taiwan Studies. Another more recent breakthrough has been the three World Congresses of Taiwan Studies (2012, 2015 and 2018) initiated by Academia Sinica, Taiwan. There are also numerous promising signs in the realm of publications, with a number of active Taiwan Studies book series created after 2000 and the establishment of the *International Journal of Taiwan Studies* in 2018.

In the mid to late 1980s academic books on Taiwan in English were quite rare. Shelley Rigger's (2002: 53) early review article found that only one or two English language books were being published per year on Taiwan's politics in the mid to late 1980s. From 1989 though there was a progressive increase in the numbers of books being published on Taiwan's politics, rising to a peak of almost 20 per year in 1999. Since Rigger's article was published the expansion in Taiwan Studies books and journal publications has continued with the Routledge Research on

Taiwan and Harrassowitz Studia Formosiana series playing key roles. Ten years after Rigger's review, Jonathan Sullivan (2011) returned to update the state of the field in a number of articles, including one with the provocative title: 'Is Taiwan Studies in Decline?' Although his methodology was different from Rigger's, his conclusions were similar on the health of the field. We also found similar optimistic results in a journal special edition collection of state of the field essays published in the newly launched *International Journal of Taiwan Studies* (Hsiao and Fell 2018).

In this book we propose an alternative way of plotting the development of the Taiwan Studies field by asking authors to revisit their earlier influential books or bodies of work. Generally we asked authors to revisit their earlier works at least ten years after the original publications. To a certain degree the chapters are autobiographical as authors discuss not only what sparked their initial research interest but also how their academic careers within the field have developed since their initial books hit the book stores.

In each case we asked the authors to address a number of themes in their chapters. First, we wanted to get a sense of the origins of their research projects and how they conducted the research design. Then they discuss the methodologies and sometimes the fieldwork they adopted to answer their core research questions. Next they briefly discuss the main findings and arguments in their respective books. Where the books had been reviewed we asked authors to outline how the books were reviewed by the critics and how they now feel about these reviews today?

Similarly we wanted the authors to reflect on how they feel about the methods and findings now. Has the study stood the test of time? Would they do anything differently if they could turn back the clock? We were also curious about what the authors did after these influential volumes. Have they continued studying the topic since and if so what are they doing differently? How have they built on their earlier studies? Have they moved into different research areas or are they still in the shadow of their earlier work?

We have selected books and published works that cut across key time periods in the development of the Taiwan Studies field. The chapters in the first part come from an era when English language academic publications on Taiwan were quite sparse. The earliest works revisited in our volume is the body of work by Michael Hsiao in Chapter 2. He revisits his early research on Taiwan's civil society and social movements that began in the last decade of martial law and has continued since. Unlike the other chapters, Hsiao is revisiting a body of work that mainly consists of journal articles and book chapters. In the next chapter sociologist Thomas Gold revisits his 1986 volume *State and Society in the Taiwan Miracle*. In the book Gold reviews Taiwan's development experience up to the mid-1980s, stressing the role of the state, but predicting that the political system would soon undergo major changes. The importance of Gold's book is seen in Rigger's (2002: 50) description of it as a classic 'that awakened the field'. While Hsiao's chapter stands out for revisiting a body of work rather than a book, Chapter 4 is the only one not written by an academic but a journalist, Simon Long. Although Long's book *Taiwan: China's Last Frontier* was published in 1991, it was mainly written in 1989. Writing for a wider audience, Long paints a vivid picture of Taiwan's political scene as it was undergoing radical transformations both in its domestic and external politics in the mid to late 1980s.

In contrast, the chapters in the second part are from a time when the idea of Taiwan Studies as a field was starting to develop in the 1990s, particularly in Taiwan as well as North America. In the United States, it was during this period that the ME Sharpe Taiwan in the Modern World series reached its peak of book publications and the Taiwan Studies organisations began to be established, such as the North American Association of Taiwan Studies and Conference Group on Taiwan Studies at the American Political Science Association. Coming out in 1997, Christopher Hughes's *Taiwan and Chinese Nationalism: National Identity and Status in International Society* was an important milestone for European Taiwan Studies. It was one of the first social science monographs on Taiwan published in Europe and would have a profound impact not only on the study of nationalism in Taiwan but also on promoting academic interest on Taiwan. The political scientist Jonathan Sullivan (2016) describes how as an undergraduate he found the book in the Leeds University Library and how this was the 'book that got me hooked on Taiwan'. Then in Chapter 6 Shelley Rigger revisits her popular 1999 book *Politics in Taiwan: Voting for Democracy*. This book was both groundbreaking in its overview of electoral politics in Taiwan but also made an important contribution to understanding Taiwan's liberalisation and democratisation processes.

The books in the third part are from what could be viewed as the golden era of Taiwan Studies, when the field expands to see Europe also become a new hub for English publications in Taiwan Studies. Key developments include the creation of three Europe based book series, large numbers of Taiwan programmes were established in European universities and of course the European Association of Taiwan Studies was first established and soon became institutionalised.

The first three books in this section were all published in 2004. First the anthropologist Anru Lee revisits her book *In the Name of Harmony and Prosperity*. Using fieldwork in sunset industry factories in Central Taiwan, her beautiful book examines changing gender and labour politics at a time when Taiwan was going through economic restructuring. Next in Chapter 8 Melissa Brown looks back on her influential book *Is Taiwan Chinese? The Impact of Culture, Power and Migration on Changing Identities*. We can get a sense of the impact of her book from the fact that the journal *Issues and Studies* decided in late 2004 to publish a book review roundtable featuring eight of the leading scholars in the field as well as Brown herself (*Issues and Studies* book review roundtable 2004). A recent study of Taiwan related courses in the United States found that it is the third most used textbook (Hsieh and Wang 2018). The third book revisited from 2004 is Joseph Wong's *Healthy Democracies: Welfare Politics in Taiwan and South Korea*. This study shows the transformative effect of democratisation on welfare system development in these two new democracies in East Asia.

4 Dafydd Fell and Hsin-Huang Michael Hsiao

Next we revisit three books that were published in 2005. First, in Chapter 10 Nancy Guy discusses her multi-prize winning *Peking Opera and Politics in Taiwan*. Guy's study uses the case of opera to reveal the intimate relationship between political change and cultural policy in Taiwan. This is followed by Fell's first book *Party Politics in Taiwan: Party Change and the Democratic Evolution of Taiwan, 1991–2004*. The volume examines how and why Taiwan's parties changed ideologically in the first decade and a half of multi-party democracy. Like Wong, Fell came to quite positive conclusions on the health of Taiwan's democracy. The third book from 2005 is Henning Klöter's *Writing Taiwanese*. The book focuses on the how, why and who questions concerning the writing of the Taiwanese or Hokkien language. In other words, it looks at how the Taiwanese language has been written in the past and present, what has been the ideology behind different writing systems, and the people or groups behind these systems. First published in 2011, Mikael Mattlin's *Politicized Society: The Long Shadow of One-Party Legacy* is the newest book revisited in our collection and also the only one with a fully revised second edition (Mattlin 2018). Like a number of the other books revisited here, Mattlin looks at post democratic transition Taiwan but argues that the roots of the country's intense politicization lie in the incomplete dismantling of the old one-party state.

To be honest, selecting which books to be revisited was not an easy task. The foremost criteria were to select books that have been popular and influential over the last three decades. In fact five of the books revisited here are among the ten listed by Sullivan (2016) in his review essay on the best academic publications on Taiwan's politics.[1] The books have also been widely used for Taiwan-related teaching courses, such as those at SOAS. There was also a personal element to the selection. For one of us editors (Fell), the books by Gold and Long were among the first he ever read on Taiwan as an undergraduate trying to find enough English language material to write a dissertation on Taiwan. Lee's research also had a major impact on him. The first time he heard her presenting her research, which would be the basis of her book, was a critical moment that helped inspire him to start his own doctoral studies on Taiwan. The books by Hughes and Rigger were highly influential on him during his own PhD research. He can still recall sitting all day in Caves Book Store (敦煌書局) in Kaohsiung to read Hughes' book as at the time the price of NT$3,000 seemed exorbitant.

The majority of the books in Part III are from the younger generation of scholars that received their PhDs in the golden era of Taiwan Studies after 2000. Another common feature is that many of the authors have played important roles in promoting the field of Taiwan Studies and have been active participants in international Taiwan Studies. Fell and Klöter, among others, for instance, were driving forces in the early development of the European Association of Taiwan Studies conferences. This contribution includes not only presenting their research but also many of the authors in our volume have been involved in the institutional building of Taiwan Studies outside Taiwan.

The chapters also can give readers a sense of the diversity of the Taiwan Studies field. Academic fields represented include sociology, public policy, musicology, linguistics, comparative politics, international relations, anthropology, migration studies, gender studies and political economy. Moreover, the majority of these revisited books adopt an interdisciplinary approach to understanding Taiwan. For many of us, involvement in Taiwan Studies is a way to break out of the sometimes narrow confines of our own disciplinary worlds. There is also much diversity in terms of the research methods scholars have typically used. Although extensive fieldwork is the basis for the vast majority of the original research, interviews, survey data, archival and content analysis have also been used by some of the authors.

We hope this revisited book will also have practical value to new and established scholars. For instance, many of the books revisited here are based on research originally conducted for doctoral studies. Thus many authors touch upon the experiences of PhD research design as well as turning PhD theses into book manuscripts, the so-called 'dethesisising' process.

The origins of this volume lie in a number of papers given on Taiwan Studies Revisited panels at the Second World Congress of Taiwan Studies that was held at SOAS in June 2015, co-organised by Academia Sinica (Taiwan) and SOAS (UK). However, only the chapters by Wong, Fell, Mattlin and Klöter were first presented at the World Congress. We then followed this up with a number of Taiwan Studies revisited lectures in London, where the speakers were then invited to contribute chapters. Chapter authors who the joined the SOAS Taiwan Studies Revisited Lecture Series were Gold, Lee, Long Hughes, Rigger and Guy.

Research origins

How did we become so passionate about the research that led to these books? For many of us it was the initial experience of visiting Taiwan for study or work that sparked our interest. However, there was often a degree of the accidental in the ultimate decision on the research topic. Gold, Hughes, Fell, Rigger, Brown and Mattlin all returned for doctoral fieldwork after earlier stays in Taiwan. Gold for instance first came to Taiwan in 1969 to study Chinese and later returned to teach English at Tunghai University in the early 1970s. Gold had originally planned to look at a PRC topic. His decision to switch his doctoral focus to Taiwan was influenced by changes in US–China relations and so he ended up following his advisor's suggestion to take Taiwan as his case. Rigger had also planned to do her dissertation on China and specifically on its minority politics; however, this plan had to be dropped following the Tiananmen Incident in 1989. Having previously been in Taiwan as an undergraduate she made the decision to switch her research topic and location. In fact the Tiananmen effect on Taiwan Studies features in a number of chapters. Brown recalls for instance how in the aftermath of Tiananmen it was impossible to get free fieldwork access to rural Chinese villages, so research in Taiwan made sense for an anthropologist.

We also see the accidental nature of the origins of our research interest in cases where some of us actually changed our topics after arriving in Taiwan to start our

6 Dafydd Fell and Hsin-Huang Michael Hsiao

fieldwork! For instance, Guy arrived planning to research the composition and performance of newly written Peking opera but found that as a result of political changes her 'dissertation topic had basically evaporated'. Instead she shifted her focus to how political policy had affected Peking opera in Taiwan. Lee states how she came to Taiwan for fieldwork in the mid-1990s with an interest in gender and the global economy and planned to research the conditions of laid-off female factory workers. However, on discovering the challenges of finding a systematic set of interviewees, she had to radically change her approach and topic. Instead it was the chance introduction to a boss of a textile factory in Changhua County that led her to what would be her fieldwork location for the next two and a half years. This was where she would go on to develop her research on how traditional family culture and the developmentalist discourse shape the lives of Taiwanese women workers.

A common thread in a number of chapters is how Chinese Studies in the UK almost completely ignored Taiwan compared with the United States, where going to Taiwan for language training was much more common. Hughes, Fell and Long recall the lack of discussion of Taiwan in their courses. Despite being a Cambridge Chinese graduate, Long first became interested in Taiwan through work first as a banker and then a journalist for the BBC and Economist Intelligence Unit in the 1980s. We again see the accidental nature of the origins of research interest in Fell's chapter, as originally he had been due to do language training in Beijing but due to the Tiananmen Incident most UK universities switched to sending their students to Taiwan. That initial experience of studying Chinese in Taiwan when the country was going through a slow transition away from authoritarianism was critical for Hughes and Fell in sparking their research interest. Unfortunately, the majority of UK universities soon switched back to sending their Chinese language students to the PRC rather than Taiwan.

In a number of cases our authors had been in Taiwan for their graduate studies and wanted to then study the country in greater depth. Mattlin for instance describes the feeling that during his three months researching in Taiwan for his MA thesis he was just 'scratching the surface of understanding Taiwanese politics'. Similarly, Klöter talks of how when he was an exchange student at National Taiwan University, a course reading sparked his interest in the topic of written Taiwanese.

From PhD to book manuscript

With the exceptions of the chapters by Hsiao and Long, all our books are to a greater or lesser extent based on our PhD dissertation research. In fact even Long's book went through a similar revision process, though in that case his equivalent starting point was an Economist Intelligence Unit special report on Taiwan (Long 1989). However, the degree of revisions and adjustments in the 'dethesisising' process varied significantly.

In some cases, such as Klöter's *Written Taiwanese*, there were only limited revisions involved in the thesis to book transition. Since there was often a gap between the completion of the PhD and the book publication, a number of the books needed some updating. For instance, Fell needed to add a new chapter to cover the four years between the end of his fieldwork in 2001 and the completion of the manuscript in 2004. The time our authors took over the revision process also saw much variation. In the cases of Fell's and Long's conversion they were able to complete the process in just over a month. Long describes the process as 'the most intense and grueling exercise in "churning in out" I have ever endured'. In contrast, most authors spent at least a year on their conversion. Brown talks of the difficulties in writing in the midst of challenging early post PhD years as an academic and becoming a mother. In fact many high quality PhDs never get published as new graduates are under so much pressure in teaching new courses, university administration work, as well as the need to get their early publications out. In these circumstances, it can be very hard to find the time needed to complete a book manuscript, and instead many have concentrated on journal articles.

The requirements for a PhD dissertation are quite different from those of academic monographs. In fact, most academic publishers will no longer send unrevised PhD dissertations for peer reviews with a view to being published. Unsurprisingly, in a number of chapters we hear how publishers tried to steer the direction of the revised manuscript. Academic publishers are also looking for ways to reach a broader readership. Two of the most common requests are to reduce the footnotes and to remove the literature or theoretical overview chapter. Brown explained how this posed a dilemma as she needed to get the book published but omitting a theoretical chapter could undermine her job prospects in anthropology departments. While Fell chose to integrate his theoretical discussions into the other chapters, Brown's solution was to place the theory chapter at the end of the book.

Of all the books reviewed here, the one that probably had the greatest degree of change from the PhD dissertation was that by Gold. In this case though he had originally planned to publish a revised version of his dissertation, his publisher encouraged him to transform his historical chapter into a stand-alone manuscript. He recalls his frustration at not being able to bring in enough of the original rich detail of his dissertation into the book. Rigger also recalls similar pressure to broaden her book's appeal. She notes how while today it would be possible to publish a book on Taiwan's local politics, she was strongly advised against this back in the mid-1990s. Her solution was to shift the focus to offering a detailed account of Taiwan's democratic transition. However, as she admits, there are some chapters that are closer to her dissertation focus on local politics, clientelism and electoral systems. In a similar vein, Brown recalls how she was pressured to change her book's title to include China or Chinese in order to make it more marketable.

Linking our work to social science theories and ongoing debates

Rigger has argued that Taiwan is attractive to many scholars as it 'offers a manageable testing ground for a vast array of social science theories' (Rigger 2002: 53–54). The desire to both engage with and contribute to theoretical debates is another of

8 Dafydd Fell and Hsin-Huang Michael Hsiao

the common themes in our revisited chapters. This linkage with theory has been critical for how we have enabled our research to reach wider audiences and for our career development. For example, Hsiao's recent work on Taiwan's tripartite linkage of the middle class, civil society and democracy making is placing the Taiwan case study in the wider context of Asia's democratic transformation experiences. He further demonstrates that Taiwan Studies can contribute to regional as well as global theorising in social sciences.

One of the theoretical themes that features in many of our chapters is democracy and democratisation. Rigger, Hsiao and Fell all engage in the debates over how best to explain democratisation. While Rigger stresses the role of authoritarian era elections as a driving force for democratisation, Hsiao has focused on the roles of civil society and progressive middle class and Fell stresses the role of party competition. In other chapters, democracy has been treated instead more as an independent variable for change. For instance, Guy shows the transformative effect of democratisation on the fate of the once heavily subsidized Peking opera in Taiwan. Similarly, Hughes shows the impact of democratisation on debates over nationalism in Taiwan. Wong takes a comparative approach to argue that democratisation not only led to the initial establishment of universal health insurance in Taiwan and South Korea but also the deepening of their welfare states.

A number of our books also engage in the debate over how to assess the quality of democracy, a topic that has received growing attention in the comparative politics field as the numbers of democratic transitions have dried up. Fell and Wong both come to positive conclusions on the health of Taiwan's democracy. In contrast Mattlin argues that Taiwan's democracy is threatened by intense politicization and claims that a key reason was that its very gradual democratic transition left much of the old one party state intact.

Book reviews

Academics are often very sensitive to how their work is reviewed both in the cases of blind peer review but also book reviews. We often take criticism personally. However, we thought it would be interesting to see how our authors reflect on the book reviews after the passage of time.

A number of the authors in the book reflect on how they attempted to address issues raised in their book reviews in their subsequent research. A number of reviews of Guy's book stated they wished she had given greater attention to the personal stories of the artists and the Peking opera audiences. In her next book on the American soprano Beverly Sills, she gave detailed attention to the personal stories of her fans (Guy 2015). In response to criticism on his neglect of party organisation, Fell notes how his first post *Party Politics in Taiwan* research project looked at inner-party candidate selection mechanisms.

A number of the book reviews raised questions on the authors' assessments of Taiwan's democracy. Fell and Wong were challenged for overstating the success of Taiwan's democracy, while Mattlin's first edition was critiqued by some for being overly pessimistic. As Mattlin is the only book with a fully revised second edition, he has had the chance to directly adjust in response to his reviews, and interestingly his second edition (2018) reaches more positive conclusions. Fell notes a similar pattern in the case of his second book, *Government and Politics in Taiwan*. While the first edition that was published in 2011 (the same year as Mattlin's first edition) came to relatively pessimistic conclusions on the state of democracy, his second edition (Fell 2018) was much more upbeat and positive.

Both Wong and Mattlin were challenged over their attempts to argue that the Taiwan experience could be generalised beyond East Asia. Wong recalls how his linkage between democracy and the welfare state was challenged in Latin America. This led Wong to refine his argument and engage in broader comparative research subsequently. Similarly, Mattlin was challenged on his argument that the Chinese Communist Party might look at Taiwan for lessons in political transformation both by reviewers and in some of his book talks. Once again it appears that timing matters. As Mattlin explains back in 2011, it still looked possible that the CCP might follow the path of the KMT in gradual political liberalisation. Writing in 2019, he notes that this no longer seems a likely scenario.

A final theme that featured in some of the book reviews was to question the book titles. This was especially the case for Brown's *Is Taiwan Chinese?* As discussed earlier she had been under intense pressure from her publisher to include China or Chinese in the title. Naturally the new title helped book sales but of course left her open to challenge, as she admits, 'I never directly answer the title question.' Fell was also criticised in one review for using the title *Party Politics in Taiwan* as he only covered the dimension of party ideological change and neglected a range of topics that a comprehensive study of party politics should deal with. Once again Fell notes that it was the publisher's desire to broaden the marketability of the book that led to this title.

Certain authors suggested alternatives to book reviews. In addition to positive reviews, Hughes recalls the many emails received expressing gratitude 'for the detailed and dispassionate explanation I provided of the linkage between Taiwan's complex domestic politics and cross-Strait relations'. Hsiao takes the frequent citation of his work as an alternative to book reviews, noting that his work on social movements in the 1990s appears to have been the most cited back then. In contrast, Brown is critical of what she calls 'dismissive engagement' of a part of some in the Taiwan Studies community that have ignored or dismissed her work despite its extensive reviews in academic journals. In fact, Brown's book was by far the most reviewed book revisited in this volume.

Subsequent research: In or out of the shadow?

We also wanted authors to reflect on how their careers had developed since publishing their first books on Taiwan. Did they develop very different research trajectories or remain in the shadow of their first books? Would they be pressured to shift their focus away from Taiwan towards publishing on China? This is an important question raised by Lev Nachman in a recent forum in the *International Journal of Taiwan Studies*. He reports being told by his advisor that focusing on Taiwan as a graduate student would be 'career suicide'. He asks whether a better solution is to 'market ourselves as China scholars for the sake of our careers' (Nachman 2018: 386). Since our early Taiwan publications we have all remained in the Taiwan Studies field. Our chapters strongly show that rather than being career suicide, it can be a career enhancing decision to have a research focus on Taiwan.

Many of us have been affected by the change from being a PhD student to a regular faculty academic. The demands of university teaching and administration have led us to adjust our research methods. A number of us reflect on how we have no longer been able to do the same kind of lengthy in-depth fieldwork that featured in our first books. This is one of the reasons why few of us have published a second PhD style research monograph. A number of us have instead tried to reach broader audiences, such as in the case of Rigger's *Why Taiwan Matters* and Fell's *Government and Politics in Taiwan*. Another strategy for broadening our appeal has been to place Taiwan in a comparative perspective. For instance, Wong's second book *Betting on Biotech* expands the comparison beyond South Korea and Taiwan to include a third Asian Tiger, Singapore. Similarly his article with Dan Slater (2013) on transitions away from authoritarianism compares Taiwan's experiences with those of South Korea and Indonesia and suggests these have potential lessons for China.

Although many of us need to cover China in our teaching, it is noteworthy that none of us has abandoned our Taiwan research focus. In his work at the BBC and then later *The Economist*, Long has continued to cover both Taiwan and China in his writings. Gold notes how he has at times tried to focus his research on China, but keeps getting pulled back to Taiwan and has continued to publish on Taiwan. In fact Gold promises that his much anticipated second book will be called *Remaking Taiwan: Society and State since the End of Martial Law*. Hughes' (2006) second book was *Chinese Nationalism in the Global Era* but he has also continued to publish widely on Taiwan's identity politics. We hear about scholars being pressured to drop Taiwan most frequently in the United States, but Rigger has published three more books on Taiwan since *Politics in Taiwan*. She also tells us about her plans for new research on youth attitudes in Taiwan. The one example of an author doing something that seems completely different was Guy's book *The Magic of Beverly Sills*, which looked at the American soprano and her fans. Guy notes how she had planned to write her second book on political music in Taiwan, especially related to social movements. However, she became disillusioned by the negativity and ugliness of much of this music in the second Chen Shui-bian presidency and so shifted her attention to the beauty of Beverly Sills. Fortunately for the Taiwan Studies field, Guy has returned to her research on Taiwan's music in recent years. A more common strategy has been for us to maintain our focus on Taiwan but to look for new topics that we find exciting. For instance, Lee has developed a series of publications that look at the cultural politics of mass rapid transport systems and high speed rail on Taiwan.

The majority of us have attempted to build on the foundation of our first books by further developing these topics of research. For instance, Lee maintained her interest in gender and labour in Taiwan. One of her major subsequent research projects has looked at the establishment of the Memorial Park for Women Labourers in Kaohsiung City, as a way to explore the intersectionality of labour, gender, the state and family. Brown has also continued to build on *Is Taiwan Chinese?* in multiple publications that look at identity change in Taiwan and China in different historical periods. Similarly, Klöter explains how he has expanded his socio-linguistic approach in research on Taiwan's language policy as well as the language ideology of television advertisements. Although Fell has also moved into some new areas such as social movements and migration, his research remains party focused. The major difference is that he has tried to cover a much broader range of topics related to parties such as party candidate selection, small parties, party switching, party mergers and party systems.

Since both of us editors have long been intimately involved in the construction of international Taiwan Studies institutions, it is very encouraging to read our contributors talk of the role that bodies such as EATS and NATSA have played in their subsequent research. For instance, Klöter talks of how his research has been enriched by the interdisciplinary dialogue in the Taiwan Studies field.

Concluding remarks

The way the Taiwan Studies field has developed since the first works reviewed here from the 1980s is quite remarkable. This success is rooted in its close relevance to contemporary humanities and social sciences. By revisiting these influential volumes we aim to offer an alternative perspective on the development of the Taiwan Studies field. We hope that the readers will be inspired not only to read the original works revisited here but also our subsequent bodies of work. We hope that the diverse strategies our authors have taken to not only survive but also to thrive in the field will offer some useful lessons for those at an early stage in their careers. Just as those of us in the golden era of Taiwan Studies were inspired by the pioneers of the field, we hope that this volume can encourage the next generation of Taiwan Studies scholars.

Note

1 These are the books by Rigger, Gold, Hughes, Fell and Brown. Sullivan lists 20 publications but also includes some journal articles and edited books.

References

Chang, Sung-sheng Yvonne and Fell, Dafydd. 2019. 'Developing Taiwan Studies Teaching Programmes in Europe and the United States: The Experience of SOAS University of London and University of Texas at Austin'. *China Quarterly* doi:doi:10.1017/S0305741019000031

Fell, Dafydd. 2008. 'The Role of SOAS in the Development of European Taiwan Studies'. *Taiwan Studies in Global Perspectives*. Santa Barbara, CA: Center of Taiwan Studies, UCSB, 1–15.

Fell, Dafydd. 2011. *Government and Politics in Taiwan*. London: Routledge.

Fell, Dafydd. 2017. 'The Golden Age of Taiwan Studies?' *Taiwan Sentinel*. October 24 2017. https://sentinel.tw/golden-age-global-tw-studies/

Fell, Dafydd. 2018. *Government and Politics in Taiwan*. London: Routledge.

Guy, Nancy. 2015. *The Magic of Beverly Sills*. Urbana and Chicago: University of Illinois Press.

Hsiao, Hsin-Huang Michael and Dafydd Fell. 2018. 'Introduction: The State of the Field of Taiwan Studies'. *International Journal of Taiwan Studies*, 1(1): 5–10.

Hsieh, Ta-Yang and Yu-li Wang. 2018. 'One-year Findings of the Taiwan Syllabus Project'. Interim report presented in 'Roundtable #1: How to Teach about Taiwan: Findings from the Taiwan Syllabus Project', at the North America Taiwan Studies Association Conference, Austin, TX, May 25, 2018; available online at https://taiwansyllabusprojectnatsa. wordpress.com/.

Hughes, Christopher. 2006. *Chinese Nationalism in the Global Era*. London: Routledge.

Issues and Studies Book Review Roundtable 2004. *Issues and Studies* 40, 3/4, 453–509.

Long, Simon. 1989. 'Taiwan: Politics versus Prosperity'. Economist Intelligence Unit.

Mattlin, Mikael. 2018. *Politicized Society: Taiwan's Struggle with Its One-party Past*. Copenhagen: NIAS Press.

Nachman, Lev. 2018. 'Response 3. Forum: State of the Field of Global Taiwan Studies'. *International Journal of Taiwan Studies*, 1(2): 385–387.

Rawnsley, Ming-yeh. 2017. 'Developing Taiwan Studies as a Sustainable and Diverse Field'. *Taiwan Sentinel*, November 22, 2017. https://sentinel.tw/developing-taiwan-studies/

Rigger, Shelley. 2002. 'Political Science and Taiwan's Domestic Politics: The State of the Field'. *Issues and Studies*, 38(4): 49–92.

Rigger, Shelley. 2011. *Why Taiwan Matters: Small Island, Global Powerhouse*. Lanham: Rowman & Littlefield Publishers.

Schubert, Gunter. 2017. 'Securing a Golden Age of Taiwan Studies'. *Taiwan Sentinel*. November 7 2017. https://sentinel.tw/securing-golden-age-taiwan-studies/

Slater, Dan and Joseph Wong. 2013. 'The Strength to Concede: Ruling Parties and Democratization in Developmental Asia'. *Perspectives on Politics*, 11(3), 717–733.

Sullivan, Jonathan. 2011. 'Is Taiwan Studies in Decline?' *The China Quarterly*, 207, 706–718.

Sullivan, Jonathan. 2016. 'The 20 Best Academic Publications on Taiwanese Politics'. *Asia Dialogue*. http://theasiadialogue.com/2016/01/04/the-20-best-academic-publications-on-ta iwanese-politics/

Wong, Joseph. 2011. *Betting on Biotech: Innovation and Limits on Asia's Developmental States*. Ithaca: Cornell University Press.

PART I
1980s–early 1990s

PART I

1980s–early 1990s

2

MY JOURNEY OF SOCIAL MOVEMENTS AND CIVIL SOCIETY RESEARCH REVISITED

Hsin-Huang Michael Hsiao

Introduction

I began my personal attention to and involvement in exploring and studying Taiwan's social movements issues in the early 1980s. I returned to Taiwan to work in Academia Sinica and National Taiwan University from the United States right after having completed my PhD degree in Sociology in 1979. Soon, with direct or indirect participant observation in various emerging social movements and protests, I began to engage in the theoretical debates on the concept of civil society when it was first introduced to Taiwan's intellectual circle in the late 1980s. It has been a long time since I started my sociological journey exploring social movements and civil society in the 1980s. However, my long-term interest and involvement in this topic did not emerge out of my doctoral research back in State University of New York at Buffalo. Over the past nearly four decades, my research works and theoretical thinking have also gone through the following twists and turns.

1. The first turn is from a citizen-intellectual's concern and advocacy to a professional sociologist's serious observation and reporting (1980s).
2. The second shift is from preoccupation with empirical research to the intention to generate plausible theoretical propositions (1990s).
3. The third shift is from the specific social movements and study of civil society to establish the theoretical connection between social movements and civil society dynamics on the one hand with the middle class and democracy on the other (since the 2000s).

In this revisited essay, I will initially concentrate on the first two interesting turns in my research on social movement dynamics and civil society organisations, and then direct my reflection on how the two changes have impinged on the third shift

16 Hsin-Huang Michael Hsiao

to develop the tripartite links of the middle class, civil society and democratisation in the context of Taiwan's experience.

The first turn, in the 1980s: Concern and observation

My first book in Chinese on Taiwan's social movements was entitled *Taiwan's Consumers' Movement: Theory and Practice* (Hsiao et al. 1982). It was a co-edited volume with two of my former students, containing more than 50 essays on the subject written by a variety of authors, mostly since the late 1970s, when many serious consumer problems and victims began to catch the attention of the public and the media. I wrote ten related essays in that volume, most of them from the viewpoint of a concerned citizen and for the purpose of consumer consciousness and advocacy for the grassroots consumers' movement and government consumer policies. Some of them were deliberate attempts to bridge the gap between academic writing and popular essays.

The following ones were most relevant: 'From Consumer Consciousness to the Consumers' Movement', 'From Money's Value to Human's Value: The Next Step for Taiwan's Consumers' Movement', 'For Advocacy of the Consumers' Movement in Taiwan' and 'A Dialogue with Professor Sidney Wolinsky'. In addition, the criteria for selection of the collected essays basically followed the frame of reference pointed out in my above articles. This book did make some contributions to raise public awareness, facilitate the social movement and even pressure the government's policy response. My role was as a concerned sociologist at that time, but the consumer issues were also my personal concern, and I had also been personally involved in the formation and establishment of the Consumers' Foundation of the ROC (1980), the first genuine urban middle-class-based social movement organisation ever set up in Taiwan.

Two years after the publication of that book for a wider public audience, I then wrote a book chapter in Chinese titled 'Consumer Problems and Consumers' Movement' in an edited book on *Taiwan's Social Problems* by Yang and Yeh (1984). That article was written from a sociological perspective on social movements to analyse the rise of mass consumption society as the background giving rise to consumer problems, the growing citizens' consciousness of consumer problems, and finally the formation of consumers' movement organised by new middle-class professionals and intellectuals (Hsiao 1984: 217–248). Looking back, this article may be the first research piece on any social movement in Taiwan.

My second book, also in Chinese, on Taiwan's social movements was entitled *We Have Only One Taiwan: Anti-Pollution, Eco-Conservation, and Environmental Movements*, and was published in 1987 (Hsiao 1987). It collected all of my semi-academic writings on three major environmental issues facing Taiwan and the related movements. At that time, I first identified three critical environmental problems, namely pollution, nature depletion and nuclear power safety, and also detected two streams of Taiwan's emerging environmental movements: local anti-pollution protests and nature conservation campaigns. By 1987, the growing concern about nuclear power pollution and safety was more and more evident, and the controversy over the construction of the fourth nuclear power plant had already come to the surface, but an organised anti-nuclear movement had not yet been staged on a big scale and in a public manner. This book collected 56 long and short essays on the subject that I wrote between 1980 and 1987.

All of the articles were written from the analytical angle of environmental sociology, which I first officially introduced to university teaching in Taiwan in the early 1980s. Like the previous book on the consumers' movement, the way I approached the environmental movement was that it was the worsening environmental problems that gave rise to the public reaction and collective action toward the formation of policy solutions to those social problems. (With that conviction, early on, in 1982, I had previously written a piece titled 'From Environmental Problems to Environmental Movements' to openly argue that sociological connection.) In the 1987 book, I also included several essays discussing the results of social surveys I had conducted on public environmental consciousness and values in 1982, 1983 and 1986. I discovered a steady growing trend of public awareness about the seriousness of the problems and even the victim consciousness caused by the above three major environmental problems. From those survey data, I then began to build the linkage between the objective environmental issues, public consciousness raising and the rise of environmental movements, as argued in my various essays collected in this volume.

One interesting side story about the publication of this book deserves to be mentioned. When I began to approach a couple of potential publishers, they were very reluctant to accept the book for publication, not because of the quality of the subject matter, but because of the title of the book. At that time, the title I insisted on using, *We Have One Taiwan*, was considered too politically sensitive for the publishers to risk. Finally, Yuan Shen (圓神出版社) was courageous enough to accept it for publication and agreed with my other insistence to use a map of Taiwan as the book cover. After this incident, my following few books on the environment and sustainable development in the 1990s all used a Taiwan map on the cover, and they no longer faced any hesitation from the publishers.

My third book (in Chinese) published in the 1980s was titled *Taiwan's Future Trends* (Hsiao 1989a). It was a volume with 12 collected essays that I had written between 1988 and 1989. The subject of the majority of the articles was related to Taiwan's ongoing mega social transformations. In *Taiwan's Future Trends*, I grasped and depicted several significant trends of societal transformation in Taiwan between the end of World War II in 1945 and the end of the 1980s. The first three were all related to social class changes: the creation of the small farmers, the birth of an industrial working class, and the rise of the middle classes. I also predicted the coming crystallisation of the social class structure in Taiwan and the inevitable formation of a class society and its growing class inequality and social deprivation. The fourth trend was the birth of different kinds of social movements and political protests for democratic reforms. In the conclusion, I expected to observe the coming of the changing state and society power relations and the shift from an authoritarian political culture to a participatory political culture in the decade to come.

The other three Chinese essays were actually written in response to the newly imported concept of 'civil society' in Taiwan in the late 1980s. I was actively engaged in the ongoing debates on how to translate the English words into Mandarin Chinese, what really constituted its contents and meanings, and how we could utilise this new discourse to understand, interpret and advocate for the emergence of grassroots social protests and organised social movements. The three essays were 'The Anti-dominance Character of Civil Society: The Nature of Social Movements', 'Social Movements and Social Enlightenment' and 'Political Freedom and Economic Equality: The Current Missions of Social Movements'. All of them were published in the then popular and recognisable intellectual magazine, *China Tribune*. I even chaired a couple of panel discussions on the exact same theme for that magazine in 1989.

Concerning the debates on the proper translation of 'civil society' into Mandarin Chinese, there were several translations used in the late 1980s when the concept was brought into Taiwan's intellectual community. That included 'minjien society (non-governmental society)' (民間社會), 'city-dweller society' (市民社會), 'bourgeois society' (布爾喬亞社會), 'civilised society' (文明社會) and 'citizen society' (公民社會). On many public discussion occasions, including invited lectures, media interviews and published writings, I strongly advised the use of 'minjien society' as the most suitable Chinese translation on the grounds that all the others are too limited in meaning, too Western in connotation, or too restricted in implications for the expected current social and political transformation.

The rationale for my preference to adopt 'minjien society' (民間社會) to stand for 'civil society' in local language were twofold: it not only could clearly demonstrate the 'non-official and non-governmental aspect of the self-autonomous mobilization and formation of social forces for change', but also could signify the 'joint effort of those different grassroots protests and organized movements to make demands of and put pressure on the authoritarian KMT state'. Since then, I even coined the term 'minjien social force' (civil social force, 民間社會力) to represent the collective pressures from different classes, sectors and localities on the authoritarian government to transform, that is, minjien society assumed the mission to stand against the authoritarian state. In that sense, the concept of 'minjien society' was also given a 'political' mission to unify all fronts to exert further collective pressures for large scale social reforms and the establishment of political democracy. Admittedly, that was indeed derived from my normative motivation as a concerned intellectual to push for democratic transition and democratic institutionalisation.

What was the link between my empirical concern regarding emerging social movements and my normative expectation of the introduction and popularisation of the 'imported concept of civil society' at that time? I was quite clear in my mind that the central dynamism of the civil society (minjien social force) should come from the various social movements that had already arisen and taken the stage to demand their respective causes of change and reform. To me, only in this way, by connecting the dynamics of local social movements with the crux of

Social movements and civil society research revisited   **19**

the conception of civil society, could the transportation of this Western discourse have any indigenised significance and even make a contribution to the real world.

In that year, 1989, I further elaborated the above concerned citizen's keen observations into more sociological discourse and published two more related academic papers. The first appeared in an edited book (in Chinese) *Taiwan's Emerging Social Movements* by Hsu and Sung (1989), entitled 'The Analytical Framework of Taiwan's Emerging Social Movements' (Hsiao 1989b: 21–46). In that chapter, I used the empirical evidence to prove the social problems – social movements link, as I had previously argued in the early 1980s. I also engaged in a typological analysis by means of two criteria of 'capability of internal resources mobilization' and 'degree of external social impact' on the 14 newly rising social movements in Taiwan as of 1987. The 14 social movements included were: 1. the consumers' movement, 2. local anti-pollution protest movements, 3. nature conservation movement, 4. women's movement, 5. student movement, 6. aborigines' ethnic movement, 7. New Testament Church religious movement, 8. labour movement, 9. farmers' movement, 10. teachers' movement, 11. handicapped and disadvantaged welfare group protests, 12. military veterans' welfare movement, 13. political prisoners' human rights movement and 14. mainlanders' home-visiting movement. From the above two-dimensional analysis, I categorised the 14 social movements into various typologies ranging from victim-centred movements to middle-class-supported movements, and from the relatively weak movements to the relatively strong movements.

In another book chapter (in Chinese) also published in 1989, I provided a more detailed sketch of the 17 social movements between 1980 and 1988. Besides the above listed 14 movements, I also added three more that took place in 1988, they were: the anti-nuclear movement; the black-listed Taiwanese home-visiting movement; and the Hakka ethnic movement. In that publication, I pointed out that among all the social movements, there existed a clear desire to change the 'historicity' of the current society and to reshape the long-lasting state–society power relations (Hsiao 1989c: 9–32). Later in a journal article in English in *The Australian Journal of Chinese Affairs* (now *The China Journal*) in 1990, I further drew the following overall characteristics of Taiwanese social movements as seen at the end of the golden decade of civil society forces. All the social movements took the state as the object of protest, they expressed a strong collective victim consciousness and the class conflict was not the dominant factor in most of the movements. All the movements had developed into the stages of consolidation and even institutionalisation in less than a decade in that the movements had established their organisations and associations to sustain their momentum. They had also created a new political market by exerting certain visible political influence, they were quite autonomous in facing the rise of political opposition, but they themselves had formed various degrees of coalition and alliance among themselves and, finally, as the significant result of and rooted in the demanding civil society, a new kind of participatory political culture had begun to appear in Taiwan (Hsiao 1990). This journal article was widely read by academics outside Taiwan, and a revised version was also published as a chapter in the book *Political Change in Taiwan*, co-edited by Cheng and Haggard (Hsiao 1992a). The above two English publications and the following several articles also written in English somehow brought me to a wider readership in the English language world. I was then recognised as a serious sociologist in Taiwan as well as a Taiwan studies scholar.

In retrospect, the above factual observations from my standpoint as a concerned intellectual greatly helped me to grasp the reality of the world of Taiwan's social movements in the 1980s. Without the personal concern and commitment to understand and to support the rising social movements, I could not gain the trust of the social movement organisations' leaders and thus to hear and see many important scenes and happenings in my participatory observation studies on site, then later turn the field observations into published writings. The accumulation of quite a few of the above semi-academic and academic writings in the 1980s also provided the solid empirical grounds for me to theorise my research on social movements and civil society in the following decade.

The second turn, in the 1990s: Empirical studies and eye on 'changing state-society' relations

It is quite true that for the decade of the 1980s, I closely observed many protest events and advocacy meetings, and analysed publications relevant to the many rising social movements mentioned above. A decade of personal concern and observation indeed provided me with many insights and a deeper understanding of Taiwan's emerging social movements and the formation of civil society. But I must admit that I was quite attached to those social movements, meaning I paid very close attention to their voices and appeals and even tried to advocate for their legitimacy on their behalf. My sociological reasoning is based on my theoretical conviction of 'changing state-society relations', in which I considered it to be the collective pressure generated by a variety of social movements that finally challenged the long-lasting authoritarian state-dictated state-society power relations. In a 1991 article (in English), I began to explore the connection between economic change and class transformation on the one hand, and the rise of social movements on the other hand, in Taiwan in the 1980s (Hsiao 1991: 127–140).

The structural contexts for such rising social movements were capitalist economic development and the consequential social class change, especially the birth of the first-generation small farmers in the 1950s, and the second-generation working class and first-generation new middle class in the 1980s. The three new classes began to engage themselves to either express their grievances over social injustices they had experienced and demand governmental policy changes (such as anti-pollution protests, and the farmers' movement and labour movements among farmers and workers) or exert pressure for social reforms at large (such as the consumers' movements, nature conservation movement, indigenous ethnic movement, Hakka ethnic movement, judicial reform movement and journalists' autonomy movement from the new middle class). Although the social movements staged by farmers and workers did involve class interests, many others initiated by new middle-class professionals and intellectuals went far beyond their own class interests. The suppressed civil society under the authoritarian Kuomintang (KMT) state in the past three decades finally began to mobilise its various elements and constituencies to demand changes to the imbalanced state–society relations.

With the above 'changing state-society power relations' perspective in mind, I embarked on a series of case study writings on various social movements in the next few years in the 1990s. The social movements on which I actually published their case history and sociological analysis during that decade included the labour movement, farmers' movement, urban residents' movement, social welfare movement and, of course, environmental movements.

The social movements initiated by labourers and farmers were very much in my head when I began to observe the emergence of social protests in the 1980s. The way I saw the breakout of the two social movements was from my ongoing investigation of the social class transformation to detect the rise of small farmers and the industrial working class in the 1950s and 1960s, respectively. The land reforms policy in the early 1950s created the small independent farmers, and the import-substitution industrialisation and export-oriented industrialisation policies in the 1950s and 1960s created two generations of the new working class.

I then associated the making of the labour movement in the 1980s with the changed social character of the second generation of Taiwanese working class in a book chapter (in English) on labour movements (Hsiao 1992b). The second-generation working class, unlike their predecessors, were uprooted from their rural base, and realised that their economic interests and livelihood lay in the urban industrial sector. In contrast, the first-generation workers were migrant workers who were the surplus agricultural population, yet they still maintained close ties with the farm economy. Their class interests were ambiguous, and they felt they could always return to the social support of their families in case of job loss in the factories. However, the new breed of workers began to challenge the authoritarian system of control over unions by means of staging many labour disputes, through which to express their collective protests and activism. In addition, the labour activists even dared to reform the existing union structure as well as establish new independent and autonomous grassroots quasi-unions free from KMT party control. Furthermore, in the late 1980s the labour movement entered a new stage of development that could be characterised as a 'surge' in both quantity and quality. However, I also detected that, at that time, the major concern of the labour movement was primarily centred on individual workers' economic interests, and not on working-class political power. To me, it showed a limit to the unionisation of Taiwan's workers and their collective labour activism (Hsiao 1992b: 151–167).

In another published book chapter (in English) on the farmers' movement, I also linked the rise of farmers' collective protests with the significant political character of post-land-reform small independent farmers' nature, which had evolved from a 'demobilized' class to a 'self-mobilizing' group since the mid-1980s (Hsiao 1994a). From my previous studies of the political and social impacts of the KMT state's

22 Hsin-Huang Michael Hsiao

land reforms policy, I discovered and published extensively that the bulk of post-land-reform small farmers were primarily contented and conservative. As already pointed out above, even those rural exoduses to the urban–industrial sector to become workers remained conservative and dependent. The agrarian society in the post-land-reform era was basically demobilised and controlled by the authoritarian state of the KMT through the control mechanism of the farmers' association and irrigation association and localised party apparatus in the countryside. No mobilisation and no protests in the countryside ever occurred before the 1980s.

The farmers' organised protests in the mid-1980s were triggered by the importation of a large quantity of US Sunkist oranges. It was the full-time economic crop farmers, who grew local fruits like oranges, who voiced their grievance and anger toward the import policy. In other words, the traditional rice farmers, most of whom were actually part-time farmers, did not fire the first shot in Taiwan's farmers' movements. In the above paper, I also discovered the success of the 'upward confrontation' of the joint protests of different farmers against the state, but the failure of the 'downward reform' of their own local rural organisational structure, which was deeply dictated by the local factions, closely associated with local elections, and again controlled by the authoritarian state. Like the labour movement, the Taiwanese farmers' movement remained a 'commodity reform movement' concerned primarily with issues such as pricing and marketing of farm products and the protection of farm land, and to a much lesser extent rural political reforms (Hsiao 1994a: 202–218).

I later also published two articles, both in English, on the urban citizens' movement in 1997 and 2002, respectively. In the two articles, I explored three types of urban dwellers' collective protests, against environmental pollution and skyrocketing housing prices and defending their living spaces and communities, all taking place in metropolitan Taipei.

Regarding the local anti-pollution protests and defence of living spaces, I conducted a content analysis on 274 protest cases based on newspaper reports in 1980–1996 and case studies occurring during that period of time. The statistical analytical variables included protest objectives, tactics and results. The case studies focused on how local residents self-mobilised to protect their living environment from ill-planned, large urban development projects. The issues of class conflict and social justice were explored in these cases. From both the quantitative and qualitative analyses, I discovered that urban Taipei residents have openly expressed their discontent over a deteriorating urban environment and challenged the top-down political structure that has long deprived them of the right to participate in the decision-making process of public affairs. The urban protests also confirmed the repeatedly highlighted significance of 'locality' in environmental movements worldwide. The urban citizens' 'war for survival' mainly responded to excessive development and obvious deterioration of their urban habitat, and they collectively claimed their right to control their own communities (Hsiao 1997a: 392–405, Hsiao 2002: 76–90).

Social movements and civil society research revisited   **23**

As for the 'urban non-homeowners protest movement', it protested against systematic manipulation and speculation by real estate development firms and the resulting unaffordable housing process for ordinary, salaried middle-class households. A staged large-scale protest took place on August 26, 1989, and received massive media coverage and the government's attention. The protest organisers deliberately de-politicized the event and staged the protest like a fun-loving carnival event. However, the actual policy impact was quite limited, as the movement did not sustain its momentum to put further organisational pressure on the concerned government agency and the speculating capitalist class after the protest and media effects. The movement failed to launch an effective and continual policy debate on the issue. Due to its original decision to maintain its political neutrality and autonomy, it was unable to gain any substantive support from the political opposition and other social movement organisations. This movement ended by turning itself into a soft-line rental service to assist low-income individuals and families with their rental rights (Hsiao 1997a: 406–410).

In the year 2000, I co-edited another Chinese language book, *Social Welfare Movements in Taiwan* (Hsiao and Lin 2000), and for that volume I wrote a chapter portraying the origins, changes and succession of Taiwan's social welfare movements since the 1980s (Hsiao and Sun 2000: 33–70). In the next year, I also had a revised English article published in an edited volume titled *Understanding Modern Taiwan: Essays in Economic, Politics and Social Policy* by Aspalter (Hsiao 2001: 169–204).

In that article, I documented the developmental histories of five types of grassroots social welfare movements in the 1980s and 1990s and how they in fact succeeded in pushing a revision and reformulation of the government's new social welfare policy agenda by means of effective movement strategies. The five related specific movements were: the disabled welfare movement; women's welfare movement; elderly welfare movement; children's welfare movement; and youth welfare movement. Each movement was initiated, organised and strategised by at least one well-organised association, foundation or alliance of movement groups. Behind each movement organisation there were always a number of new middle-class professional activists playing the key organisational roles. In a way, the social welfare movement could be characterised as a mobilisation of critical social work and social welfare professional activism, backed by a large amount of popular support from the general public. The democratic electoral system that was installed along with the political transformation has greatly helped in getting the increasing welfare demands by the various movements' organisations adopted by both the transforming KMT and opposition DPP and their candidates in a number of elections.

Between 1986 and 1996, a sequence of strategic changes was also observed among the various social welfare movements' organisations. In their objectives, they initially demanded needed relevant welfare laws, and later called for law revision and oversight. For effective appeals, they not only demanded that separate welfare issues be solved, but they also asked for policy institutionalisation. In terms of their organisational mobilisation, they started with struggles by separate organisations and later shifted to several strategic alliances so as to multiply their collective pressure on the state. Moreover, one more evident change was that, in the early years, street protests were often staged to catch the public's and the state's attention; later they opted for peaceful policy debates and persuasion. In addition, I also witnessed the shift among their choice of movement strategies, from mere advocacy to the state moving to offer direct services to the concerned needy individuals and disadvantaged groups. Like other social movement organisations, among a variety of social welfare movements, over a decade of organisational development, there was a leadership transition from the founding activist members to the next echelon of movement professionals (Hsiao 2001: 169–204).

Among my studies of various social movements, the environmental movement has been my central work, as I published a larger number of empirical research findings on the subject in the 1990s. As mentioned earlier, I turned my attention to the local anti-pollution protests in the early 1980s. In the 1990s, I devoted a series of articles in both Chinese and English to the quantitative analysis of local protests dating back to 1980. Also, as already pointed out above, the database was the content-analysed newspaper clippings on reports of various local anti-pollution protests up to 2000. I published journal articles and book chapters in both Chinese and English reporting the analysis for the different phases, two on the period of 1980–1991 (Hsiao 1994b; Hsiao, Milbrath and Weller, 1995), one on 1980–1996 (Hsiao 1999a) and one on 1980–2000 (Hsiao 2002).

Looking back at the above four articles on local anti-pollution protest movements in the two decades of 1980–2000, it is interesting to highlight some important features that remain significant.

1. The fundamental social psychological factor behind the collected 2,622 cases of local anti-pollution protests has always been 'victim consciousness'.
2. The collective expression of the individual victims' grievances and suffering from pollution and other environmental hazards may have spurred local citizens to challenge the local and even central governments over their failure to solve the pressing issues facing many localities.
3. The collective victims' consciousness then turned into social and political pressure on the authoritarian state to make necessary policy reforms, and that in turn helped facilitate political liberalisation at the local level.
4. At the initial phase the protests targeted the existing industrial pollution factories for compensation; later that turned into protesting the presence of any potentially polluting industrial facilities. The nature of collective protest changed from 'compensational protests' to 'preventive protests'.
5. The local protests have been a widespread emerging social phenomenon throughout the two decades before 2000 and even beyond.
6. It has been observed that there could have been potential escalation of violence-prone anti-pollution protests, if the polluters and the concerned local governments had failed to respond to the issue in a timely and responsive manner.

Social movements and civil society research revisited   25

7. It was found that many local industries and factories were the immediate result of the past ill-planned industrialisation policies advocated by the authoritarian developmental state.
8. The primary actors in all protests were the local residents, who effectively maximised the mobilisation capability of existing local social networks such as neighbourhoods, clans and lineages, temples and schools to stage the protests so as to demonstrate the powerful social cohesion behind the protests.
9. The timely support from the outside concerned intellectuals, journalists and a few environmental NGOs were also crucial to the success of the protests.
10. The series of local anti-pollution protests did in fact push the law-making process for two important environmental laws, the 'Pollution Conflict Resolution Act' (1994) and 'Environmental Impact Assessment Act' (1996).

I have already identified three types of environmental movements in Taiwan: anti-pollution, nature conservation and anti-nuclear-power generation in the late 1980s, as I have openly addressed them separately in different writings. But not until 1999, when I wrote a book chapter in English titled 'Environmental Movements in Taiwan' (Hsiao 1999b: 31–54) did I deliberately put the above three streams of Taiwanese environmental movements together. I have characterised each of the three streams from the political economy perspective, and also pointed out the contributions the environmental movements have made to Taiwan's democratisation, the role of business in environmental movements, and the anti-nuclear movement.

In the conclusion, I assessed the three streams in terms of the following variables: public support, normative conflict and policy impact. All in all, the anti-nuclear movement has been the most politicized, with contrasting ideology and platforms of different political parties on the nuclear power plant issue. The KMT was in the pro-nuclear power camp, while the DPP held the anti-nuclear stance.

The nature conservation movement has garnered the most support among the middle-class female population and the literary community. The anti-pollution protests were widely engaged in by farmers and the working class. The joint force of the three streams, then, has constituted the totality of Taiwan's environmental movements.

In 1995–2000 and beyond, I also began to take on two new tasks and challenges for myself in the research on social movements and civil society. The first one is to look at Taiwan's current social movements and civil society forces and dynamism in a longer historical perspective. The second one is to situate Taiwan's civil society organisational momentum in a broader comparative analytical framework.

For the former, in 1995 I published a co-authored piece in Chinese titled 'The Rise, Fall and Transformation of Taiwan's Social Forces in the Past 100 Years'. In that article, I tried to theorise on the manifestation of social forces in the following ways: it is a reconsolidation of collective consciousness; it is a redistribution of power; and it is also a rearrangement of human organisations. The three aspects (dimensions) of social forces actually reflected my previous empirical studies and documentation of various social movements including collectivity of civil society's relative power and their relations with the existing political centres. Taiwan was colonised by Japanese imperialism in 1895, as it was abandoned by the Ching empire when it was defeated by Japan's empire. My paper aimed to examine how civil society forces worked in the century under different political centres (Japanese colonialism, Chinese Nationalist authoritarian rule and the democratisation era after the lifting of martial law in 1987).

The paper concluded that, during those 100 years, Taiwan's civil society forces experienced a clear rise and fall and later even self-transformation in different historical phases. Taiwan's society was under an outside colonial state's total control from 1895–1919. From 1919–1937, Taiwan's civil society was led by young intellectuals to launch a series of demands for colonial reform movements, including farmers' and labour movements, as well as the call for modern democratic legislative reform for colonial Taiwan. Between 1938 and 1945, Taiwan was trapped as an imperial subject under Japan's strict rule during the war mobilisation and control, and no grassroots protests or demands were permitted. After World War II, Taiwan was taken over by the KMT regime from the outside, and thus began the decades of authoritarian and 'White Terror' rule between 1945 and 1980. Finally, after the 1980s, Taiwan's civil society once again regained the strength to self-mobilise by staging various social movements in the 1980s, as I have already eye-witnessed and documented in the 1980s and 1990s (Hsiao 1995: 110–149).

For the latter, I began to classify social movements in Taiwan utilising both an objective typology on movements' capacities and a typology of the public's subjective acceptance (i.e., awareness and support) of social movements. Through a comparative interpretation of the two typologies, I believe, I was actually able to help to clarify social movements' dynamism in Taiwan in the 1990s. The result was first published as a journal article in English (Hsiao 1997b), and its revised version appeared again as a book chapter (Hsiao 2011).

Later, I also published a co-authored paper in Chinese based on a comparative research project on the civil society organisations in Taipei (Taiwan), Hong Kong, Guangzhou and Xiamen (China) in 2004. It aimed to portray and characterise the emerging civil society organisations (CSOs) in Taipei, Taiwan in comparison with three cities in contemporary Hong Kong and China. Surveys of CSOs in these four cities were conducted by different researchers in the respective locations. The results show that the organisational strength of CSOs in Taipei has been very different from that in Hong Kong and China. Taipei's CSOs are quite autonomous from the state and have performed an advocacy role in the larger society. Hong Kong's CSOs are pluralistic in nature and appear to be cooperative toward the government. In contrast to Taiwan and Hong Kong, CSOs in China are still in an infant stage of development. The state's direct control and dominance over the civil organisations are evident, as all organisations lack the feature of autonomy, which is necessary to demonstrate any advocacy capability. Guangzhou's civil organisations are most concerned about their own survival and, as a result, they tend to be dependent on various levels of government bureaucracy. Similarly, most

Social movements and civil society research revisited   **27**

of the civil organisations in Xiamen are newly established, and all face limitations and restrictions from the state.

In the final analysis, Taiwan's CSOs have developed beyond being autonomous, and have demonstrated social and political reform capability. Hong Kong's CSOs are well developed in philanthropy and social services, yet remain limited in their ability to change the state–society power relations. Finally, China's sustained authoritarian corporatist control over society shows no signs of facilitating the growth of real civil society (Hsiao, Weller, et al. 2004: 1–60). From this comparative study of civil society organisations in Taiwan, Hong Kong and China, I began to look into the issues of growing importance to me: who the key members are in and behind various kinds of civil society organisations, and under what types of political systems can such organisations contribute to the process of democratic transition.

The above historical and comparative studies of Taiwan's social forces and its civil society's organisational strength that I undertook in the late 1990s and early 2000s have really equipped me not only to theorise based on my previous research on social movements and civil society, but also to move further to develop the tripartite links of the middle class, civil society and democracy both empirically and theoretically since 2000.

The third turn, since the 2000s: Theorising on the tripartite middle class – civil society – democracy links

My theoretical sociological concern on the social movements and civil society research was 'changing state-society relations', and all the writings in that decade were around studies, historical analysis and comparative perspective on specific movements in the decade of the 1990s. Into the 2000s, I pushed the issue further and tackled the question of what direction or destiny the changing state–society power relations should ideally lead to. I was convinced that the end result should be democratic transition and democratic consolidation. And that normative inclination has taken me to engage myself to solve the puzzle of the tripartite links of middle class – civil society – democracy after 2000.

Before and after the first regime change, in 2000, my research on civil society and social movements had demonstrated how they indeed had contributed to pressuring the KMT regime to lift the martial law (1987), the ban on free press (1988) and the ban on political parties (1990). I also discovered that the advocacy civil society organisations and social movements had become politicized, taking side with the opposition DPP in the late 1990s in various major elections. With evidence, in three related English articles, I asserted that the strategic alliance of pro-democracy civil society organisations and social movements with the opposition DPP had helped the DPP win the presidential election and make the first regime transition possible in 2000 (Hsiao 2003: 180–191; 42–57; Hsiao 2005a, 2005b). In another co-authored English article titled 'Civil Society and Democracy-making in Taiwan: Reexamining the Link' (Hsiao and Ho 2010), I

28   Hsin-Huang Michael Hsiao

empirically demonstrated that, from the 1970s to 2008, social movements and viable civil society have had a consistently positive impact on Taiwan's democracy-building process (Hsiao and Ho 2010: 43–64). I was convinced that the Taiwan experience between the 1980s and 2000 indeed supports the theoretical proposition of the positive connection of viable civil society – establishment of democracy as advocated by Taylor (1990), Diamond (1994), Cohen and Arato (1994), Putnam (1994) and Hsiao, et al. (1995).

However, I also pointed out that the relations between advocacy civil society and social movements on the one hand and the democratic state on the other could have turned sour after the regime change. In Taiwan's case, after the first regime change between 2000 and 2008, labour movements, environmental movements and welfare movements changed their original 'partnership' relations with the DPP government to a 'guardianship' one in critically watching and monitoring the new democratic state's related policy performance. I was rather surprised to see the sustained distrustful relations between social movement organisations and their activists and the defeated authoritarian KMT during its years as the opposition in 2000–2008. The critical civil society organisations maintained their distrustful attitudes toward the KMT, while the KMT also did not even try to extend a hand to those social movements to form a political coalition to challenge the DPP government.

My attention to the proactive and reforming role of the middle class in Taiwan can be traced back to as early as the 1980s, when I began to research a variety of social movements. As already pointed out earlier, I have noticed that for many reform and advocacy civil society organisations, the major organisational and supporting forces actually came from liberal and reformed-minded new middle-class individuals such as intellectuals, professors and professionals. Therefore, as early as the 1990s, I had already developed in my research agenda the notion that there existed a plausible connection between the liberal new middle class and pro-change social movements that constituted the core of advocacy civil society.

In my co-authored article in English in 1997, titled 'The Middle Class and Democratization', my co-author and I documented how the middle class has affected democratisation in Taiwan and South Korea since the 1980s. We concluded that it is the progressive and liberal new middle-class segments that have engaged and mobilised themselves to create the beginnings of democracy, to sustain democratic transition, and finally to deepen democratic consolidation by means of diverse and viable mobilisation strategies and tactics which extend beyond the mere casting of votes (Hsiao and Koo 1997). It was also hinted that the liberal and progressive new middle class did not speak or act alone and individually. They have organised themselves so as to exert their collective pressure on the authoritarian regimes for democratic reforms. Our article confirmed the positive link between the middle class and democratisation, as has long been advocated in the related literature on the middle class and democracy since the 1960s (Lipset 1963, 1964; Moore 1966).

But my research has gone beyond the general theorising of the classical bilateral connection of the middle class on two important fronts. First, I have specified the kind of middle class that has performed the democratising role. Second, I have also indicated that the progressive and liberal new middle-class individuals have chosen to support or join various pro-democracy civic organisations and social movements to openly express their democratic demands. At critical junctures, as already pointed out above, the liberal new class-backed advocacy civil society and social movement organisations even openly rendered their political support to the pro-democracy opposition parties. In another article in English I published in 2012, titled, 'Social Foundations of Political Vitality', I went further to develop the theoretical links among the middle class, civil society and democracy in the case of Taiwan in 1980–2010 (Hsiao 2012: 37–56). Looking back, I should have added a subtitle such as 'the tripartite links of middle class – civil society – democracy in Taiwan' to that piece.

In that article, I deliberately termed the key ingredients of Taiwan's political vitality to exactly be the required links of middle class, civil society and democracy-making processes in the past four decades. I summarised four direct lessons from Taiwan's experiences in theorising the above connections.

1. Simply having a large, upwardly mobile, affluent middle class will not be enough to secure democratisation. It is necessary to have an adequate number of liberal and progressive middle-class intellectuals and professionals to envision the prospect of democracy even under authoritarianism.
2. Simply having a sizable ordinary non-governmental civic organisation may not be sufficient. It is essential to develop adequate numbers of diverse advocacy and pro-democracy social movement organisations to exert pressure collectively on an authoritarian regime for progressive changes to happen.
3. It is essential that the liberal and progressive middle class be actively involved in various advocacy and pro-democracy social movement organisations and even play a leading role in fulfilling the democratic function of civil society organisations.
4. It is necessary to have the existence of an effective political opposition party to challenge directly the authoritarian rule so that the progressive middle class can render their political support while the advocacy civil society organisations can further develop or forge a strategic democratic coalition with it (Hsiao 2012: 54).

Finally, in the most recent English publication, I once again systematically documented, with more empirical evidence, how the adequate liberal and progressive new middle class, by means of organising, joining or supporting the diverse advocacy and pro-democracy social movement organisations, have contributed to the different stages of democracy-making history between 1960 and 2016. The five historical phases are divided to analyse how joint forces of advocacy, that is, the liberal new middle class and civil society, have been influencing, at various stages,

30 Hsin-Huang Michael Hsiao

the formation and reformation of Taiwanese democracy-making history. They are: before the 1980s, the 1980s, the 1990s, 2000–2008 and 2008–2016. In retrospect, Taiwan's experience over the past 50 years or so has, to a great extent, confirmed the positive tripartite links of middle class, civil society and democracy-making, and of course, with the necessary specifications as stressed above (Hsiao 2019a).

Conclusion

I am quite glad to have this opportunity to review and reflect on my previous research works on social movements and civil society in Taiwan. I do not have a direct way to know Taiwanese sociologists' and the social science community's responses to and critiques on my works by means of book reviews, as my publications on social movements have been mostly journal articles and book chapters rather than a single book. The rationale behind this choice of publishing option was simply the 'time factor', as only single journal articles and book chapters could keep up with the changes in Taiwan's social movements and civil society scene. However, I am pleased to see my various works have often been referred to and cited by scholars who have worked in similar research areas over the years. To me, that was an alternative way to review my related academic works. My most frequently cited works were my publications in the decade of the 1990s on the empirical studies of many specific social movements and activated civil society forces.

That seems to coincide with the beginning of the indigenisation of sociological research inside Taiwan and the rise of Taiwan studies overseas. If I may reflect on this, I think I was considered to be an informed as well as a critical observer from inside Taiwan, and a concerned social scientist who was able to publish in English to communicate with outside academic circles on this emerging social phenomenon amid Taiwan's great transformation since the 1980s. I am happy to have served my role in that capacity adequately over the years. It was particularly true, in retrospect, of my series of English journal articles and book chapters on the rise of overall social movements and protests as well as the depiction and analysis on labour movements, farmers' movements, environmental movements and the welfare movement in the 1990s.

I was fortunate enough to have the rare life chance to return to Taiwan after my doctoral degree in 1979 in time to personally witness the golden decade of social movements in the 1980s, the dialectic relations between activated civil society and the democratic transformation processes in the 1990s, and finally the historic regime changes and democratic consolidation since 2000. The broader contextual timing was great, and I am happy that I have been quite insistent on grasping every chance to observe and to publish what I have observed in the past three decades. My role in all this has been a mix of being an activist, advocate and observer, and in the most part, being a concerned supporter and serious scholar.

I have enjoyed my past roles as a witness-sociologist between 1980 and 2000, and many of my writings and publications are the products of my sociological eyewitness and investigatory reports. Because of that, I am flattered to be considered a forerunner of social movements and civil society research in Taiwan. Looking back, I feel strongly that my personal concern about and commitment to the rise of citizens' legitimate protests and organised social movements since the 1980s was undeniably the internal driving force. My sociological training as well as insight were, of course, my effective tools. My works on social movements and civil society are written from a sociological perspective with intended theoretical concern and solid empirical evidence. The methods of collection of the necessary data I employed over the years have been a combination of secondary data analysis, content analysis of newspaper reporting, participant observation and survey data analysis.

The third turn in my journey of social movements and civil society research, to theorise what I have done so far, in contrast to the previous two shifts from being concerned to observing and to empirical study, is a different story. I am no longer a helpful story teller and provider of empirical evidence to my colleagues both locally and globally in this particular field. I have decided to develop a constructive and even critical dialogue with the existing and popular theoretical discourses in sociology and social science in the past decade or so. My deliberate decision has been to relate my research findings of social movements and civil society to two other important fields, the middle class and democracy, on which I have also worked over the years. To verify and to construct the typological analysis of the tripartite links of the middle class, civil society and democratisation in Taiwan, in particular, and in Asia, in general, is exactly what I have been doing over the past few years (Hsiao 2019b, 2019c).

I do hope I can make a useful contribution to the three related sociological research areas: middle-class politics, civil society dynamics and democratic transformation. To be sure, without my past intensive and extensive studies of social movements and civil society activism in Taiwan, there would be no way I could somehow smoothly link my theoretical ambition to the other two research subjects of middle class and democratisation. Finally, I probably would not change my mind or the course of action in my past pursuit of social movements and civil society research if I were given the chance to do it again. I am still convinced that a scholar's personal passion and commitment to the research subject are crucial and can't be undermined.

Bibliography

Cohen, J. L. and A. Arato. 1994. *Civil Society and Political Theory*. Cambridge: MIT Press.

Diamond, Larry. 1994. 'Rethinking Civil Society: Toward Democratic Consolidation'. *Journal of Democracy*, 5: 4–17.

Hsiao, H. H. Michael. 1984. 'Consumers Problems and Consumers Movement' (in Chinese). In K. S. Yang and C. C. Yeh (eds), *Social Problems in Taiwan*. Taipei: Chu-Liu Book Company, 217–248.

Hsiao, H. H. Michael. 1987. *We Have Only One Taiwan: Anti-Pollution, Consecration and Environmental Movements* (in Chinese). Taipei: Yuan-Hseng Publishing Co.

Hsiao, H. H. Michael. 1989a. *The Future Trends of Taiwan* (in Chinese). Taipei: The Society University.

Hsiao, H. H. Michael. 1989b. 'The Analytical Framework of Taiwan's Emerging Social Movements' (in Chinese). In Cheng-Kuang Hsu and Sung Wen-Li (eds), *Taiwan's Emerging Social Movements*. Taipei: Chu-Liu Book Co. 21–46.

Hsiao, H. H. Michael. 1989c. 'Exploring Taiwan's Emerging Social Movements: Autonomy and Resource Distribution' (in Chinese). In Taiwan Research Fund (ed), *Monopoly and Exploitation: Political Economy of Authoritarianism*. Taipei: Taiwan Research Fund, 9–32.

Hsiao, H. H. Michael, 1990. 'Emerging Social Movements and the Rise of a Demanding Civil Society in Taiwan'. *The Australian Journal of Chinese Affairs*, 24 (July), 163–180.

Hsiao, H. H. Michael. 1991. 'The Changing State-Society Relations in the ROC: Economic Change, the Transformation of Class Structure, and the Rise of Social Movements'. In Ramon Myers (ed), *Two Societies in Opposition*. Stanford: Hoover Institution Press, 127–140.

Hsiao, H. H. Michael. 1992a. 'The Rise of Social Movements and Civil Protests'. In Tun-Jen Cheng and Stephan Haggard (eds), *Political Change in Taiwan*. Boulder, Colorado: Lynn Rienner Publishers, 57–72.

Hsiao, H. H. Michael. 1992b. 'The Labor Movement in Taiwan: A Retrospective and Prospective Look'. In Denis F. Simon and Michael Y. M. Kau (eds), *Taiwan: Beyond the Economic Miracle*. Armonk: M. E. Sharpe, 151–167.

Hsiao, H. H. Michael. 1994a. 'Political Liberalization and the Farmers' Movement in Taiwan'. In Edward Friedman (ed), *The Politics of Democratization: Generalizing East Asian Experience*. Boulder, Colorado: Westview Press, 202–218.

Hsiao, H. H. Michael, 1994b. 'The Character and Transformation of Local Environmental Protests: 1980–1991' (in Chinese). In Taiwan Research Fund (ed), *Environmental Protection and Industrial Policy*. Taipei: Vanguard Publication Co , 550–573.

Hsiao, H. H. Michael, 1997a. 'Urban Movements' (in Chinese). In Y. M. Tsai and Y. H. Chang (eds), *Urban Society of Taiwan*. Taipei: Chu-Liu Book Co., 391–413.

Hsiao, H. H. Michael, 1997b. 'Social Movements and Civil Society in Taiwan: A Typological Analysis of Social Movements and Public Acceptance'. *The Copenhagen Journal of Asian Studies*, 11, 7–26.

Hsiao, H. H. Michael, 1999a. *Taiwan's Local Environmental Protests Movement: 1980–1996* (in Chinese). Hong Kong: Cross-Strait Relations Research Center.

Hsiao, H. H. Michael, 1999b. 'Environmental Movements in Taiwan'. In Yok-Shiu Lee and Alvin So (eds), *Asia's Environmental Movements*. New York: M. E. Sharpe, 31–54.

Hsiao, H. H. Michael, 2001. 'Taiwan's Social Welfare Movement since the 1980s'. In Christian Aspalter (ed), *Understanding Modern Taiwan: Essays in Economic, Politics and Social Policy*. London: Ashgate, 169–204.

Hsiao, H. H. Michael, 2002. 'Taiwan's Local Environmental Protest Movements (1980–2000): A Historical and Spatial Analysis' (in Chinese). In *Newsletter of Sustainable Taiwan*. Taipei: Committee of Sustainable Development Research, National Science Council, 4(2), 34–68.

Hsiao, H. H. Michael, 2003. 'NGOs and Democratization in Taiwan: Their Interactive Roles in Building a Viable Civil Society'. In David Schak and Wayne Hudson (eds), *Civil Society in Asia*. Hampshire, UK: Ashgate, 180–191.

Hsiao, H. H. Michael, 2005a. 'NGOs, the State, and Democracy under Globalization: The Case of Taiwan'. In Robert Weller (ed), *Civil Life, Globalization, and Political Change in Asia: Organizing between Family and State*. London: Routledge, 42–57.

Hsiao, H. H. Michael, 2005b. 'Civil Society, NGOs and Democratization in Taiwan: 1980–2005'. *Third Sector Review*, 4, 2–26.

Social movements and civil society research revisited 33

Hsiao, H. H. Michael, 2011. 'Social Movements in Taiwan: A Typological Analysis'. In Jeffrey Broadbent and Vicky Brockman (eds), *East Asian Social Movements*. New York: Springer, 237–254.

Hsiao, H. H. Michael, 2012. 'Social Foundations of Political Vitality'. In Steve Tsang (ed), *The Vitality of Taiwan*. London: Palgrave Macmillan, 37–56.

Hsiao, H. H. Michael, 2019a. 'The Tripartite Links of Middle Class, Civil Society and Democratization in Taiwan: 1980–2016'. In H. H. Michael Hsiao (ed), *Middle Class, Civil Society and Democracy in Asia*. London and New York: Routledge.

Hsiao, H. H. Michael, 2019b. 'Comparing the Tripartite Links of Middle Class, Civil Society and Democratization in Asia: Positive, Dubious and Negative'. In H. H. Michael Hsiao (ed), *Middle Class, Civil Society and Democracy in Asia*. London and New York: Routledge.

Hsiao, H. H. Michael (ed). 2019c. *Middle Class, Civil Society and Democracy in Asia*. London and New York: Routledge.

Hsiao, H. H. Michael, Y. P. Cheng and Joan Lei. (eds). 1982. *Consumers' Movement in Taiwan: Theory and Practice* (in Chinese). Taipei: Times Culture Publishing Co.

Hsiao, H. H. Michael and Ming-Sho Ho. 2010. 'Civil Society and Democracy-Making in Taiwan: Reexamining the Link'. In Yin-wah Chu and Siu-Lun Wong (eds), *New Democracies: Deepening, Reversal, Non-liberal Alternatives*. London: Routledge, 43–64.

Hsiao, H. H. Michael, H. M. Huang and H. J. Ong. 1995. 'The Rise and Fall of Social Forces in Taiwan: 1895–1995' (in Chinese). In Taiwan Research Fund (ed), *One Hundred Years of Taiwan*. Taipei: Vanguard Publication Co., 110–149.

Hsiao, H. H. Michael and Hagen Koo. 1997. 'The Middle Class and Democratization'. In Larry Diamond, Marc Plattneret al (eds), *Consolidating the Third Wave Democracies*. Baltimore: Johns Hopkins University Press, 312–333.

Hsiao, H. H. Michael and Kuo-Ming Lin (eds). 2000. *The Social Welfare Movements in Taiwan* (in Chinese). Taipei: Chu-Liu Book Company.

Hsiao, H. H. Michael and Hwa-Jen Liu. 2002. 'Collective Action toward a Sustainable City: Citizens' Movements and Environmental Politics in Taipei'. In Peter Evans (ed), *Livable Cities: Urban Struggles of Livelihood and Sustainability*. Berkeley: University of California Press, 67–94.

Hsiao, H. H. Michael, Lester Milbrath and Robert Weller. 1995. 'Antecedents of an Environmental Movement in Taiwan'. *Capitalism, Nature, Socialism: A Journal of Socialist Ecology*, 6(3) (September), 91–104.

Hsiao, H. H. Michael and C. H. Sun. 2000. 'The Transformation and Succession in Taiwan's Social Welfare Movements since 1980s'. In H. H. Michael Hsiao and K. M. Lin (eds), *The Social Welfare Movements in Taiwan*. Taipei: Chiu-Liu Publications, 33–70.

Hsiao, H. H. Michael, Robert Weller, et al. 2004. 'Civil Society Organizations in Taipei, Hong Kong, Guangzhou and Xiamen' (in Chinese). *Third Sector Review*, 1, 1–60.

Hsu, Cheng-Kuang and Wen-Li Sung (eds). 1989. *Taiwan's Emerging Social Movements* (in Chinese). Taipei: Chu-Liu Book Co.

Lipset, Seymour Martin. 1963. *Political Man: The Social Bases of Politics, Garden City*. New York: Anchor Books.

Lipset, Seymour Martin, 1964. 'The Changing Class Structure and Contemporary European Politics'. *Daedalus*, 93(1), 271–303.

Moore, Barrington Jr. 1966. *Social Origins of Dictatorship and Democracy Lord and Peasants in the Making of the Modern World*. Boston: Beacon Press.

Putnam, Robert. 1994. *Making Democracy Work: Civil Tradition in Modern Italy*. Princeton, NJ: Princeton University Press.

Taylor, Charles. 1990. 'Modes of Civil Society'. *Public Culture*, 3(1) (Fall), 95–118.

3

STATE AND SOCIETY IN THE TAIWAN MIRACLE REVISITED

Thomas B. Gold

Introduction

I am at the stage of life where I am looking backward more than forward and am grateful for the invitation to reflect on work done more than 30 years ago. It is particularly gratifying to see the development of Taiwan Studies throughout Europe where there was little or no history of interest in the island. I want to use this opportunity to share with students in particular the process of coming up with a research project, including reflecting on how it relates to one's own personal values, presuppositions and experiences, as well as the historical era when the work is undertaken.

I will first review the backstory to the book, *State and Society in the Taiwan Miracle* (Gold 1986), and hope not to be overly self-indulgent. Next I will look at what has changed regarding the topic in the intervening three decades, and conclude with my current research on Taiwan, which is to bring the story up to the present (whenever that will be!) and to address a different set of theoretical issues.

Motivation for starting the project

I started studying Chinese as an undergraduate in 1967 on a dare. Up until the 1980s, Chinese was offered primarily only at major research institutions. I matriculated at Oberlin College, a small four-year liberal arts school in rural Ohio. It happened that Oberlin had a strong missionary tradition and a band of missionaries near Taigu County in Shanxi Province had the misfortune to be killed (martyred) during the 1900 Boxer Rebellion. The school erected the Shansi Memorial Arch in the centre of campus to memorialise them and with the assistance of alumni H. H. Kung (Kung Hsiang-hsi, brother-in-law of Chiang Kai-shek), established the Ming Hsien Middle School in Taigu. Beginning in 1908, every year Oberlin alumni were selected to go to Taigu to teach at the school.[1]

State and Society in the Taiwan Miracle revisited   35

Not long after the establishment of the People's Republic of China (PRC), the Shansi representatives, along with most other foreign missionaries and teachers, were expelled from the mainland. A dozen of the programmes banded together to establish Tunghai University in Taichung, Taiwan, under the auspices of the United Board for Christian Higher Education in Asia. Vice President Richard Nixon participated in the laying of the cornerstone in 1953. Oberlin resumed sending Shansi 'reps' in 1955 to Tunghai.

Several of us who took a course in Asian (primarily Chinese) History taught by Prof. Ellsworth Carlson, who had been a Shansi rep and also lived in China for much of World War II, were so intrigued by the material that we dared each other to actually enrol in Beginning Chinese. At that time it was extremely rare for Chinese to be taught outside of major research universities. It seemed a thoroughly impractical thing to do. Studying Chinese had nothing to do with being farsighted, as some people claim in hindsight. This was during a very tense period of the Cold War and Americans could certainly not go to mainland China or even conceive that it would ever be possible. The only place to go to learn Chinese as a living language was Taiwan. I made my first trip in the summer of 1969, spending two weeks in Taipei and eight at Tunghai. I liked Taiwan so much that I applied for and received the Shansi Fellowship to teach English at Tunghai from 1970–1972.

The 1969 trip was my first opportunity to travel abroad. Besides Taiwan, I went with my student group to Hong Kong and Japan. In addition to the heat and culture shock, it was the first chance I had had to live in a foreign language country. It was also my first trip to a developing country and I was very impressed at the diligence and long hours that people put into their work, especially small enterprises. Their ability to '*chiku*' (eat bitterness) was astounding. At Tunghai, besides teaching English, I continued to study Mandarin and added Taiwanese as well. I confess that I really knew little about Taiwan politics (such as they were) although I was aware that some of my students were pressing me to discuss the Vietnam War and reporting on me to somebody or another, probably military officers (*jiaoguan*) stationed on campus and in the boys' dorms. Foreign teachers played a game of guessing who were the spies. I did not question the '*waisheng/ bensheng*' distinction (i.e., whether you or your ancestors came to Taiwan province from the mainland after 1945 or had been there for generations). After a few of my Taiwanese friends were interrogated by the police because of something I might have said or they might have done, I avoided any mention of politics and focused on building friendships with my students, some of whom proved invaluable as informants and connections when I returned in 1977 to do fieldwork for my dissertation. One lesson I absorbed was 'politics is dangerous' and something to avoid if possible.

This was a particularly momentous, frightening and negative period for Taiwan. I can't go into detail, but one of the major trends included the rise of Chiang Ching-kuo, son of Chiang Kai-shek, through the Kuomintang (KMT) and state organisations as his father's health failed. Young Chiang had built and enforced the authoritarian apparatus on Taiwan and many intellectuals feared that his eventual assumption of power would be bad for any possible move toward political liberalisation. The Vietnam War was still raging and many American troops were stationed on Taiwan, including Ching Chuan-kang air base near Taichung, or came to the island for Rest and Recreation, which provided a big boost to the sex industry. Then there was a series of severe diplomatic setbacks, as National Security Advisor Henry Kissinger made a secret trip to Beijing in July of 1971, which set the stage for President Nixon's trip in February the next year, resulting in the Shanghai Communiqué that opened the door to eventual normalisation of relations between Beijing and Washington. Following this, the ROC withdrew from the United Nations when it was clear that the United States would no longer oppose the admission of the PRC. Both sides opposed dual recognition, so when one went in, the other went out. Subsequently, other important countries such as Japan and Canada shifted recognition to Beijing. These events caused some degree of panic on the island and some of my better-off students' parents moved away to safer venues such as Singapore. Finally, there was a movement of students critical of the government for not being assertive enough against Japan's claims to the Tiaoyutai (Senkaku) Islands that the ROC also claimed.

This was all high-level politics and macro-level structural changes whose significance I couldn't appreciate at the time, to be honest. I didn't have the skill set – concepts, theories, methods – to do that. I didn't start to develop those until I entered the PhD programme in Sociology at Harvard in 1975, with no background in Sociology! After two years in Taiwan, as part of my Shansi Fellowship, I spent another year at Oberlin taking courses, including one on 'Racial and Ethnic Minorities in Asia and Africa' taught by the eminent sociologist Milton Yinger. I wrote a paper on Overseas Chinese in Southeast Asia, something that had intrigued me during two trips to the region. I was accepted to the Masters Program in Regional Studies – East Asia at Harvard, intending to go on for a PhD in History and East Asian Languages (HEAL). Soon after arriving, Sociology Professor Ezra Vogel, a close friend of Yinger, approached me about joining a group he was organising of Sociology graduate students working mostly on China. After a bit he suggested I go into Sociology instead of HEAL, arguing (persuasively) that my personality was more suited to Sociology. It took me two years to come around, but I took his advice and plunged into this new field.

I read social theory, much of which is about social change and what makes social change possible. This was a highly charged topic at the time of the Vietnam War and Cultural Revolution. The legacy of the anti-Vietnam War protests was pervasive, as were romantic notions of the Cultural Revolution and China's call for self-reliant development, Watergate, and disgust with US politics at home and around the world.

The main theoretical approaches to look at social change were modernisation theory and dependency-world systems theory.

Modernisation theory grew largely out of the structural-functionalism work of Talcott Parsons (1964). He dissected societies into structures each of which had a function to perform to keep the equilibrium in balance internally and in relation to

State and Society in the Taiwan Miracle revisited **37**

its external environment, and permit the social organism (he used biological metaphors) to survive. As the division of labour in societies grew more complex in the process of modernisation, societies faced a range of challenges to integrate all the parts, and required capable leadership to guide the process. Modernisation theory focused on harmony, guiding a transition from tradition to modernity, with the United States as the paramount case. Structural-functionalism dominated American social science and policy. America's official goal was to bring the good things of modern life (as in the United States) to the backward, tradition-bound rest of the world. Clearly however, with Vietnam as a prime example, it wasn't working.

Dependency and world-systems theory, derived from Marx and Lenin, approached these problems from a very different perspective. They focused on imperialism, and how it established and maintained structures that took over underdeveloped economies for the benefit of the developed ones, resulting in poverty, inequality and exploitation. This was not done out of good will, as modernisationists asserted, but to ensure a supply of resources, cheap disciplined labour, markets and outlets for capital. The only way out of these structures was through struggle and the adoption of Chinese-style self-reliance. Mao Zedong, Ho Chi Minh, Kim Il Sung and Fidel Castro were inspiring exemplars of this struggle. Most of the theories and data actually came from Latin America and, to a lesser extent, Africa, with US-backed dictatorships; Asia rarely came up. So there was space to bring Taiwan into the debate.

In thinking about these issues in relation to the only case I knew first hand, it was clear that, yes, Taiwan's economy was dependent on the world system (what we'd now call 'highly globalised'), yet, unlike the other cases, it had minimal income inequality. There was even an emerging middle class. The state appeared able to exert control over multinationals rather effectively, and Taiwan had a lively private entrepreneurial class. Without doubt, the KMT state practised hard authoritarianism, and it was clear that this tight control served the Cold War American business and military interests, but even then there were indications that the system might liberalise and actually implement its democratic, but suspended under Martial Law, constitution.

When it came time to pick a dissertation topic, my adviser, Ezra Vogel, said, 'no one has tested these theories on Taiwan; you know Taiwan, why don't you do that?' So I did. I had planned to do a PRC topic but at that very time US–China relations took a dive, so I accepted Prof. Vogel's suggestion. I ended up in 'Taiwan Studies' – a subfield that didn't really exist – purely by accident.

I was also very influenced by another professor, Theda Skocpol, especially her work on state strength and her concept of the 'relative autonomy of the state' (Skocpol 1979). She introduced me to the work of her grad. school colleague, Peter Evans, whose manuscript on Brazil (elaborating work by Fernando Enrique Cardoso (and Faletto 1979)) developed the concept of the 'triple alliance' among multi-nationals, local capitalists and the state, with multinationals the strongest, and the

38 Thomas B. Gold

state pretty much its puppet to suppress workers and create a good investment climate for multinationals.[2]

I phrased my research questions to try to understand the historical evolution of domestic private business (the local, mostly Taiwanese, bourgeoisie) in an environment shaped by the very powerful émigré state and multinationals. It was a comprehensive political economic sociological approach. As I interviewed businessmen, officials and foreign investors I tried to discern how each perceived the others and how they strategised in this environment. I was interested in their stories as well as their mindsets. There was virtually no social science literature on Taiwan that I could engage with. Economists had begun to notice the island's development. Examples are Fei, Ranis and Kuo (1979), Galenson (1979), Ho (1978) and Lin (1973) but they neglected the political context almost entirely. An article by anthropologist Hill Gates (1979) is the first time I saw the word 'dependency' used in reference to Taiwan.

My main finding was that the role of the state in Taiwan was very different from that in Brazil and the other 'dependent' societies. It enjoyed a tremendous amount of autonomy from social forces and multinationals, enabling it to push a number of policies. Although the KMT state was an often brutal Leninist-style dictatorship, it nonetheless created channels and opportunities for upward mobility among all citizens, though the playing field was very uneven well into the 1970s.

Main methods and fieldwork

I returned to Taiwan in the summer of 1977 to begin fieldwork after an absence of five years. I used a variety of means to identify people to interview. Understanding the importance of *guanxi* (connections), I started with the families of students from Tunghai, as well as people with Harvard ties. Many of my interviews were based purely on cold-calling people I identified from the media, recommendations of other interviewees (snowball technique) and biographies of successful business people. At that time, as Taiwan began to feel more confident economically, several series of biographies of successful businessmen, especially rags-to-riches stories appeared and I used them to identify potential interview subjects as well as pertinent topics to discuss. Some days I would interview a local businessman, a government official and a foreign investor or banker. I also had connections to journalists and academics as well as politicians

When I had left in 1972 there was great pessimism about Taiwan's international standing after the Nixon trip and Shanghai Communiqué. But Taiwan survived the Nixon effort at normalisation with the PRC, which remained unconsummated. It was not until January 1, 1979 that Beijing and Washington established full diplomatic relations. Taiwan (ROC) also survived the withdrawal from the UN and the ongoing loss of diplomatic relations. Taiwan weathered the loss of South Vietnam and communist victories in Cambodia and Laos.

One major transition had occurred during my absence: Chiang Ching-kuo's assumption of top positions in the party and state. To my great surprise, this man

State and Society in the Taiwan Miracle revisited   **39**

most closely identified with the authoritarian apparatus, had reinvented himself as a modest man of the people, visiting and eating with farmers, workers, fishermen and small entrepreneurs, dressed casually in a windbreaker. The first item on the Sunday evening news always featured his visits of that day. This was a stark contrast to his aloof and stern father.

One final observation was that the middle class had expanded exponentially. The material standard of living of my former students and friends experienced noticeable improvement. But politically, things had not changed much.

This situation changed dramatically: two months after I returned. Taiwan experienced its first popular protest since the 2–28 uprising of 1947. This took place in Chung-li when a former KMT rising star, the Hakka Hsu Hsin-liang, decided to run for county magistrate against the party's own nominee. This violated party discipline and Hsu was expelled. Meanwhile, a number of students, lawyers, intellectuals and average citizens rallied to protest obvious efforts by the KMT to manipulate the vote. These activists had been coalescing into a movement known as the *dangwai*, or 'outside the party', with *party* referring to the KMT. It was illegal to organise new parties, so this became a non-party opposition 'party'. The movement continued to grow over the course of my research year and I interviewed most of the leading figures through various connections.

Also during that year, there was an explosion in the cultural field of what became known as *xiang-tu wen-xue*, or 'nativist literature'. This included writers such as Huang Chun-ming, Wang To, Wang Chen-ho, Cheng Ying-chen and Yang Ch'ing-ch'u (whose work I translated into English), as well as the writer-turned choreographer, Lin Hwai-min, whose Cloud Gate Dance Ensemble attracted sold-out audiences, mostly young, to its performances. The significance of these artists was that their works focused on Taiwan *qua* Taiwan, not as the temporary seat of the Government of the Republic of China, nor as the repository and protector of Chinese culture, nor as the beacon of freedom for the enslaved people of the mainland. No, it was just about, and reflecting, the common people of Taiwan, the sort of people Chiang Ching-kuo was eating noodles with, who had a chance to tell their own stories. I interviewed the leading figures in this movement as well.

In other words, there was a great deal of change afoot – albeit largely disorganised – from below, that is, society, where up to that point the mainlander-dominated exiled KMT party-state had pretty much had free rein to manage society (economy, politics, education, culture) from above for the previous three decades.

Methods-wise, I used the year to interview people from all sides of the 'triple alliance', as well as cultural figures, journalists and my former students. I was fortunate to audit a weekly class taught by K.T. Li (Li Kuo-ting), the father of the Taiwan miracle, at National Taiwan University. He invited key figures from the state, business and education fields to discuss their experience. I dashed up after class to proffer my business card and arrange to interview them at a later date. Most were extremely happy to meet me. This was an exuberant period for the Taiwan Miracle and people were excited to tell their part of the story.

40 Thomas B. Gold

So, in sum, I tried to get a balanced, all-sided picture of Taiwan's development, including archival work on the Japanese era. What was then the Provincial Library held a rich collection of material from the Japanese colonial period. I consulted newspapers as well as yearbooks and other government publications that provided data as well as texture to that time. It could be head-spinning to interview an array of people from wildly differing experiences and perspectives on the same day.

China interlude

In the meantime, after returning to the United States after short trips to South Korea and Japan for some comparative insights, I was selected to join the first group of American government-sponsored exchanged students to go to China. I spent a year from February 1979 through February 1980 at Fudan University in Shanghai.

Again, timing was everything.

After being selected in the fall of 1978, President Carter suddenly announced in December that the United States and PRC would establish full diplomatic relations on January 1, 1979. This meant a breaking of diplomatic ties with the ROC on Taiwan as both sides maintained a strict One China Policy and forbade dual recognition.

Then the December 1978 Third Plenum of the 11th Central Committee of the Communist Party shifted the focus of the party's work to the Four Modernizations. Though I had planned to control myself and *not* discuss Taiwan during that year, I discovered that there was great interest in the Taiwan experience and what China might learn from it in terms of opening to the outside world for trade, maybe even direct investment, and opening a window for private business, especially by farmers. All of this is normal now, but was absolutely revolutionary in 1979.

This helped me appreciate Taiwan even more – how what we'd now call a 'failed state' (the ROC on the mainland) had regrouped, pledged itself to a fresh start, purged its most corrupt elements and made an implied social contract with the people under its control, and brought about what I called a miraculous achievement of economic development and social transformation, albeit still under a hard authoritarian martial law regime.

I largely structured the dissertation (Gold 1981) following Peter Evans' (1979) *Dependent Development*. He began with a demonstration by workers; I began with the Chung-li Incident and what it revealed about contradictions in the process of development. After a historical overview I selected three economic sectors to illustrate the dominant role in each sector of one of the three main actors: the textile industry dominated by local capital; the electronics industry dominated by multinationals; and the petrochemical industry dominated by the state. I tried to show how the state not only used ownership of key upstream sectors but also a variety of other tools to shape and stimulate the economy as well as suppress any political or labour opposition.

The book

I wrote *State and Society in the Taiwan Miracle* mostly during 1984–1985. It was intended to be the historical chapter in a revised version of my dissertation, but an editor at the publisher M.E. Sharpe contacted me and encouraged me to expand the chapter into a stand-alone monograph, which I did. By that time, there were actually a few scholars analysing Taiwan from a dependency or world-systems perspective. I found that many of them attributed everything that had happened in Taiwan to external actors: first the Japanese empire, and then American imperialism. Taiwan's state and society had virtually no agency. More balanced work came from scholars such as Cumings (1984), Gates (1979), Hsiao (1981) and Simon (1980). But I put forth what I called, after Cardoso and Faletto (1979), a 'comprehensive framework'. This meant a 'historical-structural approach' taking into consideration the complicated intertwining of politics, social structure and the economy, and their integration with external forces.

After reviewing the theoretical debate between modernisation and dependency/world systems theories, and the positions of the emerging group of scholars applying these theories to Taiwan,[3] the book is mainly chronological. I focused on key turning points: Japanese colonialism; the chaotic interregnum after the Japanese withdrawal at the end of World War II up until the KMT government moved to Taiwan; the Import Substitution phase of the 1950s; Export Orientation phase of the 1960s and the rise of Chiang Ching-kuo; and the industrial upgrading and emergence of the political opposition from the mid-1970s until the mid-1980s. My focus in each chapter was how the state – Japanese colonialist, KMT mainlander neo-colonialist – established hegemony over society from top to bottom, but also provided channels for upward mobility, primarily through business and education. I did not shirk from discussing the February 28, 1947 Incident or the authoritarian nature of the KMT regime, topics that had been neglected in the studies of the economy that were then coming out. To my mind, the authoritarian regime was a key factor that could not be overlooked, especially because it was *developmental* and not kleptocratic, as most other dictatorships (including the KMT itself on the mainland) were.

Because the book was chronological, I could not fit in the three case studies. I presented an abbreviated version of them in my chapter, 'Entrepreneurs, Multinationals and the State', in the volume, *Contending Approaches to the Political Economy of Taiwan*, edited by Winckler and Greenhalgh (1988). I had another chapter in that book where I presented material about the Japanese era, entitled, 'Colonial Origins of Taiwanese Capitalism'.

To be honest I was frustrated that I did not include much of the rich detail about the cases and the people I interviewed in the book. I was already teaching at Berkeley and coming up for tenure, so I wanted to get a book out, even though it was not the revised dissertation I had intended to write.

A publisher in Taiwan approached me in 1985 about translating the book into Chinese, but after reading the manuscript, decided that the material about the political system, especially 2–28, was too sensitive and decided not to go ahead.

42 Thomas B. Gold

In October 1986, six months after the book came out, I went to Taiwan with a film crew to do a documentary about Land Reform's contribution to Taiwan's development ('Taiwan: Winds of Change'). It was to be very positive about Taiwan's experience, yet upon arrival at the airport I was taken to a back room and asked what I was doing; and upon departure I was removed from the plane by some security personnel until the crew insisted I board, as a signal that I was on the 'gray list'. During the trip I had visited friends from the *dangwai* who had just the month before established the Democratic Progressive Party (DPP), which was still illegal under Martial Law. To everyone's surprise, Chiang Ching-kuo decided not to suppress it. I'm not certain why I was on this list. It could have been my long association with dissidents on Taiwan and meeting them in the United States. I was not prevented from entering Taiwan or from leaving. I was not warned about anything or intimidated beyond being taken to the back room. My next trip, in 1987, was right after the termination of Martial Law and there were no problems entering or exiting.

At the end of the book, I made the following statements:

> The Party's admirable success at leading economic development and social change from a position of autonomy created the conditions for the withering away of its dictatorship. It has made marked strides toward political modernization, and the far-flung repressive apparatus has become anachronistic. (p. 121)
>
> Party rank and file came increasingly from college-educated young people who joined primarily for careerist reasons and were reluctant to submit to democratic-centralist discipline, an anachronism in a complex industrial society. (p. 129)

I used the term 'anachronistic' (or variants) twice. In fact, Taiwan had already become an unlikely case supportive of modernisation theory's predictions, as famously articulated by Seymour Martin Lipset (1959), namely, that urbanisation, education and the rise of a middle class were highly correlated with demands for democracy; not causal, but the two went together.

On July 1, 1987, Chiang Ching-kuo declared the lifting of Martial Law. The next month I attended a conference at National Taiwan University and mentioned 2–28 and Martial Law in my prepared remarks. I had to stop myself and declare, 'I can't believe I'm saying this in public in Taiwan!'

Reviews

With one exception, the reviews of the book were positive, highlighting its contribution to development theory and bringing the Taiwan case to a larger audience. M.E. Sharpe, under the leadership of Douglas Merwin, became the go-to publisher of books on Taiwan.

Time passes

It's now more than 30 years since the book came out. I tried and failed to add a few chapters for a second revised and updated edition, but did manage to publish more than a dozen articles and book chapters about different aspects of change in Taiwan. I'm not good at revising – I prefer to do something new. One article, 'Taiwan Society at the Fin de Siecle' (Gold 1996), presented an overview of social change over the decade since the end of martial law. I did several that looked at the formation of a distinct Taiwanese identity, mainly through literature and other forms of popular culture along with the emergence of civil society (Gold 1993, 1994). In the 1988–1989 academic year, while I was a National Fellow at the Hoover Institution, I participated in a study group on civil society comprising scholars from around the globe. I began to apply the concept to work on China and Taiwan (Gold 1994, 1996). I have also addressed cross-Strait relations from a number of perspectives, beginning with the initial posturing in the 1980s to the influence of Taiwan and Hong Kong popular culture in China, and the role of foreigners as a bridge between the two societies. But the main focus has been on political change: the weakening of the KMT party-state and the rise of society (Gold 2000, 2007). This has involved a shift in theoretical interests, which I elaborate on below.

The intellectual debates that formed the basis of the dissertation and book are not central to the sociology of development or terribly compelling to me anymore. I have been identified as part of the 'developmental state' school greatly influenced by Chalmers Johnson's *MITI and the Japanese Miracle* (Johnson 1982). As I see it now, there is no dominant theory or paradigm in the development field, except maybe, and very ironically, the Beijing Consensus, especially considering the attraction of Maoist self-reliance to dependency and world systems devotees way back when.

I think the story about Taiwan now is socio-political, not economic. There are now a lot of books and articles about democratisation, much of it out of SOAS and much now published by Routledge Taiwan was clearly part of what Samuel Huntington (1991) called 'The Third Wave of Democracy'. I was honoured to present a paper at the self-congratulatory 1995 conference in Taipei on the Third Wave (Gold 1997). Keynote speeches were given by President Lee Teng-hui as well as theorists and activists from around the world. It was Taiwan's 'coming out party', and an important element of Taiwan's soft power.

The field of Taiwan Studies has grown from virtually nothing. The European Association of Taiwan Studies and North American Taiwan Studies Association have become major fora for scholarly exchange.

In the intervening years I have tried many times to focus my research on China, but Taiwan is *so* interesting in so many ways, and I keep receiving invitations to conferences and programmes in exotic places, that I haven't been able to disengage. In my courses on Development and Globalization I always include lectures and readings that introduce Taiwan both as an example of a successful developmental

44 Thomas B. Gold

state with tremendous improvements in standard of living, quality of life and relative income equity, and, now, a transformation from authoritarianism to democracy.

I have been developing a book called *Remaking Taiwan: Society and the State since the End of Martial Law*. I see it as more than another study of political democratisation, something very well researched by colleagues around the world, especially in Taiwan itself. The central theme is how the balance of power has shifted from the state (or, party-state when I wrote *State and Society*) to society. In terms of theory I've turned to the French sociologist, Pierre Bourdieu (and Wacquant 1992), and my Berkeley colleague Neil Fligstein, and their work on social fields[4]:

> A strategic action field is a constructed mesolevel social order in which actors (who can be individual or collective) are attuned to and interact with one another on the basis of shared (which is not to say consensual) understandings about the purposes of the field, relationships to others in the field (including who has power and why) and the rules governing legitimate action in the field. A stable field is one in which the main actors are able to reproduce themselves and the field over a fairly long period of time.
>
> *(Fligstein and McAdam 2012: 9)*

Examples of such fields include economic, political, cultural, educational, etc. Each field comprises a number of positions and the players need to have a common goal and collaborate in order to accumulate whatever resources (what Bourdieu calls 'capital') are at play in the field. Each field has a set of rules, what sociologists call 'institutions', that govern behaviour in the field. The fields are socially constructed and need to be maintained and reproduced over time. Ideally, from the point of view of the leadership, the rules become legitimised, that is, accepted and taken for granted. However, challengers might emerge to change the rules and positions. What I'm trying to do in the book is to examine the process by which the form of capital in key fields that had been effectively monopolized by the KMT mainlander elite through the Leninist party structure, became increasingly dispersed among other actors, mainly Taiwanese of all class backgrounds. So 'democratisation' is more than a political concept alone. Furthermore, I want to trace the process by which capital accumulated in one field, say economic, was 'invested' to accumulate capital in another, say political field. This might result in challenges to the rules of the other field.

An area of particular interest to me is the cultural field, and its ties to symbolic power and what I called 'the quest for identity'. As we know, when the central government retreated to Taiwan, one of its goals was to use the island as the base for a counterattack against the communist-controlled mainland. Because the people on Taiwan had just experienced 50 years of Japanese colonialism, the KMT felt it had to remake them into Chinese, to be more specific, as anti-communist loyal citizens of the KMT-led ROC. When the Cultural Revolution attacked much of Chinese culture, the KMT determined to make Taiwan the major repository of Chinese culture and its citizens well-versed in all aspects of it.

The KMT did not expect to be holed up on Taiwan very long, but we know how that has turned out. Meanwhile, through the compulsory education system, Taiwanese mastered the body of knowledge needed to advance into the government bureaucracy through the civil service exam. As older mainlanders died off and their children – basically sons – left Taiwan or took careers outside of politics, Taiwanese began to replace them. This was one avenue of 'Taiwanisation' or 'indigenisation' of the state, and, eventually, the party, as Chiang Ching-kuo realised that he had no choice but to recruit Taiwanese, like Lee Teng-hui, into the highest echelons of political power.

With the rise of the PRC and shrinkage of Taiwan's international space, the type of themes and issues initially explored by the *xiangtu* figures began to dominate the cultural space and lead the exploration and definition of a distinct 'Taiwanese' identity. This spilled over into political life, as candidates for office, with some exceptions, needed to demonstrate their grounding in Taiwan by speaking Taiwanese, or, in some cases, Hakka, at political events.

So, symbolically, the basis of regime legitimacy in Taiwan has been dramatically remade. The landslide election of Tsai Ing-wen in 2016 and the subsequent discombobulation of the KMT are evidence. Meanwhile, Beijing watches this process with fear and without sympathy or understanding.

Trips to Eastern Europe, helped by EATS conferences, have provided me with rich comparative experience for this project. In September 2018 I convened a workshop at Berkeley on the theme 'Constructing Post-Imperium Identity: Taiwan and Eastern Europe' that drew scholars from Taiwan as well as several countries in Eastern and Central Europe.

End

I would not do anything different with the project I began 40 years ago. It addressed important issues of the time and I was glad to bring the Taiwan case to the attention of Latin America and Africa-focused scholars. I think the book holds up well. My point is that, for me at least, the issues have changed and I have engaged with a new set of theories to analyse what has happened and continues to happen. Nonetheless, it is extremely gratifying to see the burgeoning of Taiwan Studies across societies and disciplines. The newly founded *International Journal of Taiwan Studies* is a major achievement, but it is also important to note that articles on Taiwan appear in a range of other disciplinary journals. While Taiwan Studies is not about to supplant Chinese Studies, it is beginning to stand on its own as a distinct field attracting top notch scholars.

Notes

1 For more background, see Jacobson (2008).
2 Published as *Dependent Development* (Evans 1979; Princeton: Princeton University Press).
3 A great boost to my dissertation and book came from a conference held at Columbia University in December 1980. The ensuing volume did not appear until 1988 (Winckler and Greenhalgh 1988).
4 My first effort to incorporate Bourdieu and fields appears in Gold 2000.

References

Bourdieu, Pierre and Loic J. D. Wacquant. 1992. *An Invitation to Reflexive Sociology*. Chicago: University of Chicago Press.

Cardoso, Fernando Henrique and Enzo Faletto. 1979. *Dependency and Development in Latin America*. Berkeley: University of California Press.

Cumings, Bruce. 1984. 'The Origin and Development of the Northeast Asian Political Economy: Industrial Sectors and Political Consequences'. *International Organization*, 38(1), Winter, 1–40.

Evans, Peter B. 1979. *Dependent Development: The Alliance of Multinational, State and Local Capital in Brazil*. Princeton: Princeton University Press.

Fei, John H. C., Gustav Ranis, and Shirley W. Y. Kuo. 1979. *Growth with Equity: The Taiwan Case*. New York: Oxford University Press.

Fligstein, Neil and Doug McAdam. 2012. A Theory of Fields. Oxford: Oxford. University Press.

Galenson, Walter, ed. 1979. *Economic Growth and Structural Change in Taiwan*. Ithaca: Cornell University Press.

Gates, Hill. 1979. 'Dependency and the Part-Time Proletariat in Taiwan'. *Modern China*, 5(3), July, 381–408.

Gold, Thomas B. 1981. 'Dependent Development in Taiwan'. Unpublished PhD dissertation. Harvard University.

Gold, Thomas B. 1986. *State and Society in the Taiwan Miracle*. Armonk: M.E. Sharpe.

Gold, Thomas B. 1993. 'Taiwan's Quest for Identity in the Shadow of China'. In Steve Tsang, (ed.), *In the Shadow of China: Political Developments in Taiwan since 1949*. London: Hurst, 169–192.

Gold, Thomas B. 1994. 'Civil Society and Taiwan's Quest for Identity'. In Stevan Harrell and Chung Chun-chieh (eds), *Cultural Change in Postwar Taiwan*. Boulder: Westview, 47–68.

Gold, Thomas B. 1996. 'Taiwan Society at the Fin de Siècle'. *China Quarterly*, 148 (December), 1091–1114.

Gold, Thomas B. 1996. 'Civil Society in Taiwan: The Confucian Dimension'. In Tu Wei-ming (ed.), *Confucian Traditions in East Asian Modernity: Moral Education and Economic Culture in Japan and the Four Mini-Dragons*. Cambridge: Harvard University Press, 244–258.

Gold, Thomas B. 1997. 'Taiwan: Still Defying the Odds'. In Larry Diamond, Marc F. Plattner, Yun-han Chu, and Hung-mao Tien (eds.), *Consolidating The Third Wave Democracies: Regional Challenges*. Baltimore: Johns Hopkins University Press, 162–191.

Gold, Thomas B. 2000. 'The Waning of the Kuomintang State on Taiwan'. In Kjeld Erik Brødsgaard and Susan Young (eds), *State Capacity in East Asia: China, Taiwan, Vietnam, and Japan*. Oxford: Oxford University Press, 84–113.

Gold, Thomas B. 2007. 'Is the Party Over? Taiwan's Kuomintang from Power to Opposition'. In Robert Ash and J.Megan Greene (eds), *Taiwan in the 21st Century: Aspects and Limitations of a Development Model*. London: Routledge, 249–271.

Hsiao, Hsin-huang Michael. 1981. *Government Agricultural Strategies in Taiwan and South Korea*. Taipei: Academia Sinica Institute of Ethnology.

Huntington, Samuel P. 1991. *The Third Wave: Democratization in Late Twentieth Century*. Norman: University of Oklahoma Press.

Jacobson, Carl W. 2008. *One Hundred Years in the Life of Oberlin Shansi*. Oberlin: Oberlin Shansi.

Johnson, Chalmers. 1982. *MITI and the Japanese Miracle*. Stanford: Stanford University Press.

Lin, Ching-yuan. 1973. *Industrialization in Taiwan*. New York: Praeger.

State and Society in the Taiwan Miracle revisited   **47**

Lipset, Seymour Martin. 1959. 'Some Social Requisites of Democracy: Economic Development and Political Legitimacy'. *American Political Science Review*, 53, March, 69–105.

Parsons, Talcott. 1964. 'Evolutionary Universals in Society'. *American Sociological Review*. 29(3), June, 339–357.

Simon, Denis Fred. 1980. *Taiwan, Technology Transfer and Transnationalism: The Political Management of Dependency*. Unpublished PhD dissertation, University of California, Berkeley.

Skocpol, Theda. 1979. *States and Social Revolutions*. Cambridge: Cambridge University Press.

Winckler, Edwin A. and Susan Greenhalgh, eds. 1988. *Contending Approaches to the Political Economy of Taiwan*. Armonk: M. E. Sharpe.

4

REVISITING *TAIWAN: CHINA'S LAST FRONTIER*

Simon Long

It is both an illuminating and a chastening experience to look back on work done three decades ago: illuminating because so much of what I wrote about then has faded from my memory; and at least some of it strikes me as perceptive and correct. Chastening because much, with retrospect, also seems naive, misguided or just plain wrong.

I was reminded, oddly, of the 2016 Brexit referendum in the United Kingdom. I voted 'remain', and had assumed that I had done so as well in the first Brexit referendum in 1975 – the first time I ever voted. Only recently did I realise that in fact I probably voted to leave. That was what you did if you were a young leftie as I was at the time, like Jeremy Corbyn and Diane Abbott.

Similarly, on dipping into this book again there are moments of sheer shock: did I really think that? And there is incredulity at how much the world has changed. It talks of 'Peking' for example. At the time of writing I worked for the BBC, which was one of the last media hold-outs against the use of 'Beijing'.

The incredulity also covers the enormity of the changes that China, Taiwan and the world have undergone since I wrote the book.

One passage, for example, reads: 'The number of Taiwan residents who slipped into mainland China in this period is unknowable. Some estimates went as high as 10,000 a year by the mid-1980s' (Long 1991: 204).

A common estimate in recent years has been that more than 1 million Taiwan-born people are now in China at any one time.

Or take another: 'The KMT has for the foreseeable future abandoned any hopes of recovering the mainland militarily' (Long 1991: 239).

Well, at least that was true, if nowadays it sounds an other-worldly notion.

This retrospective chapter will begin by my describing the origins of this book and how it came to be written – and my own involvement with China and Taiwan. I will then go on to consider six factors that I think I gave too much weight to; and one that I underplayed. I will then look at the conclusion of the book, a final chapter called "What next? Scenarios for the future" and see how it has withstood the transformations of the past three decades.

The origins of the book

My own involvement with Taiwan and China progressed through various stages of ignorance.

A first phase began when I studied Chinese at Cambridge in the 1970s and in Beijing and Nanjing from 1976–1977. Studying Chinese was not at the time a common choice. When I went to China on a British Council scholarship, I was part of a group of 15 students: most people completing a Chinese course as an undergraduate got a place.

I was one of very few students at Cambridge – in fact I think I may have been the first – to specialise in post-1949 Chinese history in the second part of the tripos. My history teacher was a Cultural Revolution defector, whose main job, tucked away unseen on the top floor of the Oriental Studies faculty at Cambridge was to work on a Chinese–English dictionary. (I am not sure what became of it).

Looking back at that period now, it is shocking to me how much of the modern history I was taught, even at an institution and in a faculty steeped in anti-communism and conservatism, was the victor's version – especially about the civil war, but also, in retrospect, about the 1950s. A lot of this was a consequence of the work of a collection of Americans – Edgar Snow (1937), Jack Belden (1950), Graham Peck (1941, 1950), Theodore White (1947) and Annalee Jacoby. With the academic literature about the Chinese revolution seeming comparatively arid and China itself largely cut off, such books provided a sense of documentary reality and truth. And the broad picture they gave of the revolution was one in which the Communists were, basically, the good guys, and the Kuomintang (KMT) government a corrupt and cruel regime with fascistic tendencies.

Similarly, Bill Hinton's (1966) epic of land reform, *Fanshen*, described a revolution that, harsh though it was, seemed to have started with honourable intentions. *Fanshen* was made into a play by David Hare (1976) at the time I was a student, a production of which was staged in Cambridge. Years later, he became a friend in Beijing.

The picture of revolutionary China they provided was a big influence, not just on me and on the young graduate students who first taught me modern Chinese history, and so introduced me to the books. It coloured both the academic and popular consensus. To recall quite how remote and isolated China was in those days, it is worth noting that when I went to Beijing as a student in 1976, my fellow Caucasian students and I were routinely assumed to be Albanian.

The modern Chinese history course I later followed at Nanjing University – known as the history of the two line-struggle – by definition confined history to the intra-party conflicts. The contradiction with the KMT was one with the enemy. Taiwan was seen as a benighted fascist autocracy. It was part of my study in neither country.

50 Simon Long

Back at Cambridge, more academic literature on the resistance to Japan and on the civil war – I was particularly impressed by Harrison's (1972) *The Long March to Power* and Lucien Bianco's (1971) *The Origins of the Chinese Revolution* – similarly reinforced the prejudice that, if the Communist party had gone wrong under Mao with the Great Leap Forward and the great famine and then with the Cultural Revolution, that it had started out as somehow pure. The KMT, however, had been a corrupt Leninist monstrosity since 1924. Later books such as that by Frank Dikötter (2013) on 1950s China, and Jay Taylor's (2009) biography of the Generalissimo were an eye-opener to me.

With the country hardly covered at all in my studies, my general impression of the place was of a nasty right-wing, repressive regime, run by a rather comically loopy and vindictive dictator and then by his son, about whom I knew little.

The second phase was when I started visiting Taiwan in the early 1980s – as a banker. Bizarrely, as a fresh graduate I had been head-hunted by a London merchant bank in 1979. The logic was that the Bank of China had just signed a large facility from UK-government backed borrowing – from the Export Credits Guarantee Department, ECGD – to finance a huge range of large industrial and infrastructural projects the Deng Xiaoping influenced government had drawn up. My bank saw itself as one of Britain's leading arrangers of ECGD credits and was appalled not to be on the list of eligible banks. It felt it needed to do something to show it had an interest in China. Having failed to cajole anyone to leave the foreign office, they ended up with hardly any choice in the matter. I was probably the only available recent UK graduate in Chinese studies.

Of course, I ended up doing no business at all in China; though, as was the custom at the time, we gave the Chinese quite a lot of free advice. I spent much of my first years dealing with Nigeria, in fact, which was an education of a different sort. I was involved, however, in doing some business in Taiwan – the financing of a cement plant built by a UK contractor called Cementation, which was acquired by the conglomerate Trafalgar House, which I think went under in the 1990s, long after I had stopped paying attention.

It was in that capacity that I first visited Taiwan in 1981. As an indication of how little known here Taiwan was then: my credit card was stopped during the visit and when I asked my bank why, I was told, and I am not making this up: 'I'm afraid your card has been stolen by a Chinaman.' I was then moved to Singapore and visited Taiwan a few times on marketing trips. I began to know a bit more about the place, and to like it a lot, though Taipei, where I spent most of the time, struck me as seedy, polluted and dangerous – if only in crossing the road. It was the first place I had been where I did not have confidence that if a driver could stop to avoid hitting me, he would do so.

The third phase was when I became a journalist. Having returned to London with the bank, I joined the BBC World Service as what was called then a Topical Talks Writer for the Far East Service. My job was to go in each day and write one or sometimes more commentaries on the day's events in East Asia. We were a team of two or three and basically our subjects would be dictated by the news.

International issues – the Cambodian peace process, the South China Sea disputes, the Koreas, were grist to our mill. So of course were US–China relations and the Taiwan question.

It was a much simpler job, I should explain, than it would be now, if only because of the paucity of sources – we had no access to the local press; just the Summary of World Broadcasts, news wires, the British newspapers and the BBC's own resources. After a few months I became as well-informed about what was going on in Asia as almost anybody in London – which is to say, almost totally ignorant.

At that time I was also commissioned as a freelance outside contributor by the Economist Intelligence Unit, a sister company to the one I now work for, to write their quarterly economic reports on Taiwan. The EIU did this for almost every country in the world, as a subscription service for businesses. At the bank, for example, I had been a consumer – finding them the best thing to read on a plane on my way into a country I had not been to for a while. Writing for them was largely a derivative exercise based on piles of government statistics and news cuttings they would send me. But it was fairly chunky – about 12,000 words each quarter. I had to follow Taiwan quite closely. All the more so as there was also a more substantial annual publication called a Country Profile, which attempted to provide a fairly comprehensive overview.

They then asked me to produce what they called a Special Report – a five-year forecast of what was likely to happen in Taiwan – sold at some ludicrously high price to a limited number of interested parties. This was 'Taiwan: Politics versus Prosperity' (Long 1989). The title betrayed the report's central point. Over the years, I had become fairly good at making short-term forecasts for the Taiwan economy. Basically, I just tinkered a bit with the government's own projections. But it was obvious that the big questions were not over the sectoral distribution of GDP, the future of the exchange rate or income velocity of money: they were over Taiwan's international status.

Clearly this had been a huge international issue at the time of the Kissinger and Nixon visits to China, and again with the formal switch of US diplomatic recognition in January 1979. But when I was writing, nearly a decade later, a lot had changed yet little had been written about it. The best book on the topic was Ralph Clough's (1978) *Island China*, written in 1978. So I thought I should expand on that section of the EIU report in book form. The idea appealed in part because I was fatigued by a fairly intense period of the slog of daily journalism with deadlines always looming – with the extra pressure of the EIU reports (at some point I graduated to writing the China one instead – an even more arduous task). I longed, as many journalists do, for the time and space to get into a subject in depth and to write about it at length. It appeared almost like taking a holiday – much of the research was already done, from the 'Politics versus Prosperity' work, so I could, I thought, spend a fairly leisurely six months doing in-depth research, writing beautiful sentences and working my way through some of the savings I had accumulated as a banker. Ah, such illusions!

52 Simon Long

Anyway, having concocted this plan, I needed a publisher. So I wandered into the offices of MacMillan, chosen for no better reason than that they happened to be in a part of Bush House, the office block in London where I then worked with the BBC. I received a kind hearing, was asked to submit a synopsis – which I did at some length, mercifully, since it was to prove indispensable to me when I came to write.

The synopsis led to a contract, a small advance and a date for the submission of the manuscript. I then negotiated leave of absence from the BBC to research and write the book. This was in March 1989, and my leave was due to begin in June.

I was on a cycling holiday in Sicily the following month, when the first protests broke out in Beijing following the death of Hu Yaobang. Hearing about them on a short-wave radio (if anybody remembers what that was), I was sad not to be there, but had no sense that this was something different from similar student protests, say, in 1986.

By the time I got back to work, however, it was obvious this was a much bigger deal. I was sent to Beijing to reinforce the BBC's bureau there. I stayed through the occupation of Tiananmen Square, the imposition of martial law, the clearance of the square on June 3–4, the sputtering of resistance after the massacre and the emergence of a new Communist Party leadership. I ended up leaving at the end of June, having been offered a job as the World Service's Beijing correspondent – i.e., being asked to stay on. I accepted and then returned briefly to the UK, which I did via Japan and Taiwan – a trip which features in the book – for a few days in each. In the UK, I found myself with about a month to sort out my affairs and my house, make arrangements for my absence and – as I remember, rather panic-stricken – to write the book.

So what I had planned as a break from the daily grind of churning out journalistic copy, in fact became the most intense and gruelling exercise in 'churning it out' I have ever endured.

The circumstances are reflected in some of the book's shortcomings. Its sources, for example, are limited. It relies mainly on the existing secondary literature on Taiwan, largely in English, as held by the SOAS library in London, and on my previous reporting for the BBC (especially from the brief visit in the summer of 1989) and for the Economist Intelligence Unit. This had been quite extensive, and I had a large volume of notes and cassettes to work with. But because, with the BBC, I was usually making English-language radio programmes, there was a bias towards English-speaking interviewees.

Looking back, I have to ask myself why I would undertake something so, well, mad, when one of my reasons for being drawn to writing a book – taking some time out – had so definitively vanished. I have a congenital hatred of letting people down, but I must have known that the publishers would have been neither surprised nor especially disappointed had I asked to be relieved of my contract – or asked for a long extension for the delivery date.

Examining my motives three decades later, I can at least guess at four of them:

1. As a bibliophile, I longed to see a book on my shelves with my name on the spine. And I have to say this is the only one of my quartet of aims that I can with confidence say I achieved.
2. To fill what seemed to me a surprising and important gap in the literature.
3. To give expression to the Taiwan side of a story that was in most media coverage and academic research at the time seen as a kind of offshoot either of China's domestic politics, or as an aspect of Sino-American relations. (The book's title, *China's Last Frontier*, was taken from a statement by China's Communist Party Chairman Hu Yaobang. I used it to explain the importance of the issue and the Chinese view; not to endorse it.)
4. To explain the Taiwan issue to the satisfaction of expert and general reader alike, and to make some helpful prognostications as to how it might evolve, or even be resolved.

Obviously, it is only the third and fourth of these that are of any lasting importance, my apologies for dragging you through this long autobiographical preamble. I did so not because I think I was so unusual, but to explain an obvious anomaly: how did such an unqualified person come to write a book on Taiwan?

Setting aside the paucity of shortages, some factual sloppiness and stylistic infelicities that the time pressures do not excuse, the circumstances in which the book was written also explain a number of features.

1 The Beijing massacre

The most obvious is that the Beijing massacre of 1989 weighs more heavily than it would if the book had been written at a different time. That excess weight seems to me to lead to three different sorts of error in the book's analysis.

The first is in how far-reaching and long-lasting the diplomatic and geopolitical consequences of the massacre would be. You have to remember that most Western governments abruptly curtailed contacts with Beijing and imposed sanctions. When governments subsequently sought to re-establish contacts – as America's did through its national security adviser Brent Scowcroft, and Britain's through a foreign-office Mandarin, Sir Percy Cradock – they did so secretly, and when the clandestine visits were reported, were pilloried for them.

Despite that, looking back at the book, I was surprised that in fact I did not fall too much into the error of thinking either that the rift with the West would endure; nor that tentative opening of cross-strait ties that had just begun was now definitively ended. I certainly did not foresee, however, just how brief that interlude would be.

The second distortion the massacre brought was in my pessimism about the reopening of cross-strait ties. In Taiwan the KMT government, as I reported in the book, felt 'vindicated' in its view of the Communist regime as irredeemably brutal. The prospect of cross-strait talks seemed distant – though I noted that, earlier in 1989, Lien Chan, then the foreign minister, had floated the idea of 'one country –

54 Simon Long

two governments' (Long 1991: 223). Beijing had immediately dismissed this as 'splittism' by another name. But it could have been seen as at least laying the basis for talks. I wrote that, with an apparently pragmatic line in control in Beijing, it did not seem inconceivable that in the fullness of time some basis for negotiation with the Communists over Taiwan's future could be found. I went on that, as of the morning of June 4, 1989, it did seem inconceivable (Long 1991: 224). In fact, the forecasts I go on to make in the last chapter make clear that I did not think they would be inconceivable forever. I certainly, however, had no inkling that they would take such big strides so soon.

The third distortion is subtler: an implicit view of China as being both much weaker than it turned out to be, and far more unstable politically.

This is not something that I directly tackled at the time, probably because it did not seem to be much of an issue. The Chinese economy, having overheated in the late 1980s was poised to enter a period of retrenchment, insipid growth and, for some, considerable hardship. That period did not last long – symbolically it ended in early 1992 with Deng Xiaoping's *nanxun*, and the extraordinary prolonged period of growth that only accelerated this century, after the accession to the World Trade Organization. Looked at from today, the tendency is to see the Chinese economy in a 40-year time frame, as one continuous spurt of rapid growth. This book was written during the one rupture in that sequence. That China would inevitably become one day the world's biggest economy was far from as obvious then as it is now. Even China bulls thought that the growth of the 1980s was unrepeatable, a one-off unleashing of productivity as millions left the land for work in factories.

Meanwhile, the regime seemed doomed. It was one of the few to resist a wave of popular uprisings that swept Asia and then Eastern Europe and the Soviet Union in the late 1980s and early 1990s. The Philippines in 1986, South Korea the following year, one after another Eastern European country in 1989 and 1990, Taiwan itself the same year, the components of the Soviet Union in 1991, Thailand in 1992, etc. The only hold-outs were Burma in 1988 and China the next year. And the reason both held out was not necessarily repeatable: in both places the army was willing to shoot as many people as it took; and, at least in China, not everyone believed they would be ready to do so a second time.

Moreover, in terms of the scale of popular participation, the uprising in China was probably exceeded only by that in Burma. On the official account at the time, serious turmoil afflicted more than 90 cities. With the collapse of the Soviet Union, the shrinking of the "socialist world" to China, Cuba, Laos, Vietnam and North Korea seemed to spell its end. Fukuyama's declaration of 'the end of history' was only one hubristic assertion of what seemed to many simply a statement of fact.

Seeing China as a weak power then also coloured another of my prejudices: that Taiwan is less secure when Beijing has a weak government than a strong one. A weak one, I thought, and argued in the book, would be more prone to attempts to garner popularity by appealing to a nationalistic cause. And Taiwan was the greatest nationalist cause of all – the last unfinished business of the civil war. The biggest concessions Chinese leaders have made on issues of national sovereignty, it seems to me, came in the days of Deng Xiaoping's paramountcy in the 1980s: the nine-point offer to Taiwan in 1981 and the joint declaration with Britain on Hong Kong in 1984.

I think you have to wait until 2015, and Xi Jinping's meeting with Ma Ying-jeou in Singapore, to see another act of such geopolitical heterodoxy from a Chinese leader – albeit on a much more limited scale.

It now seems to me my prejudiced assumptions might be wrong, and that an unchallenged Xi Jinping dictatorship, at a time of American distraction or erratic carelessness, might actually be a period of great peril for Taiwan.

But back to 1989 and *The Last Frontier*. Little or none of this underestimation of China's future power and stability is in the book. But I think it underpins quite a lot of the narrative and analysis. The word 'China' had very different connotations then, for both me as a writer and, I imagine, for most of my readers, from those that it would have now.

2 The constitution

Other mistakes of interpretation cannot be excused by the pall cast by the massacre. For example the second distortion: I lent far too much significance to Taiwan's constitutional links with the mainland.

As a journalist, of course, I relished the idea that Taiwan's legislature was stuffed with geriatrics purporting to represent mainland constituencies; I loved to visit the department for the recovery of the mainland, or the department for Mongolian and Tibetan affairs. All were vivid ways of highlighting the absurdity of Taiwan's position. I did realise that they were, as I wrote 'not crucial', and that removing them need not bring disaster. But I also thought they mattered: that once they were removed the elaborate fiction that sustained Taiwan's international status would be more exposed, and hence a serious spanner would be thrown in the works of the status quo. In fact, of course, their removal was, in retrospect, relatively trouble-free and posed no threat to the basic tenets of the fiction.

3 Diplomatic recognition

Third, I similarly gave too much importance to the issue of diplomatic recognition. Of course, by the time I wrote this book, Taiwan had already lost the big battles for diplomatic recognition: the UN seat, ties with the US, Japan and the big European countries. Indonesia and Singapore had just established ties with China. In April 1990, I noted in what must have been one of the last updates I was allowed, it had just 26 diplomatic partners. And of these, I noted 'four stand out in importance: Saudi Arabia, South Africa, South Korea and the Vatican'. Of those, of course, there is only one to go, and the Vatican's switch, too, seems only a matter of time.

When I was based in Hong Kong for the BBC in the early 1990s, I covered the South Korean switch of recognition in 1992. That did seem a big deal. Taiwan's

56 Simon Long

government, after all, presented itself, like South Korea's, as representing part of a single divided country. That the other part was under communist dictatorship and its security relied on American guarantees –explicit for South Korea, more tenuous for Taiwan – made the two seem even more like parallels. And of course Taiwan's history had been closely bound up with Korea's for a century – in both 1895 and 1950, events in Korea had determined Taiwan's fate.

But again, after the initial shock, the loss of these big diplomatic partners did not seem such a good deal. Few think they have made Taiwan more or less secure.

4 Hong Kong

Fourth, and similarly, I overestimated the importance of Hong Kong and Macau. I still think it is true that a big motive behind Deng's concessions in signing the Joint Declaration on Hong Kong was that it would be a dry-run for the much bigger and more important task of bringing Taiwan back to the fold. So I assumed then that there would be no drastic moves on Taiwan before the reversion of Hong Kong in 1997 and Macau in 1999.

I think many in China really thought that these would prove attractive models to Taiwan's people. They just did not get either Hong Kong or Taiwan. The illusion may have persisted for a few years, but by 2007, the tenth anniversary of the handover, had largely disappeared. I wrote a long report for *The Economist* [1] to mark the anniversary and spent a few days in Taipei asking how it looked from there. (The best part of that trip was seeing former friends and contacts from the DPP ensconced in positions of power). Some people in Hong Kong clung to the forlorn hope that China would make concessions because it could not afford to let it go too wrong because of the message it would send Taiwan. Some in China might conceivably have had similar ideas, though I think by then greater realism had set in. In Taiwan, Hong Kong was already largely seen as irrelevant.

5 The Long March generation

Another consideration that proved largely irrelevant was generational change among China's leaders. I, like many, had thought that the Long March generation might feel pressure to resolve the Taiwan issue in their lifetime, not trusting younger generations to treat this sacred mission as seriously as they did. Well, if they did feel that pressure, they overcame it. And it seems to me there is little evidence that subsequent generations are any softer on the necessity of Taiwan being brought under Chinese sovereignty.

6 Taiwan politics

It might seem perverse to include domestic political developments in Taiwan in a list of factors whose importance I overestimated. Clearly, I seriously underestimated the extent and speed of political change in Taiwan. I confidently asserted: 'There is no reason to believe that in the foreseeable future, the DPP could achieve an electoral majority' (Long 1991: 230). But I suppose that is my point – the political changes were far more drastic than I expected, and posed, in theory, far more of a challenge to the status quo with the election of a government whose origins are in the independence movement. But with the exception of the escalation surrounding the 1996 presidential election, tensions have rarely reached crisis point. China has had to learn to live with a democratic Taiwan. Much has happened in Taiwan politics that I did not expect, notably the speed with which the DPP rose to power and the KMT entered a serious decline, and China's emergence as an almost explicit participant in domestic Taiwan politics.

The missing link

If those were the issues whose importance I gave too much weight to, there were obviously also those that I did not consider enough. By far the greatest of these, I think, was the impact of greater contacts between Taiwan and the mainland. Not only did these develop at a pace and to an extent I simply could not foresee, but their political impact was perhaps more clear-cut than I might have supposed. Although I noted in the book that one of the few ways in which Taiwan did not act like an independent country was in its lack of direct ties with the mainland, I did not foresee that increased contacts would foster a sense of separateness in another way: by enhancing a sense of a unique Taiwan identity.

I was in Taiwan in 2014, during the Sunflower protests, and was struck there (as I wrote at the time)[2] as I would be later in the year during the Umbrella protests in Hong Kong, by how it was the young – the generation that had grown up with daily contact with mainland people and mainland culture – who were most conscious of their difference, of being Taiwan people first, Chinese second, if at all.

Conclusion

So, finally, let me turn to my conclusion back then. And the surprising thing is that, for all that is changed, the scenarios I explored are much the same as I would put forward if I were writing now. I listed six possibilities for the future of Taiwan's international status.

    i   The status quo persisting.
   ii   Reunification on Beijing's terms, i.e., one-country, two-systems (I don't recall, by the way, why I used the term 'reunification', which the early parts of the book show to be a misrepresentation. Perhaps just out of habit).
  iii   Unification on Taiwan's terms.
  iv   Independence.
   v   A successful Chinese invasion.
  vi   Unification on a compromise formula, preserving Taiwan's de facto independence.

I knew enough even back then not to make the classic forecaster's mistake of attaching a date to my predictions. So at least I am not wrong yet. Of the six outcomes, unification on Taiwan's terms – or rather the KMT's terms – under the three principles of the people, is even less likely now than it was then. All the other five remain possible, yet all remain in a sense highly unlikely. The most probable outcome in say one, two or five years' time must presumably be now, as it was then, some version of the status quo. But is it the most likely in 20, 30 or 50 years' time? Can China's leaders for ever pretend that reunifying Taiwan is both a sacred mission and one they can afford to put to one side for now?

If the status quo is unlikely, so, thankfully, is invasion. In the book, I list the various circumstances in which China has said it might resort to military force, of which the most likely was and is a unilateral declaration of independence. I don't think it has ever retracted any of the six. Indeed it may have added some. And, the technological edge that I ascribed to Taiwan's armed forces 30 years ago has probably been eroded. But I think invasion is perhaps even more unlikely now than when I was writing. It would have completely unforeseeable consequences and would jeopardise Xi Jinping's great rejuvenation of the Chinese nation. And even under a DPP government, as its officials have said in interviews in London, the priority is 'not to give China an excuse to attack us'.[3] The same officials expect pressure to come from infiltration and cyberattacks.

Independence, sadly, I still think is not on the cards, barring the collapse of central power in China. Even if the Communist Party were to lose power, a successor government is unlikely to have the legitimacy to relinquish the claim to Taiwan.

So that does leave the prospect of some negotiated settlement as, still, perhaps one of the least unlikely outcomes. I was as shocked on reading my last chapter as on realising I had voted for Brexit to remember that this is what I had declared as the most likely outcome back then. I was even more shocked to read myself describing it as an 'optimistic' outcome. But in replicating the thought processes I went through then with the knowledge of what has happened since, I find myself drawing similar conclusions. I would certainly not put a date on it now either.

In Xi Jinping's remarks on Taiwan, in his report to the Communist Party Congress in October 2017,[4] three things struck me: the topic only merited about 3 minutes of his 3½ hours; he dropped references his predecessors have made suggesting the views of the people of Taiwan were a factor – that they were expected to lead reunification; and that, although his warnings of intolerance to any manifestations of splittism were fierce, he did not seem in a hurry.

Since Taiwan's voters seem to have developed a sophisticated understanding of the delicacy of the status quo, it seems unlikely that Taiwan will give him cause to carry out those threats.

The other risk is posed by Donald Trump. His taking a congratulatory call from Tsai Ing-wen and general transactional approach should terrify Taiwan, it seems to me. Taiwan officials in 2017–2018 like to say that relations with the United States are better than at any time since 2000; and that they have received high-level assurances that Mr Trump will not discuss Taiwan with China. But suppose he is offered a deal he thinks he cannot refuse?

Taiwan's tragedy remains a continued inability to decide its own destiny.

Notes

1 https://www.economist.com/sites/default/files/special-reports-pdfs/9359087.pdf
2 https://www.economist.com/asia/2014/03/29/on-the-antlers-of-a-dilemma
3 Off-the-record interview with senior officials, in London, November 2017.
4 http://www.xinhuanet.com/english/special/2017-11/03/c_136725942.htm

References

Belden, Jack. 1950. *China Shakes the World*. New York: Harper.
Bianco, Lucien. 1971. *Origins of the Chinese Revolution. 1915–1949*. London: Stanford University Press.
Clough, Ralph N. 1978. *Island China*. Cambridge: Harvard University Press.
Dikötter, Frank. 2013. *The Tragedy of Liberation: A History of the Chinese Revolution 1945–1957*. London: Bloomsbury Publishing.
Hare, David. 1976. *Fanshen*. London: Faber and Faber.
Harrison, James Pinckney. 1972. *The Long March to Power*. Santa Barbara, CA: Praeger Publishers.
Hinton, William. 1966. *Fanshen: A Documentary of Revolution In a Chinese Village*. London: Monthly Review Press.
Long, Simon. 1989. 'Taiwan: Politics versus Prosperity'. Economist Intelligence Unit.
Long, Simon. 1991. *Taiwan: China's Last Frontier*. London: MacMillan.
Peck, Graham. 1941. *Through China's Wall*. London: Collins.
Peck, Graham. 1950. *Two Kinds of Time*. Beijing: Foreign Languages Press.
Snow, Edgar. 1937. *Red Star Over China*. London: Gollancz.
Taylor, Jay. 2009. *The Generalissimo: Chiang Kai-shek and the Struggle for Modern China*. Cambridge: Belknap Press of Harvard University Press.
White, Theodore and Annalee Jacoby. 1947. *Thunder out of China*. London: Gollancz.

PART II

1990s

5

REVISITING *TAIWAN AND CHINESE NATIONALISM: IDENTITY AND STATUS IN INTERNATIONAL SOCIETY*

Christopher R. Hughes

It would be nice to be able to claim that *Taiwan and Chinese Nationalism: Identity and Status in International Society* was the result of a well-thought-out research plan. A more honest account is that it was the outcome of the author being lucky enough to be in the right place and at the right time. This makes it very much a snapshot of Taiwan at a particularly exciting period in its own political history, which occurred as the world entered the post-Cold War period.

To explain how I decided on the topic, it is necessary to say a bit about the circuitous route that brought me into contact with Taiwan. As an undergraduate and graduate student, I had studied intellectual history with a special focus on the history of political thought. An initial interest in China had been sparked when I had touched on Chinese philosophy and art. I had also come into contact with nationalist theory, especially when I studied under Elie Kedourie and Kenneth Minogue at the London School of Economics (LSE). One book that had made a particularly deep impression was Joseph Levenson's monumental trilogy, *Confucian China and Its Modern Fate*, which opened my eyes to the remarkable story of the identity crisis involved in China's painful transition to modernity (Levenson 1958).

In the early 1980s I also decided to start to learn Mandarin Chinese at evening school and with a private tutor. This was partly due to academic inquisitiveness but also because China was beginning to become more accessible for travellers and increasingly salient in the media in the early years of Deng Xiaoping's policy of 'Reform and Opening'. I then took the leap in 1986 and spent just under a year backpacking around most of China, including Xinjiang and Tibet. I think the first time Taiwan entered my consciousness was when someone waved a Taiwanese bank note in front of me on a train and asked what they could do with it in a rather nervous fashion.

Those were the heady days when the government of the reformist CCP general secretary, Hu Yaobang (胡耀邦), unleashed an explosion of creative and eclectic

64 Christopher R. Hughes

thinking across the arts and politics. I became involved with the movement of young experimental artists and planned to help them to gain exposure for their work in the UK. To develop my knowledge further, I registered for the MA Area Studies (Far East) at the University of London's School of Oriental and African Studies (SOAS) in 1987, taking courses in Chinese politics, art and archaeology and mediaeval philosophy.

There were no courses in Taiwan studies in those days. I even recall the great Mao scholar, Stuart Schram, refusing to allow a student to give a presentation on the topic in his class on Chinese politics. But Taiwan began to become a story in the news when Chiang Ching-kuo (蔣經國) passed away. With my interest further stimulated by talking to Taiwanese students I decided to travel to the island to improve my language skills at the Mandarin Training Centre at National Taiwan Normal University.

Taiwan was an exciting but confusing place to be in 1988. After Chiang's death, Lee Teng-hui (李登輝) had taken over the Presidency. The situation was quite surreal, as demands for democratisation grew while the parliamentary chambers were populated by representatives who had been elected in China in the 1940s and refused to relinquish power until they could return there to hold new elections. The social infrastructure had deteriorated badly after decades of neglect by a ruling party who proudly proclaimed that its aim was not to stay in Taiwan but to 'unify China under the Three Principles of the People', as billboards outside government buildings constantly reminded the population. It was not hard to understand why people should ignore such abstract political principles and take to the streets to demand better governance. In the crowded suburb of Yungho (永和), where I lived, there were no public spaces, no metro system and very few outlets that resembled modern shops. The contrast with thriving Yongho today, with its restored parks and good transport links attests to the often-overlooked achievements of democracy at the local level.

As I began to think about doing a PhD, it was obvious that the focus would have to be related to democratisation in some way. How I looked at this was also influenced by the comparison of what I had witnessed in China. Much like in Taiwan, society there had been boiling over with demands for political change as a new generation refused to accept the myths of the past. This came to a bloody end when dissent was crushed in the 1989 Beijing Massacre. At the time I was sitting in Chiang Kai-shek Memorial Plaza, where the crowds had been in contact with the students in Tiananmen Square through a video link to a large screen. To this day I do not know what happened to the friends I had made during my visit there, some of whom were students at the Beijing Academy of Fine Arts, where the 'Goddess of Democracy' was constructed.

The questions began to grow, therefore, as to how these societies could relate to each other as they moved in such different directions. The contrast only became starker when students in Taiwan occupied the Chiang Kai-shek Memorial Plaza to call for elections to the National Assembly. When the KMT literally wheeled its veteran members into the chamber to oppose the demands for change, President

Lee eventually threw himself behind the calls for reform. Democratisation in Taiwan entered a new and exciting stage just as China was put under martial law and the Communist Party began to look anew to Chinese nationalism to rebuild its legitimacy.

Theory, methods and fieldwork

With a whole set of vague questions starting to gel in my mind I decided to return to London and get the academic training to undertake a more systematic analysis. In stark contrast with the flourishing of Taiwan studies in the UK today, it proved almost impossible to find a supervisor. It was by pure luck that I happened to be listening to the radio one day and there was an interview about Taiwan with Michael Yahuda, a world-leading expert on Chinese foreign policy in the International Relations Department at the LSE. I contacted him, and after some discussion he agreed to supervise me. This was a generous decision because neither of us had a clear idea about how to approach the complex and rapidly developing situation in Taiwan.

The first problem with framing the research was the lack of secondary academic literature. When I conducted my initial bibliographic search the results were paltry, to put it generously. I think there were only two books of much use in the various libraries attached to the University of London. One of these was Thomas Gold's *State and Society in the Taiwan Miracle* (Gold 1986), without which I would not have known where to start; the other was Chiu Hungdah's *China and the Question of Taiwan: Documents and Analysis*, a 1973 book on the ROC and international law, which was extremely useful and important for background information, but somewhat out of date (Chiu 1973). Other books, such as George Kerr's (1965) *Formosa Betrayed*, were very useful for gaining insights into Taiwanese identity, but very out of date. In general, though, the study of Taiwan had been dominated by the Cold War concerns with geostrategy and security studies, with little work done on deeper issues of social and political change.

Deciding to do a PhD on an unfolding situation does also have advantages. The greatest is that it is much easier to make the claim of originality that is required for a successful thesis. I would not have been so lucky if I had come to the topic a few years later, when a new wave of books by pioneering authors such as Alan Wachman (whose early death was a tragic blow to all of us) and Shelley Rigger was appearing, triggered by interests similar to my own (Wachman 1994; Rigger 1999).

Luckily the theoretical approach I decided to take ensured that my work would add to that literature, rather than just restate what began to be published. While students often bemoan an apparent preoccupation with theory in the social sciences, I cannot stress enough how important this was in helping me to make sense of the mass of empirical evidence being generated in Taiwan. Having struggled in my first year, my eureka moment came when I joined the seminar on nationalism held every week at the LSE by Anthony Smith and James Mayall. This was a

66 Christopher R. Hughes

crowded and intensely interesting group of students and faculty, inspired by the nationalist movements that were breaking the political mould around the world after the Cold War. It rekindled the interest in nationalism that I had earlier developed when studying under Elie Kedourie and Kenneth Minogue.

It was while working in this context that it suddenly became clear to me that what I was really interested in were the implications of democratisation in Taiwan for Chinese nationalism. This question might seem rather obvious today, but throughout the Cold War nationalism had been eclipsed by the struggle between the superpowers, with a few brave exceptions, such as Benedict Anderson (1991 [1983]) Elie Kedourie (1960) and Anthony Smith (1986). Even the study of Chinese nationalism did not become a serious subject of academic study until the wave of books that was triggered by the 'new nationalism' of the 1990s.

I was fortunate, therefore, that the debates of the post-Cold War years certainly provided some concepts to bring to the study of Taiwan. Anderson's idea of the nation as an 'imagined community' was particularly useful for focusing on the *politics* of national identity. Anthony Smith's distinction of 'ethnic' and 'civic nationalism' was also useful for developing this question, insofar as it showed how the claim made by the CCP and the KMT that the populations on the two sides of the Taiwan Strait were obliged to unify due to blood ties, which has very different implications from the voluntaristic form of 'civic nationalism' upon which the liberal concept of citizenship is based (Smith 1986).

It was Ernest Gellner's definition of nationalism as the principle that 'the political and the national unit should be congruent' that eventually provided a simple starting point for designing the research programme (Gellner 1990: 1). When applied to Taiwan, this would become the question of what would happen when the political unit of 'Taiwan' no longer claimed to be congruent with the national unit of 'China'.

When faced by big and complex questions, such simple concepts are necessary for providing a clear thread to guide research. The complexity of my subject matter was certainly growing as identity politics, both ideationally and institutionally, began to be reshaped by the exercise of sovereignty through the ballot box in Taiwan. This provided an opportunity to develop theory, as Gellner's principle, which implies there can be no room for compromise, was challenged by creative political thinking that effectively loosened the bonds of ethnic Chinese nationalism in novel ways.

Another advantage of using nationalist theory was that it allowed me to avoid getting bogged down in the fruitless arguments over rival historical claims over the status of Taiwan. At the start of the book I thus make it clear that I am only interested in how history was politicized by the two parties, not in trying to define Taiwan's identity and status by finding some kind of archival proof. This meant that the first task of the contextual paragraph was thus to explain how the Chinese claim to Taiwan became a criterion for the leadership legitimacy of the two parties in the Chinese civil war, when the prospect of gaining control over the island arose during World War II. The fact that I included evidence that the Communists had not seen Taiwan as part of China before this, including Mao Zedong's 1936 remark to Edgar Snow that it should be helped in its struggle for independence from Japan, like Korea, probably explains why the work has never been honoured by publication in China (Snow 1978: 128–129).

The key claim to originality, however, would be to show what happened when ethnic Chinese nationalism collided with the forces of democratisation that were shaping a more civic conception. This led to one of the most exciting periods of my research, when I began to look at how people in Taiwan had been addressing the problems raised by theorists of nationalism for many years already. In this respect, it would be fair to say that a figure like Dr Peng Ming-min was some 20 years ahead of Anderson and Smith. As early as 1972, he had explored the relationship between political community and national identity in ways that challenged ethnic nationalism, publishing them during his exile in Canada in *A Taste of Freedom* (Peng 1972). This should be compulsory reading for all students of Taiwan and of nationalism in general.

Central to Peng's argument was the very modernist proposition that Taiwan should be understood as a 'community of shared destiny' (命運共同體). By this he meant that there was no more of an obligation for people who identify as Chinese to all live in one China, any more than there is such an obligation for the Anglo Saxons scattered through Britain, the United States, Canada, Australia and New Zealand to live in one state. Thanks to a collection of *Dang Wai* magazines on microfilm held at the British Library, I was able to trace how this loosening of the bonds between ethnic and political identity was further developed by the most brilliant of Taiwan's dissident thinkers in the 1970s. These ideas were ultimately appropriated for the KMT in the 1990s by Lee Teng-hui, who recast Peng's conception of the nation as the Kantian conception of *Gemeinschaft* (生命共同體) and avoided the use of the concept state (國) by referring to Taiwan as a 'political entity' (政治實體).

Bigger than this historical challenge was how to follow the way in which these basic conceptions of national identity were being changed by the process of democratisation unfolding in Taiwan. Having been able to secure funding for my research from what was then the Economic and Social Research Council of the United Kingdom, I could do this in situ. Living in Taiwan I could take full advantage of the remarkable flourishing of journalism that took place as political constraints were eased.

I developed a systematic method of building up a card index (personal computers were still rudimentary!) from reading several newspapers every day, representing views across the political spectrum. These included the *United Daily News* (聯合報), *China Times* (中國時報) and the KMT's official organ *Central Daily News* (中央日報); for the opposition, there was the *Independence Morning Post* (自立早報) and *Independence Evening News* (自立晚報). As important as the record of events in these newspapers were the editorials and opinion pieces that provided remarkably high-quality analysis and debates of government policies, political struggles and the profound issues of national identity politics. Finally there was the appearance of

68 Christopher R. Hughes

substantial monographs by leading political actors, as figures such as President Lee Teng-hui and DPP Chair Hsu Hsin-liang (許信良) who attempted to explain their thinking on key issues relevant to my research. As an increasing number of books on Taiwanese identity and history had appeared, there was now an embarrassment of riches when it came to research material.

All of this contextual material was extremely useful for understanding the significance of the more mainstream sources of academic research, such as the statements, policy papers and election campaign materials issued by the government and political parties. By asking how these debates were addressing and shaping the basic concepts and principles of nationalist theory, it was not hard to develop the hypothesis that democratisation in Taiwan was stretching the idea of 'one China' but it was not clear towards what it was moving. Rather than assume that Chinese ethnic nationalism would be replaced by an equivalent kind of Taiwanese nationalism, it was more interesting to explore what would happen if external constraints forced something different to emerge. I decided to call this a 'post-nationalist' identity, because it would be based on subjective loyalty to the island but was still shaped in significant ways by the demands of Chinese nationalism.

This led to the second dimension of the research, which was to ask how democratisation and the practice of sovereignty in Taiwan could be compatible with the international system of sovereign states. The importance of this question was evident in the early 1990s as war erupted in the Balkans over secessionist movements from the former Yugoslavia. Given that the Chinese Communists were increasingly relying on nationalism to claim legitimacy after Tiananmen, it was important to ask whether creative thinking and diplomacy on both sides of the Taiwan Strait would be able to avoid a descent into conflict. Even more interesting from the perspective of International Relations theory was to ask whether the international system itself could be flexible enough to adapt to whatever Taiwan was becoming.

The theoretical framework for this part of the thesis was influenced by James Mayall's *Nationalism and International Society* (Mayall 1993). Rooted in the English School approach to understanding world politics that was dominant at the LSE in those days, this focused on the international political dynamics that arise when the system of legally sovereign states is challenged by demands for self-determination made by sub-state or trans-state communities.

In the 1990s, as economic globalisation began to accelerate, it appeared that new political dynamics were creating opportunities to loosen the bonds of sovereignty and identity that a dynamic economy such as Taiwan might be well placed to exploit. The final part of the research was thus to look at how the restrictions of statehood imposed by international society were being weakened by Taiwan's diplomacy, resulting in a unique situation in which the island was neither recognised as part of 'China' or as an independent sovereign state. It was to describe this phenomenon that I coined the term 'intermediate state'.

The concept was actually inspired by a passage in Hedley Bull's seminal International Relations book, *The Anarchical Society*, where he discusses the alternatives

Taiwan and Chinese Nationalism revisited **69**

to the current Westphalian international system of sovereign states and remarks: 'the appearance of entities that remain transfixed between two statehoods might signal the decline of international society' (Bull 1993: 267). This struck me as a very important proposition that the case of Taiwan appeared to contradict, because it was thriving in every way in a condition of being transfixed between the two possible statehoods of the PRC and a Taiwan enjoying diplomatic recognition from major states and the UN. By showing that democratisation had stretched the meaning of 'China' and that pragmatic diplomacy had allowed Taiwan to thrive in international society without diplomatic recognition, I could thus contribute to both nationalist and International Relations theory by proposing that the new concept of a 'post-nationalist entity in an intermediate state' was needed to categorise Taiwan.

My choice of theory was thus very much a product of the immediate post–Cold War period. My method was determined to a large extent by fast-changing circumstances. My training in intellectual history also steered me away from trying to evaluate the rational coherence of arguments over concepts such as 'nation' and 'state' in favour of an analysis of how these were deployed in the political strategies of people who were thinking and acting to resolve a variety of problems in a fast-changing situation. To paraphrase what Joseph Levenson recommended in his book on the fate of Confucianism, it was not a history of thought that was required, but an understanding of how people were thinking, that could reveal all the creativity, imagination and constructive ambiguity that this involves.

Once I had a clear research question, the best way to do this was to just absorb, catalogue and analyse as much information as possible in the immediate environment. While such an approach might not sound particularly scientific, it has produced outstanding results in other cases. Perhaps the best example is the twentieth century's foremost China watcher, Simon Leys (the pen name of Pierre Ryckmans), who prided himself on being able to predict more about what would happen in China than the best-trained social scientists by merely talking to Chinese friends and reading the daily newspapers from that country (Leys 1989).

This method is certainly even more necessary when you are living through a period of fast political change. Like most foreign scholars doing research in Taiwan at the early stage of their career, I benefitted immensely from talking to people whom I met not just socially but also through work. This included as an English teacher for adult learners, and as a translator at the Government Information Office-sponsored multilingual magazine *Sinorama* (光華雜誌). It was enlightening and uplifting to witness how journalists and editors reacted to the shifting political environment, taking advantage of the growing confusion in the ideological guidelines from above to branch out into areas that were formerly considered taboo. This would be a research project worth conducting in itself.

Whereas I had started the research with a dearth of material, the main problem had become one of keeping up with the tidal wave of information and knowing where to stop. It was only by having a clear set of questions rooted in nationalist theory that this could be made manageable. This could allow me to mine the data to

70 Christopher R. Hughes

gain insights into how political actors were changing the meaning of nation, state and sovereignty as they pursued power and legitimacy in a democratising system.

Main findings and arguments in the book

The main finding of the project was that the processes of democratisation, domestic political negotiation and compromise and diplomacy had shown how malleable the idea of the nation could become. This could be demonstrated by tracing in detail every painful step in the search for ways to navigate around the concept of the Chinese nation that had been used to legitimate the rule of both the KMT and the CCP. While fully understanding the desire of many people in Taiwan to reject Chinese identity, it was clear that threats from conservative forces inside Taiwan and from the Chinese Communists meant that the instability followed by a declaration of independence was a price too high for most people. It was equally important to recognise that political actors and decision-makers could not ignore the positive economic possibilities presented by being part of a transnational Chinese identity.

It was my hope that combining categorising Taiwan as 'a post-nationalist entity in an intermediate state' could capture the dynamics of what appeared to be an enduring situation. Although this somewhat convoluted formulation came to me at the end of the research, it seemed to be a way to challenge the assumption that Taiwan had to choose between being either part of 'China' or recognised as 'independent', both of which terms are rarely defined. All the domestic and international dynamics appeared to be pointing to the fact that it would have to find its own, unique way to survive between these two possibilities for the foreseeable future.

I also hoped that this concept could contribute to the broader debates on nationalism. This is because the idea of a 'post-nationalist' identity can be understood as going beyond an inherited national identity but is not the same as entirely negating it. The evidence supported this in the case of Taiwan, because ways were being sought to keep 'Chineseness' as a valued part of many people's identity, so long as it was separated from the principles of statehood and political legitimacy.

I also hoped that the idea of the 'intermediate state' could contribute to debates in International Relations theory, especially as notions of statehood were becoming increasingly elastic under the impact of globalisation. Rather than assume that Taiwan was posing a threat to the international system (as many of its critics were trying to say and Bull's comments would seem to imply), it was more interesting to explore how 'pragmatic diplomacy' was creating a new kind of international dispensation. This could be seen in the use of imaginative concepts, such as the 'substantive relations' forged with Japan and the United States and the 'reciprocal recognition' used to build links with small states. Then there was the host of creative practices that Taiwan's politicians and diplomats began to develop in order to create international space, such as 'dollar diplomacy' and even the 'vacation diplomacy' used to maintain links with Southeast Asian states by sending government personnel there for their 'holidays'.

Taiwan and Chinese Nationalism revisited **71**

By looking at Taiwan in this way it was possible to side-step the temptation to make a moral judgement about whether Taiwan ought to be either independent or unified with China. Instead, such a perspective made it possible to evaluate how Taiwan was actually using its often-understated economic, diplomatic and cultural strengths to create a special niche in the international system. Those strengths were especially evident on the economic side in the 1990s, when Taiwan still had a lead over the PRC in many respects. Moreover, by developing the flexible concept of a 'political entity' (政治實體) instead of 'state', it was well-placed to align with trends that were eroding the nation-state, namely regionalisation, globalisation and the 'Third Wave' of democratisation. When the Lee Teng-hui administration was forced by opposing domestic and international pressures to propose that there might be something called 'one China', but that Taiwan and the PRC had different governments within it, something quite revolutionary was happening from the perspective of International Relations theory.

It is my greatest regret about the book that the concept of Taiwan as a 'post-nationalist identity in an intermediate state' was not taken up more broadly by academics. I still think this is useful for explaining the situation that has been created as political actors in Taiwan have had to meet the challenge of explaining and articulating the nature of Taiwan's unique international situation to widely different audiences at home, in the PRC and in international society more generally. The need to ameliorate pressures maintaining the myth of 'one China', while making it clear that sovereignty is practised by the people of Taiwan through the ballot box, has not gone away since the book was published.

While the lack of diplomatic recognition is undoubtedly a source of great frustration for the majority of people in Taiwan, it is to the credit of the island's politicians and policy makers that creative thinking has allowed a pluralist form of post-nationalist identity to emerge on the back of a flourishing civil society at home. At the same time, despite periods of tension and often vicious rhetoric from Beijing, both sides of the Taiwan Strait have benefited enormously from the forging of special economic and cultural links. The consolidation of Taiwan's subjectivity might have been constrained by the attraction of the Chinese economy and enduring family and cultural links, but the result has been a metamorphosis of identity politics rather than the kind of collapse into communal violence seen in other parts of the world since the Cold War.

When faced by pessimism concerning Taiwan's future that seems to be pervasive on both sides of the Taiwan Strait, I thus like to point out the remarkable achievements that have been made by avoiding the assumption that only zero-sum outcomes are possible. This has become even more important to recognise as democratisation and the lack of diplomatic recognition has forced Taiwan to continue to deconstruct nationalism, while there has been a hardening of ethnic Chinese nationalism in the PRC, due to the ideological crisis of the CCP and the political and cultural impact of globalisation. The case of Taiwan thus provides rich insights into the possibilities for crisis management, building international stability and even for the development of nationalism in China itself.

Given that events have borne out my hypothesis, I would not have approached the project any differently with the benefit of hindsight. This is also due to the practical reason that developing and using a more sophisticated methodology would have been very difficult due to the fact that I was really running to keep up with events. It should also be remembered that there was virtually no secondary literature to draw on, given the speed of change. Finally, it is easy to forget just how sensitive the topic was at the time.

It should be clear from the above, however, that working on an unfolding and sensitive topic does have great advantages. I was delighted and surprised when the PhD thesis was awarded the British International Studies Association prize in 1997, despite the fact that it was not possible to include the Taiwan Strait crisis that developed from the summer of 1995 through the first presidential election in 1996. The pleasure of receiving this accolade was only accentuated by the fact that my fellow research students at the LSE had treated my topic as a bit of a joke, wondering why I was bothering to work on such an insignificant issue as a faraway, authoritarian-ruled island.

The Straits crisis of 1995–1996 may well have helped me to get the contract to publish the thesis as a Routledge monograph. The fact that the quick return to the *status quo ante* made it relatively easy to integrate those events into the text seems to attest to the robustness of my main hypothesis about the durability of the political dispensation. I was very pleased to be able to summarise the core of my argument in a single chapter in a volume on Asian nationalism edited by Michael Leifer (Hughes 2000). I certainly regret that I did not do more to build on the growing interest after publication, due to pressures of job-hunting and family. I would urge all scholars to avoid making that mistake, no matter how overwhelmed you might be with other tasks and issues.

I was very pleased to have a glowing review from Professor June Dreyer at Miami University, however. As more scholars in the United States began to pay attention to Taiwan after the crisis, I also received emails expressing their gratitude for the detailed and dispassionate explanation I had provided of the linkage between Taiwan's complex domestic politics and cross-Strait relations. The work has steadily gained more attention as Taiwan has become one of the most important case studies in the social sciences and Taiwan studies has grown from strength to strength. I was delighted when a second edition was published as a much more affordable softback in 2014 and then as a Kindle version. I am absolutely delighted to have played my part in the growing community of academics who have put Taiwan on the academic map in the 1990s.

The field has developed in ways that were unimaginable when I started my project, especially with the very advanced methods used by scholars working on topics from elections, cultural and anthropological studies of identity, or political economy research into the role of the Taishang. My main consolation is that Taiwan has continued to develop its unique status and identity and avoided the kind of violent conflict witnessed in so many parts of the world over identity politics and nationalism, even as China's power has grown to exceed what most people expected when I was doing my research in the 1990s.

Taiwan and Chinese Nationalism revisited   **73**

Equally positive is the way in which ethnic Chinese nationalism has been deconstructed in Taiwan and replaced by a post-nationalist identity that has exceeded all expectations in its degree of liberal diversity and social pluralism. This has been an immense source of power in itself, as the international system has to accommodate the existence of a significant entity that is neither a part of the PRC nor a state that enjoys diplomatic recognition. Central to this is the behaviour of the most important actors, namely Taiwan, the PRC and the United States. Perhaps most remarkable of all is the way in which the concept of Taiwan as a 'community of shared destiny' that was coined by Peng Ming-min, the father of the independence movement, and appropriated by Lee Teng-hui in the 1990s, has now been taken up and applied to PRC diplomacy by none other than PRC President Xi Jinping!

Overall, therefore, the book might be considered a snapshot of the early stage of a remarkable process that is still unfolding. I have taken every effort to keep on top of developments down to the present day. In particular, I have made it a priority to be present in Taiwan for every presidential election, although I had to miss the 2016 contest due to my duties as Head of Department at the time. I have also attended countless conferences and workshops on cross-Strait Relations over the years, in both Taiwan and the PRC. I have used the information from this fieldwork to produce a series of journal articles that explore the relationship between elections and the formation of identity in Taiwan, with some special emphasis on how the PRC adapts to this and takes part in shaping it (Hughes 2002, 2009, 2008, 2011, 2014). As my status in the academic profession has improved, I have also had the benefit and pleasure of being able to gain more access to members of the political elite. Of course, we have some very important LSE alumni in Taiwan.

As my academic research and teaching have developed to cover the international politics of the Asia-Pacific region, however, I must also be honest in admitting that I cannot pretend to be able to compete with the growing number of scholars who have focused entirely on Taiwan throughout their careers. Most humbling is the amazing work conducted by Taiwanese social scientists themselves. When confronted by such formidable competition, my best hope for doing anything valuable is to continue to try to identify the cutting-edge themes that nobody else is yet working on.

I still believe that the fate of Taiwan will to an important degree determine and be determined by the evolution of nationalism in China. However, given the now abundant work on Chinese nationalism, I have chosen to focus more specifically on the problem of Chinese militarism. This issue has become increasingly salient in recent years yet remains shockingly under-researched. Taiwan is also an important case study in itself for understanding the political dynamics of militarism, having been the subject of intense militarisation under both the Japanese occupation and KMT administration. It thus presents a case for understanding not only the political dynamics of using military values and practices to discipline a society but, even more importantly, it is the only case of de-militarisation in a society that was shaped by the hegemony of Chinese nationalism for several decades. Exploring the

74 Christopher R. Hughes

political dynamics of how Taiwan's democratisation has achieved this would perhaps be a most fitting sequel to *Taiwan and Chinese Nationalism*.

References

Anderson, Benedict. 1991 [1983]. *Imagined Communities*. London: Verso.

Bull, Hedley. 1993. *The Anarchical Society: A Study of Order in World Politics*. Basingstoke and London: Macmillan.

Chiu, Hungdah ed. 1973. *China and the Question of Taiwan: Documents and Analysis*. New York and London: Praeger.

Gellner, Ernest. 1990. *Nations and Nationalism*. Oxford: Basil Blackwell.

Gold, Thomas B. 1986. *State and Society in the Taiwan Miracle*. Armonk NY and London: M.E. Sharpe.

Hughes, Christopher R. 2000. 'Postnationalist Taiwan'. In Michael Leifer (ed), *Asian Nationalism*. London: Routledge, 63–81.

Hughes, Christopher R. 2002. 'Challenges and Opportunities for Unification after Taiwan's 2000 Presidential Elections'. In Haacke, Jürgen and Preston, PeterW. (eds), *Contemporary China: the Dynamics of Change at the Start of the New Millennium*. London: Routledge-Curzon. 157–174.

Hughes, Christopher R. 2008. 'The 2008 Legislative Yuan Election and the Complex Nativisation of the KMT'. *Taiwan Perspective* 118: 1–6.

Hughes, Christopher R. 2009. 'New Trends in Taiwan's China Policy'. *International Spectator*, 44(2): 59–74.

Hughes, Christopher R. 2011. 'Negotiating National Identity in Taiwan: Between Nativisation and De-sinicisation'. In Ash, Robert, Garver, John W. and Prime, Penelope, (eds), *Taiwan's Democracy: Economic and Political Challenges*. New York and London: Routledge. 51–74.

Hughes, Christopher R. 2014. 'Revisiting Identity Politics under Ma Ying-jeou'. In Cabestan, Jean-Pierre and deLisle, Jacques (eds), *Political Changes in Taiwan Under Ma Ying-jeou: Partisan Conflict, Policy Choices, External Constraints and Security Challenges*. Abingdon: Routledge. 120–136.

Kedourie, Elie. 1960. *Nationalism*. London: Hutchinson.

Kerr, George H. 1965. *Formosa Betrayed*. New York: Houghton Mifflin.

Levenson, Joseph R. 1958. *Confucian China and Its Modern Fate* (three volumes). London: Routledge and Kegan Paul.

Leys, Simon. 1989. 'The Curse of the Man Who Could See the Little Fish at the Bottom of the Ocean'. *New York Review of Books*, 20 July, 1989. Online at ChinaFile: www.china file.com/library/nyrb-china-archive/curse-man-who-could-see-little-fish-bottom-ocean

Mayall, James. 1993. *Nationalism and International Society*. Cambridge: Cambridge University Press.

Peng, Ming-min. 1972. *A Taste of Freedom: Memoirs of a Formosan Independence Leader*. New York: Holt, Reinhart & Winston.

Rigger, Shelley, 1999. *Politics in Taiwan: Voting for Democracy*. London and New York: Routledge.

Smith, Anthony. 1986. *The Ethnic Origins of Nations*. Oxford: Basil Blackwell.

Snow, Edgar. 1978. *Red Star over China*. Harmondsworth and New York: Penguin.

Wachman, Alan M. 1994. *Taiwan: National Identity and Democratization*. Armonk NY and London: M.E Sharpe.

6

POLITICS IN TAIWAN: VOTING FOR DEMOCRACY REVISITED

Shelley Rigger

Given the rapid accumulation of new scholarship, even in a smallish corner of the academic universe like studies of Taiwan politics, it is rare to go back and reread (or read) older work. It's all we can do to keep up with the new work that is coming out constantly, so we tend to reference older scholarship, but not really read it. And rereading one's own previous work is a painful process, at least for me. I focus on the mistakes, the erroneous predictions, the word choices that I never would have made had I not been exhausted and on a deadline. But when I finally made myself do it, I discovered that revisiting *Politics in Taiwan: Voting for Democracy* (Rigger 1999) was revealing in a number of ways, a few of which might even be interesting to people who are not its author. In particular, revisiting the book gave me some insights about how people who observe politics closely tend to (mis) remember history, how the demands of publishing shape what a book becomes, how quickly Taiwan has changed in the past 25 years, and how not everything came out the way I expected.

Misremembering history

As a political scientist, I admire and envy historians' command of and care for historical detail. Those of us who pay close attention to the minutiae of contemporary politics – and here I am thinking of political scientists (not all, but many), policy-makers, activists and journalists – have a tendency to reshape our 'knowledge' about the past to fit what we know about the present. Rereading *Politics in Taiwan*, I was struck by how often some of the events I reported in that book are mis-characterised in the historical summaries political scientists write today, and in journalists' and policy makers' shorthand versions of the past.

One concrete example of this phenomenon is the frequency with which people assume the Taiwan Solidarity Union (TSU; a strongly pro-independence political party) is an offshoot of the Democratic Progressive Party (DPP). In fact, the TSU broke from the Kuomintang (KMT) after the 2000 presidential election. But because the shorthand description of the KMT is 'pro-unification', it's easy to forget that the KMT had (and continues to have) a diverse membership. It hasn't been an ideological monolith since the 1960s, if it ever was. *Politics in Taiwan* describes in detail how the KMT built its legitimacy in Taiwan by enabling (and also manipulating) grassroots elections. In the process, it brought a wide range of Taiwanese into the party, including many (in fact, a majority of KMT members and a large majority of its voters) whose ideological convictions were minimal.

The book includes a number of other forgotten truths – historical facts that don't exactly jive with contemporary realities, and as a result are often misremembered. For example, Lee Teng-hui, who is the face of hard line Taiwan independence activism today, supervised the writing of the National Unification Guidelines and ordered the creation of the National Unification Council. Throughout his presidency (1988–2000) he never deviated from the KMT's position that unification was the destiny of the Republic of China. Today he's thought of as a leading proponent of Taiwan Independence, and many authors project that preference into the past, insisting that he was a 'hidden independence advocate' from the beginning of his career. But the historical record includes little evidence to support that line of argument; if it's true, Lee hid his secret extremely well. Another example of historical misremembering, one from my second book: In 2000, the presidential candidate whose positions were most favourable toward engagement with the mainland was the DPP candidate, Chen Shui-bian.

This tendency to misremember – to rewrite history in our minds to make it coherent with contemporary realities – is partly a consequence of political science's disciplinary focus on the present. But it may also be an occupational hazard of living in the twenty-first century. In this era, history is moving extremely quickly, forcing us into a kind of compressed retrospection. The swift pace of events means that things can be ontologically old – old in our knowing and being – but not temporally old. In terms of years, that is, they happened recently, but there is an enormous amount of intervening activity that makes them feel distant.

Historians are used to thinking in terms of centuries, perhaps because it used to take a hundred years for enough change (and enough evidence of change) to accumulate for a historian to really digest it. How long had the industrial revolution been underway before historians coined the phrase? At what point did scholars begin to see the rise of the United States as a potential challenger to Britain's global domination? Now the Internet declares a technological revolution every 18 months; not 20 years after Mao's death, 'The Rise of China' was an accepted fact.

Whether it is because the pace of events has actually accelerated or because new information technologies allow us to know about more events than would have been possible in previous centuries, this compression of time can cause us to be confused, displaced from historical reality. The 'retrospective smoothing' I'm describing helps us resolve our confusion and displacement; it imposes a linearity and consistency on the past that elides and overlooks contradictory details.

Another way to understand 'retrospective smoothing' is as the social scientist's search for patterns. The trend line is up and down, but if we graph it long enough we can identify a trajectory, a directionality, and from there it's very tempting to infer inevitability, intention, even a plan. As social scientists we are often called upon to speculate about the future based on inferences we are making about the past. The problem comes when, instead of revisiting the past, we assume we remember it because it was just a few years ago, and we end up misrepresenting the past, present *and* future.

I see this happening in how quickly we forgot that the KMT has never been an ethnic party: as much as the DPP might like to paint it as the '49er' (*waishengren*) party, most of its votes come from native Taiwanese (*benshengren*). Another example: Tsai Ing-wen. There is an enormous amount of speculation about Tsai – what she wants, where she would like to lead Taiwan, what her goals are, and I think retrospective smoothing has influenced that speculation and made it unreliable. It begins with a fact: Tsai worked for Lee Teng-hui, and she worked for him during the crafting of the two-states theory (*liangguo lun*), in which Lee asserted that there was a 'special state-to-state relationship' between the mainland and Taiwan. It's entirely possible that Lee was trying to find a formula for moving cross-Strait relations forward by establishing a platform for ROC–PRC relations, but Beijing – which at that time imagined that getting Taiwan to give up on identifying as the Republic of China (ROC) would somehow help its cause – rejected Lee's idea and accused him of advancing the independence cause.

Beijing decided Lee was pushing independence, and Tsai was associated with Lee, so Tsai became an independence advocate by association. And now that she is president, the People's Republic of China (PRC) government is convinced that she is looking for a backdoor to independence. But the claim about Lee is questionable, and the extension of that claim to Tsai is even more so. When Lee did come out as an independence advocate a few years later, observers backdated his views and concluded that he had always supported independence, making everyone who had worked for him guilty by association. If we allow for the possibility that Lee was not trying to achieve independence all along, but was pushed to that position by the PRC's stonewalling and changes in Taiwan's domestic politics, then we also need to reconsider the characterisation of Tsai Ing-wen. This presentist tendency, which ignores the complexity and contingency of history, feeds a narrative about Tsai that unnecessarily limits the range of policy options available to the PRC.

Another example of this false memory syndrome is the widespread delusion that there was a golden age of cross-Strait relations back in the days when a firmly pro-unification KMT was in charge and there was no tension between Taiwan and the mainland. This delusion posits that it was only when the DPP was founded, and Chen Shui-bian was elected, and the Taiwan independence movement emerged from the shadows that cross-Strait relations began to deteriorate.

Anyone with a clear memory of what cross-Strait relations were like between 1949 and 1987 knows this narrative is nonsense. When Chiang Kai-shek was

78 Shelley Rigger

president, both sides bristled with military hardware. The two sides skirmished with live fire more than once. Meanwhile, there was no communication between the two sides – no trade, no travel, no talks. Taiwanese were taught that the PRC was governed by Communist bandits who were destroying Chinese culture and imposing a foreign-inspired totalitarian nightmare on the Chinese people. Meanwhile, the Chinese Communist Party (CCP) insisted that it would 'liberate' Taiwan from the fascist KMT by force. The two sides absolutely did not need the DPP to hate each other.

If there was a golden age in cross-Strait relations, it was short: maybe 1987 to 1995. That interval began with Chiang Ching-kuo's decision to lift the prohibition on cross-Strait communication and ended with the first round of PRC military exercises aimed at deterring Taiwan independence. It encompassed the bilateral meetings between Taiwan's Koo Chen-fu and the PRC's Wang Daohan at which the two unofficial representatives hammered out agreements that enabled cross-Strait trade and investment. At the time, no one thought of those years as a golden age, and the political relationship soured quickly (although economic ties thrived).

My aim is simply to point out the analytical distortions that can happen when we fall into narratives that make sense in the context of later events and forget what really happened. Rereading a book written in the late 1990s reveals that tendency, but one of the things I was relieved to discover in rereading *Politics in Taiwan* is the extent to which it resisted the binaries – such as independence versus unification – and oversimplifications that have infected Taiwan studies to a distressing degree. Even though I was writing the book during the heyday of independence activism, I worked hard to deconstruct the concept and ended up producing a relatively complex account of the independence issue. Likewise with national identity, which the book treats as a complicated and contested phenomenon. What I realised on rereading it is that the way Taiwan's political development unfolded was less linear, less pre-determined, than the standard three-paragraph introduction to Taiwan history would lead one to believe.

From dissertation to book

Another observation that emerged for me in rereading the book is how much the demands of publishing shaped the book I ended up writing. *Politics in Taiwan* was trying to do several things. One thing it was trying to do, and this is very important, was to turn a dissertation into a book. To be specific, it was trying to turn a dissertation about clientelism in four county and city executive elections in 1985 and 1989 into a book that someone might want to read. A scholar could write a book on clientelism in Taiwan's local elections today, but back in the 1990s, I had advice from serious people, and that advice was, broaden the topic.

In many disciplines, one of the most important steps a scholar takes early in her career is to transform her dissertation into a book, which is almost always more difficult than she expects. A dissertation is, at its heart, a demonstration of a newly minted scholar's ability to do original work within a discipline. As such, it needs to

Politics in Taiwan: Voting for Democracy revisited   **79**

combine new data and old theory to craft a novel argument. A book, in contrast, can take many forms and approaches, but it needs to appeal to an audience, to fill a niche in the available scholarship. For many dissertation writers, making the journey from dissertation to book requires both whittling down and broadening out: whittling down the theoretical regurgitation and data dumping, broadening out the topic to fill a larger niche.

My dissertation was a classic example of the genre – a detailed study of grassroots organisation in eight local elections, four in 1985 and four in 1989 – but that was far from my intention when I began postgraduate study. I had studied Taiwan as an undergraduate, including spending a summer there researching a senior thesis on the ROC government's policy toward Taiwan's Aboriginal peoples, but I expected to write my PhD dissertation on mainland China. Motivated by my interest in minority politics and my admiration for the anthropologist Dru Gladney, I decided to write about Islamic minorities in China's northwest. I was working on a prospectus for this study in the spring of 1989.

By the time I went to bed on June 4, 1989, I knew that my dissertation plan would have to change. Islamic minority politics was a sensitive topic, and even anodyne research in the PRC was suspended that summer, for how long, no one knew. If I wanted to keep moving toward my degree, I needed a new project. A fortuitous encounter with Stephan Haggard, a political scientist from the University of California at San Diego, provided the answer: Marry my interest in Chinese-speaking societies to the burgeoning political science literature on democratisation in a case study of Taiwan's democratic transition.

Because I was writing a dissertation, and not a book, I needed to narrow the topic and sharpen the theoretical focus. I chose a 'scientific' research design: comparing local executive elections in four municipalities where the opposition candidates' performance differed from 1985 to 1989. The idea was to identify attributes of the four municipalities (Taipei County, Hsinchu City, Tainan County and Kaohsiung County) that would align with hypotheses in the democratisation literature to explain the differences in opposition performance.

As you might have guessed, the data had a different idea. My research quickly showed that the variables of interest to the democratisation literature could not explain why in Hsinchu City opposition candidates won in 1985 but lost in 1989, while in Taipei County the pattern was reversed. The real reason for the opposition's wins and losses, I discovered, lay in the minutiae of grassroots political mobilisation such as local factionalism and, above all, vote brokerage and vote buying, behaviour that centred on a fascinating cadre of political activists, the *tiau-a-ka* (*zhuangjiao in Mandarin*). To provide the required theoretical spine for my study I turned to theories of clientelism, and in particular to institutional explanations for clientelistic political behaviour. My dissertation became a comparison of the grassroots political consequences of the single, non-transferable vote (SNTV) system in Taiwan and Japan.

As soon as my dissertation was completed I pivoted to the work of turning it into a book. There was urgency to the task. The democratisation literature was accumulating fast, and if I wanted to contribute, I needed to get my book into that space quickly. Also, I was still hoping to break out of the Taiwan 'pigeonhole' and shift my attention to mainland politics – studying the emerging village committee elections seemed like a logical move. Unfortunately, though, my dissertation was too focused on clientelism to be of interest as a Taiwan case study, and too focused on Taiwan to be of interest as a study of clientelism. What to do?

In the end, I decided to open the manuscript up, to make it a case study of democratisation, focused on Taiwan and animated by a theoretical perspective I discovered relatively late: Bolivar Lamounier's idea that elections themselves can be a driving force for democratisation in authoritarian states that hold elections. Lamounier's theory, while rooted in the Brazilian experience, worked well in the Taiwan case. I am still convinced that elections were a driving force in Taiwan's democratisation, and I still like the phrase I coined – mobilisational authoritarianism – to describe the KMT-led regime.

The result is a book that tries to do a lot, perhaps too much. First, it wants to be an account of Taiwan's democratisation, so there are chapters aimed at telling the story of the transition, starting around 1972 and ending with Lee Teng-hui's victory in the first direct, democratic presidential election in 1996. Second, there are chapters that look a lot like dissertation chapters, piling up details of local politics in Taiwan, including more about SNTV and clientelism than most readers could possibly have wanted.[1] And third, it has the Lamounier argument threaded through it.

The most fundamental way the dissertation shaped the book was its methodology, which was qualitative and ethnographic. The 'data' for the dissertation was gleaned almost entirely from interviews: scores of conversations with politicians, campaign aides and grassroots campaign activists. None of it was pre-packaged for my analytical treatment. Most of the literature on elections, then and now, takes a quantitative approach. Very few studies of elections, whether from Taiwan or other countries, use the venerable approach developed by Richard Fenno, 'soaking and poking'. My decision to soak and poke instead of load and code for the dissertation determined the kind of book I could write: an analytical narrative.

Those methodological choices ensured that the book would be a case study, rich in descriptive detail, rather than a hypothesis-testing exercise. All of the 'political science-y' features of the dissertation are diminished in the book. I abandoned the comparison with Japan, except in a few places where it helped reinforce my arguments about SNTV. Likewise, telling Taiwan's story comprehensively and coherently required expanding beyond the four elections at the heart of the dissertation. Those cases provide a disproportionate share of the evidence in the book, but they are not what the book is about. The revision also reduced the emphasis on clientelism (although, as I said above, there is probably still more about clientelism than most readers want or need).[2]

Choosing a qualitative method for the dissertation and book also put me outside the mainstream of electoral studies, which is dominated (for good reasons) by 'number crunchers'. The quantitative work on elections can teach us a lot, but qualitative studies also have value; for example, if I had used quantitative methods I

Politics in Taiwan: Voting for Democracy revisited **81**

would never have uncovered the phenomenon of the *tiau-a-ka* and its position as the lynchpin of Taiwan's grassroots politics. Just before my dissertation was completed, articles appeared in *Ethnology* and *China Quarterly* that identified the *tiau-a-ka* phenomenon and described it in much the same way my dissertation did. The author of those articles, Joe Bosco (1992, 1994), is not a political scientist, but an anthropologist; it makes perfect sense that the anthropologist got the jump on the political scientist on this issue.

When Fenno was soaking and poking, he was seeking to understand electoral mobilisation from the candidate's perspective, as was I. But qualitative methods can advance electoral studies in other ways as well. Above all, open-ended engagement with candidates, campaign aides and voters can help us identify questions that would not otherwise have made it onto our surveys. For example, traditional voting models don't normally produce surveys that include 'my boss told me to' as a response to the question, 'why did you vote?' or 'my grandfather divvied up the votes of our household and told everyone which candidate to vote for based on how much money each one gave us' as a response to the question 'how did you select which candidate to vote for?' But in Taiwan in the 1980s, many people's decisions were influenced by factors like these, and versions of these response categories were added to some surveys as a result of ethnographic work. We also learned, though, that some things that we know are happening are very hard to capture in a survey, even when a question designed to uncover them is included in the questionnaire.

The pace of change

Rereading *Politics in Taiwan* also confirmed my very unscientific gut feeling that the pace of change in Taiwan has been extraordinarily rapid. Many Taiwanese are perpetually dissatisfied with the rate and extent of political progress, or at least that's what they tell me. Even after a big political victory there is very little celebration – people are on to the next thing. I was amazed, for example, at how little attention Taiwanese media and activists paid to the success of the anti-media monopolisation campaign in 2012–2013. You have to really dig to find out that, in the end, the media merger the movement was formed to oppose did not, in fact, go through. The movement got a lot of coverage, but when the merger plan fell through, the activists moved on to other issues.

Politics in Taiwan came out in 1999. It begins with the campaign rallies the night before Lee Teng-hui won the first direct presidential election in 1996. It then goes back to tell the story of how Taiwan reached the point of electing its president. My second book, *From Opposition to Power: Taiwan's Democratic Progressive Party*, was published two years later in 2001. It begins with the rallies the night before Chen Shui-bian was elected in 2000. Both books begin with a presidential election. They were published only two years apart. But they reveal a massive transformation of Taiwan's political landscape. *Politics in Taiwan* gives zero credit to the possibility

82 Shelley Rigger

that the DPP might come to power within a few years. I did not see it coming. Yet, two years later I literally wrote the book on how it happened.[3]

Another example of rapid change that is evident in a rereading of *Politics in Taiwan* is the evolution of Taiwan's political institutions. The book, because it is based on a dissertation about the political consequences of the SNTV electoral formula, spends a lot of time on SNTV. It was written at a time when political scientists were taking Evans, Rueschemeyer and Skocpol's (1985) advice to 'bring the state back in' and think about institutions. SNTV turned out to be a very interesting institution, and a whole cottage of industry emerged to understand the political consequences of SNTV. And then, suddenly, both Japan and Taiwan abandoned SNTV for national elections (Taiwan still uses it in some local elections, and for the election of Aboriginal legislators; Japan still uses it in its upper house elections).

When SNTV disappeared I was a bit wistful. Even though the scholarship suggested that the incentives built into SNTV produced unhealthy behaviours among politicians and voters, I was sad to see that chapter close. But how I feel about it is immaterial; in a very few years, Taiwan's institutions changed fundamentally, and its politics changed with them. The DPP has gone from opposition to semi-power (Chen Shui-bian's presidency was a period of divided government), back to opposition, and then back to power again – this time, under Tsai Ing-wen, with a DPP majority in the legislature and DPP control of most of the island's municipal governments.

Taiwan has changed rapidly in the past 25 years, and so has the academic literature about it. That, too, is evident from rereading *Politics in Taiwan*. The quality and quantity of scholarship available today would have made for a very different book compared with what I was able to put together in the late 1990s. For example, the book includes a section on elections during the Japanese colonial period. It argues that this early experience with electoral competition, even though it was very limited, made it easier for Taiwan to embrace elections under the KMT and to build the repertoire of behaviours and expectations that helped drive the democratisation movement many decades later. That section of the book relies on just a handful of sources, mainly a book chapter in Chinese by Chen Ming-tong and Lin Jih-wen (Chen and Lin 1998). Today, a reader would be justified in looking at that section and thinking, why are there so few sources here? Didn't the author do any research? And the answer is, those were the only sources available back in the early 1990s. Today there is a huge historical literature on the colonial period, but when I was writing *Politics in Taiwan*, historians were just getting started.

Another academic trend that was just getting started was survey research on political topics. I relied a lot on the Academia Sinica's Social Change Surveys, which had been going for a long time by the time I started researching my dissertation. But we need to keep in mind that during the authoritarian period, even academic surveys had to avoid sensitive issues. The Social Change Survey did touch on some of the issues of interest to me, but there were many topics we would love

Politics in Taiwan: Voting for Democracy revisited   **83**

to know about today that could not be raised in a survey in the 1970s or 1980s. And even if they *had* asked those sensitive questions – questions about attitudes toward 'China', the KMT, the political system – the answers would not have been valid. Taiwan was a highly repressive polity in the 1970s and 1980s; people went to jail for saying or writing the wrong thing. During the martial law period (1947–1987), surveys on controversial topics were unlikely to uncover respondents' true preferences.

This question of 'true preferences' is also interesting to me after watching Taiwan politics evolve so quickly and so extensively over the past 25 years. When I first visited Taiwan in 1983, martial law was still very real. I was asking questions about politics all summer long, but no one mentioned the Kaohsiung Incident, which had happened just two and half years earlier. I was living with a Taiwanese (*bensheng*) family in Hualien, and I naively asked the grandfather a question about Chen Yi's crackdown in 1947 (what we now call the 228 Incident). He claimed to have no idea what I was talking about, which was confusing enough to make me drop that line of questioning. It mortifies me now to think how much discomfort I must have given him, purely out of my own innocence and inexperience.

At any rate, if a pollster had asked them, both the grandfather and his son would have said they were KMT-supporting Chinese who favoured unification – and their answers would have been motivated only partially by fear. For many Taiwanese, embracing a 'Chinese' identity and supporting unification were natural responses to decades of indoctrination. Meanwhile, they supported the KMT because, in their city, the KMT was made up largely of people like them – *benshengren* who had come up through local elections processes – and having good connections to the city government made their lives easier. Ideas about independence, Taiwanese identity, and so on were simply not available to them. And as for 'China', in those days it really did mean the ROC. The PRC was a distant abstraction. Taiwanese had no contact with the mainland until 1987, and it wasn't real to them in the way it is today. As I wrote in *Why Taiwan Matters* (Rigger 2011) and in Yeh Wen-hsin's edited volume *Mobile Horizons: Dynamics across the Taiwan Strait* (Rigger 2012), the meaning of 'China' has changed in the last 25 years. That makes it risky to compare attitudes across time. We don't know which is changing: the answer to our question, or the meaning of the question itself.

New research methods and directions

Given the pace of change on the ground in Taiwan, it's important to stay flexible. My own research has evolved away from the tight focus on elections and democratisation that defines *Politics in Taiwan*. That's partly due to changes in Taiwan, but it also reflects constraints that my 'day job' as a professor at a teaching-intensive institution imposes on my scholarship. Researching *Politics in Taiwan* was a leisurely undertaking. I spent a full year in Taiwan, from January to December of 1991, researching the dissertation. And even with all that time, what really made it work was the intervention of one of the very first people I met, the DPP politician Chen

84 Shelley Rigger

Chu. She opened every door that I needed to get the research going; without her, neither the dissertation nor the book would have been possible.

One of the careers I had imagined for myself as a young person was in the human rights field, so before I went to Taiwan I met with someone at Human Rights Watch (HRW) in the United States to see if there was anything I could do for them while I was in Taiwan. In fact, they didn't need me at all, but the woman I spoke to asked if I would visit the Taiwan Association for Human Rights (TAHR) and see how it was getting along. I don't think HRW ever imagined I could do anything for them, but I think they knew exactly what they were doing for me when they made that request. In any case, their introduction allowed me to get a meeting with the head of the TAHR, and that was Chen Chu.

From the moment I met her, Chen Chu treated me as a member of her tribe. She was infinitely generous, inviting me to dinners, letting me hang around her office to meet young activists, but, most importantly, she knew all the DPP candidates and politicians I was hoping to study. I wanted to interview the candidates from 1985 and 1989 in Hsinchu City, Taipei County, Tainan County and Kaohsiung County, and her name was magic. The doors just popped open for me because I came with Chen Chu's endorsement. Now, of course I realise that she was their martyr, their hero, their most beloved person. But it took some time to figure that out.

And once I was connected with the DPP candidates they turned around and did the same thing for me. For example, Li Tsung-fan was the DPP candidate in Tainan in 1989, and he was hugely helpful to me. It worked like this: Someone from his office would call to say: 'Take the 2 o'clock train, the Taipei to Tainan. A guy will pick you up there and show you around for a while, introduce you to some people.' I would pack a bag for a few days, ride down to Tainan, and get off the train. It wasn't hard for the driver to know which disembarking passenger was me! So, a car pulls up alongside me and the window on the passenger side goes down and the head comes out, 'Are you Dr Shelley?' I climb in and off we go.

I didn't know where I was sleeping, I didn't know where I was eating, I didn't know who the next person was that I was going to talk to. I didn't know who was driving and where we were going, but every single one of those people was generous and hospitable. This is, I believe, what research methods people mean by 'snowballing' – one source leads to the next source, leads to the next source. Another way to understand it is, if you're a political scientist doing ethnographic field research about local politics, you can't be afraid to get into a car with a complete stranger and spend a night in his house. That's what your job is; it's totally fine. The same basic pattern happened in Kaohsiung and Hsinchu, and also Taipei County, although in the north I didn't need the overnight bag.

It is important, too, to stress that while my point of contact with the local candidates was a DPP figure, Chen Chu, the folks who toured me around for field research took me to visit the KMT as well as DPP. In fact, it was in a KMT office that I learned the term that ended up being at the heart of my dissertation, *tiau-a-ka*. I had never heard of *tiau-a-ka*; nor had I ever registered the word *zhuangjiao*

The Mandarin pronunciation, which is how it is normally written). I must have encountered it when I was reading newspapers in the National Central Library reading room. I probably looked it up and the definition made no sense, so I just went right over it: '*Zhuang jiao, zhuangjiao* ... I don't need this, I get the gist of the article, so I'm moving on'.' But in one of my interviews I was sitting with a village officer of the China Youth Corps (*Jiu Guo Tuan*). And even though we're speaking Mandarin, he keeps dropping in this Taiwanese (Hoklo) phrase, '*tiau-a-ka*'. Finally, I asked him, 'Could you please explain this word? What is *tiau-a-ka*?'

As soon as I asked the question, he and my DPP 'chauffeur' exchanged a look as if to say, 'Uh-oh, someone just told her the secret code!' From then on, everywhere I went I began by asking relatively soft, superficial questions and once the interview was warmed up I said, 'So, talk to me about *tiau-a-ka*.' As soon as I learned the magic word my conversations moved to a different level. They understood that I knew what I was talking about, and they went much deeper.

That kind of research takes time; it requires the leisure to be wrong, to be slow, to go back again and again and again. Once a scholar has a teaching position, it is very difficult to do that sort of work. The day job forces you to change your research method. That's part of what makes quantitation so attractive: You can download a dataset from anywhere and manipulate and analyse it in the comfort of your office. But as I am never going to be a quantitative political scientist, that option has not been available to me.

Most of my projects since *Politics in Taiwan* have included field research, but I've had to be much more efficient. When I received a grant to study the DPP it included funding to buy myself out of a semester of teaching. I spent the summer in Taiwan collecting material, but because it was only a couple of months, I had no time to soak and poke. I had to move quickly so I hired a research assistant, Jesse Lan. Working with Jesse was great in many different ways, but one of the many things I learned from him is that having a second set of eyes and ears can be enormously helpful in an interview. I was interested in the potential for generational turn-over in the party, so I asked about it in all my interviews. One day, Jesse asked me, 'Do you notice how they all change their body language when you ask about generational change-over?' In fact, I was so desperate to understand, take notes, and make sure I wrote down what I didn't understand so I could ask him later that I did not notice their body language changes at all. Jessie explained that the respondents hated that question because they didn't think of themselves as the 'older generation' and they were not ready to hand off power to younger people. I would not have gained that insight without Jesse. If I'd had unlimited time, perhaps I would have, but when you're working fast because your research time is limited, you need to let people help you.

Much of my recent work, and the project I hope to do next, tries to bridge quantitative and ethnographic methods. I'm interested in youth attitudes, both because understanding how young people see their situation is important for envisioning how things may develop in the future and because I think young voices are consistently ignored and misconstrued, not just in Taiwan, but

86 Shelley Rigger

everywhere. In Taiwan, though, there's a particular problem. I'm convinced that the survey questions that were developed back in the late 1980s and early 1990s mean something different to young people from what they do to older respondents. For a 20-year-old to say 'I'm Taiwanese' in 1992 meant something very different from what it does now. But we continue to ask the same survey questions because we want continuity across time. The project I started in 2005 uses focus group research to dig beneath the surface and find out what young people are thinking and feeling that isn't captured by the survey data. That method requires time, too, so I've only been able to do it during sabbaticals, but it takes less time than the ethnographical work that I did for my dissertation.

Detours and dead ends

Needless to say, *Politics in Taiwan* has its share of analytical failures. One that stands is the book's overestimation of the KMT's resilence. In the democratisation literature, authoritarian ruling parties typically end badly. One feature of the Taiwan case that was noteworthy was the KMT's ability to reinvent itself and thrive in the democratic period. Bruce Dickson (1997) wrote an entire book on this process, *Democratization in China and Taiwan: The Adaptability of Leninist Parties*. *Politics in Taiwan* was at pains to understand how the KMT pulled off this feat, so it emphasises the ways in which democratisation strengthened the ruling party, and underemphasises the challenges the transition posed to the KMT. I also was influenced by the historical moment in which I was writing.

In the early 1990s, Lee Teng-hui and the KMT received a great deal of credit for Taiwan's democratisation. Lee himself was nicknamed 'Mr. Democracy', a characterisation he happily embraced (and encouraged). Democratisation helped Lee secure his position against conservatives in the KMT – he was able to resist pressure from the right because he was so popular with voters. At the same time, democratisation helped the KMT indigenise (Lee was known for 'Taiwanising' the KMT), and that process was at its peak in the early 1990s. I did not anticipate that the indigenisation process would wane, but after its 2000 presidential election defeat, the KMT split. Instead of deepening, indigenisation became a source of intraparty conflict. It is one of the factors that drove the competition between Ma Ying-jeou and Wang Jin-pyng, which in turn contributed to the KMT's defeat in the 2016 presidential and legislative elections.

Politics in Taiwan asserts that the KMT had a big electoral advantage in the 1990s. That is no longer the case, but it's worth remembering; it wasn't just the case that an authoritarian party can't remain in power after democratisation. Unless we keep this history in mind, we may have difficulty understanding both the KMT's fall in 2016 and its future potential, as its revival in the 2018 local elections attests. How the KMT lost its grip on electoral politics, and to what extent, are important questions. They have political answers, but they may be linked to institutional changes as well. Political scientists have sophisticated tools for connecting demographic and ideological variables to electoral outcomes, but do our research

Politics in Taiwan: Voting for Democracy revisited **87**

methods allow us to give appropriate weight to mobilisation? Are we paying enough attention to the parties' ground game? Parties within parties, factions within factions, do we know how reform has changed behaviour relative to all the other drivers?

In short, Taiwan's recent political history is a story of multiple variables changing simultaneously: institutions, ideology, resources, social norms, mobilisational practices. Are we confident that quantitative methods alone can adjudicate the relationships among all these variables? Survey-based research consistently identifies the national identity issue (variously defined) as the most important variable for explaining voting behaviour. But there is precious little variation on this 'variable' among certain age groups. Once identification as 'Chinese' falls below the margin of error in the survey, how can we use it to explain voting behaviour? To move through an impasse like this requires an openness to new information, even new categories and kinds of information. That openness is often found in interdisciplinary work, area studies and qualitative methods. If *Politics in Taiwan* has been helpful for understanding anything, it is thanks to its holistic, open-minded approach and deep engagement with its subject.

Notes

1 Speaking of SNTV: One thing I really regret about *Politics in Taiwan* is, why did I not use 'SNTV'? Where did I get the idea to call the electoral system SVMM, an acronym that no one else has ever used before or since? Luckily, I can't remember so I can blame only myself.
2 Editor's (Fell) note: My students have consistently told me how much they enjoy the local politics parts of Rigger's book.
3 Full disclosure: I did not see the DPP victory coming. The idea to write about the DPP belongs to Allan Song, a program officer at the Smith Richardson Foundation, who offered me funding to study the DPP. It was Dr Song, not me, who foresaw the possibility that the DPP might win a national election in the near future. He also recognised that if that happened, policy makers, journalists and scholars would be caught off guard, because very little information was available about the DPP in English at that time. His prescience was a boon to me and my readers.

References

Bosco, Joseph. 1992. 'Taiwan Factions: Guanxi, Patronage, and the State in Local Politics'. *Ethnology*, 31(2), 157–183.
Bosco, Joseph. 1994. 'Faction versus Ideology: Mobilization Strategies in Taiwan's Elections'. *China Quarterly*, 137, 28–62.
Chen, Ming-tong and Lin Jih-wen. 1998. 'The Origins of Taiwan's Local Elections and the Changing Relations between State and Society'. In Chen Ming-tong and Zheng Yung-nian (eds), *Basic Level Elections and Socio-Political Change on Both Sides of the Strait*. Taipei: Yuedan Publishing Company, 23–70.
Dickson, Bruce. 1997. *Democratization in China and Taiwan: The Adaptability of Leninist Parties*. Oxford: Oxford University Press.
Evans, Peter B., Dietrich Rueschemeyer, and Theda Skocpol. 1985. *Bringing the State Back In*. Cambridge: Cambridge University Press.

Fenno, Richard. 1978. *Homestyle: House Members in their Districts*. Glenview, IL: Scott, Foresman and Company.

Lamounier, Bolivar. 1989. 'Authoritarian Brazil Revisited: The Impact of Elections on the Abertura'. In Alfred Stepan (ed.), *Democratizing Brazil: Problems of Transition and Consolidation*. New York: Oxford University Press, 43–79.

Rigger, Shelley. 1999. *Politics in Taiwan: Voting for Democracy*. New York: Routledge.

Rigger, Shelley 2011. *Why Taiwan Matters: Small Island, Global Powerhouse*. Lanham, MD: Rowman and Littlefield.

Rigger, Shelley. 2012. 'Redefining China: From the China Inside to the China Outside'. In Wen-hsin Yeh (ed.), *Mobile Horizons: Dynamics across the Taiwan Strait*. Berkeley: Institute of East Asian Studies, 48–73.

PART III
2000s towards a golden era

7

IN THE NAME OF HARMONY AND PROSPERITY AND BEYOND

Gender and labour as a (renewed) research agenda

Anru Lee[1]

This chapter revisits my book, *In the Name of Harmony and Prosperity: Labor and Gender Politics in Taiwan's Economic Restructuring* (Lee 2004), with the aim to (1) understand the circumstances under which the book was produced; (2) reflect on the issues that it addressed at the time of publication and questions remaining to be tackled; and (3) explore future research agenda. I start with a prologue to contextualise the research on which my book was based. This is followed by a brief overview of the literature on gender and global industrialisation, with a focus on how my work is positioned in the literature. The title of my book, *In the Name of Harmony and Prosperity*, reflects the emphasis on the entwined significance of the patrilineal familial cultural ideal and the developmentalist discourse in shaping the lives of Taiwanese women workers. The third section considers issues, especially concerning the role of the state, that were important or subsequently became important but not covered in my book. In the fourth section I offer the establishment of the Memorial Park for Women Laborers in Kaohsiung City, one of my current research projects, as an example to explore the intersectionality of gender, the state and family. The chapter ends with a brief conclusion.

Prologue: How and why I started the research

In the early 1990s I came to Taiwan, beginning the research on which my book, *In the Name of Harmony and Prosperity*, was eventually based. To borrow Dickens's famous quotation, 'It was the best of times, it was the worst of times,' the 1990s was indeed a time of mixed blessings.[2] After four decades of authoritarian political control, the Democratic Progressive Party was illegally established in late 1986, preceding the lift of martial law in mid-1987. Concomitantly, the late 1980s and onwards were characterised by a successive wave of social movements (Hsu and Sung 1989). Much of the long-accumulated civil discontent was finally released in the form of rallies, protests and street demonstrations. Political change rarely occurs as an isolated phenomenon but, rather, as an integrated part of the larger transformation. In Taiwan, the rise of the middle class as a result of a successful export-oriented economy was considered a key factor to democratisation (Hsiao 2006). Yet, at the same time, the wealth and prosperity brought about by the success also began to change the contour of Taiwanese society and economy. By the late 1980s, concurrent with political liberalisation, Taiwan was experiencing a rapid economic restructuring, namely capital outflow and deindustrialisation. The changing demographic profile, the rising labour costs and the increasingly stringent environmental codes and labour regulations – all of which were parts of the social transformation – together with intensified global competition, propelled Taiwanese manufacturers to seek alternative strategies. Many of them closed down their factories and turned to then-booming real estate or retail businesses, or they sought other production sites by relocating their factories to Southeast Asia and China. In this process, a substantial number of workers – predominantly women in labour-intensive industries – were laid off illegally or let go without proper compensation. Accordingly, many of the labour protests started in the late 1980s and corresponding scholarly research focused on severance and retirement payments owed by employers (Bo 1993; Ho 1992; W. Lin 1998; Shin-kong 2003).

My general interest in the issue of gender and global economy brought me to Taiwan in the mid-1990s. At the time, I was also concerned about the conditions of laid-off women workers, and my original research was to understand their situations after plant closures. However, soon enough, this research agenda had to be revised. Immediately, finding workers affected by plant closures presented a great challenge, as very few factories kept their employee records – let alone tracked the employees' whereabouts – after the shutdown. Consequently, even when I was able to use the snowball method to find and interview ex-factory workers (mostly in the metropolitan Taipei area), the data collection was at best sporadic, and the collected data was unsystematic and did not provide a rounded picture. The holistic perspective so fundamental to anthropology was sacrificed as a result. At the end, differing from the approach of the then-existing literature that tended to concentrate on labour activism surrounding one single factory in urban areas (e.g. Hsia and Jeng 1992), I decided to look for a geographical place – a town, a village or a district – wherein I could focus not only on industrial workers and their families but also the social system within which their lives took on shape and meaning (cf. Nash 1989).

The subsequent development of my research sounds like a typical ethnographic field story. After much seeking and consulting, sociology colleagues at Tunghai University in Taichung, who were conducting a series of studies on the organisation, network and transition of small-scale enterprises in central Taiwan at the time, pointed to me the possibility of Homei as my research site. Later, with the help of a classmate of the sister of a college friend of mine, I was introduced to the boss of Treasure Island, the factory that became the epicentre of my research. I lived in Homei for nearly two and half years (September 1993 to December 1995), first

In the Name of Harmony and Prosperity revisited **93**

staying with the family of my college friend's sister's classmate who ran a small textile factory, but later moving to the dormitory of Treasure Island. After my departure at the end of this period, I made regular return trips to Homei, to follow up on its economic changes over time. My knowledge about women textile workers is derived primarily from ethnographic fieldwork, namely participant observation and the everyday chats and conversations I had with them. Additional insight was gained from talking to other Homei residents, either through formal interviews or informal discussions. I also visited other textile factories, in Homei and elsewhere in Taiwan, to obtain an understanding of the larger economic context within which Homei's textile industry is embedded.

Homei appeared to be ideal, as it was a place that maintained a strong sense of community whose (non-agricultural) economic life had been dominated by one single industry.[3] Its long history in textile production and the congregation of numerous textile and related factories in a relatively well-defined location offered a unique opportunity to analyse the enduring impact of the global economy on Taiwan through the life course of a particular industry. By looking at the change in regional economy and production organisation, I was able to study the inter-connected issues that bear on the restructuring of the Taiwanese economy, the relationship between industrial transformation and social life, and the consequences of economic restructuring on individuals, the family and community.

Taiwan in the literature of gender and global industrialisation

'Gender and global capitalist expansion' is a well-established area of academic interest and policy concern, and Taiwan has been an integral part of the literature. As one of the 'Asian Tigers', Taiwan had been a global manufacturing powerhouse. The export-processing zones in Kaohsiung were the first of their kind in the world. They were established in the 1960s to attract foreign direct investment, which proved crucial to Taiwan's post–World War II economic development. The manufacturing jobs created by the factories inside the export-processing zones and elsewhere in Taiwan had not only contributed to the success of Taiwan's export-oriented economy but also helped to bring employment opportunities to many families, especially those with young daughters (Arrigo 1980; Diamond 1979; Kung 1994).

Taiwan is not unique in this regard, however, but a part of the broader phenomenon of global industrialisation that has shown to be a gendered process (Mills 2003). Ubiquitous in many parts of the world in recent times has been the employment of young women in the global assembly line. This incorporation of women workers into factory work exemplifies the larger process of flexible accumulation in late capitalism (Harvey 1991), which is characterised by the deployment of increasingly heterogeneous work forces and the utilisation of multiple modes of production. The variety of industrial situations linked to flexible accumulation raised anew questions about workers' relations with, and their responses to, capitalist transformation (Cairoli 2012; Chow 2002; Kim 1997; C. Lee 1998; Pun 2005; Salzinger

2003). Specifically, as women emerged to be the major labour force in global factories, models of regulation based on gender ideologies have been developed to control labour. These ranged from direct despotic labour management in large firms (Fernandez-Kelly 1983; Kim 1997; Ong 1987) to paternalistic control in small-scale, family-centred factories (Salaff 1981; Wolf 1994). The latter is particularly true in Taiwan, where young women's role in the family made them an ideal source of cheap labour essential to Taiwan's early export industrialisation (Gallin 1984, 1990; Greenhalgh 1994).

Past literature has pointed out that the family as a corporate unit to which family members contribute their labour and income, under the authority of the eldest male household head, has been a dominant ideology especially in the heyday of Taiwan's rural industrialisation in the 1970s and 1980s (Cohen 1976; Harrell 1985; Niehoff 1987; Stites 1982, 1985). The recruitment of young women into factory work was a welcome new development to farming families because their daughters now were no longer economic liabilities. Rather, they brought in much needed cash income into the family (Hu 1984). Elsewhere in the world the new economic role of women is sometimes perceived as a transgression of proper cultural codes and thus a source of moral anxiety (Mills 1999; Ong 1987, 1997), which at times led to violence against women (Belair-Gagnon, Mishra and Agur 2014; Livingston 2004; Lynch 2007; Wright 1999, 2007). As a contrast, my work shows that female industrial employment was readily accepted in Taiwan, subsumed under the idea of working daughter as filial daughter (A. Lee 2009). Furthermore, female industrial labour was cheap and disposable mainly because only young, single women were considered suitable productive workers. Once married, the woman's primary responsibility was to bear a son for her husband's families with whom her welfare, dead or alive, now lay. In other words, for the Taiwanese patrilineal family, the role of women changed from productive to reproductive in nature upon marriage. One might argue that in this type of family system there is a progression of rights and obligations throughout the lifecycle as well as belated gratification for women. That is, just as a woman's brothers and their wives were enjoying the fruit of her labour, after marriage, she would also be enjoying the fruit of her husband's (unmarried) sisters' labour. However, what would happen to a woman if she was unmarried or if she did not get a chance to get married before she died?

Elsewhere I argue that, if the patrilineal familial ideology had constituted the foundation of the cultural-cum-capitalist logic in post-World War II Taiwan, the act of non-marriage – voluntary or not – represented a slippage from the process of social reproduction. It was a 'subaltern practice', a moment when the paradox of the patrilineal family and the incongruities in industrial production were revealed (A. Lee 2008). These paradoxes and incongruities are discussed in detail in my book. *In the Name of Harmony and Prosperity* centres on a juncture when the smooth reproduction of the female manufacturing labour force throughout most of the post-World War II era was disrupted, primarily due to the decreased willingness of young single women to consider industrial work as their first choice of employment. By the 1990s, in Homei and elsewhere in Taiwan, many of the female

(junior) high school graduates expected (by factory owners) to enter factories preferred to work in the rapidly expanding service sector, which they considered to be
more modern, prestigious and providing better chances for upward mobility. Or
they chose to continue their education in preparation for a white-collar profession,
as their families were no longer in urgent need of their labour and incomes. This,
in turn, had a profound impact on the remaining female work force. In my
research, I observed an increase in employment opportunities for married women,
who were previously considered as less dependable because of their domestic
responsibilities, but now were regarded as more reliable because young women
were no longer available. Young women were said to be leisure- and consump-
tion-oriented and, unlike hard-working Taiwanese in previous generations, preferred to take time off for fun as opposed to working overtime for money. The
discourse of 'good workers' had changed, in other words. I also observed that
young women who chose to work in factories tended to have a strong sense of
economic independence because industrial employers needed them. Some even felt
that they could choose to remain unmarried and support themselves with their
wages. However, these women's optimism was soured by the introduction of foreign workers to the country. I also discovered that daughters working for their
family factories were caught in a dilemma. On the one hand, they were eager to
pursue the better opportunities for personal advancement outside the family factories. On the other hand, however, their families urgently needed their labour,
not only because family members had always been the core work force of Taiwan's
family businesses, but also because their families had difficulties recruiting female
workers. As a result, family loyalty was recurrently called on to secure a daughter's
cooperation, often at the expense of her desire to have a life of her own, even
though a daughter was never considered a true member of her father's family.

As I characterised at the beginning of this chapter, the 1990s was the best and
worst of times, a time full of contradictions. On the one hand, it was a time when
Taiwanese society was enjoying general prosperity as a result of a successful export-
oriented economy. The phrase 'One's ankles are flooded with Taiwanese money'
(台灣錢淹腳目) speaks to the large amount of wealth accumulated over the past
few decades seeking venues of investment. Much money was poured into the
then-booming stock and real-estate markets, causing the rise of a bubble economy.
On the other hand, the economic success was also its own worst enemy. The
industrial reorganisation, including plant closure/relocation and recruitment of new
sources of labour, addressed in my book reflects the renewed strategies of industrial
capital accumulation under the changing socio-economic contour of Taiwan. In
terms of gender and labour relations, permeating in Taiwan at the time was the
industrial employers' lament for labour shortage (of young single women), while
many middle-aged, senior workers were unlawfully laid off or lost their jobs
without proper compensation. Yet, concurrently, married women became the new
favourite workforce among many small manufacturing producers such as in Homei,
because young single women were no longer available. In family-centred factories,
the labour of unmarried daughters was considered even more essential than before.

96 Anru Lee

However, the family remained patrilineal in nature, and daughters were not permanent members of the family, although their family loyalty was constantly called upon even if they remained unmarried throughout their lives.

All of these, of course, reflect the capitalist attempt to renew the process of capital accumulation in the transition from an industrial economy to a post-industrial economy. But they were not just about capital accumulation in a strict economic sense. Revealed in my book are the complex interdependent connections between gender, labour, the family and community. Therefore, on the issue of gender and global industrialisation, we should focus not only on cultural distinctions based on locale, or the interaction of gender and other stratifying factors within a socio-cultural system, but also on how gender can produce different effects and meanings over time under different historical-economic circumstances. This is especially evident in Taiwan where the economy transformed within a few decades from one based on agriculture to one centring on manufacturing, but has now moved towards the direction of service industries. The pattern of labour deployment, as well as the labour available for deployment, differs at each of these stages. Moreover, given the short span of time involved, the impact of these transitions can be observed during the work life of one single individual, as illustrated in the life stories in my book.

The state, labour and gender: An unfinished business

My book emphasises the interplay of Taiwanese patrilineal family and global capitalist expansion and how women as workers, daughters and mothers found agency under these powerful structural constraints. It investigates the dialectic relationships between culture and economy. While I am by and large satisfied with what I was able to accomplish – and probably would have not done anything differently had I gone back in time – I now think that the role of the state might be more sufficiently addressed in the book. In their review articles of my book, Anita Chan (2005) and Hill Gates (2005) each point out the salience of the state in understanding the economic life in Taiwan. Chan's comment focused specifically on the issue of migrant workers, whereas Gates noted the overall effect of the powerful state in shaping the Taiwaneses' life experiences. In the following, I elaborate on each of their points vis-à-vis my own work, and discuss how their points are addressed in the current literature or how they might be addressed in literature.

The issue of foreign labour/migrant workers

Chapter 6 of my book, 'Guests from the Tropics', tackled the issue of foreign labour/migrant workers, one of the most dramatic trends in Taiwan's economy after the official introduction of foreign labour policy in the late 1980s. Chan (2005) stated that, while my book paid great attention to labour exploitation based on gender inequality, it did not sufficiently discuss the exploitation faced by migrant workers. As a part of an ethnography that attends to the politics of industrial reorganisation embedded in a particular community, chapter 6 is in sync with other chapters that adopt a locally centred perspective. Accordingly, the situations of migrant workers were understood through the discourses and practices of local entrepreneurs, workers and residents. However, Chan's critique is helpful in the sense that it reminds us of the significance of the state in shaping the conditions of migrant workers in Taiwan, even though the critique itself did not involve the state directly. By naming members of the non-Taiwanese work force as 'foreign laborers' but not 'migrant workers' in the official language, the Taiwan government has readily provided a framework to conceptualise these people's legal, political and economic statuses in particular ways. All of these, in turn, became a part of how local populations in Homei perceived and regarded these migrant workers. Indeed, the state was an integral part of the story, which should be fully studied.

Fortunately, migration (including labour and marriage migrations) has been one of the most dominant topics of research in Taiwan Studies in recent years, and many excellent scholarly works have been produced accordingly. To name a few, Tseng and Wang (2013) and Wang (2001, 2011) reviewed and provided critiques of Taiwan's immigration policy. The political economy and socio-cultural impact of foreign labour have inspired a tremendous amount of literature, especially regarding foreign domestic and care worker migration (Cheng 2003 and Lan 2006 are prime examples).

The state, kinship and family

Chan's critique primarily concerns global labour exploitation, which points to the explicit and brutal force of the state. In contrast, Gates's comment touched upon not only the direct, despotic control of the state but also policies seemingly unrelated to but indeed bearing great impact on the sphere of kinship and family life.

Gates (2005) stated that the 'patrilineal family ideology' so emphasised in my book did not simply bubble up from millions of Taiwanese expressing values, but it was shaped and consolidated as much by the state as by individual families. She wrote in her review of my book:

> I am uncertain ... of the utility to social analysis in general of counterposing 'economy' and 'culture' (even when they interact dialectically). I am fairly certain that to employ this dichotomy in East Asia, and most of all in China-derived societies, leaves out something of great importance. That something is the highly conscious use that Chinese states, through their elites, have made of kinship and gender by shaping it as the bottom level of a political-economic hierarchy encompassing the social whole.
>
> *(Gates 2005: 299)*

Highlighted in Gates's review was the household registration system that the post-World War II Nationalist (KMT) government inherited from its Japanese colonial predecessor. The household registration system was of course implemented for the

98 Anru Lee

purpose of demographic governance – or, in Foucault's term, 'biopolitics' (Lin and Tseng 2014). Under the KMT rule, and until very recently, Gates pointed out, households based on patrilineal membership were the basis of all individual identity. They were not optional. Registration as a household member with a specific relationship to the household's head was a key element in social management and political control. As such, kinship and gender relations were administrative as much as customary.

Gates's concern, of course, was not confined to the realm of kinship and gender but extended to the omnipresence of the Taiwanese state. Specifically, under the KMT's authoritarian rule and even at the democratic present, the state sector (including those recently privatised state enterprises in which the government continues to be a major stock holder) constitutes an enormous segment of the economy. For Gates, the 'nonmarket sphere' that spanned from state enterprises and military complex to individual registered households presented considerable material backing to the market, and it gave its own hierarchical logic to a great variety of human experiences including economic ones in Taiwan (Gates 2005: 299). For me, this insight points to the need for a more careful examination of the explicit policy and implicit influence of the state that bridges my proposed dichotomy of culture and economy. Two issues that deserve further research spring to mind: The first one, of course, involves the power of administrative/bureaucratic forces such as the household registration system in regulating one's social membership. This, as Gates reminded us, in turn has the effect of outlining one's rights and obligations vis-à-vis both the state and the family. The central topics dealt with in my book, such as why a woman participated in the industrial labour market and how she might exert an agency of her own, were shaped by these rights and obligations and the sense of self-identity and subjectivity derived from them.

The second issue relates to the state's role in the famous 'Living Rooms as Factories' (客廳即工廠) campaign. Scholars working on Taiwan's post-World War II development all agree on the significance of this campaign. It is considered a turning point in Taiwan's export-oriented economy wherein the then-reserved female labour force in primarily rural areas was successfully mobilised for industrial production. This not only gave Taiwanese manufacturers a large number of cheap and highly adaptable workers but also helped them to create an exceedingly decentralised and flexible production system that lent them a competitive edge on the global market. While the exploitive nature of this campaign regarding gender relations is well studied (Hsiung 1996), much less clear is how individual families actually turned their living rooms into factories. I am not talking about why they did it. Given the general poverty and lack of employment possibilities at the time, it is easy to understand why the Taiwanese embraced any opportunity to make money. Rather, I am asking how the campaign was waged. For example, the conventional wisdom about 'Living Rooms as Factories' is that it was a part of the Adequate Plan (小康計劃) advocated by Hsieh Tung-min (謝東閔), the Governor of Taiwan Province (1972–1978), to eradicate the enlarging urban–rural discrepancy and the ensuing wealth gap due to the take off of Taiwan's export economy. In the plan, (rural) women were encouraged to use their living rooms as a workplace, take on industrial piecework, and increase their family revenues accordingly. However, particularly at the local level, who was doing the encouraging? How was the encouragement done? Was 'Living Rooms as Factories' mainly a governmental advocacy decree? Or were there specific policies (e.g. tax-related incentives) to steer the society in that direction? These are all questions left unanswered in the current literature.

It is worth noting that the campaign is normally understood and phrased as 'Living Rooms as Factories', including that used in the current 'Your Home is A Factory' (家庭即工廠) exhibition at the National Museum of Taiwan History.[4] However, on the 'In-depth Travel around Taiwan' webpage of the Ministry of Culture that introduces the campaign and Governor Hsieh who presided over the campaign, a distinction is made between 'Living Rooms as Work Arenas' (客廳即工場) and 'Living Rooms as Factories' (客廳即工廠).[5] It is emphasised on this Ministry of Culture webpage that the provincial government was pursuing a campaign of the former but not the latter. Therefore, the webpage cautions that people will be making a big mistake if they think the 'Living Rooms' campaign was about moving in motors and machines to build a factory at one's house for, as a matter of fact, it was about doing small assembling jobs in one's own living room.

For my purpose here, the fact that this distinction has to be made and disseminated by a cabinet-level government agency is meaningful as it points to a slippage between the intended goal of the state and unintended consequences (although, in this case, the planned goal of 'Living Rooms as Work Arenas' appeared to be as successful as the unintended consequence of 'Living Rooms as Factories'). The slippage presents an opportunity to understand the strength (and insufficiency) of administrative/bureaucratic forces in shaping the economic life of Taiwan. Once again, 'Living Rooms as Work Arenas and/or Factories' did not simply bubble up from millions of Taiwanese expressing self-interests, but it was shaped and consolidated as much by the state as by individual families. Questions such as 'What government policies were originally put in place to facilitate the discourse and practice of "Living Rooms as Work Arenas"?', 'What regulations were developed to ensure the success of the campaign?', 'How effective were these regulations?', 'How did these regulations – or the lack thereof – enable the mushrooming of factories in the countryside of Taiwan?', and 'Why did the government allow the establishment of numerous factories in the middle of farm fields if this was not the original plan?' are all questions that should be explored further in order to attain a full picture of Taiwan's recent economic history and the intricate relationships among gender/culture, labour/economy and the state.

Gender, labour and the state revisited: The case of the Memorial Park for Women Laborers

In the previous section I raised two issues regarding the state derived from my book that deserve further research. Although I have not yet begun exploring these issues systematically, I have been working on a 'Twenty-five Ladies' Tomb/ Memorial Park for Women Laborers' project that brings together three areas crucial to understanding the current gender dynamics: popular religion (especially pertaining to ancestor worship), feminist activism and the state. The Tomb/Park project represents my effort to contemplate how Taiwan can continue to make substantial contributions to the discussion of gender and global capitalism despite the fact that it is no longer a manufacturing-based economy. While women's incorporation into the global labour market and its impact on the individuals and societies involved continue to be significant topics of worldwide academic and policy concerns, there seemed to be a decrease of interest in women workers in Taiwan Studies as Taiwan moved into a post-industrial era. As a result, my book was published at the tail end of the literature. Taiwan is no longer recognised as a vital part of the conversation on the persistently important issue of gender and global capitalism. A close look at the renovation of the Twenty-five Ladies' Tomb, however, reveals that 'women workers' could be a crucial signifier with or without a corporal body to labour. This enables us to (re)evaluate the significance of women workers, in real life and theoretically, and thus provides us with renewed research agendas on gender and global capitalism in Taiwan Studies.

In this section, I use the transformation of the Twenty-five Ladies' Tomb to the current Memorial Park for Women Laborers as an example to demonstrate how we might conceptualise the intersected issues of gender, labour and the state within the context of post-authoritarian and post-industrial Taiwan. My previous approach to gender and global industrialisation focused on the transformation of political economy in local societies. The Tomb/Park project, however, attempts to understand the political and cultural dimensions of this transformation, including the meaning of industrialisation as a crucial component of modern nationhood (c.f. Moon 2005). In this section I explain why and how I started this project and present my preliminary findings. I propose that the economic contributions of women workers do not always derive from their productive roles but also from the symbolic capital they help to create as icons in a post-industrial, culture-led urban economy (such as that of Kaohsiung).

Why and how I started the Tomb/Park project

After I finished the research in Homei, on which *In the Name of Harmony and Prosperity* was based, I directed my focus to urban areas, especially Taipei and Kaohsiung, the two largest cities in Taiwan.[6] This move was informed by the theoretical observation that post-industrial cities – but not (de-)industrialised hinterlands – have emerged to be the critical site of global competition in late capitalism (Sassen 2001). I was interested in understanding how the place-making and infrastructure-building practices in Taipei and Kaohsiung characterise the two cities' efforts to be a part of the current global economic ordering (A. Lee 2007, 2012, 2015; Lee and Tung 2010). The renovation of the Twenty-five Ladies' Tomb to the Memorial Park for Women Laborers, it seemed to me, presented a good opportunity to connect my previous research to my current theoretical interest.

The Twenty-five Ladies' Tomb (旗津二十五淑女墓) was the collective burial site of female workers who were drowned during a ferry accident on their way to work at Kaohsiung's export processing zones in 1973. Of the 70 plus passengers on board, all 25 who died were unmarried young women. Taiwanese culture shuns unmarried female ghosts who have no husband's ancestral hall to rest in peace. This made the tomb a fearsome place. Since the early 2000s, the Kaohsiung Association for the Promotion of Women's Rights (高雄市女性權益促進會 [hereafter, KAPWR]), a major feminist group in Kaohsiung, had urged the Kaohsiung City government to rename the tomb to remove the stigma of unmarried female ghost and to reflect the productive role of the deceased young women. The feminists' call, however, was not answered until urban tourism became a prominent part of the Kaohsiung City government's developmental plan. As part of an effort to reinvent the city's economy, the Kaohsiung Mayor's Office finally allocated money to clean up the gravesite and remake it into a tourist-friendly 'Memorial Park for Women Laborers' (勞動女性紀念公園) in 2008.

People involved in the renovation process included the families of the 25 deceased women, the Kaohsiung City government and the KAPWR, all of whom had different considerations and therefore diverse expectations regarding the purpose and the future of the tomb. Elsewhere I detail the contention and contestation during the renovation process (Lee and Tang 2016). Here, I briefly delineate the sequence of events and ask why and how the renovation happened in the way it did at the time. Specifically, I orient my thinking around approaching 'women workers' as a metaphor, and trace the change in its meaning and implication at different historical junctures leading to the tomb renovation whilst 'women workers' assumed a postmortem central role in both the feminist intervention and the Kaohsiung City government's discourse at a time when manufacturing was no longer the primary sector of female employment.

Partly because the duty of a faculty member made it difficult to take prolonged research leaves but primarily because the scale of the Tomb/Park project is no longer confined to a small town but covers a city of a few million people, I used different research methods instead of the long-term community study emphasised in my Homei research. My collaborator for the project, Dr Anna Wen-hui Tang at the Sociology Department of National Sun Yat-sen University in Kaohsiung, is herself a core KAPWR member and one of the chief instigators behind the KAPWR's campaign for the renovation of the Twenty-five Ladies' Tomb. Her experience and observation lent the groundwork for our research. While our concern for the subject matter is ongoing, we conducted a month of intensive ethnographic field research (from mid-December 2012 to mid-January 2013) that included both formal interviews and participant observation/informal conversation. We conducted formal interviews with families of deceased women (mostly parents or elder siblings). We also interviewed Kaohsiung City government staff involved in the tomb renovation and core KAPWR members active in the KAPWR's tomb renovation effort. In addition to formal interviews, we also engaged in daily, informal conversations and participant observation with the people we met in

102 Anru Lee

Kaohsiung and elsewhere in Taiwan. In these conversations we were particularly interested in learning about the knowledge ordinary citizens have about the 25 ladies, their collective burial and the refurbished memorial park, as well as how they used the park. We also collected government documents and newspaper and magazine articles in relation to the ferry accident, the Twenty-five Ladies' Tomb and the tomb renovation.

Deceased women as enlightened beings: Families telling the story

Shortly after the ferry incident, the Kaohsiung City government intervened and helped to settle the pension and compensation issue. The city government also helped to find a plot of land big enough to accommodate the graves of all these 25 women after their families decided to have them buried in one location. Parents of the deceased also began to address these women as 'sisters' and refer to the collectivity as a 'sisterhood'. Later, in 1988, because the land of the tomb site was acquired for the expansion of the Kaohsiung Port by the government, the tomb, along with other graves from Chong-chou Village, where the families of the deceased lived, was relocated to a new seashore site. This time the Kaohsiung City government also erected a memorial gateway (inscribed with 'The Twenty-five Ladies' Tomb') for the new site. Compared with the original burial ground, which was at a fairly remote corner of Cijin Island that not many outside visitors would usually go to, this new location is right beside a main road of Cijin. It sits facing the Taiwan Strait, enjoying a scenic view of the coastline. The public land across the road from the tomb has been renovated and made into a part of the Cijin Tourist Port Area since the relocation of the Tomb.

As far as the Kaohsiung City government was concerned, the ferry incident had come to a relatively satisfactory conclusion. For the families grieving for their lost daughters, however, there was still unfinished business. Specifically, where and how to place the spirits of those who died unmarried presented a great challenge to these families.

A few years after the ferry accident, some members of the grieving families began to report paranormal incidents. At first, the young women would come back to their family members' dreams, and say that they were now learning to become 'enlightened beings', and that they wanted their families to have their 'god statues' made. After this, some families began to experience health problems. As soon as the family made their deceased daughter a 'god statue', all the problems were gone and everybody (in the family) was cured. Before long, 22 out of the 25 deceased young women had had their 'god statues' made.

The transcendence of these deceased women from being maiden ghosts unable to be incorporated into their patrilineal ancestral shrines to becoming pious beings who could be welcomed to join the pantheon worshipped at the altars of their fathers' houses provided their families with a culturally sanctioned solution to care for their daughters in the afterlife. However, efficacy was evidently an issue in the minds of the families when their deceased daughters requested to have their god statues made. The variation in where and how these women's god statues are placed illustrates the ambivalence that many parents of the deceased felt – and continue to feel – about their daughters' said elevated religious position (Lee and Tang 2017). Despite that, many of the god statues were welcomed into their fathers' houses and revered as someone with a pious status, they were not placed in the family altar along with these women's patrilineal ancestors and other gods worshipped by the families. Instead, they were placed in a separate altar of its own on a different floor of the house. As a result of this ambivalence, the deceased's parents were continuously anxious about the eternal fates of their daughters and worried that these young women would be forgotten after the passing of their aging parents.

Deceased women as worker heroines: Feminists framing the discourse

Just as the unwed status of these deceased young women caused the biggest worry for their parents, it was also the popular cultural and religious assumptions associated with their maiden identity that were at the centre of the feminists' critique. In 2004, right before the Ching-ming Day, the KAPWR called a press conference, in which they rallied for the reconstruction of the Tomb. The then-KAPWR Secretary published a newspaper op-ed article, entitled 'Women Who Cannot Go Home', in which she commented on the custom that Taiwanese married women could only commemorate the ancestors of their husbands but not those of their natal families. Essentially, the KAPWR activists emphasised the role of these 25 women as manufacturing workers who helped to build Taiwan's economic miracle; and they died on their way to work. Therefore, their deaths were job-related. KAPWR feminists also stressed that a focus on these women's work roles would also help to advance the public's recognition that Taiwanese women have made great contributions to the economic growth of the country.

KAPWR's effort to refashion the image of the tomb was more than a posthumous recognition of the deceased women. It was also a critique of a core feature of the Taiwanese patriliny, which treasures sons as true and permanent members, but regards daughters as outsiders and thus temporary associates, of their father's family. This symbolic differentiation has provided a framework on which many gender-based practices, including the preference of young women for industrial work, are justified. KAPWR's activism therefore represented a strategic choice borne out of the particular patrilineal familial context of Taiwan. Globally, it also resonates with feminist movements' efforts worldwide to rectify women's history by rewriting and valorising the contribution of women.

From remembering to memorialising: The state as the arbiter

The Kaohsiung City government was slow to respond, however. It was not until early 2006 that the Kaohsiung Mayor's Office revealed the 'Cijin: An Island for Tourism' project, which was part of the city's larger plan to reinvent the city's

104 Anru Lee

deindustrialised economy by developing urban tourism. To ensure the overall success of the Cijin project, given the Taiwanese aversion to cemeteries, changing the public image of the tomb site was essential. The Twenty-five Ladies' Tomb was to be transformed into a 'Memorial Park for [All] Women Laborers'.

Initially, many of the deceased's families simply could not understand why the government wanted to dig up their daughters once again. When these families were eventually persuaded to accept the idea, they wanted the Tomb to be renovated into something like the Eighteen Lords Temple (十八王公廟). The Eighteen Lords Temple was originally 'a simple roadside shrine for unidentified bones – the sort that sits unattended and almost unnoticed all over the countryside' but, thanks to the said power and efficacy exhibited by the 18 lords, since the 1980s it has grown into one of Taiwan's major temples (Weller 1994). From the perspective of these families, the Eighteen Lords Temple resembled the Twenty-five Ladies' Tomb in the nature of its ghostly spirits who also suffer from the lack of a proper place on an ancestral altar. Its success in attracting a large number of worshippers and, accordingly, enjoying exuberant incense burning seemed to present the best kind of prospect for the Twenty-five Ladies' Tomb for these families. The parents were concerned that no one else in the family would be making regular offerings to their daughter-gods after they passed away.

However, it had always been the position of the Kaohsiung Mayor's Office that there should be no trace of the tomb left after the renovation. In the end, the government prevailed. As a result of the renovation, the individual graves of these young women were removed, and trees and meadows were planted. At the centre of the park is a sculpture of a Buddhist lotus on a pedestal. On 3 September 2008, 35 years after the fatal ferry accident, the Memorial Park for Women Laborers was inaugurated. The words of then-Kaohsiung Mayor Chen Chun (陳菊), '[Let's] Remember our sisters who labored [and] Wish for a city of happiness' (懷念勞動姊妹，祈願幸福城市), were inscribed on the pedestal of the Buddhist lotus sculpture. The inscription also explains the park's purpose:

> Resting in peace here are twenty-five women who gave their lives in the labor front [...]. In 1973, they died while on their way to work. The Kaohsiung City government helped to bury the deceased together at the time, and named the collective entombment 'The Twenty-five Ladies' Tomb,' as an important documentation of the contemporary life of Cijin and a witness to the sacrifices the working-class people made for Taiwan's economic development. However, the term 'Lady' carried stereotypical gender ideologies that ignored both the economic contributions of women workers and the urgency of safety issues in the workplace [...]. On the recommendation of the Kaohsiung Association for the Promotion of Women's Rights and other groups, the current Kaohsiung City government decided to rectify the site as the 'Memorial Park for Women Laborers' to commemorate the twenty-five martyrs who died on their jobs [...]. We hope that we can work together to build a

country for working people and a city of happiness, so that the sacrifice made by the deceased women will not be in vain.[7]

Since then, the Kaohsiung City government has held an annual spring memorial ceremony around the time of Ching-ming in front of the lotus sculpture. In the first few years, only the families of the deceased were invited to attend, along with Mayor Chen Chu and her staff. Since 2012, however, the city government has begun to mobilise local school children to perform at the ceremony, playing taiko drums and recorders and reading poetry. The city government hoped that, by participating in the memorial ceremony, the children would learn about the history behind the women's deaths and also enjoy the park. In other words, this was a further attempt of the city government to redefine the site as a 'recreational space', not a 'home of the dead'. The annual spring memorial service is also the occasion that the Kaohsiung City government employs to (re)assert its commitment to workplace safety for all job-related activities including the commuting to and from work.

On the intersectionality of gender, the state and family

There is no doubt that it was the feminists' persistent effort that pushed the government to act. Yet, the Kaohsiung City government had its own agenda and different constituencies to respond to. It did not actively act on KAPWR's call to change the appearance of the tomb site until the development of urban tourism in Cijin became an integral part of the city's plan to reinvent Kaohsiung's deindustrialised economy. In addition, the inscription engraved on the lotus sculpture at the refurbished park is revealing for, from the city's perspective, it serves multiple purposes. It highlights the economic contribution of the deceased women and recognises them as a part of the larger history of Taiwan, thereby addressing the concern of the feminists. It also emphasises the government's commitment to gender equality and workplace safety, which helps to enhance the aura of Kaohsiung as a modern city and its municipal administration as a reform-minded, progressive government. On the emotional level, the portrait of the deceased as noble workers dying on their jobs also has the (intended or unintended) effect on promoting Kaohsiung's urban tourism. After all, what could be a better symbol than the image of 25 young women dying tragically on their way to work to characterise the romance and pathos of Kaohsiung's past as a blue-collar city? The very act of memorialisation, therefore, also embodies the effect of place-making and city-marketing crucial to a successful remaking of Kaohsiung's city economy.

The state played a prominent role in shaping the meanings and purposes of (a) the story of the 25 young women and the ferry incident that took their lives, (b) the collective burial of these women, and (c) the renovated park where their final resting place is situated. However, there is a twist in this case. In the public voices of the KAPWR feminists and the Kaohsiung City government, the 25 deceased young women became emblems and their individuality is subsumed under the

106 Anru Lee

symbolism they now collectively represent. This does not exclude any private reading of how they should be remembered, such as that echoed in the quiet voices of their families. Thus the park in its current existence allows different interpretations to coexist. The annual spring memorial service deployed by the city government to (re)affirm the official memory of the deceased is also the occasion that gives the deceased the recurring acknowledgement and reverence sought by their individual families. Public memorialisation advocated by the feminists and the private remembrance essential to the deceased's families are both attained via the mediation of the city government.

Beyond *In the Name of Harmony and Prosperity*: Thoughts on gender and labour in post-industrial Taiwan

This chapter has a dual goal: to look back and reflect on my book and to look forward and develop a future research agenda. In the first three sections of this chapter, I discussed the context under which my book was published and issues derived from the book remaining to be explored. As the Taiwanese economy has gradually moved from one primarily based on manufacturing to a service-oriented one, new circumstances create new social realities that, in turn, pose new theoretical and practical questions. The family and state continue to be relevant factors in shaping social life including gender and labour conditions, but in ways different from those in previous times. In this concluding section, I thus move beyond my book, follow the Tomb/Park case study presented in the former section, and offer some thoughts on what theoretical and political insight this particular case represents to us.

First of all, as small as a local case like the renovation of the Twenty-five Ladies' Tomb might be, its implications echo the larger process of economic globalisation and resonate with the experience of many deindustrialised communities around the world. The recent development of Kaohsiung (and urban Taiwan in general) conforms to the worldwide trend of place-making as an economic strategy (Smart and Smart 2003). In a deindustrialised setting, this often involves employing and appropriating elements from the industrial past as attractions to promote tourism and entice capital investment. The Tomb/Park case study thus points to a new research direction by facilitating our conceptualisation of 'women workers' as not only an essential means of capital accumulation under global industrialisation but also an emerging site of cultural production and consumption in the flexible accumulation in today's post-industrial world.

Concomitantly, and yet paradoxically, the increasing commercialisation and commodification of the past has also generated a renewed public interest in labour history in various places.[8] In this light, a case study of the Twenty-five Ladies' Tomb that tells the story of factory women gives a much needed gender perspective to this revived academic interest in labour history. It also dovetails with global feminist endeavours of rewriting and revalorising women's history as a political movement for gender equality. The writing of women's labour history or rewriting

In the Name of Harmony and Prosperity revisited   **107**

of labour history with a critical gender viewpoint is especially important, given the strong cultural disapproval faced by neophyte female global assembly line workers and the resulting violence against them around the world, as previously discussed in this chapter. One crucial irony about factory women in Taiwan as illustrated in the Tomb case, however, is that they were first and foremost regarded as filial daughters but not industrial workers. In other words, their productive role was primarily an extension of their familial role. Past research including my own has critically examined how this perception facilitated the exploitation of Taiwanese women in capitalist industrial production. Yet, it is also undeniable that it was the perception that young female workers were sacrificing themselves for the welfare of their families which gave rise to the powerful affect we observed in the Tomb case and other similar stories; and this, in turn, propelled the parents of the 25 deceased young women to advocate for their daughters' wellbeing in the afterlife. It seems to me that there is a lesson to be learned here for global feminist movements seeking a positive recognition of female industrial labour. The Taiwanese experience suggests that affect towards working women informed by a cultural understanding of these women not as 'women workers' but as 'devoted family members' might bear political potency upon which feminists seeking gender equality could strategise. This, of course, requires a nuanced and expanded understanding of women workers' history as the history of their families and of their communities and the keen awareness that women's productive role is intricately enmeshed in a complex web of social roles.

Notes

1 Anru Lee was a Fulbright Visiting Scholar at the Anthropology Department, National Taiwan University, while completing the current chapter. She is grateful for the generous support of Fulbright Taiwan and her host institution that made this writing possible.
2 Several authors in this volume also echo this sentiment (e.g. Joseph Wong, Chapter 9).
3 As a matter of fact, Homei is not the only place with this characterisation in central Taiwan, where there is a long artisan tradition and cottage industrial history. For example, the sock industry in Shetou and the metal fittings/hardware industry near Lukang, both of which are also in Changhua County, are good cases for studying Taiwan's modern economic/industrial development.
4 The National Museum of Taiwan History website (http://the.nmth.gov.tw/English/Deta il.aspx?id=256) (accessed 29 June 2016).
5 The Ministry of Culture website (http://travel.culture.tw/template/StrokePage.aspx? Sid=71) (accessed 29 June 2016).
6 Regrettably, I have not gone back to Homei for an extended stay to update my previous research findings since I moved my research focus to urban areas.
7 The original text is in Chinese. This is the author's translation.
8 This seemingly encouraging development has also prompted a sense of urgency among labour historians and labour studies scholars (Klubock and Fontes 2009), as this 'nostalgic (re)construction of the past' is rarely reflective but inevitably highly selective and generally idealised and sanitised for public consumption (Taska 2009). As a consequence, the redevelopment of industrial heritage sites often leads to what Christine Boyer calls 'double erasure' (Boyer 1996). That is, the first erasure happens when a place loses its primary reason for being – for example, as a locale of industrial production – and a

108 Anru Lee

second erasure occurs when the creation of museums or other cultural facilities, the restoration of historic spaces, or staged celebration or commemoration further removes places and events from the realm of everyday experience and re-places them in the realm of abstraction and representation (Stanton 2006: 112).

References

Arrigo, Linda Gail. 1980. 'The Industrial Work Force of Young Women in Taiwan'. *Bulletin of Concerned Asian Scholars*, 12(2), 25–38.

Belair-Gagnon, Valerie, Smeeta Mishra, and Colin Agur. 2014. 'Reconstructing the Indian Public Sphere: Network and Social Media in The Delhi Gang Rape Case'. *Journalism*, 15(8), 1059–1075.

Bo, Lan-zhi. (柏蘭芝). 1993. 'Restructuring, Gender, and Local Spatial Transformation' ['經濟再結構中的婦女就業變遷與地域空間轉化: 台北縣成衣業關廠女工再就業的個案研究']. Master's thesis. Taipei: National Taiwan University.

Boyer, Christine. 1996. *The City of Collective Memory: Its Historical Imagery and Architectural Entertainments*. Cambridge, MA: MIT Press.

Cairoli, M.Laetitia. 2012. *Girls of the Factory: A Year with the Garment Workers of Morocco*. Gainesville, FL: University of Florida Press.

Chan, Anita. 2005. 'Reviewed Work: In the Name of Harmony and Prosperity: Labor and Gender Politics in Taiwan's Economic Restructuring by Anru Lee'. *The China Journal*, 54, 201–204.

Cheng, Shu-ju. 2003. 'Rethinking the Globalization of Domestic Service: Foreign Domestics, State Control, and The Politics of Identity in Taiwan'. *Gender and Society*, 17(2), 166–186.

Chow, Esther Ngan-lin. (ed.). 2002. *Transforming Gender and Development in East Asia*. New York: Routledge.

Cohen, Myron. 1976. *House United, House Divided: The Chinese Family in Taiwan*. New York: Columbia University Press.

Diamond, Norma. 1979. 'Women and Industry in Taiwan'. *Modern China*, 5(3), 317–340.

Fernandez-Kelly, M. Patricia. 1983. *For We Are Sold, I and My People: Women and Industry in Mexico's Frontier*. Albany: SUNY Press.

Gallin, Rita. 1984. 'Women, Family, and the Political Economy in Taiwan'. *Journal of Peasant Studies*, 12(1), 76–92.

Gallin, Rita. 1990. 'Women and the Export Industry in Taiwan: The Muting of Class Consciousness'. In Katherine Ward (ed.), *Women Workers and Global Restructuring*. New York: ILR Press, pp. 179–192.

Gates, Hill. 2005. 'Book review: In the Name of Harmony and Prosperity: Labor and Gender Politics in Taiwan's Economic Restructuring by Anru Lee'. *American Anthropologist*, 107(2), 298–299.

Greenhalgh, Susan. 1994. 'De-orientalizing the Chinese Family Firm'. *American Ethnologist*, 21(4). 746–775.

Harrell, Stevan. 1985. 'Why Do the Chinese Work So Hard? Reflections on an Entrepreneurial Ethic'. *Modern China*, 11(2), 203–226.

Harvey, David. 1991. *The Condition of Postmodernity*. Oxford: Blackwell.

Ho, Yang-tang. (何燕堂). 1992. 'Form and Mobilization of Labor Collective Struggle: The Case Study of the Struggle for Plant-closure of Xin-Guang' ['勞工集體抗爭行動的形式與動員: 新光士林廠關廠抗爭的個案研究']. Master's thesis. Taipei: Soochow University.

Hsia, Lin-ching and Tsuen-chyi Jeng. (夏林清與鄭村棋). 1992 'On the Front Line of Union Strike: An Inquiry about the Far-East Textile Union Strike on May 1989 from the Strikers' Perspective' ['站上罷工第一線: 行動主體的角度看1989年遠化5月罷工抗爭的發生及影響']. *Taiwan: A Radical Quarterly in Social Studies* [台灣社會研究季刊], 13, 63–108.

Hsiao, Hsin-huang Michael. (ed.). 2006. *The Changing Faces of the Middle Classes in Asia-Pacific.* Taipei: Center for Asia-Pacific Area Studies, Academia Sinica.

Hsiung, Ping-chun. 1996. *Living Rooms as Factories.* Philadelphia: Temple University Press.

Hsu, Cheng-kuang and Wen-li Sung. (徐正光與宋文里). (eds). 1989. *The EmergingSocial Movements in Taiwan* [台灣新興社會運動]. Taipei: Juliu chubanshe [巨流出版社].

Hu, Tai-li. 1984. *My Mother-in-Law's Village: Rural Industrialization and Change in Taiwan.* Taipei: Institute of Ethnology, Academia Sinica.

Kim, Seung-kyung. 1997. *Class Struggle or Family Struggle? The Lives of Women Factory Workers in South Korea.* Cambridge: Cambridge University Press.

Klubock, Thomas Miller and Paulo Fontes. 2009. 'Labor History and Public History: Introduction'. *International Labor and Working-Class History*, 76, 2–5.

Kung, Lydia. 1994. *Factory Women in Taiwan.* New York: Columbia University Press.

Lan, Pei-chia. 2006. *Global Cinderellas: Migrant Domestics and Newly Rich Employers in Taiwan.* Durham: Duke University Press.

Lee, Anru. 2004. *In the Name of Harmony and Prosperity: Labor and Gender Politics in Taiwan's Economic Restructuring.* Albany: SUNY Press.

Lee, Anru. 2007. 'Subways as a Space of Cultural Intimacy: The Mass Rapid Transit System in Taipei, Taiwan'. *The China Journal*, 58, 31–55.

Lee, Anru. 2008. 'Women of the Sisters' Hall: Religion and the Making of Women's Alternative Space in Taiwan's Economic Restructuring', *Gender, Place and Culture*, 15(4), 373–393.

Lee, Anru. 2009. 'Shaping One's Own Destiny: Global Economy, Family, and Women's Struggle in The Taiwanese Context'. *Women's Studies International Forum*, 32(2), 120–129.

Lee, Anru. 2012. 'Global is National: The Cultural Politics of the Mass Rapid Transit Systems in Taiwan'. In Bi-yu Chang and Henning Klöter (eds), *Imaging Taiwan: Identity Representation and Cultural Politics.* Wiesbaden, Germany: Harrassowitz, pp. 127–148.

Lee, Anru. 2015. 'Space, Mobility, and Identity: The Politics and Poetics of Urban Mass Rapid Systems in Taiwan'. In Julie Cidell and David Prytherch (eds), *Intersecting Places: Transport and Mobility in the Production of Urban Space.* New York: Routledge, pp. 153–171.

Lee, Anru and Wen-hui Anna Tang. 2016. 'Female Ghost or Worker Heroine? Gender, Space, and Feminist Intervention in Contemporary Taiwan'. *Social Politics*, 23(3), 415–436.

Lee, Anru and Wen-hui Anna Tang. 2017. 'Gender, Popular Religion, and the Politics of Memory in Taiwan's Urban Renewal: The Case of The Twenty-five Ladies' Tomb'. In Zayn Kassam (ed.), *Women in Asian Religions.* New York: Praeger, pp. 135–148.

Lee, Anru, and Chien-hung Tung. 2010. 'How Subways and High Speed Railways Have Changed Taiwan: Transportation Technology, Urban Culture, and Social Life'. In Marc Moskowitz (ed.), *Popular Culture in Taiwan: Charismatic Modernity.* London and New York: Routledge, pp. 107–130.

Lee, Ching Kwan. 1998. *Gender and the South China Miracle.* Berkeley: University of California Press.

Lin, Thung-hong and Hui-jiun Tseng. (林宗弘與曾惠君). 2014. 'The Politics of Hukou: A Comparative Study of the Household Registration System in China and Taiwan' ['戶口的政治: 中國大陸與台灣戶籍制度之歷史比較']. *Mainland China Studies* [中國大陸研究], 57(1), 63–96.

Lin, Wen-ting (林文婷). 1998. 'The Community of Resistance: An Empirical Research of Fu-Chang Factory' ['抵抗的社區: 社會運動中的女性勞工經驗, 以福昌紡織電子廠員工關廠抗爭為個案']. Master's thesis. Taipei: National Taiwan University.

Livingston, Jessica. 2004. 'Murder in Juarez: Gender, Sexual Violence, and the Global Assembly Line'. *Frontiers: A Journal of Women Studies*, 25(1), 59–76.

Lynch, Caitrin. 2007. *Juki Girls, Good Girls: Gender and Cultural Politics in Sri Lanka's Garment Industry*. Ithaca: ILR Press.

Mills, Mary Beth. 1999. *Thai Women in the Global Labor Force*. New York: Routledge.

Mills, Mary Beth. 2003. 'Gender and Inequality in the Global Labor Force'. *Annual Review of Anthropology*, 32, 41–61.

Moon, Seungsook. 2005. *Militarized Modernity and Gendered Citizenship in South Korea*. Durham: Duke University Press.

Nash, June. 1989. *From Tank Town to High Tech: The Clash of Community and Industrial Cycles*. Albany, NY: SUNY Press.

Niehoff, Justin D. 1987. 'The Villager as Industrialist: Ideologies of Household Manufacturing in Rural Taiwan'. *Modern China*, 13(3), 278–309.

Ong, Aihwa. 1987. *Spirits of Resistance and Capitalist Discipline: Factory women in Malaysia*. Albany: SUNY Press.

Ong, Aihwa. 1997. 'The Gender and Labor Politics of Postmodernity'. In Lisa Lowe & David Lloyd (eds), *The Politics of Culture in the Shadow of Capital*. Durham: Duke University Press, pp. 61–97.

Pun, Ngai. 2005. *Made in China: Women Factory Workers in a Global Workplace*. Durham: Duke University Press.

Salaff, Janet. 1981. *Working Daughters in Hong Kong: Filial Piety or Power in the Family?* New York: Columbia University Press.

Salzinger, Leslie. 2003. *Genders in Production: Making Workers in Mexico's Global Factories*. Berkeley: University of California Press.

Sassen, Saskia. 2001. *The Global City: New York, London, Tokyo*. Princeton: Princeton University Press.

Stanton, Cathy. 2006. *The Lowell Experiment: Public History in a Postindustrial City*. Amherst and Boston: University of Massachusetts Press.

Stites, Richard W. 1982. 'Small-scale Industry in Yingge, Taiwan'. *Modern China*, 8(2), 247–279.

Stites, Richard W. 1985. 'Industrial Work as an Entrepreneurial Strategy'. *Modern China*, 11(2), 227–246.

Shin-kong. (新光關廠抗爭戰友團). 2003. *The Battle Against the Shin-Kong Spinning Plant Closing: Stories of Workers of Shi-Lin Factory* [那年冬天, 我們埋鍋造飯: 新光士林廠關廠勞工生命故事及抗爭實錄]. Taipei: Taipei City Department of Labor Education and Cultural Division.

Smart, Alan, and Josephine Smart. 2003. 'Urbanization and the Global Perspective'. *Annual Review of Anthropology*, 32, 263–285.

Taska, Lucy. 2009. 'Labor History and Public History in Australia: Allies or Uneasy Bedfellows?' *International Labor and Working-class History*, 76, 82–104.

Tseng, Yen-fen and Hong-zen Wang. 2013. 'Governing Migrant Workers at a Distance: Managing the Temporary Status of Guest Workers in Taiwan'. *International Migration*, 51(4), 1–19.

Wang, Hong-zen. (王宏仁). 2001. 'Social Stratification, Vietnamese Partner's Migration and Taiwan Labour Market' [社會階層化下的婚姻移民與國內勞動市場: 以越南新娘為例]. *Taiwan: A Radical Quarterly in Social Studies* [台灣社會研究季刊], 41, 99–127.

Wang, Hong-zen. 2011. 'Immigration Trends and Policy Changes in Taiwan'. *Asian and Pacific Migration Journal*, 20(2), 169–194.

Weller, Robert. 1994. 'Capitalism, Community, and the Rise of Amoral Cults in Taiwan'. In Charles F. Keyes, Laurel Kendall, and Helen Hardacre (eds), *Asian Visions of Authority: Religion and Modern States of East and Southeast Asian Societies*. Honolulu: University of Hawai'i Press, pp. 141–164.

Wolf, Diane Lauren. 1994. *Factory Daughters: Gender, Household Dynamics, and Rural Industrialization in Java*. Berkeley, CA: University of California Press.

Wright, Melissa. 1999. 'The Dialectics of Still Life: Murder, Women, and Maquiladoras'. *Public Culture*, 11(3), 453–473.

Wright, Melissa. 2007. 'Femicide, Mother-activism, and the Geography of Protest in Northern Mexico'. *Urban Geography*, 28(5), 401–425.

8

TIGERS ON THE MOUNTAIN

Assessing *Is Taiwan Chinese?* in 2018[1]

Melissa J. Brown

一山不容二虎 (*Yishan burong erhu*).
One mountain cannot sustain two tigers.

In 2018, Xi Jinping consolidated his hold, for life, on the leadership of the PRC Party-state. After an anti-corruption campaign that conveniently destroyed his political opponents, Xi got the approval of the PRC Standing Committee, which was rubber-stamped by the People's Congress, to remove term limits from the presidency – term limits that Deng Xiaoping had set up during the 1980s to ensure that there would be no further Mao-like emperors of the PRC. I begin consideration of Taiwan's identity – and the 2004 book I wrote about it – with this dramatic change to an increasingly authoritarian PRC Party-state because collective identities result from processes of social negotiation and this move to emperorship coincides with an increasingly aggressive Chinese imperialism that affects not only Taiwan but also the Pacific Rim, Central Asia and beyond.[2]

In this context, assessing *Is Taiwan Chinese?* and whether the main conclusions I drew there – both about Taiwan identities and about processes of identity formation – still hold is particularly salient. Although the PRC appears ready to take Taiwan – by a 'sharp' power gambit if not (yet) by full military force – the PRC Party-state has consistently failed to recognise its inability to control collective identities, with the result that its manipulation of identities frequently takes unexpected turns (Brown 2010). And the Party-state understands Taiwan's collective identities even less than the identities within the territories it does control.[3]

Taiwan's identities have moved in amazing directions during the twenty-first century – moving away from nationalism and toward a simultaneously locally rooted and globally reaching cosmopolitanism. In building such a 'glocal' cosmopolitan community, Taiwan's people are showing the world a way forward beyond the war-mongering trap of ultranationalism. It remains to be seen whether

Taiwan's cosmopolitanism will effectively counter the PRC's imperialism, but it is worth considering how this cosmopolitanism grows out of the identities and the processes I discussed in *Is Taiwan Chinese?* That 2004 book still provides insights into both the Taiwanese identity forged in the 1990s and the sociopolitical processes forming that identity. Although in retrospect we can see how Taiwan's subsequent cosmopolitan trajectory came out of the 1990s and those processes, *Is Taiwan Chinese?* did not predict that trajectory and thus it merits an update.

The main findings of *Is Taiwan Chinese?*

There are two kinds of claims in *Is Taiwan Chinese?* – empirical claims about specific identities in both Taiwan and China and theoretical claims about general processes of identity formation and their implications for collective action. In order to understand the empirical claims, we must first realise two fundamental theoretical points: (1) identities are fluid and changeable, not fixed as ideologies claim, and (2) the people who share an identity are variable, not homogeneous as ideologies claim. There is a lot to unpack in these two deceptively simple statements.

First, ideologies, which usually take the form of narratives of unfolding, work to manipulate specific identities in order to serve current political purposes. These narratives portray identities of individuals as fixed by birth – to particular parents (ancestry) and in a particular culture. These narratives also imagine collective identities as the inevitable result of some primordial essence that is rooted in antiquity and merely unfolds according to some internally driven destiny. People construct narratives about the unfolding of their own groups (charter myths) and also about the unfolding of other groups, which they may idolise or villainise. The interweaving of ancestry and culture in these narratives is often deterministic to the point of racism – fuelling, for example, anti-immigrant sentiment.[4]

But fluidity and changeability of collective identities come from identities' actual formation through *social* (including political and economic) processes, not some predestined unfolding of genes (ancestry) or culture. Social circumstances shift constantly – when different political factions gain power, when technological 'revolutions' reorganise production and economic dynamics, when environmental disasters destroy populations and resources, and so on. Thus, when we realise that identities are socially constructed, it is no longer surprising that identities change. Sometimes people are involuntarily reclassified by external sources (fluidity): the borders of identity shift around a community, whose populace has not changed in ancestry or cultural practices. Sometimes people voluntarily negotiate a new self-label (changeability): these people push across the identity border, perhaps embracing or discarding some cultural practices.[5] Whatever way that people end up with a new identity label, the new label marks – both reflects and invites – different social experience; thus, over a very short time, these people authentically belong to the 'new' classificatory group.

A second main theoretical point recognises that there is variation within any and every human group – what is remarkable is not the existence of individual

114 Melissa J. Brown

variability but rather the social processes that form a single collective identity across ubiquitous variation. Social experience builds on but is different from lived experience: lived experience refers to the actual experiences of specific individuals, whereas social experience refers to negotiations over power positions. Thus, social experience is passed down across generations, perhaps as oral history or written law, with particularly galvanising events passed down in more detail and for longer periods. The 2:28 Incident was galvanising for Taiwanese and Mainlanders – not only for those who lived through the tumultuous events of 1947, but also for younger generations because martial law, which arose out of those events, shaped all aspects of Taiwan's society for decades. When individuals' lived experiences are both similar to the lived experiences of others and connected to the social experience of a labelled group, those individuals develop an authentic collective identity under that label.

Is Taiwan Chinese? presents these theoretical claims by using empirical ethnographic and historical evidence to unpack actual identities and practices in Taiwan from the seventeenth through twentieth centuries, with comparison to identities and practices in the mountains of Hubei. Ironically, I began this research in the early 1990s without much interest in identities. My goal was to examine how cultural changes move across communities. Like most anthropologists of the time, I assumed that identity was based on culture, so I chose to work in communities with historical evidence of identity change in order to track cultural changes. Even though most anthropologists interested in Chinese-speaking groups wanted to work in the PRC – even after the massacre at Tiananmen Square in 1989 – many had difficulty getting into rural field sites (leading to a default shift in China anthropology's focus to urban areas, where researchers were stuck waiting to get permission to go into the countryside); if they got permission, they were often allowed no more than a few weeks' time in a government-specified locale. I wanted to devote research attention to anthropological methods in small (and therefore rural) communities, not swallow whatever access was dictated as a political price of even seeing a rural site. I had already spent enough time in Taiwan (12 months in 1987–1988, 3 months in 1989) that I knew access to research sites would not be an issue there, so I chose to work in Taiwan. (I planned to do postdoctoral research in the PRC to counter anti-Taiwan sentiment among US academics that would create problems in applying for 'China' jobs.)

Being able to spend 12 months in my research sites and develop research methods for tracing community changes via the practices of individuals led to unexpected findings. My doctoral field research in Taiwan (12 months in 1991–1992, 2 months in 1994) benefited from the research sponsorship of the late Pan Inghai 潘英海 and the Institute of Ethnology (IOE, Minzuxue yanjiusuo 民族學研究所) at Academia Sinica. With Pan's considerable help, I was able to arrange living arrangements in two of the four communities where I interviewed; I met important community members in all four sites, including spirit mediums and small business owners; and Pan was able to get permission for me to take photocopies of local Japanese-period household registers to IOE for archiving.[6] Historical sources – Japanese-period household registers and ethnological reports – and the secondary literature on both the late nineteenth century and early Japanese period labelled quite a few villages on Taiwan's southwestern Jianan plain as sinicised indigenous peoples (using the pejorative term *shufan* 熟番, lit. cooked barbarians). Moreover, ethnographic research during the 1980s, by Pan Inghai (1994) and by John Shepherd (1986), showed that an annual festival devoted to an indigenous goddess – variously called Thai Tsoo 太祖, A-li Tsoo 阿立祖, or A-li Bu 阿立母 – was still maintained in three communities. I chose these communities so that the ongoing festivals might serve as a segue to other indigenous-derived practices and beliefs.

But discussing the communities' Austronesian heritage explicitly proved more difficult than I had expected. My first two months in the field were devoted to participant observation: I attended the annual festivals and got a sense of contemporary quotidian life. During that time, several community members told me about changes in practices over recent decades. But they also informed me that although the village had once been Austronesian – using the derogatory term 'savages' (*fanzi* 番仔, T. *hoan-a*), the only ethnonym they had at the time for plains Aborigines (*pingpu zu* 平铺族) – all the Austronesians had left, having migrated into Taiwan's high central mountains. They explained that the Hoklo 副佬 (Han漢[7]) villagers who remained continued worshipping the Austronesian deity because she belongs to this place and she is powerful (*ling* 靈).

These comments attest to villagers' Han identity in 1991, and they helped me develop my interview questions, but the individuals who made these comments could neither tell me who introduced the newer practices nor why people adopted them. Moreover, historical records show no such mass migration, and the Japanese-period household registers identify most villagers as Austronesian – including the parents and grandparents of some of the middle-aged men telling me that all the Austronesians had emigrated. Despite their surprise that their reports were not sufficient, I pursued a social-science approach to tracking change.[8] I worked with a local woman in each village to interview every (mentally capable) elderly woman and man still living in the community, using a semi-structured oral questionnaire about practices and beliefs relating to marriage, childbearing, funerals, religious worship, livelihood and household structures.[9] Rather than asking these elders about community practices in general, I asked them about specific practices and beliefs they had observed – the first wedding they remember seeing, the first funeral, their own marriage, and so on – taking care to date these events (using their relation to major events in the community to determine an approximate year). By putting the specific lived experiences of all these villagers together, I could track change in the community, across time and across households, with information on the connections between households. And by interviewing every elderly person, I found key individuals: the woman who was the first Hoklo bride to marry into one village, the woman whom the last woman spirit medium to Thai Tso had wanted to train to be spirit medium after her, a man whose grandfather had told him many oral history stories about life during the late Qing period. I linked the

116 Melissa J. Brown

oral reports to Japanese-period household registers and cross-checked differing oral accounts of some events.

But I was unable to get people to talk explicitly about their non-Han heritage for several months – until by chance, I asked a stalling question in a Longtian interview and got back an unexpected answer. One elderly woman responded to a question about whether her mother or grandmother bound her feet not just with 'no' (the Japanese household registers were clear that Austronesian women did not bind their feet) but with the statement, 'we savages didn't bind feet' (T. *guan hoan-a bo pak-kha* 我們番仔沒幫腳). Asking that question of other elders, including going back to follow up with previously interviewed people, allowed the elders themselves to bring up that derogatory non-Han ethnonym and thereby allowed me to ask direct questions about their memories of that non-Han identity in their youth.

Working to trace changes in practices, beliefs and identity in this way, I realised that several of the assumptions I had brought to the research were wrong. The purported link between identities and culture is ideology, not empirical reality. The actual dynamics of identity formation and cultural change are distinct. Social identity processes more often drive cultural change than vice versa. And authentic identities matter to people, because identities succinctly encapsulate people's social and lived experiences.

In *Is Taiwan Chinese?*, I present these points in relation to Taiwanese society.[10] I show that identities had changed and were continuing to change in Taiwan throughout the twentieth century. People in southwestern Taiwan who had been considered, circa 1900, as acculturated 'savages' were accepted by 1930 as Han (specifically, as Hoklo). These people took the 'long route' to Han identity because their language and most of their cultural practices had already become like their Hoklo Han neighbours' by 1900; even about 10 per cent of the people in these communities had patrilineal Han ancestry. Yet despite these cultural and even ancestral shifts, they were still not considered Han in 1900. It took the socio-political fallout of a regime change – the Japanese colonial annexation of Taiwan – to shift identity around them so they became Han.

During my analyses, I used these ethnographic and historical demography materials (interviews, observations, Japanese-period household registers, and Japanese-era ethnological reports) to identify both the specific Austronesian practices and beliefs that had lingered long and also the distinct processes that changed identity, practices, and beliefs during the early twentieth century.[11] With a more complete and ethnographic-based understanding of twentieth-century changes, I revisited historical accounts of the Dutch, Zheng and Qing eras to search for evidence of such patterns in those earlier periods.[12]

As during the twentieth century, regime change had also been necessary for seventeenth-century identity change. Mass migration of Han immigrants and marriage of Han (and Dutch) men to Austronesian women occurred under Dutch colonial rule of Taiwan, but it required the context of settler-colonial regimes, under first the Zheng and then the Qing, to motivate people to take the 'short route' to Han identity. Patrilineal Han ancestry allowed people – whom the Dutch

Is Taiwan Chinese? revisited   **117**

had treated as economic and political allies, some of them with Dutch in-laws and many with Austronesian language skills and practices – to negotiate Han identity. It was clear that these identity shifts were driven by changing social experience: mass migrations, widespread ethnic intermarriage (perhaps 40 per cent of southwestern population under Dutch rule), but above all new regimes with new policies.

When I wrote *Is Taiwan Chinese?* (primarily 1997–2001), Taiwan had just completed democratisation – which itself constituted a regime change – and identities were still in flux, as new democratic policies were enacted. Between 1987 and 1996, when democracy was in process but not yet completed, a consolidation began of pan-ethnic national identity as Taiwanese. Lee Teng-hui and others called it a 'new Taiwanese' (*xin Taiwan ren* 新台灣人) identity and consciously included both ethnic Taiwanese – Hoklo, who were about 65 per cent of the population at the time, and Hakka (H. 客家; *kejia*), about 15 per cent of the population – and also Mainlanders (*waisheng ren* 外省人), who were about 17 per cent of the population. This new identity also included many descendants of plains Aborigines, largely without realising it because most of them had already taken on an ethnic Taiwanese identity (and thus their percentage of the population is unclear). The remaining 3 per cent of the ethnically documented population at the time were mountain Aborigines (*gaoshan zu* 高山族) and their inclusion in this new Taiwanese identity was at first ambiguous.[13]

The question was not so much *whether* to include Taiwan's indigenous Austronesian peoples but *how* to construct a narrative of unfolding that would encompass both Austronesian and Han peoples. This issue was a problem during the mid- to late 1990s, and it brought attention to my research. When I began field research in 1991, most people in Taiwan had never heard of plains Aborigines (*pingpu zu*, lit. plains clans)[14] – not only in Taiwan generally, but also in the communities where I interviewed. The elderly people who recalled being called 'savages' in their youth, as well as the next generation in middle age, had never heard such a polite and empowering term. And young people – high school and college students who heard me talking with their grandparents about the past – had no idea of their family's non-Han heritage. But by 1994, these same communities were participating in a pan-Taiwan revival of *pingpu zu* heritage that celebrated plains Austronesian peoples as the 'real Taiwanese' (*zhenzhengde Taiwan ren*真正的台灣人) (cf. Pan Inghai 2000).

This inclusion moved unevenly. There were reassertions of difference and even a brief revival of the derogatory term 'savages' (much to my horror). But a narrative developed within a few years of ethnic Taiwanese as descendants of immigrant Han men and Austronesian women, bringing Austronesians as laudable ancestors into the narrative of Taiwan's unfolding as a distinct country. As with most narratives of unfolding, there is some historical basis for this narrative, but ideological narratives reshape historical evidence to suit contemporary political purposes. In the early 2000s, this narrative was taken to the point of claiming that over 90 per cent of ethnic Taiwanese have substantial Austronesian genetic ancestry, even though historical and genetic evidence indicates much more modest and regionally variable contributions. The highest percentage is likely 40 per cent, and this high estimate is strictly for that part of southern Taiwan that was settled by Han during the seventeenth century (Brown 2004a, Chen 2008). Under Chen Shui-bian's administration (2000–2008), Austronesians were more readily included in this ideological narrative of Taiwan's unfolding.

Instead, the tension swung to whether Mainlanders should be included. Mainlanders' social experience changed, from holding the privileged position of not considering themselves ethnic at all to finding Taiwanese suspicious of them unless they explicitly indicated their allegiance to Taiwan: the need to state 'I love Taiwan' (*wo ai Taiwan*我愛台灣) in daily discourse was palpably uncomfortable for many Mainlanders under Chen's administration. The discomfort came from how much Mainlanders' own identity shifted during the regime-changing process of democratisation. It was not merely that political power was no longer exclusively vested in Mainlanders – that shift had already begun during the 1970s' 'Taiwanisation' of the Nationalist Party, which started under authoritarian rule (Chang 1994, 2000). Discomfort also came from many Mainlanders who travelled to the PRC during the early 1990s, when it first became possible for them to do so, and found the PRC a foreign country. Forty years of CCP rule had radically changed the people, society and infrastructure of the PRC from depictions of the China left behind in Mainlander collective memories. The contemporaneous reality of the PRC convinced many Mainlanders both that their imagined China is gone and that their identity is Taiwanese. This realignment fuelled the new Taiwanese identity in the 1990s and created tensions in the early 2000s when politically driven questions arose about Mainlanders' place in that identity. It is important that Mainlanders' embrace of Taiwanese identity was driven by their social experience not only in Taiwan but also in the PRC.

Taiwan is not the only place where social experience and identity have changed since the last time that Taiwan and all the territories of the current PRC were uncontestably ruled by a single government. I included a comparison chapter about the PRC in *Is Taiwan Chinese?* because the processes of identity formation and change were the same on both sides of the Strait but the outcomes were not: different regime trajectories led to different outcomes. With the considerable help of Dong Luo 董珞 and Wu Xu 吳旭, I was able to conduct postdoctoral research (1995–1996) in the Enshi Tujia-Miao Autonomous Prefecture (Enshi Tujia-Miaozu zizhizhou 恩施土家苗族自治州) in Hubei among people, called Tujia 土家 in the contemporary PRC, whose history bears important structural resemblances to plains Aborigines and their Han descendants in southwestern Taiwan.

The Tujia originate in part of the mountainous border of the Sichuan basin – in Hubei, Hunan and Guizhou provinces and parts of rural Chongqing municipality. There have been waves of immigrants to these mountains from the Yangzi River plains (Chang *yuan* 长原) over millennia, driven by multiple states' attempts to consolidate political power over Sichuan by dominating this mountainous border (through military control and sinicisation of the population). Many immigrants from the plains were convicts and the soldiers who guarded them –

Is Taiwan Chinese? revisited **119**

disproportionately men. With each new wave, the people already in place were 'locals' (*tu* 土) to the newcomers, whose families over time intermarried and became locals to the next immigrants. Dynastic regimes had loose enough control in this area that whichever specific regime was in power made little difference in how this pattern played out, only to differences in how frequently the waves of migration occurred. Even the 1937 retreat of the Nationalist government to this mountainous area – the central government to Chongqing, the provincial government to Enshi – followed the pattern, with these refugees merely the newest wave of immigrants. During the war, these purportedly sophisticated urbanite refugees took a strongly pejorative view of the people already in the mountains as 'local trash' (*tumanzi*土蠻子) – backward hicks, but nevertheless Han (Brown 2002, 2004a, 2007).

Regime change to the PRC's Party-state government, however, changed the longstanding pattern, largely because of its Stalinist-derived policy to systematically identify all ethnic groups and classify all individuals as a member of one officially recognised ethnic group (*minzu shibie* 民族识别). Ethnologists with a mandate from Beijing travelled to the Southwest, though they relied heavily on Confucian notions of what constituted Han identity rather than on the Stalinist principles that were supposed to guide them (Brown 2003, cf. Harrell 1995). This method identified 90 per cent of the PRC's population as Han, despite 'regional' differences among Han in language, customs, territory and economic production (Stalin's guiding principles for identifying a distinct ethnic group). This method also identified all the mountain peoples in the Enshi area as Miao – a non-Han ethnic category.[15] People considered 'locals' (*tu*) were horrified, preferring to be considered backward Han than Miao. Through a personal connection to Zhou Enlai, one local secured a re-examination of locals' identification.[16] In 1957, after several years' reconsideration, the ethnic category of Tujia – neither Miao nor Han, and thus a new ethnic minority category – was officially established for locals in this region.

This timing is crucial to subsequent social experience and identity formation. The identification of Tujia as an official ethnic category occurred only one month before the Anti-Rightist Campaign put a moratorium on the entire ethnic identification (*minzu shibie*) project. As a result, in Enshi and other predominantly Tujia areas in the mountains around the Sichuan basin, the classification of every individual resident into officially approved ethnic categories was not implemented until the early 1980s – in many places, not until after the 1982 census. Thus for two decades – a period that saw widespread violent Han chauvinism – 'locals' continued to think of themselves and to be treated as Han, thereby escaping the assimilationist persecutions rife in other minority areas between 1957 and 1978. In other words, locals remained socially Han through those turbulent times and until the mid-1980s, when many were shocked to find a non-Han ethnic label (Tujia) on their national identity card (*shenfen zheng* 身份证).[17]

During the mid- to late 1980s, social experience changed in the PRC and Taiwan – both undergoing what were essentially regime changes that reshaped

Tujia and Taiwan Mainlander identities. Taiwan was democratising, which meant that ethnic representation in the government would move in the direction of population proportions. Mainlanders, at about 17 per cent of the population, could no longer expect to hold the majority of government offices. Thankfully, Taiwan decided not to get into the business of classifying every one of its citizens ethnically, though there is a certification process for people in those specific indigenous categories that confer affirmative action benefits within Taiwan.

During this same period, the PRC, which had abandoned Maoism, was embracing capitalism, with students and intellectuals pushing for democratic reforms. The PRC forcefully implemented the one-child policy for Han yet allowed minorities to have two children – in order to portray the overwhelmingly Han Party-state to the world as a responsible 'older brother' looking after 'younger sibling' ethnic minorities (and so as not to be accused of genocide when it desperately needed economic investment). There were other affirmative action benefits to minority status as well – not only for individuals, such as getting spotted points on the college entrance exam, but also for local governments, most importantly getting additional economic development funds if the population under their administration had a specified percentage of minorities (Brown 2002). Thus, individuals and local governments in the PRC have incentives to seek minority identities (up to a point), requiring central and local governments to remain engaged in fixing the borders of ethnic identities.

The social experience of Tujia in the PRC and that of Mainlanders in Taiwan both changed from what each had experienced in previous decades and diverged from each other. Mainlanders could embrace a Taiwanese identity, but because of the regime change to electoral democracy they had to negotiate their identity in daily social interactions – quotidian affirmations of their self-identification with Taiwan. Because of the communist regime change, Tujia were told what they were and were expected to 'get used to it' (Brown 2004a, 2010). Moreover, local government officials (at least in Hubei) designed the classification method to label as Tujia that percentage of the population that would maximise economic development funds – by having enough Tujia to receive funding but not so many as to trigger centrally mandated Han immigration. The contrast between the Taiwan regime's observational approach to ethnic identities and the PRC regime's manipulative approach could not be starker; the difference in impact on identities could not be greater.

These contrasting ideological approaches to ethnic identities influenced disparate national identities. In *Is Taiwan Chinese?*, I explain that the closer ideologies are to actual identities, the more effective the ideological narratives are in motivating people to act, and I examine the implications of this tension between ideologies and identities for the political debate about Taiwan's future, from the vantage point of 2001. At that time, there were three kinds of competing ideological narratives selectively presenting the historical events to manipulate national identities; they were aimed at various audiences.

The PRC created two interwoven narratives – the first about its own unfolding as a nation-state, the second about Taiwan's unfolding as separate from the PRC. Both narratives emphasise China's 'century of humiliation' (*bainian guochi* 百年国耻) from foreign – Western and Japanese – imperialists, a rhetorical strategy that stokes an anti-foreigner form of Chinese ultranationalism by invoking PRC citizens' galvanising social experiences of the early twentieth century and World War II. Both narratives are aimed primarily at PRC citizens and are used to justify aggressive PRC international engagement, including against Taiwan: foreign imperialism devastated China, having ripped away Taiwan; Taiwan must be returned; China must be aggressive to prevent being victimised. These narratives resonate very little with Taiwan citizens and only in a minimal way with the global community, but for now, they still resonate with PRC citizens, feeding ultranationalism.

By contrast, the third kind of narrative has been much more successful on the international rhetorical stage. Various political actors in Taiwan created narratives about Taiwan's unfolding as a separate nation-state, which they aim primarily at Taiwan's citizens and diaspora but also at an international audience: Taiwan was exploited by a series of colonising regimes – Dutch, Zheng, Qing, Japanese, Nationalist – but Taiwan has proven resilient and independent by combining Austronesian and Han cultures and peoples, Japanese culture and technological innovation. These narratives resonate both for Taiwanese and for international visitors to Taiwan, who can see the valorisation of Austronesian, Han and Japanese cultural heritages and also Taiwan's de facto political independence: its own currency, its own economic success, its own government, its own independent press. Even PRC citizens who visit Taiwan experience these differences.

Taiwan's narratives resonate because they are closer to people's current social experience and thus closer to people's actual identities than the PRC's narrative about Taiwan. Moreover, the ideological power of *both* the PRC's narratives is time-sensitive, because the social experiences of the first half of the twentieth century are less and less salient than are those of the second half of the twentieth century for people in the contemporary PRC, Taiwan and the world – hence, the PRC Party-state's recent demands that Western businesses (airlines and such) incorporate PRC ideological narratives into the maps and place names they use. This economic bullying suggests that the PRC realises it is losing the rhetorical battle, but how far is it willing to go?

I ended *Is Taiwan Chinese?* with a consideration of how competing ideological narratives in tension with actual identities might influence different possible political trajectories for Taiwan and the PRC. My main underlying point still holds: Taiwan national identity is authentic – that is, it motivates collective action – and thus it must be taken into consideration in any proposed resolution of Taiwan's political future. Similarly, the PRC's long-term options remain the same: democratise so that Taiwan will agree to reunification, go to war to recapture Taiwan, or accept that Taiwan is independent. And given that the Party-state's primary goal is to stay in power, one would think that self-interest would lead to acceptance. I

122 Melissa J. Brown

still think that the third option remains the least threat to the CCP. Xi Jinping *has* moved the PRC even further away from democratic possibilities; he has, however, expanded military capacity and become increasingly aggressive on the international stage, militarily, economically and ideologically. It is difficult to tell whether these imperialist actions are precursors of war – perhaps to stake out China's 'sphere of influence' – or if they are tactical bullying. Xi himself may not know yet which way these actions will play out; China is on a dangerous path indeed.

In 2001, I saw Taiwan's need to persuade China to democratise or accept Taiwan's independence, and I saw leverage for acceptance in PRC citizens' ability to experience Taiwan's difference and Taiwan's enormous economic investment in the PRC. I still think that Taiwan's own example of maturing democracy and the ability of PRC citizens to visit Taiwan are effective, but they require time and some political space for PRC citizens to have at least a modicum of influence on their government. The PRC has been working to ensure that time runs out, not only by restricting its own citizens' political expression, but also by working to isolate Taiwan diplomatically and economically (via ECFA and other regional trade agreements). Here, Taiwan's economic investment in the PRC is not proving the leverage that I had thought it might. But Taiwan is radically turning the economic table in an innovative, cosmopolitan way that, as I discuss further below, may well work because it requires nothing from the PRC.

The politics of writing, reception and extension

Politics swirl around *Is Taiwan Chinese?* – international politics about Taiwan's future and China's rise, PRC politics about studying politically sensitive topics, and US academic politics about contested approaches (the so-called culture wars, lingering Cold War sentiment against Taiwan, and gender politics). So it is worth understanding how these politics have influenced the construction of the book itself as well as its reception and subsequent research.[18] I began writing the book in 1997 during a second postdoctoral fellowship at the University of California at Berkeley, wrote much of it while juggling my first tenure-line faculty job (as an assistant professor of anthropology at the University of Cincinnati) with family responsibility (my daughter was born in 1998), and finalised the manuscript in 2001 as an assistant professor at Stanford in the anthropological sciences department – one of two anthropology departments at Stanford, the fallout of particularly vicious culture-wars infighting during the 1990s (Gibbs 1998). My postdoctoral fellowship at Berkeley gave the University of California Press the right of first refusal on the book manuscript, but – as then Asian-studies acquisitions editor Sheila Levine informed me in 1996 – Cal Press had never yet published a book about Taiwan and it was one of the few academic presses at the time that was turning a profit.[19] That context influenced my writing.

At Berkeley, as I was framing the book, I had advice to write a book that would sell (Sheila Levine), to put China in the title (Arthur Wolf), leave out anthropological theory entirely (Fred Wakeman) and not worry that statements the PRC might view as critical would prevent future research there *as long as* the comments are published only in English (Steve Harrell, Fred Wakeman). Since US anthropology largely ignores Taiwan and even China and moreover the manuscript was going to Cal Press's Asian studies editor for review, I knew that I couldn't use the standard anthropological structure of beginning with a theory chapter (but because I was on the job market in anthropology, I could not entirely omit theory, so I put it at the end of the book). I worried a lot about Levine's explicit comment to me (and Philip Kafalas, another postdoc at Berkeley that year) that excellent scholarship was not sufficient for acceptance at Cal Press; the proposed book had to be expected to bring in revenue too. Arthur Wolf told me that Levine's statement meant I had to put China in the title; he said Stanford University Press always insisted he use 'China' in his titles for marketing reasons. I had originally planned to title the book 'At the Border to Han', as I was already using 'Han' for ethnic identity and 'Chinese' for national identity, but Levine said something with China or Chinese in the title would be more marketable. I had used the title 'On Becoming Chinese' for a 1994 paper presented at a panel I organised for UC Berkeley's annual China symposium that later became the basis of my 1996 edited volume.[20] But Stephen Murray and Keelung Hong's book *Taiwanese Culture, Taiwanese Society: A Critical Review of Social Science Research done on Taiwan* (Murray and Hong 1994) was also on my mind: Murray and Hong criticise anthropologists (especially Arthur Wolf) for, among other things, referring to Taiwan as China and Taiwanese as Chinese.[21] Moreover, having just come from six months' field research in the PRC, I was well aware not only of the political issues about use of the term 'China' but also of the plain fact that life in the PRC was nothing like life in Taiwan and had not been for a century. As a junior scholar, I felt that I needed Cal Press to accept the manuscript and publish the book, so I felt I had to work 'China' or 'Chinese' into the title, but I insisted that the title must also contain 'Taiwan' – many contortionist and lengthy title attempts that I have mercifully forgotten ensued. It was my husband, Jim Truncer, who came up with the solution: rather than making a definitive statement in the title, instead use the title to pose the question the book explores: Is Taiwan Chinese? That provocative title also meant that later, when I did get a book contract from Cal Press, I made sure that any translation into Chinese required my signature.[22]

I attribute some of the popular interest in *Is Taiwan Chinese?* to its provocative title. It was featured on National Public Radio, Radio Taiwan International, Voice of America (television with call-ins from the PRC) and in an independent documentary on the Taiwan March 2004 elections. There was a panel discussion about the book in relation to the politics of national identity in September 2004 at UC Berkeley's Institute for East Asian Studies. I was also asked to deliver the 2004 keynote speech to the northern California chapter meeting of the Formosan Association for Public Affairs. There have been negative consequences. I have never spoken publicly about *Is Taiwan Chinese?* without at least one comment from a PRC nationalist who is offended that I even question that Taiwan should belong to the PRC, let alone that I suggest the identity of Taiwanese themselves should be

124 Melissa J. Brown

taken seriously in guiding a solution to tensions over Taiwan's political future. Thus, I was quite worried about the phone calls from the PRC that the VOA wanted me to field on air. There were of course such Chinese nationalist comments, but I came away actually encouraged by the number of Chinese callers who were ready to accept the difference between Taiwanese experience and their own.

I never directly answer the title question; indeed 'one would be hard pressed to come up with a conclusive answer to the striking question' (Liang 2005: 126). I say that Taiwanese Han are both more Han than Han in the PRC (from a Confucian culturalist perspective) and have been significantly influenced by Austronesians and Japanese. I say that Taiwanese identity is real – not a political ploy – and that I think that identity will not go away any time soon. I say that collective identities – including both ethnic and national identities – are based on social experience and that the experiences of people in Taiwan and in the PRC have been different not only since 1949 but also going back to 1895. I also say that while identities do not determine the political future, they will influence popular responses to political policies. Is Taiwan Chinese? It's complicated because the response 'must always be situational, fully contingent on ever unfolding social events that have little relationship to the thread-bare dogma of culture and ancestry' (Shen Hsiu-Hua 2006: 152). This contingency bothers Cal Clark (2004), Wang Fu-chang (2004), Alan Wachman (2004), Fong Shiaw-chian (2004), Timothy Cheek (2004) and I suspect Shih Chih-yu (2004), as stated in their thoughtful contributions to the 2004 *Issues and Studies* Book Review Roundtable of *Is Taiwan Chinese?* It also bothers Ooi Su-Mei (2007) and Evan N. Dawley (2009). Clark (2004: 463) concludes his review by saying:

> In short, Melissa Brown has provided an excellent and innovative study of national identity in Taiwan and China. Her analysis, though, suggests that the question '*Is Taiwan Chinese?*' might be less central than is often assumed to the political question of whether Taiwan should be part of the PRC.

Yes! It is exactly my point that ideological rhetoric places identity – with ideology's false assumption that collective identities, both ethnic and national, are based on culture and ancestry – at the heart of what is really a sociopolitical question. When we stop obfuscating the political nature of the question and the social basis of collective identities, then we must analyse possible solutions in a very different fashion.

Should Taiwan become part of a unified China? That's not for me to say. But most of the public discussion reflects the views of the political and intellectual elite on both sides of the Strait. By contrast, *Is Taiwan Chinese?* offers insights from the social experience of ordinary citizens – primarily in Taiwan but also in the PRC – because these are the people who must live with the political policies and whose actions collectively constitute the popular response. Throughout *Is Taiwan Chinese?*, I was explicit about when I was speaking with my own voice as a researcher and when I was conveying the experiences and beliefs so generously shared with me by the people I worked among. In this regard, I must dispute Shen Xingyi's

(2006) criticism that I do not approve of the villagers of Toushe, Longtian and Jibeishua being considered plains Aborigine once again because they had previously changed to Han (p. 226) and that I imposed my belief of what people's identities should be despite their contrary expressions of identity (p. 227).[23]

There are both intellectual traditions and ideological rhetoric that claim fixed homogeneity to cultural beliefs and ethnicity.[24] *Is Taiwan Chinese?* disrupts these reifications by demonstrating variation in the cultural beliefs and the personal sense of identity not only as held by different individuals across a community but also as held by the same individuals over time. In my book, I reported the concern I heard from elderly villagers about the move by young people to reclaim an Austronesian identity; they feared being stigmatised as savages once again. But I also document that generational shift in the community and consider it in the context of larger changes in Taiwanese society that promoted Austronesian heritage as lauditory. I think Shen does not understand that I interpret this documented generational variation as indicating a transformation in progress.[25] As an anthropologist, my goal was to convey the voices of ordinary women and men, in all their rich complexity, into the mix of public debate about Taiwan's future – not because I think I can speak for them, but because they so rarely have their voices heard at all.

Although I worked hard to provide 'a balanced treatment of a politically charged topic' (Greene 2004: 831), politics influenced the book's reception.

> Diehard supporters of Taiwan-China unification and advocates of Taiwan independence share an underlying belief in the inviolability of their own narrative. To her credit, Brown's book will please neither side.
>
> *(Liang 2005: 126)[26]*

Similarly, my efforts to synthesise across academically warring theoretical perspectives also pleased neither side. By arguing that culture's role in the formation of collective identities is limited and instead political economy, or society, predominates, I discomfited those who view culture (including religion) as substantial if not predominant (Woo 2004, R. Shepherd 2004, Rubinstein 2004, Shih 2004, Chang 2005) and also those who cannot see ethnic identity as political (Ooi 2007). I also exasperated some (Fong 2004, Shih 2004, Chang 2005) with my discussion of the natural-selection implications of migration, population sex ratios and marriage. When called demographic factors these influences are read as boring and quaint, but when called evolutionary factors they are read as positivist or tautological. I think it highly likely that this theoretical synthesising, perhaps in conjunction with my position at the time in the now-defunct Department of Anthropological Sciences at Stanford, influenced the small number of reviews in disciplinary journals – five, only two of which are in anthropology journals – in contrast to the 18 reviews in area studies journals.[27]

As the creator of *Is Taiwan Chinese?*, I cannot help but see this book differently, and more personally, than others. For me, the book's 'biography' over the past two decades is woven from multiple skeins, from its social as well as intellectual threads.

These threads include my knowledge of its making, its reception in the field, how its making has transformed me, and how it has perhaps transformed the field. My eyes fall on a passage, and I am suddenly transported back to moments in its creation and its reception: my sharp gasp in the close, still room when the first Taiwanese elder self-referentially used the phrase *guan hoan-a* (T. we savages) and I realised I had finally found the question that would allow open discussion about people's former non-Han identity; the bitter cold and danger of climbing a snowy, rocky path in Hubei, at what seemed a 60-degree incline, to reach a rare Tujia dancing funeral in a mountain hamlet; the flush of elation when I first read Murray Rubinstein's (2004: 454) prediction that my book would be 'the starting point of future discussions of the very nature of identity and the role that identity as a construct plays in Chinese and Taiwanese intellectual and political life'. I am fortunate that the book has been favourably received in my lifetime and still remains popular as a teaching text and a scholarly touchstone. Of course, there were some reviewers and colleagues who took me to task or engaged in vigorous debate. Wang Fu-chang (2004: 464–66), for example, argued against what he considered the anachronistic application of an ethnic-group concept to seventeenth-century Taiwan, and I responded (Brown 2004b: 503–4) to the major issues in his thoughtful argument. Timothy Cheek, who engaged some of my theoretical claims, noted, 'One may not agree with Brown's conclusions or her (many) neologisms, but an honest scholar cannot dismiss the considerable work represented in this book without engaging it in some detail' (Cheek 2004: 497). Given Cheek's assessment, I cannot help but also remember being puzzled by what seemed to be assiduous and studied avoidance of this book in certain corners of our tightly knit field of Taiwan studies. It has been at times irritating, worrying and amusing to observe a discernible pattern of 'dismissive engagement' on the part of a few men. Some, such as Tonio Andrade, have gone so far as to borrow titles and dismiss specific arguments that were drawn from my work and were discussed by reviewers of my work in major journals – all while carefully writing around acknowledgement.[28]

Given the success of the book, am I nit-picking to mention this pointed lack of acknowledgement? Perhaps so, if it is happening only to me. And in this way, maybe the story of this book's reception and post-publication life is also the story of the maturation and diversification of professional Taiwan studies – a development Peter Kornicki welcomed, in his introductory remarks at the 2010 British Academy conference on Taiwan, as a contribution to expanding our singularly defined field. When I was a graduate student, it was not unreasonable for a scholar to know every single English-language work on their research question. Even now, this problematic expectation is the norm, despite the digital access that shows the wealth of relevant literature in Chinese, Japanese and other Asian languages, as well as European languages other than English. A decade ago, before #MeToo and perhaps in a time before we openly pondered the visible and invisible ways that valuations and systems of merit can be bent by power, we were less conscious of the significance of repetitive patterns of seemingly agentless aggression and thus

Is Taiwan Chinese? revisited   **127**

perhaps less likely to call out the dismissal of a woman's work. But we need to consider the power of dismissal, the rejection of a scholar's right to thoughtful consideration of her reasoned arguments – a right earned through the same gate-keeping degree and career mechanisms that are supposed to enfranchise all scholars equally. This technique is one of the most powerful tools of the concerted, see-mingly bloodless but insidiously efficacious war against professional women and people of colour.[29] For me – with remembrance of my book's creation and sub-sequent acclaim woven into my own biography – I cannot help but see the success of *Is Taiwan Chinese?* as one story of a growing normalisation of academic women. But it also bears remembering that justice, merit and inclusivity take constant work to materialise, even today. Graduate students today need mentors and allies – not only for professional development, but also for actively countering diversity-redu-cing exclusionary tactics. I remain indebted to Steve Harrell, Arthur Wolf, Marc Feldman, Pan Inghai, Tseng Chiu-yu, Rhoda Halperin, Rob Weller, Gail Her-shatter and Don Sutton, among others – all of whom promoted me and my work – and I hope that up and coming scholars will not be discouraged by the political injustices that factor so intersectionally into academic lineages and institu-tional prestige.

Political citation is one of these injustices and a clear symptom of dishonest scholarship. Citing or avoiding the acknowledgement of authors may be motivated by many reasons – promoting an academic lineage, claiming or excluding mem-bership in a social in-group, even influencing probable reviewers. But whatever the motivation, political citation undermines all academic research by forsaking prin-ciples of cumulative knowledge. Moreover, it has a cascading effect. Omission of a major book in the field – and especially dismissal of it without attribution – hurts the larger field of Taiwan studies. It sends a message that original research is not valued; it occludes the intellectual engagement and debate that strengthens a field and encourages new scholarship. In such a close-knit field as Taiwan studies, it is ludicrous to think that such omission is not noticed. I kept waiting for scholars reviewing Andrade's work – including those who know me personally and have even praised *Is Taiwan Chinese?* in print – to write about this omission, but there was only a careful silence. If a graduate student missed a major work in the field, any professor would call out the omission. But perhaps the professional costs of criticising political citation were too powerfully persuasive. Although only ten years ago, it was a different time. Then, I could not ask whether the occlusion of my work is gender-based, but now the #MeToo movement allows such questions to be publicly considered. And going forward, we as a field must do better.

To step back now and think about the intellectual field, I want to consider what responsibility we as a scholarly community have to academic honesty and justice. In a small well-defined field, where we know each other, what should the com-munity's reaction be to a person who, perhaps like many, is inspired by a scholar's work but does not do the right thing and cite her work? The community reaction plays out as a series of responses by individuals. An editor who queries an author for an exemplary citation of an unattributed criticism not only uses time against a

128   Melissa J. Brown

looming deadline but also risks an accusation of hubris. A reviewer who finds another scholar's work problematic must consider – in the context of the contemporary trend of positive-only book reviews in major journals – what to write or whether to drop the review. And an individual scholar considering debate over points of intellectual disagreement knows that citation and engagement – hallmarks of civil, respectful debate – invite others to read the disagreed-with work and thus risks that readers will think critically about his *own* work and perhaps find it wanting. Individual scholars are constantly confronted by such issues and, being human, do not always make the best choices. But we as a scholarly community have to encourage – both supportively and critically, as necessary – better choices. Community vigilance is crucial here, for people are more likely to behave ethically when they encounter even small reminders of community observation (Appiah 2010). A good beginning is to publicly acknowledge that these choices – made in seemingly isolated circumstances – impact our community well beyond the influence of a single book or author, and often in ways that diminish inclusivity.

I return now to the more specific reception of *Is Taiwan Chinese?* and the reviews and citations that do intellectually engage the book. In addition to the scholars and topics mentioned above, many reviews and subsequent citations emphasise the major points of the book:

- the social construction of identity (Greene, Liu, Liang, Schak, Chang, HH Shen);
- the divergence of Taiwan's and China's social experience (Lee, Woo, Liang, Lin, Ferdinand, Schak, Chang, HH Shen, Liu, Heylen, Ooi);
- the documentation that migration, intermarriage and regime change can lead to *either* a long-route or a short-route pattern of identity change (Lee, Schak, Chang, HH Shen, Heylen, Hunter);
- the critical look at the concept of Chineseness (Lee, Chang, Heylen, Rubinstein);
- the documentation of the fluidity and changeability of identity and examination of the ethnic borders (K. Li, HH Shen, Chang, Heylen, Ooi);
- the close ethnographic and historical analyses (Lee, Greene, Schak, Heylen, Rubinstein, Wang, Shen Xingyi);
- the consideration of identity on both sides of the Strait (Rubinstein, Clark, Fong, Ferdinand, Schak, Chang, HH Shen, CY Liu, Heylen); and
- the rich theoretical grounding (Rubinstein, Wang, Cheek, Ferdinand, HH Shen, CY Liu).

I have been particularly encouraged that other scholars have built on and tested some of these points – adding their own original insights to expand our understanding – for example, E. Vickers' (2010) work on Taiwan's history and identity in museums; Chen Rou-Lan's (2012) work on the contributions of shared experience to Taiwanese national identity over time; Chris Vasantkumar's (2012) work on what ethnic minority studies contribute to a critical assessment of Han identity; Emma Teng's (2013) work on hybridity and mixed-ancestry families;

Li Yi-tan's (2014) work on peaceful resolution to the distinct identities and nationalisms across the Strait; and the contributors to Arif Dirlik, Liao Ping-Hui and Chuang Ya-chung's edited volume who examine the relationship between colonialism and historical identity formation, including de-sinicisation (Dirlik et al. 2018). Moreover, in 2018, *Is Taiwan Chinese?* is the third most popular text book for undergraduate courses about Taiwan in North American (Hsieh and Wang 2018).[30]

My own work has continued to reconsider, extend and refine the findings of *Is Taiwan Chinese?* I extend the theoretical framework about the disjuncture between culture and identity, arguing that there was less cultural standardisation in late imperial China than usually assumed and that the imperial state promoted 'the ideology of cultural unity while at the same time accepting a wide range of practices and cultural ideas as Han' (Brown 2007: 116).[31] In subsequent research using this expanded theoretical framework, I argue that under Japanese rule, Han in Taiwan did not think of themselves as Japanese (Brown 2010, 2015; contra Ching 2001). And based on their similar social experience – under the colonial rule first of the Japanese and then of the Nationalists – Hoklo and Hakka and plains Aborigines, who had infamously feuded for several centuries, began to think of themselves as one group. Historical evidence suggests this identity was framed as 'Chinese' under Japanese rule, but the massacres Nationalists carried out following the 2:28 uprising destroyed that possibility. Social experience led to a different framing – *bensheng ren* 本省人, a political label that became the ethnic category of Taiwanese (*Taiwan ren*; see also Brown 2008). Moreover, although both colonial powers did shape this collective identity, neither succeeded in promoting the identity they sought. Japanese officials tried to instil a (second-class) Japanese identity, and Nationalists tried to instil a (regional) Chinese identity.

People's identity as Taiwanese formed during the martial-law period along with, and in contrast to, Mainlanders (*waisheng ren*), who largely denied that they were an ethnic group until they lost political power (Corcuff 2000; Brown 2008, 2015; Yang and Chang 2010). Identity formation was driven by the myriad changes in social experience that, for both Taiwanese and Mainlanders, accompanied the regime change of the establishment of Nationalist rule in Taiwan. Like Dutch rule, Japanese colonial rule was focused on extraction of resources. In contrast, Nationalist rule was settler colonialism (Brown, forthcoming) – with many similarities to the settler colonialism of Zheng rule in Taiwan and of Qing-era annexation of China's Southwest (e.g., Herman 2018), including the proclivity toward short-route identity change. Despite the differences in their approaches, the failure of Japanese and Nationalist regimes to manipulate the desired collective identities in their Taiwan subjects comes down to the fundamental structural violence of colonialism – the hierarchy of metropole elite over colonial subalterns. The differential social experience across that hierarchy precludes a unifying collective identity (Brown 2010).

In short, the structural basis of collective identities (both ethnic and national) might seem to lend itself to the social engineering efforts of authoritarian regimes.

130 Melissa J. Brown

But that appearance is misleading. While there have been successful instances of identity manipulation in the PRC – the Prmi and the Tujia, for example – these successes required the intervention of local governments, using officials with insider sympathies and knowledge to mediate for local benefit mandates from the central government (Harrell 1996, 2001; Brown 2003, 2004a, 2010). The PRC central government's ham-handed attempts to manipulate collective identities often results in consequences it does not want – not only among the peoples of Taiwan, Tibet and Xinjiang, but also among young, educated Han. In the aftermath of the Tiananmen democracy protests and subsequent massacre, the PRC Party-state mandated an indoctrination period for all college students, in the two weeks before the first (or in Shanghai, the second) year of college. I have been on PRC campuses during this period. Although the late-night, loud intellectual training sessions may be more effective in guiding these young minds toward unquestioning nationalistic loyalty, I must admit that I personally find more viscerally disturbing the daytime hours that thousands of incoming 17-, 18- and 19-year-olds spend learning to goosestep in unison around an athletic field (with the most promising singled out to march at the front with automatic rifles). This centrally planned social engineering effort does not just lead to loyalty to the CCP; it also fans the flame of ultranationalism – to the point where the Party-state cannot always control matters. A 2016 study examining the participation of students from three elite Beijing colleges in the September 2012 anti-Japanese demonstrations (which turned to riots) found nationalism a significant – but not primary – factor (Zhou and Wang 2016). Equally revealing in my opinion, albeit unexplained by the researchers, is that PRC citizens (who are required to participate in the before-school training sessions) were significantly much more likely to have demonstrated than ethnic Chinese students from the diaspora. The ultranationalism of Chinese youths seems correlated to the Party-state's increasingly aggressive insistence on international adherence to its narrative of Taiwan (and Kashmir and the seas east and south of China) as part of the PRC. These bullying acts only reinforce a Taiwanese collective identity as different from the PRC, but what can Taiwan do to counter this imperialist threat?

Possibilities of cosmopolitanism

Although I did not foresee an effective counter to PRC ultranationalism in *Is Taiwan Chinese?* – or even how to track nationalism across ordinary citizens in the way I had examined identity – I now think that I see possible ways forward on both those fronts. The politics surrounding identities research (discussed above) led me to pivot and examine a population-level process of change among Han: the kin-based management of girls' and women's labour in relation to the demise of footbinding across China. Yet this pivot eventually brought me back to consideration of Taiwanese national identity because of the stark difference I found in women's social engagement while analysing data from 12 inland rural provinces of the PRC (Brown et al. 2012, Brown 2016, Brown 2017, Brown and Satterthwaite-Phillips 2018).[32]

Is Taiwan Chinese? revisited **131**

In years of interviewing in both Taiwan and the PRC about household- and village-level customs, I have been struck by the distinct difference not only in acknowledging women's contributions but often even in recognising the existence of those contributions (Brown 2016). In Taiwan, both men and women often acknowledged these contributions (Brown 2003, 2004a). In the PRC, men did not acknowledge women's contributions; women often did not even realise that they had made contributions, and women who did realise could not say so in front of their men (Brown 2016, cf. Evans 2016). These observations correspond to larger cultural patterns. Uxorilocal marriage, for example, where a daughter can stand in for a son and bring a marriage and potentially grandchildren into a patrilineal household, was widely accepted during the late nineteenth and early twentieth centuries in Taiwan, somewhat accepted in parts of southern China, and not tolerated in much of northern China (Wolf and Huang 1980, Wolf 1984). Women are necessarily part of quotidian social engagements because women are part of all class and ethnic divisions within a society, so women – especially women of populous marginalised groups – are crucial, if often unacknowledged, contributors to public spheres (Brown, forthcoming; cf. Weller 1999). Politically and economically, women's status in the PRC continues to lag behind that of women in Taiwan,[33] so I returned to consideration of Taiwan history to better understand the impact of engaged women on society.

I suggest that impact is cosmopolitanism. Ordinary women have been crucial to the ebb and flow of cosmopolitanism across Taiwan's history, including its present-day zenith (Brown, forthcoming). Here I should clarify that I am using a social-science definition of cosmopolitanism – where what defines a community as cosmopolitan is whether its members engage socially across diversity (such as linguistic, ethnic or religious difference).[34] This definition means that ordinary people, even if they never leave their community, can potentially be cosmopolitan. If the majority of people in a community engage across different identities on a daily basis – in cooperative economic ventures, for example – then that place is cosmopolitan. And that focus on social experience of collective identities is where *Is Taiwan Chinese?* contributes; that analysis of the fluidity and dynamics of collective identities endures.

I think we are seeing Taiwanese nationalism in the process of becoming a glocal cosmopolitanism – simultaneously global and local. Taiwan itself is cosmopolitan, as people within Taiwan engage regularly across linguistic, ethnic, religious and other differences. But more than that, Taiwan is making global connections across differences as well – with migrant brides and migrant caregivers, with student exchanges and economic development cooperation, for example. Scott Kennedy provocatively suggested in a 2017 talk that Taiwan's 1980s–1990s economic investment in the PRC led to China's current economic growth and that Taiwan's current economic investment in Southeast Asia could lead to the development of a regional, Southeast Asian economic power (cf. Glaser et al. 2018; Brown 2004a: 249). This new 'southbound' engagement encompasses broad-based exchanges that span education, the arts, medicine and technology. These exchanges require nothing from the PRC. Moreover, if the

Notes

1 *Acknowledgements*: I thank Dafydd Fell for his gracious understanding of the family emergency that kept me from attending the 2015 World Congress of Taiwan Studies and his invitation to include my chapter in this volume. I am grateful to Saeyoung Park and Caroline Reeves for their thoughtful comments

2 Xi's attempts at an imperial Chinese reach include live-ammunition war games in the Taiwan Strait, frequent military flyovers of Taiwan, extraterritoriality demands that PRC maps including territories not under PRC control be used as official outside the PRC's borders (for example, by international airlines throughout their range)s, and increasing threats of military action if Taiwan formalises the empirical fact of its independent nation-state status. Under Xi, the PRC has also flaunted international law by using squatter-tactics in the South China Sea and Central Asia, arranged unequal development and rights for Chinese settlers across Africa, and expanded the Confucius Institutes programme that presents PRC propaganda in low-quality Mandarin Chinese-language education around the world. (On the poor quality of CI language training, see for example Link 2017.)

3 The PRC claims multiple borders that it does not control, including Taiwan; islands, shoals and rock outcrops in the South China Sea and East China Sea; and Arunachal Pradesh and the Shaksgam valley in the Himalayan mountains. (There are also disputed PRC-controlled territories in these areas.) Countries with which the PRC has territorial disputes are: Taiwan, Japan, Malaysia, Indonesia, Vietnam, the Philippines, Brunei, India, Bhutan and Nepal. In 2017, the PRC built in the South China Sea and attempted to build in the Himalayas, inciting military responses from the United States and India, among others.

4 A culture – the shared meaningful beliefs of a population – changes over time; all cultures change. But changes over time in the cultural repertoire of an individual – the constellation of cultural ideas that an individual comprehends and can act upon in a way that others consider competent – is not understood in any theoretical or systematic way. There are many individuals whose cultural repertoire changes greatly over their lifetime – they are competent in more than one culture – and there are other individuals whose competence may even be limited to a very narrow (regional) range within a culture. Such variability in cultural competence appears, like linguistic competence, affected both by a critical period of age (birth until 3, 10, 15?) during which culture (like language) is absorbed (through social interactions) and also influenced by the range of variation to which individuals are (socially) exposed.

5 Fluidity and changeability can interact, with some individuals taking advantage of social circumstances to push across an identity border and leading to a subsequent shifting of the border itself, as I describe for long-route Han in chapter 3 of *Is Taiwan Chinese?* (See also Brown 2008, 2015.)

6 The household registers from these communities are included in Arthur Wolf and Chuang Ying-chang's historical demography project (now held by the Program for Historical Demography at Academia Sinica). Computerisation of these registers was not complete until after *Is Taiwan Chinese?* was published, but I was able to use the hard copies, both for my dissertation and for the book.

Is Taiwan Chinese? revisited **133**

7 Han is commonly used in the PRC and Taiwan for the ethnic group that most Westerners think of as ethnic Chinese. Other common terms for ethnic Chinese, more frequently used in the diaspora, include Hua 華, Xia夏 and Tang唐. I do not explore the politicization of these different terms.

8 Using a methodological individualist approach requires thinking about sample size, representativeness of sampling, and sufficient structure across interviews to ensure direct comparability. During the early 1990s, such an approach was already stigmatised as 'positivist' by the postmodern side of US anthropology's particularly virulent form of the culture wars. This dismissal assumed that (a) cultural meanings and power hierarchies are sufficiently public that any well-informed resident should be able to provide relevant information and (b) structured interviews do not capture cultural meanings. I incorporated some interview techniques developed by cognitive anthropologists (e.g. D'Andrade and Strauss 1992) in order to access meanings in a structured, consistent manner.

9 I interviewed systematically in three communities that Japanese records labelled plains Aborigine and, for comparison purposes, in one labelled Hoklo (I also had a few interviews in additional communities). In the three communities that were still rural villages in 1991–1992 (when I interviewed), I interviewed people aged 70 and older. In Longtian, which had been subsumed in the small city of Guantian, I had to lower the age to 60 in order to find a sufficient number of community elders whose family had lived in the community before the Japanese colonial administration put in a railroad stop and the village became a city. The interviews took a minimum of 1.5 hours, but there were sufficient open-ended questions in every section of the questionnaire that most interviews took 2–4 hours, and some even longer. I interviewed in multiple sessions, each session lasting 1–2 hours, the length depending on the comfort and willingness of the elderly people sharing their knowledge and memories with me. Of the approximately 100 people I interviewed, only two women refused a second follow-up session – one because the interviews asked about a period in her life that was personally difficult and she preferred not to dwell further on that period and one because her son did not want her to discuss the relative poverty of her natal and marital families during the Japanese period. Everyone else agreed to multiple interviews, often with great enthusiasm.

10 My dissertation presents these points in relation to an anthropological theory framework.

11 I was fortunate to be working through these materials while Steve Harrell (my PhD advisor) was working through his ethnographic and historical materials about the sociohistorical interactions of Han and non-Han peoples in southwestern China for his 2001 book. I remain grateful for many years of fruitful and insightful discussions with Steve.

12 For historical accounts, I relied on translations into modern Chinese or English (e.g. Campbell 1903, Zhang Yaoqi 1951) and on the secondary scholarly literature in both languages (including Meskill 1979, Shepherd 1993, Pan Ying 1993). In spring 1989, when I was still doing graduate coursework, Joe Esherick was a visiting professor at the University of Washington (UW), and in response to my frustration about the limitations of the tantalising information on Dutch-era Taiwan, Joe was the first to encourage me to do the ethnographic work to figure out the twentieth century and then revisit the premodern materials. John Shepherd was also a visiting professor at UW, in 1990–1991 when I was developing my dissertation project. John was writing his 1993 book at the time, and our thoughtful conversations about Han-Aborigine intermarriage helped me think through the larger historical context of the changes I proposed to investigate. I think that I also influenced John's thinking about the social dynamics of intermarriage. While we have, over the decades, diverged in our interpretations on various points, I have always found John's historical and ethnographic research reliable, relevant, revealing and thus invaluable.

13 These proportions continue to change. In the 2008 census, Hoklo were 73 per cent of Taiwan's population, Hakka 12 per cent, Mainlanders 13 per cent, and certified 'mountain' Aborigines (receiving affirmative action benefits) 2 per cent.

14 In the context of indigenous peoples, the term zu 族 is usually considered to 'literally' mean 'tribes'. I even used this literal translation in *Is Taiwan Chinese?* but I now find this

134 Melissa J. Brown

usage problematic. The same term *zu* in the context of Han peoples is usually considered to mean 'lineages'. Why should we use a term 'tribes' that necessarily invokes a nineteenth-century conception of progressive evolution (itself an ideological narrative of unfolding) for Austronesians but not for Han? Instead, I suggest we should consider *pingpu zu* as speaking literally of 'plains clans' as most parallel to the usage for Han of *jiazu* 家族 (lineages).

15 The Miao became a catch-all designation for those peoples whom ethnologists considered not Han but whom ethnologists would not – or could not – distinguish as separate groups. There were a variety of political pressures to keep the number of ethnic categories limited (Cheung 1996, Brown 2002).

16 A local woman from the Hunan part of the mountains who worked for Zhou sought his assistance. Zhou brought in a linguistic specialist on Miao languages, who said that the native language of this local woman was not a Miao language. Zhou personally ordered the reassessment (Brown 2002, 2004a: 170).

17 Every PRC citizen's national identity card states their government-approved ethnic identity category.

18 These politics influenced the dissertation as well. For example, in 1990, I was at a Hoover Institute invited conference for graduate students writing dissertations about Taiwan and had my dissertation proposal slammed by Thomas Metzger and Ramon Myers, both apologists for the Cold War-era Nationalists. Because we all still thought that culture and identity coincided, they apparently feared that my analyses of Austronesian contributions to Taiwanese culture would fuel Taiwanese identity as not Chinese. It is a measure of just how much Taiwan's political context changed over the next decade that Ramon Myers agreed to write a positive blurb in 2004 for *Is Taiwan Chinese?*

19 That attitude of suspicion about the value of a book about Taiwan persisted at Cal Press even after the book was published. Cal Press put my book on the slow track to publication, having the final manuscript in 2001 but waiting until 2004 to publish – in fact, they were going to make me wait until 2006 or 2007 for publication until I complained. I had to fight to get Cal Press to take the book for display at the annual anthropology conference, and I could not get them to include the book in Cal Press advertisements in *The New York Review of Books* or other popular venues, even though I had worked with some University of Cincinnati undergraduates to make sure the book is accessible to those who are not familiar with Taiwan's history. Indeed, Cal Press seemed not only surprised but not particularly pleased that the book sold well enough to require four printings, dropping the book from publication, I think in 2010, even though it is still regularly used as a text in college courses. Recent discussion about the possibility of a second edition was going nowhere until I asked if Cal Press would sell the rights to another publisher, and I am still tied up in proving there is a market for the book.

20 That title has proven popular. I first used the title publicly at the 1994 Berkeley symposium and published it in my 1996 edited volume with UC Berkeley's Institute for East Asian Studies – a book that Cal Press distributed. Yeh Wen-hsin and Leo Ching titled books *Becoming Chinese: Passages to Modernity and Beyond* (Yeh 2000) and *Becoming 'Japanese': Colonial Taiwan and the Politics of Identity Formation* (Ching 2001), respectively. Both books were published by Cal Press – Ching's book was accepted after mine and fast-tracked for publication. (Indeed, the freelance copyeditor who worked on my book greatly added to the time to publication by globally changing all references from 'Taiwan Aborigines' to 'Taiwanese Aborigines,' contrary to usage in Taiwan studies but following usage in Ching's book.) Note that Ching's title allows Cal Press to subsume this book about Taiwan under a different area of study – Japan – and relegates Taiwan to the subtitle. There are also others, including Tonio Andrade's (2007) *How Taiwan Became Chinese: Dutch, Spanish, and Han Colonization in the Seventeenth Century*. (A Google Scholar search, for example, turns up 26 works with the exact phrase 'becoming Chinese' in the title between 1994 and 2018 but does not capture my 1996 chapter title or a 1995 article by Jennifer Saville; there are no works with that title before my 1994

Is Taiwan Chinese? revisited   135

presentation.) And Evan Dawley (2019) has *Becoming Taiwanese: Ethnogenesis in a Colonial City, 1880s–1950s.*

21 Indeed, their 2005 book, *Looking through Taiwan: American Anthropologists' Collusion with Ethnic Domination* (Hong and Murray 2005), mentions *Is Taiwan Chinese?* only in passing (pp. 8, 35, 53, 89, 105, 128n1), including the (p. 35) criticism that I mention conservative estimates of Taiwanese deaths in 1947, despite the fact that my 'main thesis coincides with Hong and Murray's argument that Taiwan is not China' (Sylvia Li-chun Lin 2006: 135).

22 *Is Taiwan Chinese?* has not been translated into Chinese. There were three requests to Cal Press shortly after publication but all three were from publishers in Taiwan with clear political biases, and I refused permission. One of these publishers went on to publish a book that advocates Taiwan independence and uses my English title (*Is Taiwan Chinese?*; see Xue, Dai and Chow 2005). A couple years later, I did find a published Taiwanese American author willing to do the translation, but I could not raise the funds to pay for his time.

23 Shen Xingyi (2006: 227) also criticises my discussion of footbinding, insisting that footbinding was important to Han to ensure upward marital mobility and that farm families could not afford to bind daughters' feet. Although these are commonplace and long-standing assumptions about footbinding, empirical evidence shows both to be wrong (Brown et al. 2012; Brown 2016; Brown and Satterthwaite-Phillips 2018). Shen was a surprising choice of reviewer, since her doctoral dissertation (on which she was working at the time) is about anticommunist scholars during the Korean War – not identity, plains Aborigines, or even rural communities.

24 I define 'ethnicity' as a sense of identity and as distinct from 'ethnic identity,' which is a social label.

25 The one place I express disapproval in the book is in opposition to some young (Hoklo Han) researchers referring to that Austronesian identity pejoratively. The young people of these villages have embraced an identity as *pingpu zu* (plains Aborigines), not an identity as *hoan-a* (savages). In scolding those who call the villagers 'savages', I am not imposing my belief about villagers' identity; rather, I am standing with the villagers to oppose racism.

26 See, for examples, reviews by Franklin J. Woo (2004) and Chih-yu Shih (2004).

27 By 'disciplinary,' I mean journals that publish about topical issues across regions of the world (R. Shepherd 2004, K-M Chang 2005, Heylen 2006, H-H Shen 2006, Hunter 2007). Journals that publish about a specific region of the world across disciplines I consider area studies journals (E.M. Lee 2004, F. J. Woo 2004, Greene 2004, H-M Liang 2005, Ferdinand 2005, Shen Xingyi 2006, Ooi 2007, Dawley 2009), including two reviews by Taiwan anthropologists (C-Y Liu 2006, David Schak 2005) and the eight reviews in *Issues and Studies* (Rubinstein 2004, Clark 2004, Wang 2004, Wachman 2004, K. Li 2004, S-c Fong 2004, C-y Shih 2004, Cheek 2004).

28 If building on my work to the point of titling the preface 'Is Taiwan Chinese?' – three years after my book came out – then at least give the nod of a citation!

29 The gendered language of Andrade's dismissal of my initiating capitalisation of *Aborigine* (as a term fully equivalent to *Han*) gives a sneering, disdainful tone: 'Some scholars today espouse the use of the capitalized term Aborigines to refer to the many and diverse Austronesian peoples who have inhabited Taiwan. I prefer, however, to maintain the use of aborigines as a value-neutral term meaning "original inhabitants" and reserve capitalization for specific ethnic designations, such as Favorolang, Sinkan, and Austronesian' (Andrade 2007: xviii). My position is 'espoused', an emotional verb, whereas his position is 'value-neutral,' an adjective that invokes the mantle of science. And by not citing my work, Andrade discourages others from even considering my reasoning.

30 I hope that this ongoing engagement with the book will lead to a second edition of the book, but as of this writing, I am still in negotiations with Cal Press.

31 I also expand the theoretical consideration of processes of change along other dimensions (Brown and Feldman 2009; Lipatov, Brown and Feldman 2011; Brown 2015, 2016).

136 Melissa J. Brown

32 With funding from the US National Science Foundation (Cultural Anthropology Program grants: BCS-0613297 & BCS-1238999), Stanford University and Harvard's Radcliffe Institute for Advanced Study, these three projects included my personally conducting extensive interviewing in four provinces, follow-up interviewing in another four provinces, and further extensive interviewing in two major urban centres that draw rural-to-urban migrants.
33 See, for example, Chia, Allred and Jerzak, 1997; Weller 1999; Farris, Lee, and Rubinstein 2004; Rigger 2014; and the contributions to Davis and Friedman 2014 and Harrell and Santos 2017.
34 Cf. Appiah (2006), Fewkes (2014).

References

Andrade, Tonio. 2007. *How Taiwan Became Chinese: Dutch, Spanish, and Han Colonization in the Seventeenth Century*. New York: Columbia University Press.

Appiah, K. Anthony. 2006. *Cosmopolitanism: Ethics in a World of Strangers*. New York: W.W. Norton.

Appiah, K. Anthony. 2010. *Experiments in Ethics*. Cambridge, MA: Harvard University Press.

Brown, Melissa J. 1996. 'On Becoming Chinese'. In Melissa J. Brown (ed.), *Negotiating Ethnicities in China and Taiwan*. Berkeley: Institute for East Asian Studies, University of California, pp. 37–74.

Brown, Melissa J. 2002. 'Local Government Agency: Manipulating Tujia Identity'. *Modern China*, 28(3), 362–395.

Brown, Melissa J. 2003. 'The Cultural Impact of Gendered Social Roles and Ethnicity: Changing Religious Practices in Taiwan'. *Journal of Anthropological Research*, 59(1), 47–67.

Brown, Melissa J. 2004a. *Is Taiwan Chinese? The Impact of Culture, Migration, and Power on Changing Identities*. Berkeley: University of California Press.

Brown, Melissa J. 2004b. 'Social Experience, Authenticity, and Theory' (Author Response to Book Review Roundtable of Is Taiwan Chinese?). *Issues & Studies (Special Issue: Studies of Taiwan Politics)*, 40(3/4), 501–509.

Brown, Melissa J. 2007. 'Ethnic Identity, Cultural Variation and Processes of Change: Rethinking the Insights of Standardization and Orthopraxy'. *Modern China* (special issue), 33(1), 91–124.

Brown, Melissa J. 2008. 'When Culture Does Not Affect Behavior: The Structural Basis of Ethnic Identity'. In Melissa J. Brown (ed.), *Explaining Culture Scientifically*. Seattle: University of Washington Press, pp. 162–183.

Brown, Melissa J. 2010. 'Changing Authentic Identities: Evidence from Taiwan and China'. *Journal of the Royal Anthropological Institute* (N.S.), 16, 459–479.

Brown, Melissa J. 2015. 'Collective Identities, Shifting Population Membership, and Niche Construction Theory: Implications from Taiwanese and Chinese Empirical Evidence'. In Philip Kreager, Stanley Ulijaszek, and Bruce Winney (eds), *Population in the Human Sciences: Concepts, Models, Evidence*. Oxford: Oxford University Press, pp. 331–360.

Brown, Melissa J. 2016. 'Footbinding, Industrialization, and Evolutionary Explanation: An Empirical Illustration of Niche Construction and Social Inheritance'. *Human Nature*, 27(4) (December), 501–532.

Brown, Melissa J. 2017. 'Dutiful Help: Masking Rural Women's Economic Contributions'. In Gonçalo Santos and Stevan Harrell (eds), *Transforming Patriarchy: Chinese Families in the Twenty-First Century*. Seattle: University of Washington Press, pp. 39–58.

Brown, Melissa J. Forthcoming. 'Taiwan's Intersectional Cosmopolitanism: Local Women's Contributions to Building Community in Colonial Contexts and Beyond'. In Peter Thilly and Graeme Reed (eds), *Taiwan as Global Island* (expected 2020).

Brown, Melissa J., Laurel Bossen, Hill Gates, and Damian Satterthwaite-Phillips. 2012. 'Marriage Mobility and Footbinding in Pre-1949 Rural China'. *Journal of Asian Studies*, 71 (4), 1035–1067.

Brown, Melissa J. and Marcus W. Feldman. 2009. 'Sociocultural Epistasis and Cultural Exaptation in Footbinding, Marriage Form, and Religious Practices in Early 20th-Century Taiwan'. *Proceedings of the National Academy of Sciences USA*, 106(52), 22139–22144.

Brown, Melissa J. and Damian Satterthwaite-Phillips. 2018. 'Economic Correlates of Footbinding: Implications for the Economic Importance of Chinese Daughters'. *PLOS ONE*, available online at https://journals.plos.org/plosone/article?id=10.1371/journal.pone.0201337.

Campbell, William. 1903. *Formosa Under the Dutch*. London: Kegan Paul.

Chang, Kai-Man. 2005. 'Review of Is Taiwan Chinese? The Impact of Culture, Power, and Migration on Changing Identities, by Melissa J. Brown'. *Cultural Dynamics*, 17(3), 351–358.

Chang, Mau-kuei. 1994. 'Toward an Understanding of the Shen-chi Wen-ti in Taiwan: Focusing on Changes after Political Liberalization'. In Chen Chung-min, Chuang Ying-chang, and Huang Shu-min (eds), *Ethnicity in Taiwan: Social, Historical, and Cultural Perspectives*. Taipei: Institute of Ethnology, Academia Sinica, pp. 93–150.

Chang, Mau-kuei. 2000. 'On the Origins and Transformation of Taiwanese National Identity'. *China Perspectives*, 28 (March–April), 51–70.

Cheek, Timothy. 2004. 'Is Social Theory Useful? – Reflections on Melissa J. Brown's Is Taiwan Chinese?' *Issues & Studies (Special Issue: Studies of Taiwan Politics)*, 40(3/4), 496–500.

Chen, Shu-Juo. 2008. 'How Han Are Taiwanese Han? Genetic Inference of Plains Indigenous Ancestry among Taiwanese Han and its Implications for Taiwan Identity', PhD dissertation, Department of Anthropological Sciences, Stanford University, Stanford, CA.

Chen, Rou-Lan. 2012. 'Beyond National Identity in Taiwan: A Multidimensional and Evolutionary Conceptualization'. *Asian Survey*, 52(5), 845–871.

Cheung, Siu-woo. 1996. 'Representation and Negotiation of Ge Identities in Southeast Guizhou'. In Melissa J. Brown (ed.), *Negotiating Ethnicities in China and Taiwan*. Berkeley: Institute for East Asian Studies, University of California, pp. 240–273.

Chia, Rosina C., Linda J. Allred, and Page A. Jerzak. 1997. 'Attitudes toward Women in Taiwan and China: Current Status, Problems, and Suggestions for Future Research'. *Psychology of Women Quarterly*, 21(1), 137–150.

Ching, Leo T. S. 2001. *Becoming 'Japanese': Colonial Taiwan and the Politics of Identity Formation*. Berkeley: University of California Press.

Clark, Cal. 2004. '"Is Taiwan Chinese?": Does it Really Matter?' *Issues & Studies (Special Issue: Studies of Taiwan Politics)*, 40(3/4), 459–463.

Corcuff, Stéphane. 2000. 'Taiwan's "Mainlanders": A New Ethnic Category'. *China Perspectives*, 28 (March–April), 71–81.

D'Andrade, Roy G. and Strauss, Claudia. 1992. *Human Motives and Cultural Models*. Cambridge: Cambridge University Press.

Davis, Deborah S. and Sara L. Friedman (eds). 2014. *Wives, Husbands, and Lovers: Marriage and Sexuality in Hong Kong, Taiwan, and Urban China*. Stanford, CA: Stanford University Press.

Dawley, Evan N. 2009. 'The Question of Identity in Recent Scholarship on the History of Taiwan'. *The China Quarterly*, 198 (June), 442–452.

Dawley, Evan N. 2019. *Becoming Taiwanese: Ethnogenesis in a Colonial City, 1880s–1950s*. Cambridge, MA: Harvard University Press.

Dirlik, Arif, Ping-Hui Liao, and Ya-Chung Chuang (eds). 2018. *Taiwan: The Land Colonialisms Made*. Durham NC: Duke University Press.

138 Melissa J. Brown

Evans, Harriet. 2016. 'Patriarchal Investments: Expectations of Male Authority and Support in a Poor Beijing Neighborhood'. In Gonçalo Santos and Stevan Harrell (eds), *Transforming Patriarchy: Chinese Families in the Twenty-First Century*. Seattle: University of Washington Press, pp. 182–198.

Farris, Catherine S.P., Anru Lee, and Murray A. Rubinstein. 2004. 'Introduction to *Women in the New Taiwan: Gender Roles and Gender Consciousness in a Changing Society*'. In Catherine S.P. Farris, Anru Lee and Murray A. Rubinstein (eds), *Women in the New Taiwan: Gender Roles and Gender Consciousness in a Changing Society*. Armonk, NY: M.E. Sharpe, pp. vii–xvi.

Ferdinand, Peter. 2005. 'Review of Taiwan: A Political History, by Denny Roy, AND Is Taiwan Chinese? The Impact of Culture, Power, and Migration on Changing Identities, by Melissa J. Brown'. *Asian Affairs*, 36(2), 255–256.

Fewkes, Jaqueline H. 2014. 'Living in the Material World: Cosmopolitanism and Trade in Early Twentieth Century Ladakh'. In Tim Harper and Sunil Amrith (eds), *Sites of Asian Interaction: Ideas, Networks and Mobility*. Cambridge: Cambridge University Press, pp. 44–46.

Fong, Shiaw-chian. 2004. 'Identity and the Mannheim Paradox'. *Issues & Studies (Special Issue: Studies of Taiwan Politics)*, 40(3/4), 483–487.

Gibbs, James L., Jr. 1998. 'Stanford's Anthro Department Splits'. *Anthropology Newsletter*, 39(7), 21.

Glaser, Bonnie S., Scott Kennedy, and Derek Mitchell, with Matthew P. Funaiole. 2018. 'The New Southbound Policy: Deepening Taiwan's Regional Integration'. Washington DC: Center for Strategic and International Studies.

Greene, J.Megan. 2004. 'Review of Is Taiwan Chinese? The Impact of Culture, Power, and Migration on Changing Identities, by Melissa J. Brown'. *The China Quarterly*, 179 (September), 830–831.

Harrell, Stevan. 1995. 'Introduction: Civilizing Projects and the Reaction to Them'. In Stevan Harrell (ed.), *Cultural Encounters on China's Ethnic Frontiers*. Seattle: University of Washington Press, pp. 3–36.

Harrell, Stevan. 1996. 'The Nationalities Question and the Prmi Prblem'. In Melissa J. Brown (ed.), *Negotiating Ethnicities in China and Taiwan*. Berkeley: Institute for East Asian Studies, University of California, pp. 274–296.

Harrell, Stevan. 2001. *Ways of Being Ethnic in Southwest China*. Seattle: University of Washington Press.

Harrell, Stevan and Gonçalo Santos. 2017. 'Introduction'. InGonçaloSantos and Stevan Harrell (eds), *Transforming Patriarchy: Chinese Families in the Twenty-First Century*. Seattle: University of Washington Press, pp. 3–36.

Herman, John E. 2018. 'From Land Reclamation to Land Grab: Settler Colonialism in Southwest China, 1680–1735'. *Harvard Journal of Asiatic Studies*, 78(1), 91–123.

Heylen, Ann. 2006. 'Review of Is Taiwan Chinese? The Impact of Culture, Power, and Migration on Changing Identities, by Melissa J. Brown'. *Journal of Multilingual and Multicultural Development*, 27(4), 344–346.

Hong, Keelung and Stephen O. Murray. 2005. *Looking through Taiwan: American Anthropologists' Collusion with Ethnic Domination*. Lincoln: University of Nebraska Press.

Hsieh, Ta-Yang and Yu-li Wang. 2018. 'One-year Findings of the Taiwan Syllabus Project', interim report presented in 'Roundtable #1: How to Teach about Taiwan: Findings from the Taiwan Syllabus Project', at the North America Taiwan Studies Association Conference, Austin, TX, May 25, 2018; available online at https://taiwansyllabusprojectnatsa.wordpress.com/.

Hunter, Jason. 2007. 'Review of Is Taiwan Chinese? The Impact of Culture, Power, and Migration on Changing Identities, by Melissa J. Brown'. *National Identities*, 9(4), 417–419.

Li, Yitan. 2014. 'Constructing Peace in the Taiwan Strait: A Constructivist Analysis of the Changing Dynamics of Identities and Nationalisms'. *Journal of Contemporary China*, 23(85), 119–141.

Liang, Hong-Ming. 2005. 'Review of Is Taiwan Chinese? The Impact of Culture, Power, and Migration on Changing Identities, by Melissa J. Brown'. *China Information*, 19(1), 125–126.

Lee, Emily Mei-hwa. 2004. 'Review of Is Taiwan Chinese? The Impact of Culture, Power, and Migration on Changing Identities, by Melissa J. Brown'. *The China Journal*, 52 (July), 207–210.

Li, Kuangchun. 2004. 'Identity of Mixed People and People of Mixed Identities – A Field Trip with Melissa Brown'. *Issues & Studies (Special Issue: Studies of Taiwan Politics)*, 40(3/4), 477–483.

Lin, Sylvia Li-chun. 2006. 'Review of Looking through Taiwan: American Anthropologists' Collusion with Ethnic Domination, by Keelung Hong and Stephen O. Murray'. *China Review International*, 13(1), 133–137.

Link, Perry. 2017. 'Confucius Murders Squirrels'. *Harvard Journal of Asiatic Studies*, 77(1), 163–173.

Liu, Cheng-Yuan. 2006. 'Review of Is Taiwan Chinese? The Impact of Culture, Power, and Migration on Changing Identities, by Melissa J. Brown'. *The Asia Pacific Journal of Anthropology*, 7(2), 181.

Lipatov, Mikhail, Melissa J. Brown, and Marcus W. Feldman. 2011. 'The Influence of Social Niche on Cultural Niche Construction: Modelling Changes in Belief about Marriage Form in Taiwan'. *Philosophical Transactions of the Royal Society, B* (part of a special issue on Human Niche Construction), 366, 889–900.

Meskill, Johanna Menzel. 1979. *A Chinese Pioneer Family: The Lins of Wu-Feng, Taiwan, 1729–1895*. Princeton, NJ: Princeton University Press.

Murray, Stephen O. and Keelung Hong. 1994. *Taiwanese Culture, Taiwanese Society: A Critical Review of Social Science Research Done on Taiwan*. Lanham, MD: University Press of America.

Ooi, Su-Mei. 2007. 'Review of Is Taiwan Chinese? The Impact of Culture, Power, and Migration on Changing Identities, by Melissa J. Brown'. *Journal of East Asian Studies*, 7(3), 501–503.

Pan, Inghai [潘英海]. 1994. 'Cultural Recombination and Recombinatory Culture: The Implications of the Taizu Annual Festival of Toushe Village' [文化合成與合成文化]. In Chuang Ying-chang and Pan Ying-hai [莊英章 and 潘英海] (eds), *Collected Essays on Research on Taiwan and Fujian Society and Culture* [臺灣與福建社會文化研究論文集]. Taipei: Institute of Ethnology, Academia Sinica, pp. 235–256.

Pan, Inghai [潘英海]. 2000. '"Pingpu" Consciousness in Today's Taiwan: On History and Ethnicity'. *China Perspectives*, 28 (March–April): 82–88.

Pan Ying [潘英]. 1993. 'A Short History of Plains Aborigines' [平埔族史略]. *Taiwan Wenxian*, 44(1), 113–153.

Rigger, Shelley. 2014. *Why Taiwan Matters: Small Island, Global Powerhouse*, rev. edn. Lanham, CO: Rowman & Littlefield.

Rubinstein, Murray A. 2004. 'Rethinking Taiwanese and Chinese Identity: Melissa J. Brown's Is Taiwan Chinese?' *Issues & Studies (Special Issue: Studies of Taiwan Politics)*, 40(3/4), 454–459.

Schak, David. 2005. 'Culture and Political Culture: An Anthropological View'. *Asian Studies Review*, 29(3), 301–308.

Shen, Hsiu-hua. 2006. 'Review of Is Taiwan Chinese? The Impact of Culture, Power, and Migration on Changing Identities, by Melissa J. Brown'. *Contemporary Sociology*, 35(2), 151–152.

Shen, Xingyi [沈幸儀]. 2006. 'Review of Melissa J. Brown's [評介鮑梅立] Is Taiwan Chinese? Is Taiwan Chinese? The Impact of Culture, Power, and Migration on Changing Identities by Melissa J. Brown'. *Bulletin of Academia Historica* [國史館學術集刊] 10 (December), 221–228.

Shepherd, John Robert. 1986. 'Sincized Siraya Worship of A-li-tzu'. *Bulletin of the Institute of Ethnology, Academia Sinica* [中央研究院民族學研究所集刊] 58 (Spring), 1–81.

Shepherd, John Robert. 1993. *Statecraft and Political Economy on the Taiwan Frontier, 1600–1800.* Stanford, CA: Stanford University Press.

Shepherd, Robert. 2004. 'Review of Is Taiwan Chinese? The Impact of Culture, Power, and Migration on Changing Identities, by Melissa J. Brown'. *Anthropological Quarterly*, 77(3), 611–614.

Shih, Chih-yu. 2004. 'Voting for an Ancestor?' *Issues & Studies (Special Issue: Studies of Taiwan Politics)*, 40(3/4), 488–496.

Teng, Emma Jinhua. 2013. *Eurasian: Mixed Identities in the United States, China, and Hong Kong, 1842–1943.* Berkeley: University of California Press.

Vasantkumar, Chris. 2012. 'Han at *Minzu*'s Edges: What Critical Han Studies Can Learn from China's "Little Tibet"'. In Thomas S. Mullaney, James Liebold, Stéphane Gros, and Eric ArmandVanden Bussche (eds), *Critical Han Studies: The History, Representation, and Identity of China's Majority.* Berkeley: University of California Press, pp. 234–255.

Vickers, Edward. 2010. 'History, Identity, and the Politics of Taiwan's Museums: Reflections on the DPP-KMT Transition'. *China Perspectives*, 3(2010), 92–106.

Wachman, Alan M. 2004. 'Over-identifying with Identity'. *Issues & Studies (Special Issue: Studies of Taiwan Politics)*, 40(3/4), 470–476.

Wang, Fu-chang. 2004. 'Some Reservations about Melissa J. Brown's *Is Taiwan Chinese?*' *Issues & Studies (Special Issue: Studies of Taiwan Politics)*, 40(3/4), 463–469.

Weller, Robert P. 1999. *Alternate Civilities: Democracy and Culture in China and Taiwan.* Boulder, CO: Westview Press.

Wolf, Arthur P. 1984. 'Fertility in Prerevolutionary China'. *Population and Development Review*, 10(3), 443–470.

Wolf, Arthur P. and Chieh-shan Huang. 1980. *Marriage and Adoption in China, 1845–1945.* Stanford, CA: Stanford University Press.

Woo, Franklin J. 2004. 'Review of Is Taiwan Chinese? The Impact of Culture, Power, and Migration on Changing Identities, by Melissa J. Brown'. *China Review International*, 11(1), 30–34.

Xue, Huayuan, Bocun Dai, and Mei-li Chow. 2005. *Is Taiwan Chinese? A History of Taiwanese Nationality.* Tamshui, Taiwan: Taiwan Advocates.

Yang, Dominic Meng-hsuan, and Mau-kuei Chang. 2010. 'Understanding the Nuances of *Waishengren*: History and Agency'. *China Perspectives*, 3(2010), 108–122.

Yeh, Wen-hsin (ed). 2000. *Becoming Chinese: Passages to Modernity and Beyond.* Berkeley: University of California Press.

Zhang Yaoqi [張耀錡]. 1951. *A Comparative Name List of Plains Tribes Villages* [平埔族社名對照表]. Taipei: Taiwan Province Historical Research Committee [臺灣省文獻委員會].

Zhou, Min and Hanning Wang. 2016. 'Participation in Anti-Japanese Demonstrations in China: Evidence from a Survey on Three Elite Universities in Beijing'. *Journal of East Asian Studies*, 16(3), 391–413.

9

HEALTHY DEMOCRACIES AND WELFARE POLITICS IN TAIWAN

The arguments, refinements and limitations

Joseph Wong

My first book, *Healthy Democracies: Welfare Politics in Taiwan and South Korea* (Cornell University Press), was published in 2004 (Wong 2004a). In it, I argue that, despite expectations to the contrary, industrialising Taiwan and Korea deepened their social welfare regimes, transitioning them from former welfare laggards into universal and redistributive welfare states. Though the empirical focus of the book was the political economy of health care reform, the political logic of welfare state deepening in Taiwan I presented in *Healthy Democracies* helped to explain similar social policy reforms in other areas, such as old-age income security and social care. In this respect, *Healthy Democracies* endeavoured to offer a theory of welfare state formation among late developers in Asia.

The book was motivated by an important, and until then understudied, empirical and theoretical puzzle. The welfare state literature at the time, derived mainly from Anglo-European experiences, led us to expect welfare state retrenchment. After all, this was the era of globalisation; presumed declining state capacity; increasingly segmented unions; and the demise of the political left. And yet, empirically, we saw something quite unexpected happening in Taiwan and Korea during the 1990s: the deepening, not the dismantling, of the welfare state. In fact, as I demonstrate in the book, further efforts in the late 1990s to reform and privatise the insurance carrier of the National Health Insurance (NHI) system were rebuffed, made politically impossible, despite structural pressures to retrench. The cases of Taiwan and Korea therefore presented an important puzzle that demanded an explanation. The main argument presented in the book was that democratic transition affected politics in Taiwan in ways that deepened the welfare state. *Healthy Democracies* thus recounted a basically happy story, one in which political and socio-economic equity went hand-in-hand. This chapter, over a decade later, seeks to revisit the main thesis of *Healthy Democracies*.

142 Joseph Wong

It proceeds in three parts. In the first section, I briefly review the core argument of the book, establishing the causal link between democracy and social welfare state formation in Taiwan. In section 2, I draw on subsequent work I have published (and that of others) to trace the evolution of the argument and refinements I have made to the original thesis. In the third section, I come at the core argument of the book with a very critical eye, highlighting the new challenges that have emerged in more recent years – challenges that illuminate the constraints on Taiwan's welfare state in practice, as well as the theoretical limits of *Healthy Democracies*. Specifically, I identify three contemporary challenges to the welfare state in Taiwan: rising levels of inequality, especially in the unequal distribution of wealth (rather than income); the new distributional fights between labour market 'insiders' and those employed outside formal labour markets, and the stratifying effects of extant welfare regimes; and the practical problems of delivering social welfare services efficiently and equitably to the poor, the marginalised and those who are difficult to reach.

These contemporary challenges are the focus of my current research on poverty and inequality in what can be best described as the post-welfare state political economy. Despite a critical review of my earlier work, I maintain the story I tell in *Healthy Democracies* is a justifiably happy story *for that time*, but a story that nonetheless requires fresh theoretical renovation if we are to understand the political economic pressures that are being exerted on the welfare state today.

1. From welfare laggard to welfare state

The story of Taiwan's postwar development invariably features the developmental state. Robert Wade's pioneering study of government-led industrialisation, *Governing the Market*, put Taiwan on the comparative political economy map (Wade 1990). Likewise, Stephan Haggard's *Pathways From the Periphery*, Peter Evans' *Embedded Autonomy* and Wu Yu-shan's *Comparative Economic Transformations* showed how Taiwan's developmental experience was able to overcome the presumed structural constraints of dependency theory and how Taiwan effectively transitioned to a capitalist industrial economy (Haggard 1990; Evans 1995; Wu 1994). The story of Taiwan's postwar economic development is well-trodden and need not be repeated here in depth. Rapid economic growth in Taiwan: was facilitated by a strong and capable state, one that prompted a strategic shift from import substitution industrialisation to export-oriented industrialisation; husbanded key industrial sectors and firms; fostered technological upgrading and continual industrial diversification; and, due to its authoritarian nature, maintained a disciplined labour force.

Social policy, however, does not feature centrally in Taiwan's developmental success story. And for good reason. The developmental state model was a model for postwar economic growth and not redistributive social welfare policy. Taiwan, and other late industrialising societies such as South Korea, is often considered a welfare state laggard. There is plenty of evidence to support this view. For instance, social spending, a key indicator of the state's commitment to social welfare, was very low prior to the 1990s (Chan 1997; Midgeley 1985). Cultural interpretations of Taiwanese society likewise emphasised the role played by family and kinship networks in the provision of social services, reinforcing the notion that Confucian societies were hardwired to eschew 'western' welfare state ideas (Jones 1993). And to the extent there was any social policy reform in Taiwan, much of the social policy regime was concentrated in limited social insurance schemes targeting socio-economically privileged groups, such as those serving in the military and government bureaucrats. Social insurance mechanisms were not intended to be redistributive nor were they universal. Meanwhile, social assistance programmes aimed at the very poor were primarily residual and inconsistently delivered (Ku 1997; Lin 1994). Industrialising Taiwan was not unique in these regards, as South Korea demonstrated a similar record of welfare state laggardism throughout the postwar period. Like in Taiwan, social insurance benefited government employees and formal sector workers who were by and large employed in large *chaebol* firms.

Ian Holliday contends that social policy in East Asia, including in Taiwan, served the overarching goal of aggregate economic growth. Social policy, he argues, was subsumed within the aims of growth, not redistribution (Holliday 2000). Universal programmes, notably primary and secondary education reforms launched during the 1960s, were motivated by the imperatives of labour market up-skilling. The universalisation of education in Taiwan and South Korea was understood as a kind of human capital investment rather than social policy. This point is affirmed by the World Bank in its 1993 report, demonstrating the positive impact of universal education on growth in late developing Asian economies (World Bank 1993). In terms of social insurance, benefits were limited in their coverage to only the privileged clients of the authoritarian state (see above) and economically 'productive' sectors of society. Workers employed in favoured state-owned enterprises, and later those working in large firms, benefited from social insurance. Meanwhile, self-employed workers, informal sector workers, farmers and family dependents, such as the elderly, children and the unemployed, were excluded; hence the *productivist bias* of social insurance, and the absence of redistributive social welfare policy in postwar Taiwan and Korea. The poor and vulnerable were forced to continue to rely on family and kinship networks as their social safety nets. By the late 1980s, fewer than half of Taiwan's citizens were enrolled in any form of social insurance. South Korea's developmental state did not post a much better record in terms of social policy inclusion.

Things began to change, however, during the 1990s. Social spending increased dramatically in both Taiwan and Korea. For instance, between 1980 and 2000 social security spending, as a percentage of national product, tripled in Taiwan. Beginning in the 1990s, the Taiwan government expanded coverage in health insurance, old-age income security provisions, as well as long-term care insurance. Unlike before, programmes were universal in scope, most notably with the implementation of the National Health Insurance (NHI) programme in 1995. And, even more significantly, social policy programmes were redistributive across income groups, shifting resources from the 'productive' sectors of the economy to

144 Joseph Wong

those who were earlier deemed as 'un-productive', such as dependents, the self-employed or casually employed, and the elderly. In Taiwan, the NHI's single pipe financing system ensured financial pooling. The Korean government followed suit during the late 1990s when it consolidated medical insurance funds into a single risk and financial pool. Simply put, the course of social welfare policy reform experienced an important inflection point during the 1990s, marking a transition from what was previously a productivist social policy regime towards a universal, redistributive welfare state.

Health care reform, recounted in *Healthy Democracies*, reflected this important transition. Prior to the implementation of the NHI in 1995, health benefits in Taiwan were tied to the labour insurance scheme. Labour insurance was limited in coverage to those who were formally employed and to other select beneficiaries of the state. The poor, the self-employed, and dependents were excluded. The 1995 NHI entailed, however, the creation of a universal health insurance scheme with benefits extended *to all citizens*. Within a few years of its implementation, NHI coverage was nearly 100 per cent. The programme was also extremely popular.

The NHI was publicly managed by the Bureau of National Health Insurance (BNHI), organised as a single pipe payer system. Premiums were collected by the single insurance carrier, and payments for medical benefits were redistributed across income groups and occupational categories. Premiums from the rich effectively subsidised the cost of health care for the relatively poor (Chiang and Cheng 1997). To ensure accessibility for the poor, point-of-delivery costs, such as out-of-pocket co-payments, were also minimised. As I recount in the book, efforts by the KMT government during the late 1990s to privatise the BNHI failed. The government attempted to offload from the state to the private sector. However, myriad political forces – from the opposition DPP to ruling party KMT legislators, to civil society – mounted an effective cross-class coalition to ensure the NHI remained a public entity. In short, the NHI was universal in coverage, redistributive in its effects and remained a government-managed social welfare programme.

The transformation of Taiwan's health insurance programme – and of the welfare state more generally – which began in the 1990s presented an important conundrum. The empirical evidence of what was actually going on in Taiwan did not accord with what welfare state theory at the time would have led us to expect. *Taiwan's welfare state was expanding when the rest of the world's welfare states were supposedly retrenching.* Why did Taiwan embark on a reform trajectory that deepened the welfare state, and why during the 1990s specifically? This puzzling question needed an answer, which is what *Healthy Democracies* set out to provide.

Explaining Taiwan's welfare state

One explanation for the emergence of Taiwan's nascent welfare state draws on a functionalist interpretation of Taiwan's political economic structure at the time. In this argument, the welfare state emerged during the 1990s to meet the functional imperatives that had been generated by Taiwan's postwar economic development.

Changing societies have changing needs. Indeed, modernisation and development in Taiwan entailed important structural changes that required addressing. By the 1990s, for instance, Taiwan's economy was considerably more diversified than it was during the 1970s. Society had become much more urban. Agriculture accounted for a much smaller proportion of economic productivity. Meanwhile, Taiwan was also beginning to experience the strains of hollowing out, in which its prior comparative advantages in industrial manufacturing sectors were being lost to other economies in the region. Taiwan, by the 1990s, had in many ways entered into a post-industrial phase of development, where employment was generated in widely diversified service and manufacturing sectors. The labour market in Taiwan had become increasingly segmented, resulting in growing income disparities. To be sure, inequality began to grow more pronounced during the 1990s. Though Taiwan managed the 1997 Asian Financial crisis relatively well, the downturn in the regional economy exposed its export dependence, associated with higher rates of unemployment in Taiwan, precarious employment and the incidence of poverty. Taiwan's historically low Gini coefficient began to rise.

With economic development, Taiwan's social and demographic structure had been transformed. By the 1990s, Taiwan was an aging society, with a very low fertility rate. Taiwan's net birth rate was well below the population replacement rate, resulting in a larger older population segment, comprising people who were not working but who required care. Yet, as the extended family model evolved, the number of three-generation households had declined considerably in both Taiwan and South Korea. Correspondingly, as gender norms changed and as women increasingly entered the formal labour market, combined with rising divorce rates, the number of single-female households grew as well (Peng and Wong, 2008). These social changes eroded traditional social safety nets within the family and emphasised the functional imperatives for the state to provide more inclusive social policies.

We have to be careful, however, in overstating the explanatory power of the functionalist argument in industrial East Asia. After all, the structural changes brought with industrial diversification, growing levels of inequality, and demographic shifts were evident elsewhere, such as in Latin America, other parts of Asia, and of course in Europe. And yet we did not see in other places the kind of welfare state deepening that was occurring in Taiwan and Korea. Thus, though the functionalist story is an important one to consider, and one that holds tremendous explanatory power, it alone cannot explain the emergence of Taiwan's welfare state – of why it did, when it did.

Linking democracy and welfare

In *Healthy Democracies* I identify the transition to democracy to be the key causal variable to explain the transformation of the welfare states in Taiwan and Korea. Efforts to deepen the welfare state – and the legislation of progressive policies more generally (Wong 2003) – coincided with the start of democratisation. In Korea, for instance, the

146 Joseph Wong

expansion of medical insurance to rural and urban workers occurred around the time of founding National Assembly and Presidential elections during the late 1980s. The NHI policy in Taiwan was announced in 1988, just after martial law was lifted by the KMT regime, and the NHI was implemented by the KMT government in 1995, on the eve of Taiwan's first freely contested presidential election in 1996. We know that incumbent President Lee Teng-hui implored the Legislative Yuan at the eleventh hour to pass the NHI Act in 1994 so as to not delay the implementation of the popular programme before the 1996 presidential contest; Lee sought to win votes with the NHI. The foundation for an old-age income security policy was similarly laid during the early 1990s, when candidates for both the KMT and the DPP made electoral promises to local constituencies that if elected they would push for direct subsidies to be transferred to older voters.

Elections were crucial to the politics of welfare state deepening in Taiwan. With democracy, the political incentives for both the ruling party and opposition candidates favoured a social policy reform agenda. For the opposition DPP, elections were an opportunity to diversify the issue base, with the hope of taking some votes away from KMT electoral strongholds. Prominent factions within the DPP, for instance, held to a strong social democratic ideology. From the point of view of the KMT, the transition to democracy and the institutionalisation of elections meant the ruling party had to win support, rather than rely on past practices of suppressing dissent. The KMT, as Dan Slater and I argue, drew on its developmental record from the past but also looked to develop new bases of electoral support for its redistributive promises (Slater and Wong 2013). For both parties, then, appealing to voters was critical in their efforts to assemble winning electoral coalitions. Public opinion data from that time show that welfare reform was viewed by most voters as an important policy priority. The welfare state thus proved a winning platform (Fell 2005).

Democratic transition did not only re-structure the incentives of politicians to promise welfare reform in Taiwan, it also transformed the bureaucracy. As my research in *Healthy Democracies* shows, bureaucrats had long held to a more progressive and redistributive reform agenda, though their powers to enact any such social programmes were curtailed due to the overwhelming power of the authoritarian KMT party-state regime prior to democratic transition. With democratisation, however, bureaucrats came to play a more decisive and autonomous role in social policymaking. As an institution within the state apparatus, the bureaucracy became more responsive, especially to societal actors such as social movements. Bureaucrats were also more professionalised and assertive vis-à-vis elected politicians. The bureaucracy thus gained new sources of influence in the Legislative Yuan, playing a leadership role in crafting new legislation rather than implementing programmes developed by the ruling party and the legislature.

And of course, civil society actors emerged as critical sources of political power with democratic transition. As I recount in *Healthy Democracies*, and in a 2004 article, 'Democratization and the Left', the key source of power for social movement groups in Taiwan and Korea was the development of what I call 'expert-activism' (Wong 2004b). Drawing on the knowledge of academics, technocrats and former legislators, social movement groups gained tremendous sources of expert knowledge specific to welfare reform and legislation. Consequently they were no longer simply activists looking in from the outside. Rather, their expertise gained them a seat at the policymaking table. Societal actors had an arena in which to voice their preferences. In this respect, civil society actors became key agenda-setters in social policy reform debates. In my survey work and interviews with legislators and bureaucrats in Taiwan and Korea during the late 1990s, many state elites acknowledged social movements' expertise. They also recognised how they came to rely on their civil society counterparts for assistance in drafting social policy legislation. As I recount in *Healthy Democracies*, when the KMT's efforts to privatise the BNHI failed during the late 1990s, it was a coalition of social movement expert-activists that led the charge to maintain a publicly managed medical insurance programme; legislators had little choice but to follow their lead.

The publication of *Healthy Democracies* generated many scholarly reviews of the book. Several scholars emphasised the important puzzle that the cases of Taiwan and Korea presented: the expansion of welfare states during a time of presumed retrenchment. Many echoed the key role democratic transition played in establishing the health policy reform trajectory. Some, understandably, questioned the portability of my theory and challenged the argument's applicability to cases beyond Taiwan and Korea. I was most gratified, however, by the many reviewers' affirmation of the veracity and reliability of my account of health policy change in both places. As I point out in the book, when I was conducting my fieldwork during the 1990s I had basically 'walked into' a period of intense reform. I had little secondary literature upon which to base my account. Relying on over 100 informant interviews with legislators, bureaucrats and social movement activists, I essentially pieced together the stories of reform in Taiwan and Korea. By the time Cornell University Press published in the book in 2004, I was confident of the accounts I constructed; I was pleased, nonetheless, to learn that various 'insiders' from all political camps in both places agreed with my account.

2. Refining the argument

With the publication of *Healthy Democracies*, I was – perhaps naively – convinced of the link between democratic transition and welfare state deepening. Shortly after the book was published, I was invited to speak in Chile, to a gathering of like-minded social democrats from Latin America, comprising policymakers and academics. I was hopeful – again naively – that the arguments I developed in my book would resonate with colleagues there, that they too would see the relationship between democracy and the welfare state. I was immediately made aware, however, that the causal link I drew between democracy and social policy reform did not hold in much of Latin America. Contrary to what I observed in East Asia, democracy did not bring about a welfare state in places such as Brazil, Chile and Mexico, at least not during the early 2000s. Upon situating the Taiwan case within

148 Joseph Wong

a broader comparative perspective, I was forced to refine my arguments, to both account for Taiwan's particularities and for patterns I was not seeing in other parts of the late developing world.

Fiscal capacity

My colleagues in Chile reminded me of the simple fact that Taiwan (and Korea) is rich, while Latin American countries are not. Taiwan and people in Taiwan can afford universal, redistributive, social welfare programmes such as the NHI, whereas in most of Latin America, they cannot. In their book on comparative welfare development in East Asia, Latin America and former Soviet countries, Stephan Haggard and Robert Kaufman observe that, in addition to democracy, the emergence of the welfare state in developing world contexts corresponds with strong fiscal capacity (Haggard and Kaufman 2008). Simply put, *welfare states emerged in late developing countries that had democratised and were rich*. When compared with their Latin American counterparts, the East Asian NICs enjoyed lower budget deficits, lower levels of foreign debt, and thus much lower debt servicing ratios. They had more resources – the fiscal capacity needed to finance universal social welfare programmes. In this respect, the process of welfare state development in Taiwan mirrored more closely the experiences of 'rich' postwar Japan (Kasza 2006) than it did the experiences of much poorer countries in Latin America, a point I make in a recent piece on East Asian political economy and social policy reform (Wong 2013).

Growth with equity

In addition to making it rich, a key feature of the developmental state experience in Taiwan was the fact that the distribution of income during its high growth period was relatively egalitarian, unlike in Latin America. Amidst rapid growth, the fruits of development were shared equitably in Taiwan. Several explanations account for this regional divergence.

A key distinction between the East Asia and Latin America development experiences, for instance, was land reform in the former, and the absence of such reform in most Latin American countries. Land reform during the late 1940s in Taiwan broke the landlord class, giving the developmental state more autonomy and preventing the kind of political capture of the state by the landed elite that occurred in Latin America. Moreover, early land reform encouraged more efficient agricultural productivity at the outset of the postwar period, the gains from which were used to finance Taiwan's initial industrialisation efforts. In addition, indus-trialisation in Taiwan centred on the growth of small and medium sized enterprises (SMEs), which lowered the barriers of entry to marketplace competition among small-scale commercial entrepreneurs and allowed for rapid upward socio-economic mobility. The developmental state also encouraged a full-employment strategy to absorb the labour surplus in the countryside and to ensure steady gains in household incomes. Taiwan's postwar economy thus grew between 8 and 10 per cent per year, while the distribution of income, measured by the Gini coefficient, remained around 0.3. This was consistently in-line with the Nordic welfare states, the gold standard of equitable economic growth. On the other hand, the distribution of income in Latin American countries ranked, and continues to rank, among the most unequal in the world.

The effects of growth with equity were critical with respect to the emergence of a welfare state in Taiwan. The *legacy effects* of growth with equity reduced the costs of redistribution in democratic Taiwan, making the welfare state more economically, socially and politically viable there than in its Latin American counterparts. Growth with equity reduced the costs of redistribution in three ways.

First, growth with equity narrowed the income gap in Taiwan and reduced the *economic costs* of transferring resources from the rich to the poor. In Taiwan, the gap between the haves and have-nots was simply narrower and consequently resources had much less distance to travel. Second, equitable economic growth in Taiwan mitigated the *social costs* of redistribution as well. The vast majority of Taiwanese perceive themselves to be middle class. This perception reduces the social distance between classes, making a redistributive agenda more socially viable among the majority of citizens. In highly unequal societies, on the other hand, social distance tends to be much more pronounced. Redistribution in highly socially stratified societies, such as in Latin America, not only requires the transfer of resources and wealth across income groups, but also across distinct social classes. This was mitigated in Taiwan.

Last, growth with equity reduced the *political costs* of redistribution by making social welfare programmes politically appealing across a broad distribution of voters and thus less costly for parties to attach themselves to such an agenda. In political party systems where the left and right are institutionalised and entrenched, and where voter identification maps onto the left–right spectrum, redistributive policy agendas tend to be associated with leftist parties. For parties on the right, therefore, redistributive welfare is a politically costly platform. In Taiwan, however, growth with equity nullified the left–right class cleavage and minimised the political costs for both the ruling and opposition parties to viably run on a social welfare platform. In this regard, it is significant that it was the nominally conservative KMT, and not the progressive opposition DPP, that was responsible for implementing the NHI programme in Taiwan in 1995 (Peng and Wong 2010). In January 2013, the KMT government again took the helm in launching the second-generation (2G) NHI reforms, reducing premium rates for most workers and implementing a supplementary premium for those who earned additional non-salaried incomes. The KMT touted the 2G reform as a way of reducing socio-economic disparities and financial burdens on the working poor.

Electoral competition in democratising Taiwan was structured along cleavages of identity politics and the legacies of the authoritarian regime. The social welfare policy reform agenda was neither 'owned' exclusively by the DPP or the ruling KMT. Ideological flexibility in the party system meant both parties could legitimately claim welfare reform to be their party's platform. And they did. KMT and

150 Joseph Wong

DPP politicians ratcheted up the scope of social policy reform through electoral contestation, resulting in a race to the top, rather than to the bottom (Wong 2003). Welfare state deepening came about in Taiwan in the absence of any political party programmatically committed to a leftist policy agenda. This was not only evident in the creation and evolution of Taiwan's NHI but also in other social policy initiatives such as old-age income security and, later, elderly care (Peng and Wong 2010). In other words, the birth of the welfare state in Taiwan came about despite – and arguably because of – the absence of a party on the left.

Institutional continuity

A criticism of the welfare state in Taiwan is that social welfare is by and large financed and delivered through a social insurance mechanism; Taiwan's welfare regime is not the same as the Nordic welfare state, in which redistributive programmes are financed by general tax revenues and delivered by the government. Critics point to the fact that Taiwan's social policy regime remains structured along Bismarck-ian social insurance lines, rather than adhering to the Nordic model (Esping-Andersen 1993), a criticism made of the Japanese welfare state as well (Kasza 2006). This observation is not untrue. To be sure, early on during the authoritarian period, labour insurance schemes were implemented, as critics argue, to selectively benefit clients of the state and, later, those employed in the formal sector. Furthermore, labour insurance funds were maintained separately, with little redistribution or cross-subsidisation among them. Risk and financial pooling were minimised, and those excluded from the limited social insurance programmes had no protection at all. As mentioned earlier in this chapter, by the 1980s less than half the population in Taiwan was covered by any form of social insurance.

The development of the welfare state during the 1990s, I argue in *Healthy Democracies*, resulted from the expansion of the social insurance model and, in the case of health insurance, the eventual universal coverage provided by the NHI programme. Critics are therefore correct in pointing out that universalisation was achieved through coverage expansion, with minimal structural change to the basic social insurance model. They point to institutional continuity in Taiwan's social policy regime, and conclude that what I argue to be a welfare state is in practice a chimera, a patchwork of social insurance schemes that falls short of the ideal welfare state.

Ito Peng and I, in a 2008 *Politics and Society* article, argue that the decision to expand existing social insurance structure was ideal *for Taiwan* for several reasons (Peng and Wong 2008). For one, the expansion of the social insurance model provided a quick route to universal coverage. Second, expansion and replication of pre-existing social insurance schemes lowered the transaction costs of policy reform. To have dismantled entirely the social insurance structure and replaced it wholesale with another model of social welfare financing and delivery, such as a copy of the Nordic welfare state, would have been prohibitively costly in terms of political capital, time and resources. Because social policy reform was driven, as I

Healthy Democracies revisited   151

argue, by political incentives and an electoral logic, minimising the costs of reform and expediting the reform process were critical if the government was to benefit from the political payoff of social policy reform. Structural and institutional change was difficult, and thus it made the most political sense for the Taiwan government (both the KMT and DPP administrations) to pursue a reform path to universal coverage with the least resistance.

However, Peng and I are also explicit in our argument that the absence of institutional change to the social insurance model does not preclude changing the *institutional purpose* of social insurance. Building upon the work of historical-institutional theorists such as Kathleen Thelen, Paul Pierson and James Mahoney (Thelen 2004; Pierson 2004; Mahoney 2000), we argue that over the longer term, and in the absence of abrupt institutional destruction and reconstruction, it is possible that evolutionary change in the so-called margins can nonetheless bring about *fundamental change to an institution's purpose*. The purposes of social insurance during the postwar period had evolved. We show that throughout the 1970s and 1980s the gradual but exclusionary expansion of social insurance adhered to an 'additive' reform logic – the addition of new enrollees into an existing social insurance model. During this period, the array of social insurance programmes in Taiwan was not intended to be universal in scope or redistributive. Their institutional purpose, we argue, was to be selective and exclusive. By the 1990s, however, the creation of the NHI reflected not only the universal reach of social insurance coverage but more fundamentally a change in the purpose of social insurance: from selective and exclusionary coverage to *universal and redistributive* coverage. The single pipe financing and payment system in the NHI was intended to increase risk and financial pooling across different occupational categories and income groups. The point is that, whereas earlier on social insurance stratified society, by the 1990s the impetuses for social welfare reform were *both* universalism and redistribution. The institutional purposes of social insurance had changed.

3. Resilience?

Healthy Democracies tells a happy story, and indeed, the book ends on a happy note. I conclude by writing (in 2004): 'For those concerned about the future of the welfare state and issues of socioeconomic redistribution, the recent social policy developments in democratizing Taiwan and South Korea give reason for optimism' (Wong 2004a). I expected welfare state resilience in Taiwan for several reasons. As Paul Pierson shows in his work on advanced industrial democracies, institutional path dependency makes it difficult to dismantle welfare state institutions (Pierson 1994). Too many entrenched political, economic and social interests become invested in extant arrangements, making them resilient. The same could be said of Taiwan's emerging welfare state, as evidenced by the KMT government's failed attempts to privatise the Bureau of National Health Insurance during the late 1990s. I was optimistic also because of what I argued was the normative mainstreaming of social welfare; that despite being a Confucian society, people in

152 Joseph Wong

Taiwan had come to *expect* the state to deliver social welfare programmes. I saw such ideational path dependency as another source of welfare state resilience. And, last, I saw the resilience of Taiwan's welfare state because I anticipated the ability of social policymakers to continually reform the institutional purposes of social policy, preserving the institutional form of social insurance while extending the redistributive capacity of the existing insurance schemes. I did not foresee significant change.

That was then, however. Looking ahead, I see significant challenges to Taiwan's welfare state in practice, as well as our theories to explain welfare state evolution in the contemporary era. My current research focuses on these challenges. Though my present work does not look specifically at the case of Taiwan, the new and significant pressure points on the welfare state that I see evident elsewhere mirror what is currently going on in Taiwan. What follows in this last section is a more general discussion of these emerging political economic pressures and how they affect Taiwan's welfare state. As it was in *Healthy Democracies*, the case of Taiwan presents opportunities to make important empirical observations and to do some creative theoretical work.

Inequality

The popular media has captured an important story in contemporary Taiwan: the continual rise in inequality. Everything from reactions to ECFA, to the Sunflower Movement, and to the emergence of new political parties is rooted in both perceived and real increases in inequality in Taiwan. The fact of the matter is that *income inequality* has risen in Taiwan. In 1989, the 80:20 earnings ratio[1] was 5.18 (meaning the top quintile earned 5.18 times more than the bottom 80 per cent), while in 2010 the 80:20 ratio had grown to 7.72, an increase of nearly 50 per cent in less than two decades (Chi and Kwon 2012: 904–905). In another study, using different data, the ratio of the top income quintile to the bottom quintile rose from 4.9 in 1989 to 6.2 in 2010. The Gini coefficient, a measure of wages and other income earnings, has also increased during that time period, from around 0.3 to 0.34.[2] Regardless of what data is used, all studies show an increase in income inequality.

But while earnings disparities have increased quite dramatically in a very short time in Taiwan, the redistributive effect of the government – notably through income taxation – has actually been quite effective. Whereas the pre-tax (and thus pre-transfer) 80:20 income ratio increased by nearly 40 per cent during the 1990s and into the first decade of the 2000s, the post-tax (and thus post-transfer) 80:20 disposable income ratio grew by just 15 per cent, meaning that over 60 per cent of the growth in pre-tax income inequality is mitigated through government taxes and transfers. In this regard, Taiwan performs comparatively well in reducing inequality (of disposable income) through state mechanisms (Chi and Kwon 2012).

The challenge, as I see it, is not so much in rising levels of measurable income inequality, but instead the quickly growing levels of *wealth inequality*. The first thing that needs to be pointed out is that measures such as the 80:20 ratio and the Gini are calculated from *reported* income and earnings. This means that such measures capture earnings, and specifically only those earnings from formally reported activities. Much is thus missed in the data. For instance, it is estimated in China that while the disparity between the top and bottom quintiles in reported incomes is a ratio of about 7:1, the ratio increases to about 20:1 when factoring in estimates of unreported income (Credit Suisse 2010). Thus, a much better indicator of perceived and real inequality is wealth inequality, which takes into account unreported income as well as earnings from equities, real estate, offshore investments and so on. Wealth inequality is most certainly on the rise in Taiwan and its conspicuousness is a source of political grievance.

Related to wealth inequality is the effect of wealth disparity on *consumption inequality*. The logic here is that those with more disposable income and other sources of (unreported) wealth are able to consume more and spend more. Through their increased consumption, which has a marginal effect on their overall stock of resources, consumer prices in the aggregate are raised. When prices rise, the marginal cost to consume for lower income earners is much higher. Real estate property values demonstrate the problem of consumption inequality well. For the rich, the marginal cost of purchasing a home at $1 million is low, given their stock of assets and earnings. But by making such purchases, the average cost of real estate goes up for all consumers. The middle-class consumer or the lower income earner must pay a higher price for a home, but for whom the cost, as a proportion of their household income and assets, is considerably higher. This consumption cascading effect is particularly pronounced for lower income earners, for whom the purchase of a home would either be financially debilitating or impossible. This is happening in Taiwan. The 'home price to income ratio' (PIR) increased in Taipei from 6:1 in 2002 to over 15:1 in 2013. In just one decade, the price to purchase a home increased 2.5 times more quickly than the rise in wages, disproportionately affecting lower income earners and exacerbating levels of consumption inequality.

What does all of this mean for the welfare state? A lot. The modern welfare state derives its fiscal resources from reported income. The welfare state, at its core, is a mechanism for the redistribution of income, not wealth, and certainly not market-based consumption. The fiscal model of the welfare state is thus predicated on the extraction and redistribution of resources that it can *fiscally see*, which is reported incomes and earnings generated primarily from the formal sector. It is much less effective, if at all, in redistributing wealth, and in market economies it has little redistributive effect on consumption inequality. Practically, this means the policy instruments of the welfare state need to be re-thought, expanded even. For example, Taiwan is considering (though the government has found it difficult to effectively implement) capital gains taxes and more accurate measures of wealth and income generated from self-employment. From a theoretical perspective, the compounded problem of income, wealth and consumption *inequalities* renders the welfare state an institutional anachronism.

Insiders and outsiders

The political economic logic of the welfare state's evolution is one that historically privileged formal sector workers. Recall that the welfare state first emerged in a specific historical moment: the rise of the industrial factory system. Industrial workers were employed in factories. They were formal sector workers, organised into trade unions. Wage disparities at the time were relatively small, meaning workers' preferences were uniform. Welfare state beneficiaries wanted job security and higher wages. Workers were collectively mobilised through unions and, where possible, allied with social democratic parties. The welfare state literature has long shown a positive and robust correlation between union density, union size and the presence of a social democratic party with the generosity of the welfare state. Formal sector wage earners thus benefited from the welfare state because they were labour market 'insiders'. But they also contributed to what we now see to be the stratifying effects of social welfare regimes. Labour market 'insiders' remain the welfare state's beneficiaries, while labour market 'outsiders' have been excluded (Rueda 2007).

But whereas in the past the welfare state was primarily, if not solely, concerned with formal sector workers, and thus insiders, the fact of the matter is that labour markets are increasingly segmented, dualised, along insider–outsider lines (Emmenegger et al. 2012). Formal sector workers are decreasing in number, while other kinds of workers – those who are informally or casually employed, part-time, or contract workers – are growing. The vast majority of new jobs created in OECD countries over the past two decades, for instance, have been in non-formal kinds of employment. It is expected that over half of all jobs in the club of rich nations will be non-formal. Simply put, labour market *qua* welfare state outsiders will soon constitute the majority of wage earners. The situation in contemporary Taiwan is no different. Already an economy in which a disproportionate share of wage earners are classified as self-employed, formal sector labour markets in Taiwan, such as in manufacturing, are rapidly shrinking. Young people, whose pessimism and restlessness were on full display in the recent Sunflower Movement, have little reason to be optimistic about their future employment prospects. They represent, potentially, an entire generation of welfare state outsiders.

The presence of insiders and outsiders directly impacts the political economy of the welfare state. The conflict between insiders and outsiders rests with their divergent interests and preferences, as well as their abilities to politically mobilise. On the one hand, labour market insiders continue to look to the welfare state for job security and wages. Insiders are also well organised (usually into trade unions or professional associations) and able to collectively mobilise. Outsiders, on the other hand, have different preferences. They turn to the welfare state for measures that promote labour market flexibility in the hopes that new jobs can be created. They prefer active labour market policies that disrupt the labour market status quo. In other words, job security, the key preference for insiders, is precisely what outsiders seek to dismantle. Organisationally, outsiders are at a disadvantage as well. Because they prefer flexibility, they are less likely to collectively mobilise. And because they are not organised formally, outsiders constantly confront collective action problems such as free riding (Rueda 2007).

The conflict between insiders and outsiders poses enormous political challenges, especially to political parties. Historically, social democratic parties have represented the interests of organised workers, in part because such labour market insiders have been well organised, and in part because of left parties' normative commitment to equity and egalitarianism. But whose interests do social democratic parties represent today – insiders' or outsiders'? David Rueda, in his work on OECD countries, finds that social democratic governments have continued to favour welfare state insiders because they are better organised and able to deliver the political payoff (electoral support) to the government. Outsiders, he finds, are excluded.

The context in Taiwan, for reasons I described earlier in this chapter, does not map directly onto the political economic scenario I have just laid out for the OECD, not least because the party system in Taiwan is not structured along the left–right continuum. But the conflict between welfare state and labour market insiders and outsiders is increasingly evident in Taiwan, sharpening new political cleavages among generational cohorts, occupations, gender and income groups. On the one hand, we might expect a partisan realignment among the main political parties to account for these new constituent bases and potentially winnable cleavages. Yet, on the other hand, we also have reason to expect, as we have seen in other places, that insider–outsider conflict will exacerbate inequalities, as outsiders are excluded from the welfare state and from politics more generally (i.e. the frustrations contributing to the Sunflower Movement). We can imagine, therefore, the redistributive welfare state in Taiwan becoming an instrument for stratification rather than socio-economic equity.

Reaching the unreached

The ideal universal redistributive welfare state is one that is supposed to benefit *all* citizens. The National Health Insurance (NHI) programme, as with any welfare program, is intended to equalise opportunities (in this case, for health) for all citizens through the redistribution of resources. And I argue in *Healthy Democracies* that the NHI was effective in this regard. But consider these facts. In Taiwan, aboriginal men live, on average, 10 fewer years than others – this despite the universal enrolment of all citizens in the NHI and increased access to the health care system. Yet, we also know that aboriginal men do not utilise the NHI as often as others, and that they tend to enter into the health care system much later on, when otherwise preventable conditions have become more acute or incurable. We also know the social determinants of health matter a great deal in terms of aboriginal health status. Consider also that despite the introduction of the NHI and its positive effect on utilisation rates of health care among those previously uninsured, this effect is less pronounced among rural elderly people. Despite greater access to health care facilities, older people in the countryside tend not to access the health system as frequently, constrained for instance by distance to the clinic, poverty and the lack of medical specialists (Liao, Chang and Ma 2012). Another study shows that while the NHI corresponded with an increase in health care utilisation among the elderly, especially in lower-income households, the health status of the elderly did not significantly improve, suggesting public health and preventative interventions remain insufficient and the social determinants of health are neglected (Chen et al. 2007).

These facts reveal an important limitation of the welfare state in Taiwan: the inability of the state to 'reach' those most difficult to reach, such as the impoverished, those living in hard-to-reach places, the elderly, aboriginals, migrants and the socially marginalised. By reach, I mean the actual delivery (as distinct from the supply-side provision) of social services to those they are intended to reach. In some cases, such as with the rural elderly, the problem of reach is a challenge of coverage over large spatial distances. In other cases, such as aboriginal health in Taiwan, the problem of reach is one of cultural dissonance, even ignorance, making it difficult for health interventions designed in Taipei to reach aboriginal communities. Yet in other cases, the problem of multi-dimensional poverty (i.e. slums in urban centers) makes certain segments of the population difficult to reach. If the welfare state is to be universal and redistributive, it has to reach those who are most difficult to reach (Wong 2015).

Reaching the unreached, as a principled objective of the welfare state, is easy to affirm. Who, after all, would deny such an aspiration? However, the empirical evidence suggests that reaching those most difficult to reach is costly. This point is significant. It is often presumed that the replication (i.e. universalisation) of services will achieve some economies of scale, and consequently a reduction in the cost per unit (or enrollee or intervention). Simple economics tells us that as welfare provision is expanded, the marginal cost of such expansion should decrease. But the reality is that reaching the difficult-to-reach is expensive, and the marginal cost of enrolling or reaching each additional person or providing each additional intervention actually increases, a point made recently by the WHO.

For example in 1997 the Taiwan BNHI piloted the Health Care Improvement Program (HCIP) to reach those living in rural and/or mountainous regions. The HCIP financed a fixed clinic in the A-Li mountain district. The pilot project was successful as utilisation rates among the 5,000 residents increased in the district. However, the BNHI injected an additional 7 million NTD per year for the clinic, with an average cost of over 1,400 NTD per person (Tan et al. 2005). Expansion and reach, in this case, did not translate into economies of scale and a reduction in cost; rather, reaching those 5,000 people in the A-Li district cost the BNHI more per person. The value of HCIP and the positive health effects of A-Li clinic are undisputable. But that reach is not without its costs. The HCIP example illustrates a fundamental political–economic tension in the welfare state: on the one hand, effective welfare states need to reach the unreached, yet, on the other, reaching is very costly, economically and potentially politically as well. The point is that if the welfare state in Taiwan continues to aspire to be universal in its reach and redistributive in its effects, then proponents of such a welfare state – politicians, bureaucrats, social movements – must also square the political and economic costs of reaching those who have been excluded.

Conclusion

Allow me to return to the publication of *Healthy Democracies*; it was the starting point of this chapter and the impetus for the preceding reflections.

I was relieved in 2004 that the general reception of the book was, by and large, positive. Most agreed I had gotten the 'story straight'. Some felt, quite rightly, the democracy angle was a bit overstated. Others felt I was stretching a bit when I implied democracy in other regions could result in similar welfare state outcomes. And many pointed out the particularities of the Taiwan (and South Korean) case, which made Taiwan uniquely positioned to deepen its welfare state at a time when the prevailing conventional wisdom predicted retrenchment. I was forced to do more comparative work, drawing on examples beyond East Asia. As I have recounted in this chapter, I have attempted to address these criticisms, in part by making more modest claims about the generalisability of the story I tell in *Healthy Democracies*, and also in part by doing more empirical and theoretical work on the East Asian cases. I made my arguments in 2004, and since the publication of the book I have continued to refine those arguments.

One criticism that I was unable to respond to, however, is one that has stuck with me. Some critics of the book were very dissatisfied with the happy story I tell. As it was pointed out, welfare reform was indeed a happy story for the vast majority of people living in Taiwan, but there remained a minority for whom the story was not so happy. Put another way, most came to enjoy the benefits of the emerging welfare state in Taiwan – most, but not all. Many were left out. At the time, I paid little attention to this criticism as I felt an account of how a welfare laggard had transitioned into a welfare state was one that ought to be celebrated. On balance, I felt the story was a happy one.

I fear I was quick to dismiss, and that the critics of the book drew attention to an important puzzle I was unwilling to deal with at the time. But that puzzle is precisely what I am concerned with now. And though those criticisms of *Healthy Democracies* were the most biting, they were also the most illuminating of the challenges facing the contemporary welfare state. I have attempted to account for these in this chapter: rising inequality and poverty; insider–outsider conflict; and the imperatives of reaching those most difficult to reach. But as I also point out in this chapter, the challenges of this contemporary period are ones that cannot be resolved, as they were over a decade ago; that welfare state is anachronistic when one considers that inequality is different today; poverty is more pronounced; outsiders are increasingly the norm; and the marginalised are unreached. Taiwan's welfare state is thus on a new path, one that I am hopeful *Healthy Democracies* has historically informed, but a path I fear the book has little to offer by way of any solutions, in practice and in theory.

158 Joseph Wong

Notes

1 The 80:20 ratio is the earnings ratio between the top income quintile to the income earned by the remaining income quintiles.
2 It should be noted that measures of inequality are terribly imprecise from one study to another. Hence, one should not read the data from different studies as being directly comparable, as measures and data have likely varied by study. However, what is important for our purposes in this paper is the *change in inequality over time within a study*. Presuming each study calculates inequality consistently over time (though not necessarily consistently across studies), then we can assume the data presented here demonstrates the direction and magnitude of change between 1989 and 2010.

References

Chan, Steve. 1997. 'Democracy and Inequality: Tracking Welfare Spending in Singapore, Taiwan and South Korea'. In Manus Midlarsky (ed.), *Inequality, Democracy and Economic Development*. Cambridge: Cambridge University Press, 227–243.

Chen, Likwang, *et al*.2007. 'The Effects of Taiwan's NHI on Access and Health Status of the Elderly'. *Health Economics*, 16(3), 223–242.

Chiang, Tung-liang and Shou-hsia Cheng. 1997. 'The Effect of Universal Health Insurance on Health Care Utilization in Taiwan'. *Journal of the American Medical Association*, 278(2), 89–93.

Chi, Eunju and Hyeok Yong Kwon. 2012. 'Unequal New Democracies in East Asia: Rising Inequality and Government Responses in South Korea and Taiwan'. *Asian Survey*, 52(5), 900–923.

Credit Suisse. 2010. 'Analyzing Chinese Grey Income'. Asia Pacific/China Equity Report.

Emmenegger, P.*et al*. (eds). 2012. *The Age of Dualization: The Changing Face of Inequality in Deindustrializing Societies*. Oxford: Oxford University Press.

Esping-Andersen, Gosta. 1993. *Three Worlds of Welfare Capitalism*. Princeton, NJ: Princeton University Press.

Evans, Peter. 1995. *Embedded Autonomy: States and Industrial Transformation*. Princeton NJ: Princeton University Press.

Fell, Dafydd. 2005. *Party Politics in Taiwan: Party Change and Democratic Evolution of Taiwan, 1991–2004*. London: Routledge.

Haggard, Stephan. 1990. *Pathways from the Periphery: the Politics of Growth in the Newly Industrialized Countries*. Ithaca: Cornell University Press.

Haggard, Stephan and Robert Kaufman. 2008. *Development, Democracy and Welfare States: Latin America, East Asia and Eastern Europe*. Princeton, NJ: Princeton University Press.

Holliday, Ian. 2000. 'Productivist Welfare Capitalism: Social Policy in East Asia'. *Political Studies*, 48(4), 706–723.

Jones, Catherine. 1993. 'The Pacific Challenge: Confucian Welfare States'. In Catherine Jones (ed.), *New Perspectives on the Welfare State in Europe*. London: Routledge, 198–217.

Kasza, Gregory. 2006. *One World of Welfare Capitalism: Japan in Comparative Perspective*. Ithaca: Cornell University Press.

Ku, Yeun-wen. 1997. *Welfare Capitalism in Taiwan: State, Economy and Social Policy*. Basingstoke: Macmillan.

Liao, Pei-an, Hung-hao Chang and Fang-an Ma. 2012. 'Does the Universal Health Insurance Program Affect Urban-rural Differences in Health Service Utilization Among the Elderly? Evidence from a Longitudinal Study in Taiwan'. *The Journal of Rural Health*, 28(1), 84–93.

Lin, Wan-i. 1994. *The Welfare State: A Historical-Comparative Analysis*. Taipei: Great Current Press (in Chinese).

Mahoney, James. 2000. 'Path Dependence in Historical Sociology'. *Theory and Society*, 29(4), 507–548.

Midgeley, James. 1985. 'Industrialization and Welfare: the Case of the Four Little Tigers'. *Social Policy and Administration*, 20(3), 225–238.

Peng, Ito and Joseph Wong. 2010. 'East Asia'. In Frances Castle*set al.* (eds), *Oxford Handbook of the Welfare State*. Oxford University Press, 656–671.

Peng, Ito and Joseph Wong. 2008. 'Institutions and Institutional Purpose: Continuity and Change in East Asian Social Policy'. *Politics and Society*, 36(1), 61–88.

Pierson, Paul. 2004. *Politics in Time: History, Institutions and Social Analysis*. Princeton, NJ: Princeton University Press.

Pierson, Paul. 1994. *Dismantling the Welfare State? Reagan, Thatcher and the Politics of Retrenchment*. Cambridge: Cambridge University Press.

Rueda, David. 2007. *Social Democracy Inside-Out: Partisanship and Labor Market Policy in Industrialized Countries*. Oxford: Oxford University Press.

Slater, Dan and Joseph Wong. 2013. 'The Strength to Concede: Ruling Parties and Democratization in Developmental Asia'. *Perspectives on Politics*, 11(3), 717–733.

Tan, Hsiu-fen, *et al.*2005. 'Accessibility Assessment of the Health Care Improvement Program in Rural Taiwan'. *The Journal of Rural Health*, 21(4), 372–377.

Thelen, Kathleen. 2004. *How Institutions Evolve: the Political Economy of Skills in Germany, Britain, the United States and Japan*. Cambridge: Cambridge University Press.

Wade, Robert. 1990. *Governing the Market: Economic Theory and the Role of Government in East Asian Industrialization*. Princeton, NJ: Princeton University Press.

Wong, Joseph. 2003. 'Deepening Democracy in Taiwan'. *Pacific Affairs*, 76(2), 235–256.

Wong, Joseph. 2004a. *Healthy Democracies: Welfare Politics in Taiwan and South Korea*. Ithaca: Cornell University Press.

Wong, Joseph. 2004b. 'Democratization and the Left: Comparing East Asia and Latin America'. *Comparative Political Studies*, 37(10), 1213–1237.

Wong, Joseph. 2013. 'From Developmental States to Welfare States'. In Larry Diamond*et al.* (eds), *Democracy in East Asia: A New Century*. Baltimore, MD: Johns Hopkins University Press, 31–47.

Wong, Joseph. 2015. 'Achieving Universal Health Coverage'. *Bulletin of the World Health Organization*, 93, 663–664.

World Bank. 1993. *The East Asian Miracle*. New York: Oxford University Press.

Wu, Yu-shan. 1994. *Comparative Economic Transformations: Mainland China, Hungary, the Soviet Union and Taiwan*. Palo Alto, CA: Stanford University Press.

10

PEKING OPERA AND POLITICS IN TAIWAN REVISITED

Nancy Guy

My introduction to Peking opera came over the course of the 1982–1983 academic year, which I spent in Taipei as an undergraduate student studying Mandarin Chinese at National Taiwan Normal University's Mandarin Training Center on a scholarship from the Republic of China's (ROC) Ministry of Education (MOE). Even as an undergraduate student, I thought that I might be heading for a career as an ethnomusicologist; therefore, I took the year in Taiwan, which was between my junior and senior years of university, to survey all manner of traditional performing arts. I attended quite a few Peking opera performances over the course of my ten months in Taiwan and was instantly smitten with the art form's visual beauty – the vibrant costumes, makeup, and stunning acrobatics. I had not yet fallen in love with the music – that would come later.

Back in the early 1980s there were five full-time professional Peking opera troupes in Taiwan. The Ministry of Defense supported four of these while the Ministry of Education maintained its own troupe. Between these organisations, Peking opera shows were held almost every evening at the China Armed Forces Literature and Art Activities Center in central Taipei, just a few blocks from the Presidential Palace and other buildings housing governmental offices. That I was watching military supported troupes in an armed forces theatre seemed in keeping with the general atmosphere in Taiwan under martial law. It was not uncommon in those days to see armed soldiers standing guard in front of buildings in this part of town as I rode the bus to and from the theatre.

When I returned to Taiwan in early 1987, to conduct the field research for my MA thesis, my main interest revolved around the melodic consistency and variation involved in Peking opera performance, which was practised primarily as an oral tradition in Taiwan at that time. It was not long before my focus centred on an actor, Ma Yuqi, who had been born and trained in mainland China. He was a student of Ye Shenglan, a renowned performer of the *xiaosheng* (young male) role type. Ma had been living in Hong Kong long enough to have gained a Hong

Kong passport, which made his travel to Taiwan possible. These were the days before the ban on travel between China and Taiwan had been lifted. The first time this was legally possible, albeit in a limited way, was in November 1987, when people from Taiwan who still had relatives living in the mainland could visit China. The point of reviewing this history is that Taiwan's Peking opera tradition, transplanted to the island along with the Nationalist regime in the late 1940s existed in relative isolation from Peking opera and its turbulent mid-century developments in China. The arrival of Ma Yuqi in late 1986 caused quite a stir. He performed as the invited guest with several of Taiwan's state-supported troupes. At a time when local artists sometimes performed before half empty houses, Ma's performances were consistently sold out. I bought a ticket to one of his shows from a scalper (or *huangniu*, lit. 'yellow cow') at a considerably marked up price. Newspapers reported the outbreak of 'Ma Yuqi Fever' (Ma Yuqi *re*). In reporting on Ma, my MA thesis did not take into account the political environment, or that the nature of cross-strait relations was fundamentally responsible for his instant fame in Taiwan. My interests were exclusively on the music.

With my PhD dissertation, however, which was the precursor to my book *Peking Opera and Politics in Taiwan* (Guy 2005), I laid bare the political forces that had shaped Peking opera's development in Taiwan. When I headed to Taiwan in 1991 to conduct the field research for my dissertation, I intended to study the creative practice involved in the composition and performance of newly written Peking operas. While for many decades much of the repertoire presented by the island's Peking opera troupes had been composed of traditional repertoire (i.e., works created prior to 1949 in China), Taiwan's artists did create a handful of new operas every year.

Given the connections that I had already established in the island's Peking opera world, I felt that Taiwan was a perfectly viable site to conduct my study of creative practice. What I discovered shortly after my arrival, however, was that a recent loosening of restrictions on contact between Taiwan and China had resulted in Taiwan-based troupes commissioning works from mainland artists. They were also copying 'lock, stock, and barrel' recent mainland productions from videos, which were now freely circulating in Taiwan. There appeared to be a virtual, though undeclared, moratorium on creating new operas from scratch (i.e., by that I mean without using material created by mainland artists). My dissertation topic had basically evaporated. Given this radical transformation, I turned my attention to what had caused this change. Broadening the topic further, I decided to ask how political policy had shaped Peking opera's performance tradition generally on Nationalist-controlled Taiwan. Eventually, I expanded the historical scope to include the earliest days when mainland troupes successfully toured the island during the Japanese colonial period.

How and why

My most basic research question became, 'how had the political environment shaped multiple facets of the art form as it was practised in Taiwan?' In investigating this 'how question', I looked at large- and small-scale developments from the

162   Nancy Guy

art form's institutionalisation in state-supported training schools and professional troupes, down to the details of musical practice such as how a melody could or could not be performed. Underlying the 'how question' was the pregnant question of 'why?' What motivated the Nationalist government to invest in Peking opera, especially in the years prior to the 'economic miracle' when budgetary resources were not plentiful? Following the approach Dafydd Fell employed in the reevaluation of his first book, I discuss as a conclusion to this chapter the key question of, 'so what?' In other words, I address why my examination of Peking opera on Taiwan mattered. What broader lessons about Taiwan did my study offer?

How did Taiwan's political environment affect Peking opera?

As a preface to this discussion, I must state clearly that every performing art is affected by its political environment. Autonomous art is a myth. What I did with my work was to detail the impact of the political environment on Peking opera's development in Taiwan.

In investigating the 'how question', I drew my data from a wide range of sources, including newspaper and magazine reports, several MA theses on Peking opera's history in Taiwan, interviews with performers, fans and troupe administrators, observation of many rehearsals and performances, published memoirs and government documents, primarily censorship degrees, among others sources. Employing the ethnomusicological/anthropological research method of participant/observation, I also took *jinghu* lessons from one of the island's leading *jinghu* players. *Jinghu* is the two-stringed bowed lute that serves as the leading instrument of the melodic portion of the Peking opera orchestra. My close musical relationship with my *jinghu* teacher became vital in providing me insight into the challenges faced by Taiwan's instrumentalists when they were confronted with learning to play the post-1949 mainland repertoire following the lifting of the ban on such works in 1988. Below, I discuss this issue in greater detail.

The most potent factor influencing Peking opera's development in Taiwan was its level of state support. From the 1950s through to the mid-1990s, the KMT state housed and staffed up to seven full-time troupes, and as many as four training schools. As I mentioned above, all but one of these troupes, as well as one of the schools, was under the auspices of the Ministry of Defense (MOD). The others fell under the auspices of the Ministry of Education. These state-supported troupes were charged with performing publically, primarily in Taipei, and they occasionally toured internationally. The MOD troupes also provided entertainment for the ROC's armed forces.

Keeping a tradition alive by employing its performing artists and ensuring that there is always a new generation of practitioners in training is one matter. Controlling the repertoire, and controlling the musical style with which it may be performed, is another. In chapters 4 and 5 of my book, I examined the issue of how censorship policies shaped the actual performance practice. I reported that political policies stemming from the ROC and PRC's perpetual state of civil war not only forbade contact between people from the two sides of the Taiwan Straits, but also curtailed the transference of material culture as well as the transmission of artistic knowledge. This left Taiwan's performers essentially cut off from their tradition's authoritative 'land of origin' (*fayuan di*). Anyone who entered Taiwan, particularly from Hong Kong, up through the late 1980s will recall having had the contents of their suitcases routinely scrutinised at customs for mainland Chinese-derived materials. This meant that, until 1988, it was illegal (though not impossible) for scores, librettos, musical instruments and, perhaps most importantly, audio and visual recordings to enter Taiwan from China. Performers and aficionados found ways around these restrictions sometimes, for example by bringing a cassette recording of a mainland Chinese performance to Taiwan via the United States. However, censorship policies established by the Department of Education worked most of the time to ensure that operas created in China after 1949 did not make their way to the stage (Figure 10.1).

Among the guidelines shown in Figure 10.2 is a statement that an opera must be performed according to its original, pre-1949 version, and not following a 'corrupted version created by communist bandits'. Guideline #7 (the two columns on the far left) specifically mentions that this applies to the plot, the text and the ways in which the melodies are sung.

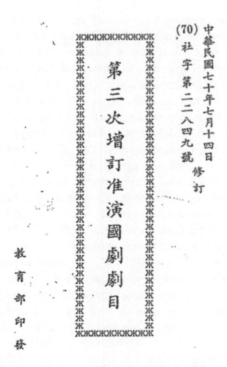

FIGURE 10.1 Cover of the 1981 decree. Jiaoyubu (Ministry of Education). 1981. *Disanci zengding zhunyan guoju jumu* (The third revised and enlarged permitted national opera titles). Taipei: Jiaoyubu Yinfa.

164 Nancy Guy

說　明

一、本次修訂之港演劇目，係以民國五十五年十二月本部頒佈暨民國六十六年十二月增訂之港演劇目為藍本，而再加修訂之。

二、凡本之主題意識，有離經叛道、違反倫常、淹沒人性或失敗主義過濃厚者，概予禁演，概不列入。

三、較生冷之劇目，其有藝術可資參考者，均予列入。

四、凡本戲中之一折改散折、醫俠上屬常情一齣單元、獨立派出，且有其專用劇名者，均予重複列入，以便查考（如見女英雄傳、社麟劇內之註明「包括紅柳村、悅米店、能仁寺……」）。

五、凡本戲之內容，可以分成若干片段，每一片段，有其習從使用之名稱者，均在個劇名內，予以註明。

六、申諸上演時，本港演劇目所有各劇，自即附屬本劇之劇本，其本屬列入者，無論為舊有或新編，均視劇目所列各劇，屬本劇之演唱為準，始得上演。

七、本港演劇目所有各劇，臨照原本演唱，其遇共匪改竄者，不得照其改竄本（包括唱詞、同句及臨詞）演唱。

FIGURE 10.2 The first seven of fourteen guidelines that preface the 1981 censorship decree. Jiaoyubu (Ministry of Education). 1981. *Disanci zengding zhunyan guoju jumu* (The third revised and enlarged permitted national opera titles). Taipei: Jiaoyubu Yinfa.

The state of separation imposed by travel bans and censorship degrees had grave consequences for the health of the tradition. While we may think of Peking opera as an art form whose main repertoire is composed of traditional works, in fact, in its heyday in the early twentieth century, it was a vibrant art form with new, often experimental repertoires being created regularly as vehicles for showcasing the strengths of its virtuosic artists. The lack of access to mainland librettists, composer/musicians or singers meant that the resources available to Taiwan's performers, such as playwrights, were limited to a very small number of artists and intellectuals who were well versed in Peking opera's scriptwriting conventions and performance practices. Qi Rushan, a prolific scholar, playwright and artistic advisor to Mei Lanfang (a male performer of female roles who was easily the most famous Peking opera performer in the twentieth century), followed the KMT to Taiwan. Writing in late 1960, Qi noted that most librettists in Taiwan had little knowledge of Peking opera and wrote scripts mainly to enter competitions. Qi claimed that these compositions were 'far from satisfying, and could never be described as brilliant. Consequently, all of the operas are just performed once or twice, and if they are staged again, no one goes to see them' (Qi 1979: 2762). This situation persisted with only a few exceptions (such as with the works of scholar and librettist Wang An-ch'i) until the late 1980s, when a major shift in policy restored contact with the mainland.

In March 1988, Taiwan's Peking opera world witnessed a seismic change with the lifting of the ban on operas created in the post-1949 mainland (provided that they met certain criteria). This new openness followed massive changes in the political climate, which began with the lifting of martial law in July 1987 and continued in late 1987 with the removal of the ban on travel to the mainland. This policy shift had enormous consequences for Taiwan's Peking opera world. I discussed these in chapter 6, 'The Musical Legacy of Isolation, the Shock of Reunification'. As I mentioned earlier, Taiwan's

Peking opera's development on Taiwan involved: 1) the degree to which the

troupes were eager to explore the repertoire that had been created in the mainland during their nearly four decades of state-imposed isolation; they even started commissioning mainland artists (including librettists, composers, set and costume designers, etc.) to compose new works for them. These mainland-created operas represented the majority of major new productions staged in the years immediately following this shift in policy.

Turbulent changes in China's own political environment (which are too numerous to mention here), had resulted in the creation of a performance style that was distinct from the pre-1949 style in several key ways: the melodies were ornamented and elaborated to a far greater degree than in the old repertoire; the more complicated melodies and harmonies required the use of written musical notation for instrumentalists. These factors, among others, caused significant difficulty for some of Taiwan's performers, especially middle-aged and senior players of melodic instruments, many of whom had little experience performing from musical notation. I observed these difficulties when I attended rehearsals of these new works. I also had numerous in-depth discussions of the situation with my *jinghu* teacher, who was himself struggling to learn and play in this new musical style.

To sum up, the two most fundamental ways in which the political environment impacted Peking opera's development on Taiwan involved: 1) the degree to which the state perpetuated the tradition primarily through the operation of professional troupes and training schools; and, 2) policies aimed at controlling the repertoire (including both what operas could be staged and how they could be performed with a special focus on melodic style), and controlling the influx of creative ideas, materials and artists. In the period under my examination, these policies were shaped most significantly by the ROC's political reactions to developments in mainland China, and to changes in cross-Strait relations.

The 'why question'

It appeared to me back when I was doing my original research (and still today), that the answer to 'why' the KMT chose to support and control Peking opera on Taiwan was rather transparent. Why the state dismantled many of its decades-old institutions in the mid-1990s was equally easy to diagnose. In my study, I asserted that it was Peking opera's potency as a symbol of Chinese culture that led the KMT to enlist the art form to promote the regime's political goals. And, it was largely the strength of Peking opera's Chinese identity, perpetuated for decades by the KMT, that made it vulnerable to attack in a democratising Taiwan.

In chapter 2, 'The Search for International Recognition', I traced the begins of the use of Peking opera as a potent and efficacious symbol of 'Chineseness' to early twentieth-century China when Qi Rushan and others helped Mei Lanfang package Peking opera for the gaze of foreign dignitaries in China. One of the earliest of these highly curated encounters took place in the banquet hall of the ROC's Ministry of Foreign Affairs in 1915. Before long, with the financial backing of Shanghai bankers, this circle of artists and intellectuals prepared Mei for his wildly successful 1930 tour of the United States.

After the 1949 split, Peking opera became an agent of soft power employed by both Chinese regimes in their international battle for legitimacy. Foreign tours to

166 Nancy Guy

Europe, the UK and the United States provided the most high-profile vehicles for this competition. From the KMT's perspective, they expected Peking opera, in its traditional 1949 form, to communicate the notion that they were the protector of Chinese culture, and hence the legitimate Chinese government, albeit in exile on Taiwan. This message also had currency domestically where the KMT needed to assert its right to minority rule. I took up this issue in chapter 3, 'Peking Opera in the Service of State Ideology'. Within Taiwan, the KMT aimed to develop a 'Chinese consciousness' (as opposed to a 'Taiwan consciousness') in the native Taiwanese citizenry through multiple policies, including increasing the exposure of the general population to Peking opera. The KMT devised several programmes aimed at strengthening and perpetuating Chinese culture (by this I mean a conglomeration of Confucian principles, Sun Yat-sen's philosophy and symbolically Chinese arts). The first of these was the New Literature and Arts Movement, which they initiated in 1965. I argue that this, like nearly all of the KMT's arts-related policies, was developed in response to developments on the Chinese mainland. As the Chinese Communist Party (CCP) set out to reform Peking opera, among other arts, the KMT reacted. The primary purpose of this movement was to disseminate the KMT's dominant ideology of mainland recovery through the performing and literary arts. The MOD commanded its Peking opera troupes to increase the number of their public performances, which would be staged in the newly opened China Armed Forces Literature and Arts Activities Center, the theatre in central Taipei in which I spent countless evenings in the early 1980s.

The second of the KMT's programmes for widespread cultural and educational intervention in Taiwan was its Chinese Cultural Renaissance, which the regime devised in response to the Cultural Revolution on the mainland. Incidentally, in my overview of works that cite my book, it appears that the greatest number of citations refer to the nine pages (66–74) in which I discuss this movement. To me, this is an indication that this cultural moment has not yet gained significant scholarly attention. Among the programmes put in place by the movement's mandate to increase the masses' general knowledge of 'national opera' (*guoju*, as Peking opera was then officially termed) were Peking opera competitions for amateur opera enthusiasts, support for amateur clubs at the elementary through college levels and an increased presence of Peking opera on television.

I concluded chapter 3 by considering the efficacy of the KMT's cultural movements. I suggested that observing differences in attitude and educational experiences of people in Taiwan with mainland Chinese might be a good place to start. While I believed that a simple comparative method might have yielded documentable differences in the early 2000s when I was writing my book, I think that the moment to observe such obvious differences has long passed following significant changes in both places over the past ten or more years. What stands as a testament to the pervasiveness of these cultural movements, however, is the backlashes they inspired. Evidence of this is found in the historical record, which I document in chapter 7, where there is a trail of vehement attacks levelled on Peking opera and its standing and title as the 'national opera' (*guoju*). A letter delivered to the Legislative Yuan in December 1983 documents an early, pointed, and well-argued attack against the 'national opera' title. These attacks escalated throughout the 1990s and led to the dismantling of most of the state-sponsored institutions, and a reorganisation and Taiwanisation of the few remaining groups in 1995.

Evaluating *Peking Opera and Politics in Taiwan*

In evaluating how the book was received, I am happy to report that *Peking Opera and Politics in Taiwan* won an award from one of the most prestigious prize-giving organisations in music, the American Society of Composers, Authors and Publishers, or ASCAP. ASCAP honoured the book with a Deems Taylor Award for excellence in writing on the subject of music (specifically with the 'Béla Bartók Ethnomusicology Award'). The book was also named an 'Outstanding Academic Title for 2006' by *Choice*, the review magazine of the Association for College and Research Libraries.

Book reviews

The book was reviewed in seven academic journals: six in English and one in Chinese. Interestingly, only one of these was a music journal, *Asian Music*; there was also a review in the theatre journal, *Comparative Drama*. The other venues were the *Journal of Asian Studies*, the *International Journal of Asian Studies*, the *Bulletin of the School of Oriental and African Studies*, the *Journal of Folklore Research Reviews* and the *Monumenta Taiwanica*. Three of the reviewers were ethnomusicologists. A historian, an anthropologist and a theatre scholar penned the other reviews while two Chinese literature scholars co-authored the Chinese-language review.

The reviews are on the whole quite positive. Generally, they each give a succinct summary of the book's contents. There are no extensive engagements or major disagreements with my approach or conclusions. There is one critical theme that is hinted at across all of the reviews, however.[1] Writing for the *Bulletin of the School of Oriental and African Studies*, ethnomusicologist Hwee-San Tan expresses this directly when she notes that I divulged little about my 'subjects as individuals' (Tan 2007: 195). In his review for the *Journal of Asian Studies*, historian Peter Carroll elaborates more fully on this apparent lacuna, writing that he would have liked to have seen more on the 'artists' self-perceptions and their role in the GMD's cultural project over the course of several decades' (Carroll 2008: 274). He also recalls that the KMT state support 'fostered large audiences that included schoolchildren and others', and wishes that I had documented how students and others viewed opera at the time. He wonders if 'specific operas enjoy[ed] particular ideological currency and popularity'. Generally, Carroll would have liked to have seen, as he puts it, 'a more fine-grained analysis of the particulars of performance and reception' (ibid.). This view is echoed in ethnomusicologist Shzr Ee Tan's review published in *Asian Music*. While her review is generally laudatory, she suggests that it would have been interesting 'for the sake of alternative perspective, to access the scene not so much from a masterful and macro "helicopter" view of power politics, than through the mindset of ground-level practitioners or audiences engaged in the proactive (as opposed to reactions) creation of socio-musical meanings in the micro-musical life' (Tan 2010: 210). Likewise, in her review for *Comparative Drama*, theatre scholar Cecilia

168 Nancy Guy

Pang writes: 'I was thoroughly intrigued by her recounting of the personal struggles shared by the Peking opera performer/musicians such as Kao Hui-lan, a male imperso-nator, and wished there had been more of those kinds of stories scattered throughout the book' (Pang 2007: 254). Shzr Ee Tan also made note of another such personal story when she commented that my

> relentless flow of arguments segues into deeply human anecdotes of how, for example, an old fiddle player is painfully berated by junior members of his socio-musical hierarchy as he struggles to read cipher notation and adjust to new, Beijing-developed florid melodic styles.
>
> *(Tan 2010: 210)*

Clearly, these reviewers would have liked to have seen a greater balance between my presentation and analyses of policies, and how these policies manifested them-selves in the lives of performers and audience members alike.

While ethnomusicologist Judah Cohen (2007) did not touch explicitly on this point in his review for the *Journal of Folklore Research Reviews*, I think he hints at a likely source of the criticism. Cohen felt that the final chapters of the book were the 'most interesting in their ethnographic detail'. I wrote these final chapters on the basis of my close contact with artists in the 1990s as they grappled to learn the repertoire, which was based on the then relatively unfamiliar contemporary main-land performance style. The first four chapters of the book were primarily histories of different topics such as the art form's history in Taiwan, its use as a political symbol, an overview of the KMT's censorship policies, etc. Almost all of my sources for these earlier chapters were written documents. It was only within my discussion of Kao Hui-lan and her career near the beginning of chapter 5, that I drew most of my data from ethnographic sources (i.e., living, breathing people with whom I had spent time and, in some cases, shared close friendships).

The idea of tracking down people in the 1990s and early 2000s who were schoolchildren in the 1970s, for example when they saw Peking opera performed at a school assembly, as Peter Carroll suggests, is intriguing. I have to admit that it never occurred to me to do so, and I agree that the study might have been richer, had I been able to include their voices. I also could have engaged more deeply with audience members who attended performances in the 1970s at the China Armed Forces Literature and Art Activities Center because many of my compadres at the same venue in the 1980s and early 1990s were those very same audience members.

The only review published in a Taiwan-based journal appeared in 2011 in *Monumenta Taiwanica*, a journal produced by National Taiwan Normal University's Department of Taiwan Culture, Languages, and Literature. Lin Feng-yi and Hsu Ying-chun from the Chinese Literature Department at Taiwan's National Central University co-wrote the review (Lin and Hsu 2011). This piece stood out from the others in that it considered my book within the context of scholarship on Peking opera published in Taiwan. It also was unique in that the authors displayed a more

Peking Opera and Politics in Taiwan revisited **169**

in-depth understanding of, not only the scene about which I wrote, but also about the art of Peking opera. The work that the authors identified as sharing the most similar focus to mine is Wang An-ch'i's *Fifty Years of Peking Opera in Taiwan* (Wang 2002). They noted that while Wang's book is richly illustrated with colour photographs and gives an excellent record of historical events, it provides little critical analysis. They report that, for this reason, *Peking Opera and Politics in Taiwan* is worthy of the attention of the local scholarly community. They praise the work for the varied sources I employed (e.g., interviews with performers, observation of rehearsals and performances, musical analyses, etc.), and how I drew larger, critical questions out of a plethora of detailed, insider information.

They did, however, have two notable points of criticism. First, they observed that the vast majority of the personal cases I used to illustrate broader points were of incidents involving performers of the *xiaosheng* (young male) role type. The authors were correct to point out that *dan* (young female) and *laosheng* (mature male) roles have been both presently and historically the most prominent – one could even say – most important role types. They also inferred correctly that *xiaosheng* is my personal favourite. Admittedly, I developed the closest relationships with performers of this role type (especially with Kao Hui-lan and Ma Yuqi) and, therefore, had the richest ethnographic material related to their trials, tribulations and triumphs. In praising the book's engaging writing style, they wrote that 'even though it is a scholarly book, the narration of events is gripping' (Lin and Hsu 2011: 112). Ironically, the example that they chose to mention as one of engaging narration was of Kao Hui-lan's enormous disappointment when censors denied permission for her Da Peng troupe to stage a performance of an opera about Qing Emperor Kangxi, a role that she had poured her heart and soul into for months. It was largely due to my close personal relationship with Kao that I was able to tell her story in a 'gripping manner'. As other reviewers also appreciated the sections in which I discussed Kao Hui-lan (Figure 10.3), it is obvious that the sharpest insights for me were gleaned through my personal contacts. That my closest relationships were primarily, though not exclusively, with performers of the *xiaosheng* role type was simply the result of serendipity and personal chemistry – both vital and inescapable elements of the very human ethnographic research method.

Their second criticism involved my use of the word 'singer' to denote a Peking opera performer. They rightly pointed out that Peking opera performers do a lot more than just sing: they narrate in a highly stylised manner (*nian*), they act (*zuo*), they do acrobatics and martial arts movements (*da*) and, of course, they sing (*chang*). They compare Peking opera performers with singers of Western opera, who, in the past, were notorious for standing and singing with little movement (mockingly termed 'park and bark'). I found this criticism fascinating, and I appreciate the writers' frustration with the failure of the English word 'singer' to capture the richness of the Peking opera performer's complete performance. In employing the word, I aimed to break up the monotony of sentences in which I needed to discuss an artist's performance, etc. I am afraid that the confines of the language do not present many good alternatives.

FIGURE 10.3 Master performer of the *xiaosheng* role type, Kao Hui-lan, in 1993 as Zhou Yu in *The Meeting of Many Heroes* (Qun ying hui). Photo by Lo Te-fen.

To be honest, I had not looked at these reviews in years. It was fascinating to revisit them. Curiously, in my second book *The Magic of Beverly Sills* (University of Illinois Press; Guy 2015), which was also about opera, just not Chinese opera, I largely focused on the often deeply personal stories of why opera and the American coloratura soprano Beverly Sills mattered in the lives of fans. I have to wonder if I might have somehow internalised the criticisms of my first book? If so, they were certainly well beneath the level of my waking consciousness. What is more likely, though, is that while I enjoy archival work, the greatest joys in my career as an ethnomusicologist have come during moments of intense engagement with people who are deeply invested in the art under my study. Hence, the most positive response to *Peking Opera and Politics in Taiwan* was in reaction to the sections that drew most directly on the experiences of the people with whom I enjoyed close personal relationships.

What came next?

Once my work on Peking opera and politics was finished, I had little interest in developing a new project on Peking opera.[2] In the years between my beginning the revisions that would turn the dissertation into a book, I launched several new research projects in Taiwan that culminated in the publication of several articles (Guy 2000, 2001, 2002a, 2002b). None of these involved Peking opera. I did not care for the contemporary performing style that by this time was dominating Peking opera performance in Taiwan partly because, in my opinion, it was often poorly executed (if not in performance, then in composition). Standard repertoire was becoming less and less frequently staged. There was certainly not enough happening in Taiwan to hold my sustained attention. And, I was not motivated at that time to move my research to mainland China.

I decided instead to turn my attention to music and politics generally in Taiwan. I took as my primary focus music and performance in the arena of political contestation, including in campaign rallies, inaugural events, etc. I also wrote about how music was used to bolster ethnic identity and a multi-ethnic, multicultural vision of Taiwan. While I believe that very important lessons about how a society functions, and how its people may respond to governing policies, can be learned through the study of the musical expression, frankly, I grew frustrated with the lack of attention that this scholarship was gaining both inside and outside of the academy. I wondered who was listening to the stories that my analyses of music were telling?

I was in the middle of putting together a book on music and social movements in Taiwan when I encountered a serious hazard of working with music and politics. In studying music, one deals directly with emotion and viscerally experienced meaning. This work is exhilarating when developments are positive, but a steady diet of negativity can be difficult to bear. I did not react well when creativity turned, to put it in the starkest terms, from love and hope to hate and destruction. Allow me to explain. In the 1990s, there was a good deal of extremely creative and highly artistic music being produced, with much of this being imbued with a beautiful, hopeful message for a brighter future for Taiwan. Specific examples include the works of Chen Ming-chang, the Blacklist Workshop, Zhu Toupi, Chen Sheng, and Lin Shengxiang and the Labor Exchange band, to name a few. However, in the year 2000 (the year in which Chen Shui-bian was elected to the presidency) Taiwan witnessed a seismic shift in popular music creativity and production. There were multiple reasons for this – not all of them involving state politics, such as the collapse of the local music industry with the rise of the mp3 and piracy. Some factors, however, were most certainly related to the political environment including the impact on creativity following China's banning of Zhang Huimei after her performance of the ROC national anthem at Chen's 2000 inaugural ceremony (see Guy 2002a). The *Taipei Times* reported on the year 2002's Golden Melody Awards with an article aptly titled 'Mando-pop's Cheerless Year' (Taipei Times 2002: 24). It wasn't long before the most innovative music was coming from the blue camp such as two strongly negative albums released in 2004 following the re-election of Chen Shui-bian: 1) *Meilidao* [Beautiful Formosa] by Luo Da-you; 2) *Mingyun de zidan* [Fateful Bullets] by the Peng Peng Yue Dui [the Bang Bang Band].

There were also the massive 'Anti-Corruption' protests, whose fury was directed at President Chen Shui-bian, staged in 2006. The music and performances staged during the 'Daobian' ('overturn Chen') rallies were absolutely fascinating, but they were also stomach turning for someone, such as myself, who did not have sympathy for the movement. Following the publication of *Peking Opera and Politics in Taiwan*, I only published two more refereed journal articles on Taiwan. One of these was 'Feeling a Shared History through Song: "A Flower in the Rainy Night" as a Key Cultural Symbol in Taiwan', which was inspired by Lee Teng-hui's singing of the old song, 'Flower in a the Rainy Night' (*Yu ye hua*) at a rally on the eve of a Taipei mayoral election in 2002. The other was 'Flowing down Taiwan's

172 Nancy Guy

Tamsui River: Towards an Ecomusicology of the Environmental Imagination', which has become a seminal work in the burgeoning field of ecomusicology. Following the ugliness and hatred of the 'Daobian' protest, I turned my interest once again to beauty and hope with my research on Beverly Sills, who died the very night that I finished writing a conference paper on the 'Daobian' protest. Since 2015, however, I have begun my re-entry into Taiwan studies, initially with my work on another environmental theme: garbage truck melodies (Guy 2019).

Reassessing *Peking Opera and Politics in Taiwan* and considering 'so what'

As one of my reviewers, anthropologist Teri Silvio, opined, the book was 'basically a coroner's report – a detailed, step-by-step description of the slow strangulation of a once-popular art form' (Silvio 2007: 143). The first lines of my book read,

> Twenty years from now, if I were to restudy the people, the places, and the performance style of Peking opera in Taiwan, I wonder what I would find. Who would be there to talk with me? What kind of Peking opera would I hear and see? When, where, and how often would it be performed?
>
> *(Guy 2005: 1)*

As of 2019, there is one remaining full-time, state-sponsored Peking opera troupe and one training programme. The training programme finds itself as a single department in a school, the National Taiwan College of the Performing Arts (臺灣戲曲學院), which includes programmes in Taiwanese opera, traditional music, acrobatics and dance, and is dominated by a curriculum in Hakka music. The professional troupe, the GuoGuang Opera Company (國光劇團), was created in 1995 to take in performers following the disbanding of the three remaining Ministry of Defense troupes. Initially, GuoGuang (whose name no longer carries the honorific name '*guoju*' – nor does it indicate that it specialises in Peking opera) was under the administration of the Ministry of Education. In 2008, it was placed under the control of the 'Council for Cultural Affairs' (CCA; 文建會), and in 2012, when the CCA became the Ministry of Culture, GuoGuang was placed under the umbrella of the Center for Taiwan Traditional Arts (國立臺灣傳統藝術中心).[3]

It is beyond the scope of this chapter to give a complete overview of GuoGuang and its current activities. Suffice to say that the troupe's greatest efforts in recent years have been on creating new works, most often with librettos written by troupe director Wang An-ch'i. These new works typically have a run of three days in the National Theater in Taipei, and they may sometimes be performed at large-scale venues in other urban areas. A look at the company's website shows that in 2016, the year that marked the GuoGuang's twentieth anniversary, was a year of an extraordinarily high number of shows. I counted 37 performances for the entire year.

In her 2011 book, *Alternative Chinese Opera in the Age of Globalization*, Daphne Lei (2011) spins a hopeful tale of Peking opera remaking itself in Taiwan in the form of what she terms 'innovative *jingju*' (*xinbian jingju*). She focuses most of her attention on the activities of the GuoGuang troupe. Lei begins with a question that seems to be directed at my 2005 book by asking: 'Is traditional Beijing opera [sic.] (*jingju*) an art form associated with hegemony or state power?' (Lei 2011: 23). She answers:

> Many young people in Taiwan today would consider the question absurd: the dated art form is usually associated with a minority group, the old Main-landers – retired soldiers and military village dwellers – who are dying out and no longer enjoy any class or political privileges. Recent changes in the political climate also make any traditional arts associated with mainland China misfits. New and innovative *jingju*, on the other hand, is a different story. This is the form the younger generation might consider fashionable, artistic, intelligent, even cool.
>
> *(Lei 2011: 23)*

Lei argues that innovative *jingju* as created by the GuoGuang troupe has adopted a strategy of effeminisation. By this she means that new plays are about women and written by women; thus they may seem 'pretty and harmless' (Lei 2011: 41). Therefore, she argues, Peking opera has become 'completely depoliticized'. Inno-vative *jingju* now offers an experience more akin to a romantic musical than tradi-tional Peking opera (Lei 2011: 40–41). Lei concludes: 'Whether veiled in political correctness or in apolitical femininity, Innovative *Jingju* pushed boundaries of *jingju* reform and extended the life of the genre' (Lei 2011: 57). 'The "feminine" creative energy miraculously rescued the dying *jingju* in Taiwan in the last decade' (Lei 2011: 63).

It is, I believe, premature to claim that the so-called '*Innovative Jingju*' has rescued Peking opera. The art form is still deeply dependent on state funding. In 2010, Taiwan's most celebrated Peking opera performers, Wei Hai-ming, Li Bao-chun and Wu Hsing-kuo, staged a public protest at the Ministry of Education against cuts in Peking opera education (Lei 2011: 183). Lei notes that this was 'the first time these actors regarded as 'national treasures' have had to take to the street in an effort to rescue their art' (ibid).

Has the passing of time (and with it the disempowering and even death of those previously associated with Peking opera under the KMT's hegemonic rule) and the form's feminisation truly turned GuoGuang's Peking opera into a depoliticized art form? Does such a thing as depoliticized art even exists? Lei offers little evidence to support her bold claim. What is clear is that without state support, Peking opera would no longer be sustainable in Taiwan.

Currently, there is one private venture involving Peking opera that is self-sus-taining, but even it is dependent on the state having supported the fundamental training of its performers. Long-time Peking opera fan, librettist and patron of the

174 Nancy Guy

arts, Vivien Huai-chun Koo (daughter of Koo Chen-fu, former Chairman of the Straits Exchange Foundation), runs a private Peking opera troupe, which is staffed mostly by recent graduates of the Chinese Cultural University's Peking opera department. They perform four nights a week under the banner of 'Taipei Eye'. Their shows, which seem to be running at a profit, are aimed largely at tourists and take place in the Koo family's theatre in the Taiwan Cement Hall on Zhongshan North Road in downtown Taipei.[4]

In addition to these Taiwan-based efforts, professional troupes from China continue to visit Taiwan, but the flow is much less than it was in the years immediately following the re-opening of cross-straits travel. Typically, the China National Peking Opera Company (中國國家京劇院) visits once a year for about a week of performances. Ticket sales have dwindled in recent years. The audience for their performances is composed largely of the old folks that used to enjoy the performances of the now disbanded MOD and MOE troupes. In fact, when I attended several of these performances in Taipei in December 2016 and September 2017, I ran into several of my favourite old opera fans.

In my book's last paragraph, I said that over the previous 15 years, I had frequently asked performers, government officials, aficionados and others to predict what they believed to be Peking opera's future in Taiwan. How the art form would make its way was becoming increasingly unclear to me. I worried that Peking opera carried with it the legacy of having been privileged under an oppressive regime. And, that this represented an added burden at a time when many traditional performing arts were struggling to remain relevant and viable parts of contemporary life (Guy 2005: 165). The key question now is whether or not state politics (past and present) are relevant beyond the question of patronage. If the state were to withdraw support altogether, the systematic training of new performers would stop, and it is almost impossible to imagine a troupe such as GuoGuang being able to offer its members full-time employment – of that, I am certain. State support can keep Peking opera in the theatre (albeit on a small fraction of evenings compared with previous decades), but it cannot make it popular. Whether or not politics has anything to do with Peking opera's level of genuine popularity in the 2010s has not been adequately studied to make an enlightened determination.

Conclusion: So what?

When I ask 'so what?', I question what lessons can be gleaned from my book. What I asserted in the conclusion as being the study's main lesson has gnawed at me over the last decade or so. As I followed Peking opera through its history in Taiwan, I noted its genuine popularity during the Japanese colonial period, and its genuine lack of popularity among many *bendiren* during the period of oppressive KMT control. I argued that Peking opera in Taiwan:

> always had a symbolic presence, standing for something other than, or in addition to, itself. The meaning of an association with the art has been one of

Peking Opera and Politics in Taiwan revisited   **175**

the most critical factors affecting its viability and popularity. The changing meanings of Peking opera (e.g., as a tie to the Chinese motherland under Japanese colonialism; as a symbol of the totalitarian regime under Nationalist rule) illuminates what is perhaps this study's most important lesson: Taiwanese people (like most people, I imagine) have never fully succumbed to oppression or coercion. The most cleverly planned and implemented programs for forced assimilation have ultimately failed.

(Guy 2005: 164)

I made this conclusion writing in the early 2000s following Chen Shui-bian's first election to the presidency. Looking back over the twentieth century, what I saw was that Taiwan had been steadily marching forward, often in the face of brutal forces of oppression. In the period surrounding the Daobian protest in 2006, I began to question the veracity of this 'lesson'. With the election of Ma Ying-jeou in 2008, I no longer believed in my own conclusion. I visited Taiwan to observe the inaugural festivities in 2008 where I sensed a general mood of resignation. The exuberant and hopeful atmosphere that I experienced in the days surrounding Chen's inauguration in 2000 was absent.[5] What I concluded from this was that the promise of strong economic ties with China – which Ma's election seemed to promise – overrode the Taiwanese electorate's desire for self-determination. Now, with the election of Tsai Ing-wen of the Democratic Progress Party, I am not sure where I stand on this point. Certainly, the situation is complex. Will my 'lesson' turn out to have been correct in the long term? Only time will tell.

There is another 'lesson', though; that I think is an important take away from the book. Tracing Peking opera's history in Taiwan, particularly during the first 50 years of the KMT's rule, we see in vivid detail the importance that Chinese regimes assign to 'symbols', and we see the lengths that they will go to in creating, disseminating, venerating or denigrating these symbols. One only needs to review conflicts over the symbols used to represent Taiwan in international sporting competitions as recent examples of the importance of national symbols in Chinese societies.[6] China simply will not allow Taiwan to enter into any international arena using the ROC's flag or the national anthem.

Capturing the intensity of passion that permeates Taiwan's political environment is a key challenge faced by scholars writing about Taiwanese society, political contestations and policy creations. Specific types of music, such as Peking opera, carry with them historical ties to past struggles and tensions. Once elevated to a 'national essence' (*guocui*) in early twentieth-century China, and named 'national opera' (*guoju*) in mid-century Taiwan, the art form, now known by the same name (i.e., *jingju*) on both sides of the Taiwan Straits, faces an uncertain future in the twenty-first century. A close look at the uses and functions of symbolically potent musical entities (from large-scale theatrical traditions to pop songs sung at political rallies) provides a direct window into the powerful emotional forces that underlie heartfelt political struggle. My book provided a detailed study of the rise, maintenance and decline of one such entity. My hope is that future work in Taiwan studies will focus

176 Nancy Guy

greater attention on the messages that the stratum of musical communication has to tell us about the inner workings and tensions within Taiwan society.

Notes

1 Not exactly along the same lines, but in a similar vein, anthropologist Teri Silvio would have liked to have seen the scope of the book broadened to include something of how Peking opera influenced other performing traditions such as '*ge zai xi*, conceptual theater and modern dance' (Silvio 2007: 144). As she points out, one of my stated goals was to access how Peking opera influenced its environment, but I mostly focus on the KMT's intended influence. I agree that Peking opera's impact on and presence in other forms of creative expression would have made for an interesting study, but, for me, that would have been a different book-length study, not an additional chapter.
2 The period of intense research for the dissertation was the 1991–1992 academic year. I returned for several months of research in 1994 before completing the dissertation, and I made a number of trips to Taipei beginning in 1998 in preparation for writing the book.
3 The GuoGuang Company, in addition to three other entities, the National Chinese Orchestra Taiwan (臺灣國樂團), the Taiwan Music Institute (台灣音樂館), Taiwan Bangzi Opera Company(台灣豫劇團), comprise this organisation.
4 The troupe performs mostly Peking opera standards such as *The Legend of the White Snake, The Legend of Eight Immortals Crossing the Sea*, and other operas that are heavy on comedy and acrobatics and are easily interpreted by foreigners and children. The 'Taipei Eye' (Taibei xipeng) programme sometimes includes a variety of traditional performing arts, including the lion dance, aboriginal dance and music, Taiwanese opera and budaixi, among others.
    www.taipeieye.com/en/aboutus/
5 I am vitally aware that this sense of optimism was not shared across all segments of Taiwan society. I shall always recall the sombre mood as I rode in a car in central Taipei with several MOD employees (whom I had known during my days of working with MOD-supported Peking opera troupes) on the eve of Chen's inauguration in 2000. I even received a phone call from Taipei to my home in San Diego from a mainlander friend (and former Peking opera performer) shortly after Chen's election victory in 2000 asking me to adopt her teenage daughter because she feared that *waishengren* (mainlanders) would be discriminated against following Chen's ascent to the presidency.
6 Writing about the gold medal victories in taekwondo of two Taiwan athletes at the 2004 Olympics, the *Taipei Times* editorial observed: 'This was a moment of enormous pride – but that pride was mixed with regret. For the flag was not Taiwan's national flag, and the music was not Taiwan's national anthem' (28 August; Taipei Times 2004a). Bowing to pressure from China, the national flag song played in place of the ROC anthem and a flag sporting a plum blossom stood in for the ROC flag. Chinese pressures against symbols of Taiwan extended beyond the Olympic stage when it pressured the Greeks to remove signs that included the words 'Taiwan' and 'Chinese Taipei'. Advertisements were removed from the Athens airport and city buses 'despite the fact that their presence was the result of perfectly legal financial transaction' (1 September; Taipei Times 2004b). There are many such examples, including organisations within Taiwan removing the ROC flag when officials from China visit the island.

References

Carroll, Peter J. 2008. 'Review of *Peking Opera and Politics in Taiwan* by Nancy Guy'. *Journal of Asian Studies* 67(1): 274–275.
Cohen, Judah M. 2007. 'Review of Peking Opera and Politics in Taiwan by Nancy Guy'. *Journal of Folklore Research Reviews*. http://scholarworks.iu.edu/journals/index.php/jfrr/article/view/2485/2361

Guy, Nancy. 2000. 'Performing Taiwan: Music, Dance, and Spectacle in the Celebration of President Chen Shui-bian's Inauguration'. *ACMR Reports* 13: 21–50.

Guy, Nancy. 2001. 'How Does "Made in Taiwan" Sound?: Popular Music and Strategizing the Sounds of a Multicultural Nation'. *Perfect Beat: The Pacific Journal of Research into Contemporary Music and Popular Culture* 5(3): 1–17.

Guy, Nancy. 2002a. '"Republic of China National Anthem" on Taiwan: One Anthem, One Performance, Multiple Realities'. *Ethnomusicology* 46(1): 96–119.

Guy, Nancy. 2002b. 'Trafficking in Taiwan Aboriginal Voices'. In Sjoerd R. Jaarsma (ed.), *Handle with Care: Ownership and Control of Ethnographic Materials*. Pittsburgh: University of Pittsburgh Press, 159–209.

Guy, Nancy. 2005. *Peking Opera and Politics in Taiwan*. Urbana and Chicago: University of Illinois Press.

Guy, Nancy. 2008. 'Feeling a Shared History through Song: A Flower in the Rainy Night as a Key Cultural Symbol in Taiwan'. *TDR: The Drama Review* 52(4): 64–81.

Guy, Nancy. 2015. *The Magic of Beverly Sills*. Urbana and Chicago: University of Illinois Press.

Guy, Nancy. 2019. 'Garbage Truck Music and Sustainability in Contemporary Taiwan: From Cockroaches to Beethoven and Beyond'. In Timothy Cooley (ed.), *Cultural Sustainabilities: Music, Media, Language, and Advocacy*. Urbana and Chicago: University of Illinois Press, 63–74.

Lei, Daphne P. 2011. *Alternative Chinese Opera in the Age of Globalization: Performing Zero*. Basingstoke: Palgrave Macmillan.

Lin, Feng-yi, and Hsu Ying-chun. 2011. 'Review of *Peking Opera and Politics in Taiwan* by Nancy Guy'. *Monumenta Taiwanica* [Taiwan xuezhi] 4(October): 109–112. http://dx.doi.org/10.6242/twnica.4.5

Pang, Cecilia J. 2007. 'Review of *Peking Opera and Politics in Taiwan* by Nancy Guy'. *Comparative Drama* 41(2): 252–254.

Qi, Rushan. 1979. *Qi Rushan Quanji (Complete Works of Qi Rushan), 10 vols*. Taipei: Lianjing Chuban Shiye Gongsi.

Silvio, Terri. 2007. 'Review of *Peking Opera and Politics in Taiwan* by Nancy Guy'. *International Journal of Asian Studies* 4(1):143–145.

Taipei Times. 2002. 'Mando-pop's Cheerless Year'. 5 May 2002. www.taipeitimes.com/News/feat/archives/2002/05/05/0000134792

Taipei Times. 2004a. 'Editorial'. 28 August 2004.

Taipei Times. 2004b. 'Rest in Peace, Chinese "Taipei"'. 1 September 2004.

Tan, Hwee-San. 2007. 'Review of *Peking Opera and Politics in Taiwan* by Nancy Guy'. *Bulletin of the School of Oriental and African Studies* 70(1): 191–193.

Tan, Shzr Ee. 2010. 'Review of *Chinese Street Opera in Singapore* by Tong Soon Lee, and: *Peking Opera and Politics in Taiwan* by Nancy Guy'. *Asian Music* 41(20): 206–211.

Wang, An-ch'i. 2002. *Taiwan jingju 50 nian* [Fifty years of Peking opera in Taiwan]. Ilan: Guoli chuantong yishu zhongxin.

11

PARTY POLITICS IN TAIWAN REVISITED

Dafydd Fell

My first book, *Party Politics in Taiwan: Party Change and the Democratic Evolution of Taiwan* was published in August 2005 (Fell 2005a). Now seems a good time to revisit it. The paperback was published in 2012, but it is well over a decade since the original publication and 18 years since the core fieldwork was conducted. After discussing the main findings of the book, I will consider how the original research has stood the test of time and how the book has affected my subsequent research direction.

As is the case for many academics, my first book was based on a revised version of a PhD dissertation. For a mid-career academic, revisiting the first book is quite an emotionally charged challenge for a number of reasons. After becoming a tenured academic with all the inevitable teaching and administrative duties, it is close to impossible to conduct the same kind of focus on a single research project and multi-year fieldwork that often goes into a PhD. Thus it can be hard to match the depth of research in a PhD-based book afterwards. In the same way as Taiwan is in the shadow of China, at times I feel under the shadow of *Party Politics in Taiwan*. I sometimes joke to students that I have been given a life sentence to analyse the election advertisements produced by the major political parties for every Taiwanese election. Moreover, since the main period covered in the book is from 1991–2001, when I was living in Taiwan, the book feels almost auto-biographical. Rereading my analysis of the 1995 Legislative Yuan campaign brings me back to the sleepless nights and nappy changing of the first months of being a father.

How?, *Why?* and *So what?*

PhD students tend to start out with very broad research interests but the key challenge in the first year of a British PhD is to quickly narrow down a clear set of

Party Politics in Taiwan revisited **179**

focused research questions and to design the research around these. Thinking about the big questions and how my material related to these was something constantly drummed into me by my PhD supervisor, Julia Strauss. Nowadays I also often suggest to my students that they should design research projects around three questions: *How?*, *Why?* and *So what?* In other words, in political science we are often measuring a political phenomenon (*How?* or the dependent variable), we need to explain the phenomenon (*Why?* or the independent variable) and we need to convince readers that our research findings matter (*So what?*).

I was fortunate in having worked out exactly what my research questions were very early on in my PhD research. They are essentially what the book seeks to examine:

1. How did Taiwan's main parties adjust their positions on the core policy spectrums in the first decade of multi-party elections? (*How?*)
2. How can we best explain the parties' changing positions (*Why?*)
3. What is the significance of these patterns of change for the state of Taiwan's democracy? (*So what?*)

In the next three sections I will discuss how I addressed these core research questions and my major findings.

The How?

Prior to starting to write the PhD, I had naturally read most of the existing literature on Taiwan's party and electoral politics. Much of this literature was and still is extremely dull. Public opinion survey data is an essential tool for understanding politics, however, the way the data is presented in Taiwanese political science is often quite off-putting for readers not trained in statistical analysis. For Europeans accustomed to short and dry election campaigns, the vibrancy, colour, passion and noise of Taiwanese elections is a source of attraction. However, the festival style of Taiwanese politics seemed absent from so much of the literature. Having lived in Taiwan through the late 1980s and most of the 1990s I was determined to find a way of bringing the colour of Taiwanese elections into my research writings. In fact one point that I make at the start of a Taiwanese politics course to the new set of students is that Taiwanese politics is never dull and is always full of surprises.

One preliminary question to consider was the time period to cover in my analysis of party change. There is much debate over when we should classify Taiwan as being a democracy. Should it be the first multi-party election of 1986, the lifting of martial law in 1987 or the first direct presidential election of 1996? I chose to start my analysis from the first full re-election of a national parliament, the 1991 National Assembly elections. Although my PhD analysis ended in 2001, the book included a chapter (chapter 7) that updated the analysis to include developments up to the 2004 presidential election. The decision on which parties to include in the analysis was quite straightforward. Since 1986, Taiwan's party system has been

180 Dafydd Fell

dominated by two parties, the Democratic Progressive Party (DPP) and the Kuomintang (KMT). However, the New Party's (NP) role as Taiwan's first significant third party for most of the 1990s made it a case worth bringing into the analysis.

Before tracking change though it was necessary to decide which issues to examine. Here I examined a combination of election advertisements, issue saliency surveys and party elite surveys to narrow down three issue dimensions: (1) social welfare, (2) political corruption and (3) national identity. Although the majority of political science literature is focused on national identity, I hoped to show that elections in Taiwan involved debate over a wider range of issues. In fact, my data found political corruption to be the most stressed issue on election advertising in the 1990s campaigns.

Once I had settled on my issue spectrums I could begin the task of measuring party positions and showing change over time. This brings me to the issue of disciplinary location, something all research projects need to make explicit. The topic meant that my study was in the field of party change, defined by Harmel and Janda (1994: 275) as 'any variation, alteration or moderation in how parties are organized, what human and material resources they can draw upon, what they stand for and what they do'. Similarly I was able to engage with the comparative politics literature on measuring party positioning, a field featuring two main approaches relying on either expert surveys (Benoit and Laver 2006) or content analysis of election manifestoes (Budge et al. 2001). Previously the only systematic way party positioning had been measured in Taiwan was using party image surveys. One key resource that I employed that was original was content analyses of election newspaper and TV advertisements. By the end of the 1990s this was the largest single spending item in election campaigns; however, this had largely been ignored by political scientists. In contrast the best analysis of Taiwanese election advertisements tended to come from advertising scholars such as Cheng Tzu-leong (鄭自隆) (Cheng 1992, 1995). Thus I attempted to track party change using a combination of qualitative and quantitative content analysis of ads. The quantitative analysis employed a revised version of the Comparative Manifesto Research Project coding scheme (Budge et al. 2001, 222–228). Once again this allowed the study to engage with the more comparative literature as well as to offer an alternative approach to test the Taiwanese party image perception of change generated from survey data.

The research material and methods meant the fieldwork year ranked as one of the most enjoyable years of my academic life. Conducting content analysis of newspaper and TV ads was extremely enjoyable once I had photocopied the originals. The collection though was hard work as it meant working through heavy stacks of newspapers in hot library storerooms. By the end of each day I tended to have backache and hands blackened with newsprint.

In order to locate party positions in each of the ten election campaigns examined over the period I took into account a range of data. First I analysed all newspaper election ads for one month prior to voting day.[1] This analysis was both qualitative and quantitative. The quantitative element looked at the proportion of issue mentions with particular emphasis on my three core issue dimensions. With total

Party Politics in Taiwan revisited **181**

issue mentions for each party for each election campaign, I was able to show changing patterns of issue emphasis over time. The qualitative examination of TV and newspaper ads was designed to extrapolate key themes and slogans from the campaign. The slogans added flavour to the analysis and by showing changing slogans it was often possible to show emphasis and positional change. I also examined newspaper reports in the final month of the campaign to get a sense of elite discourse on the three issue areas to supplement the advertising data. Although this kind of content analysis was extremely time consuming, it was to be critically useful when it came to the stage of elite interviews, as I needed to have this in-depth knowledge of the campaigns in order to be taken seriously by the interviewees. In my elite interviews I asked a range of questions to get politicians' views of their parties' changing issue emphasis and positioning, as well as their explanations for change. The final tool I brought into the equation for measuring party positioning was party image surveys, such as those carried out by the National Chengchi University Election Study Centre.

Before I began the in-depth analysis of party change on my three core issue areas I included short chapters that first reviewed the development of party politics in Taiwan and discussed the role of issues in Taiwan's electoral and party politics.

Party change on social welfare

My chapter 4 examines party change on the social welfare issue. This had not been a highly salient issue during the democratic transition period despite the fact that Taiwan's welfare provision had been highly unequal under martial law. Space opened for the issue once democratisation had been agreed on, and the DPP needed to find new issues to broaden its appeal beyond core voters.

I set up social welfare as a policy spectrum with one extreme of a Scandinavian-style welfare system of high taxes and extensive welfare provisions to the unequal limited welfare system left over from the martial law era at the other extreme. I showed how, although both parties gave attention to welfare issues, they addressed the issue differently. The sub-issue the KMT raised most during the 1990s was its achievement in introducing the popular Universal National Health Insurance programme. However, since the decision to introduce this programme occurred during the transition period, it never became a contested campaign issue. Instead the main case study I used to show patterns of change was over pensions.

The pensions issue was first raised in the 1992 legislative election but was nationally first salient a year later in the 1993 local executive elections. That year the DPP made old age allowances one of its key policy appeals. However, this should not be taken as a sign of a Scandinavian-style system as the proposed allowances were quite limited, and instead of calling for tax rises the party argued they could be funded by reducing KMT political corruption. The KMT revealed it took a conservative stance on welfare common in many other former East Asian developmental states. It countered the DPP's pensions appeal with arguments that the care of the elderly should principally be the family's duty, that such programmes would

182 Dafydd Fell

bankrupt the treasury and that they were tantamount to vote buying. Although the DPP struggled to implement its old age allowances policy where it won at the local level, it continued to advocate universal old age allowances in campaigns through to the 2000 presidential campaign. In contrast, though, the KMT gradually moved closer to the DPP's position on pensions. For instance in 1995 it brought in old age allowances for retired farmers and the Executive Yuan began researching a universal contributory pensions scheme towards the end of the decade. One episode that was especially enjoyable to research was when KMT chair and President, Lee Teng-hui (李登輝), even tried to poach the DPP's pensions appeal in 1997. Lee was not successful in this endeavour and in the next two elections the KMT returned to its more cautious stance on the issue. Thus during the 2000 presidential debates, the KMT and DPP still held sharply different positions on old age allowances. The process of convergence continued after the DPP came to power, culminating in the KMT accepting the DPP's universal old age allowance bill in 2002 and in the 2004 presidential election even attempting to outbid the DPP on the old age allowance. Of the three parties the one that did not show any signs of change was the NP, which retained the KMT's original conservative stance on welfare spending.

The social welfare issue was the first case where I argued that Taiwan's parties were following a pattern of what I called *moderate differentiation*, whereby although the parties had shifted towards more moderate positions, they have retained distinct policy-based identities. In other words, on the welfare issue the parties had moved from being quite polarised at the outset of multi-party elections towards the centre. However, they remained distinct on certain welfare sub-issues, and voters tended to perceive the DPP as the more pro-welfare party. To use John Petrocik's (2003–2004) term, voters felt the DPP *owned* the social welfare issue.

Party change on political corruption

The emergence of political corruption as a salient election issue showed parallels to those seen with social welfare. It first received heavy attention in the 1992 legislative election with the DPP placing numerous ads highlighting KMT corruption cases. In contrast, the KMT tended to try to steer clear of the issue, hoping to shift the issue agenda on to more favourable issues. Despite its high election visibility and salience, the corruption issue had received minimal attention from the national identity focused Taiwan political science community. Since political corruption is a valence rather than a positional issue, a different approach to measure change was required. Instead I adopted the framework suggested by Heidenheimer (2002: 141–154) that distinguishes between white, grey and black corruption according to the attitudes of elites and the masses. Black corruption occurs when a 'majority consensus of both elite and mass opinion would condemn and want to see punished' (152). In contrast, white corruption 'signifies that the majority of both elite and mass opinion would probably not vigorously support an attempt to punish a form of corruption that they regard as tolerable' (152). In the case of grey corruption though, some may wish to see corruption punished, the majority are ambiguous on the issue.

Party Politics in Taiwan revisited **183**

My analysis of party treatment of the corruption issue also found patterns of change. The DPP consistently attacked the KMT with allegations of political corruption and by the mid-1990s was joined in this by the KMT splinter party, the NP. The opposition parties also gradually broadened the scope of their corruption attacks adding new sub-issues such as calling for the KMT to return its party assets in the mid-1990s. The KMT did move in response to these anti-corruption appeals that were damaging its reputation. For instance, in 1994 the then Justice Minister, Ma Ying-jeou (馬英九), conducted a sweeping campaign against vote buying among grassroots politicians that mainly involved fellow KMT members, and in the 2000 presidential election KMT candidate Lien Chan (連戰) promised to end the party's involvement in profit-making enterprises (party assets). Thus I argued that corruption sub-issues were making a transition from white to grey and even black corruption. However, as with social welfare, the parties did not become indistinguishable on this issue. Repeatedly the KMT was forced to backtrack on its anti-corruption initiatives, as even today the KMT has been unable to resolve its party assets dilemma. Public opinion polls revealed that the public had starkly different images of the parties in the 1990s, with the KMT increasingly associated with corruption and the DPP seen as relatively free of corruption.

Party change on national identity

The national identity chapter was the most challenging to write. The political science literature on national identity in Taiwan is extremely rich and diverse. Moreover, it was the issue politicians interviewed most wanted to talk about. It was surprisingly, however, not the most stressed issue in election advertising, falling behind political corruption in my advertising data and behind social welfare in Liu Tsung-wei's analysis of election gazettes (Liu 2002). Although the literature on Taiwanese national identity is very rich, it had tended to be focused on public opinion surveys and elite discourses, while election advertising issue emphasis had been relatively neglected. Thus this allowed me to offer a contribution to this crowded field.

I attempted to show party change by dividing the issue into two spectrums. The first I called Taiwan independence versus unification or the TongDu issue. Here the far left incorporates calls for immediate independence; the status quo in the middle and at the far right calls for immediate unification with China. For the second (largely overlapping) spectrum, the far left featured exclusive Taiwanese identity appeals, with dual identity appeals at the centre and at the far right exclusive ethnic Chinese identity appeals. Naturally both spectrums included more moderate centre left and centre right appeals that are better captured by the term *civic nationalism*.

I showed how in the first democratic election of 1991 the parties were highly polarised on both identity spectrums. That year the DPP was calling for the declaration of a Republic of Taiwan and using exclusive Taiwanese identity appeals, locating it at the far left. In contrast, I located the KMT at the far right of these spectrums. The KMT warned of the dangers of Taiwan independence

184 Dafydd Fell

leading to Chinese invasion, called for unification under the National Unification Guidelines and made use of Chinese identity appeals such as Chiang Kai-shek.

From 1992, though, both parties moved towards the centre or centre left on these spectrums. There were of course some exceptional campaigns such as the DPP's more explicitly pro-independence appeals in the 1996 presidential campaign. However, I argued the overall trend for the two large parties was convergent. The KMT's shift was visible in its increasing use of Taiwanese identity appeals such as Lee Teng-hui's 1998 *New Taiwanese* appeal. The KMT's promotion of pragmatic diplomacy, dropping of unification references and bid to re-enter the United Nations brought it closer to the centre. Similarly the DPP swept its Republic of Taiwan appeal under the carpet in favour of what I called *diluted Taiwan independence* appeals. It also de-emphasised identity appeals in favour of new issues such as welfare, gender equality and political corruption. The degree of convergence was seen in the build up to the 2000 presidential election when the DPP's position was represented by the Future of Taiwan Resolution, while Lee Teng-hui claimed the relationship between China and Taiwan was a special state to state one.

The exception to the pattern of convergence was in the smaller splinter parties and the case I focused on was the NP. The NP was highly critical of the KMT's move away from Chinese nationalist positions and, particularly after 1998, it took a pro-unification stance even further to the right than the KMT's. In my post 2000 chapter I show how the NP continued this rightward drift through to 2004.

Why? *What explained party change?*

In the sections on explaining change I relied heavily on the final part of my fieldwork, which was an extensive set of elite interviews. I tended to interview politicians that had been involved in a series of major elections as candidates, party leaders or campaigners. I supplemented these with a number of interviews with academics.

In *Party Politics in Taiwan* I tried to apply a framework for explaining party change proposed by Harmel and Janda (1994). They propose that party change tends to occur as a result of two inner party factors: (1) leadership change and (2) changes in the factional balance of power, plus external stimulus, such as election defeat. The way I operationalised the framework was to make the distinction between election- and ideological-oriented leaders and factions. Where the former were dominant in the party, the party would respond to public opinion and poor election results by moving towards more centrist positions, closer to the median voter. In contrast, where ideological-oriented leaders and factions dominate the party we would expect priority to be placed on staying true to the party's core values, even when this might undermine electoral prospects. Moreover where ideological purity takes priority, a party may not necessarily respond to election defeat by moving closer to public opinion.

Party Politics in Taiwan revisited 185

I argued that the initially highly polarised party positions in 1991 were best explained by the inner party balance of power. The DPP had become increasingly dominated by the New Tide Faction and it had been able to push the passage of the Taiwan Independence Clause in 1991. Moreover the domination of more radical factions meant that other issues such as welfare and corruption did not initially receive much attention. Similarly, in the KMT with Hau Pei-tsun (郝柏村) the premier, the Non Mainstream Faction was influential in party positioning and appeals. Lee Teng-hui still needed to compromise with party conservatives such as over the National Unification Guidelines. At this point elections had not yet been a critical variable, as previous elections had been only partially supplementary or local elections and public opinion surveys were not yet reliable.

The external shock prompting the DPP's gradual movement towards the centre was its serious defeat in the 1991 National Assembly election. Following this setback, election-oriented leaders such as Hsu Hsin-liang (許信良), Shih Ming-teh (施明德) and Chen Shui-bian (陳水扁) contributed to the party's convergent movement. Propaganda chiefs such as Chen Fang-ming (陳芳明), Chen Wenchien (陳文茜) and Lo Wen-chia (羅文嘉) played a role in moulding the DPP's more moderate image. The new balance of power within the party also meant that the party gave greater attention to a broader range of issues such as welfare, gender equality and political corruption, as the party attempted to broaden its support base. The moderates did not always have it all their own way, as more ideological-oriented factions constrained movement towards the centre. One example was the selection of Peng Ming-min (彭明敏) as the party's presidential candidate in 1996 and his more Taiwanese nationalist campaign. However, Peng's resounding defeat allowed party moderates to push a continuation of the convergent trend that culminated in Chen Shui-bian's 2000 campaign.

There were similarities in the factors pushing the KMT towards the centre in the 1990s. For the KMT though the turning point came in 1993 with the replacement of Hau Pei-tsun with Lien Chan as Premier and the departure of a large group of Non Mainstream Faction KMT politicians to form the NP. This left Lee Teng-hui and his Mainstream faction dominant in the party and thus able to move the party closer to public opinion. In the case of the KMT, this served to improve the party's election fortunes, culminating in the 1996 presidential election victory. Despite the domination of election-oriented factions in the KMT, at times even Lee was constrained in centrist movement, such as on pensions in 1997 and on his special state to state discourse in 1999. In other words, although both parties were being led towards the moderate centre, ideological-oriented factions prevented total convergence and allowed for a degree of differentiation.

The exception to the pattern was the NP, in which ideological factions ensured the party was more consistent in its positioning. However, even in this case this was not inevitable. In the mid-1990s the party did tone down its unification appeals and broaden its appeals to other issues. It is possible the party could have taken a centre right line if Yao Li-ming (姚立明) and colleagues had come out on top in the inner party power struggle. However, following the party's poor showing in the 1998

186 Dafydd Fell

elections, Chinese nationalists such as Lee Ching-hua (李慶華) and Hsieh Chi-ta (謝啟大) took the party to the far right of the spectrum. Thus the party responded to election defeat by taking positions ever further away from public opinion.

So what?

The book clearly reached a set of positive conclusions on the state of Taiwan's democracy. First, I argued that issues matter in Taiwanese elections and that voters were generally offered genuine policy choices in elections. Thus Taiwan's elections were not just a matter of selecting personalities. However, the parties were moving from polarised to more moderate centrist positions, contributing to Taiwan's democratic stability. My argument of moderate differentiation suggested that Taiwan had a healthy pattern of multi-party competition. I also argued that the study showed that party competition was not just centred on a single divisive issue cleavage but that there were cross-cutting cleavages. For instance, the DPP could work together with the NP on issues such as opposition to nuclear power but on some national identity-related questions such as scrapping the Provincial Government structure, it was the DPP and KMT cooperating.

I went on to argue that this democratic debate over political issues had brought about tangible benefits for Taiwanese society. In other words, elections had played a key conflict resolution role. Opposition parties had raised a range of issues in election campaigns such as social welfare inequality and political corruption. The electoral debate had led to changed norms at both the mass and elite levels, leading to solutions to critical social problems. For instance, I argue that this debate led to a much more equal and universal welfare system being developed and stricter controls on political corruption. The ruling party time and again was forced to respond to public opinion and messages from election campaigns. Even on the controversial issues of national identity and cross-Strait relations with China, I argued that electoral debate pushed the parties towards a tacit consensus on many aspects of national identity question by the end of the decade. In short, the responsive nature of political parties led me to argue that democracy was working in Taiwan.

Lastly I suggested that my issue case studies showed a link between parties' issue strategies and election outcome. In other words, I argued that where parties achieved the right issue formula, they would be likely to enjoy electoral payoffs. This formula involved a mix of a moderate national identity appeal together with a broad range of salient issue appeals. In contrast, I argued that campaigns focusing solely on radical national identity positions tended to be punished by Taiwan's moderate voters. Thus for the case of the DPP the worst possible issue package came in the 1991 National Assembly election, while this could be contrasted with the more successful 2000 presidential campaign.

PhD to book transfer

Since the book is based on PhD research it is worth saying a little about the 'dethesisising' process. I know that for many this can be a very challenging

Party Politics in Taiwan revisited **187**

transition and I have seen numerous cases where scholars gave up as they became overwhelmed with heavy teaching and administration loads in their initial post-graduation posts. In my case I waited until nine months after my PhD viva before I embarked on the revisions when I was being hosted at the Graduate Institute of Political Science at National Sun Yat Sen University in the summer of 2004. Amazingly the revision process was competed in only five weeks. Looking back, a number of reasons can explain this smooth transition.[2] I received detailed revision guidelines from my PhD examiners, the initial manuscript reviewers, as well as my book series editor. In addition I had submitted an article to the *Journal of East Asian Studies* that synthesised many of the key arguments in the PhD. The feedback I received from the journal's reviewers and especially from the journal's editor Stephan Haggard was invaluable in allowing me to fine tune my core arguments.

Revisiting *Party Politics in Taiwan* today

Book reviews

The first journal book reviews for *Party Politics in Taiwan* came out in 2006. The reviewers were Chu Yun-han (朱雲漢) (Chu 2006), Shelley Rigger (2006) and Murray Rubinstein (2006). All three have been influential in my own struggle to understand Taiwan's modern political history both during the research for the book and over the last decade. It was wonderful to see them in the audience at the conference where I first presented this chapter in 2015.

Of the three, Rubinstein was the most positive. I particularly appreciated his comment that 'he makes Party Politics in Taiwan accessible and interesting to a wider audience than many other books on Taiwan's present-day political system this reviewer has read over the course of his 26 years studying Taiwan' (Rubinstein 2006: 114). Shelley Rigger was also generally positive in her review. In particular she notes that, 'This book provides a detailed and persuasive corrective to the overly-negative assessments of Taiwan's democratic development' (Rigger 2006: 174). She concludes by stating 'it is hard not to be persuaded that as Fell writes in his conclusion, Taiwan's voters are sophisticated and moderate' and 'democracy is working well in Taiwan' (176).

Rigger's main criticism lay in the way I placed political issues at the centre of Taiwan's political process. I was thus challenging her conclusion that the private face of the campaign was more influential than the public face (Rigger 1999). There are at least two reasons why we came to different conclusions on the role of issues in Taiwanese politics. First, we conducted our core fieldwork at quite different periods of Taiwan's political history. As Rigger's fieldwork was mainly in the democratic transition period of the late 1980s to early 1990s, mine came a decade later in what could be termed the democratic consolidation period. A second and perhaps more important reason for the variation is that while Rigger spent much more time in grassroots factional politics, I was primarily analysing national level election campaigning material. Thus different research methods and material contributed to different conclusions. Rigger also suggested that I was missing other

188 Dafydd Fell

important dimensions of the campaign such as the importance of candidates. This is something that I have tried to address in a number of subsequent publications. For example, in studies employing the Lees-Marshment market-oriented parties framework (Lees-Marshment et al. 2009), I included the party leadership as a component of the political project (Fell and Cheng 2009). Similarly in a number of studies examining how parties attempted to learn the lessons of defeat in the post 2000 period, I included changing leadership as a key element of change (Fell 2010; Fell and Chen 2014).

Chu Yun-han's (2006) review was the most critical of the three. He argued that the focus of the book was too narrow. For instance, he noted how the book had said little about how parties are internally organised. With hindsight I realise that a more truthful title for the book should have been something like 'Party Platform Change in Taiwan' or 'Political Issues in Taiwanese Elections'. However, now that I also serve as a book series editor I understand that the drawback of a more specific title might be to reduce the market for a book. I was aware of the importance of internal party organisation and in fact my first post-PhD project was research on candidate selection and inner-party democracy. Although I have published a number of journal articles on the topic (Fell 2006a, 2006b), I am not sure whether I will ever complete my unfinished book on Taiwanese parties' candidate selection.

Naturally my positive conclusions on the state of Taiwan's democracy laid the book open to criticism. Chu, for instance, ended his review concluding, 'the emerging pattern of competitive party politics on Taiwan is in anything but a state of moderate differentiation' (Chu 2006: 190). To a certain extent my book came out at the wrong time. The controversial 2004 presidential election and the increasingly antagonistic and polarised party system of the second Chen Shui-bian term did seem to undermine my moderate differentiation argument. My immediate response to Chu's critique is that we should treat the book as a record of the development of Taiwan's party politics between 1991 and 2001 and not what happened after I submitted the manuscript. In fact towards the end of the second Chen term even I began to be more critical of the state of Taiwan's democracy in some of my writings (Fell, 2010).

Although not something in the book reviews, a number of readers have raised questions about the book's cover. With hindsight I should have insisted on using the actual party badge colours rather than the strange shade of green used on the cover. Other readers have thought it was a book about the NP as that party badge comes at the top. However, if I had placed the DPP or KMT at the top it could have been interpreted as favouring one side.

Revisiting *Party Politics in Taiwan* after a decade

Methodology

Since the publication of *Party Politics in Taiwan* I have published a series of journal articles and book chapters that continue to address the questions of measuring and explaining party change. I have also continued to rely on a range of data sources, particularly election advertising to measure patterns of change. However, I have moved away from the earlier method of using detailed statistical content analysis of election ads to plot party change. One reason for this was the amount of time that is required to manually code the full content of ads. Another factor has been the emergence of studies that feature far more systematic statistical methods of content analysis of election advertising. The key scholar revolutionising this kind of analysis has been Jonathan Sullivan (2008, 2009) with his work on election advertising. I have tended, instead, to rely more on qualitative analysis of newspaper and TV advertising to reveal key trends in issue emphasis and positional change. While TV ads were a secondary source in *Party Politics in Taiwan*, they have become more important as it is now much easier to get access to ads as parties increasingly also use YouTube channels and social media to broadcast them. I also still use this advertising data in conjunction with interview, elite discourse and the party image survey data. A future methodological challenge will of course be the use of the Internet and social media campaigning as a tool of measuring party change.

A second basic area that has required reconsideration since 2005 has been the parties to examine. After the NP's collapse in 2001 it no longer made sense to give the party the same level of treatment as I had in *Party Politics in Taiwan*. Although the Taiwan Solidarity Union (TSU) and People First Party (PFP) emerged as significant parties in the 2001 and 2004 elections, by the time *Party Politics in Taiwan* was published even these new challenger parties were in decline. The PFP was the most successful of these challengers and for a while looked to have the potential to become the largest Pan Blue party. One further challenge in studying the PFP was its overwhelming focus on personality and vague stance on issues. The decline of these new challenger parties culminated in the virtual disappearance of all small parties in 2008. These changes in the party system made the kind of time-series analysis of the smaller parties together with the DPP and KMT less effective. Instead since 2005 I have published a number of articles that look either at small parties overall or individual small parties (Fell 2005b; Fell 2006; Fell 2014). I have argued that the growing alienation of voters in the advent of the Sunflower movement of 2014 makes the analysis of potential alternatives to the mainstream parties all the more important.

The third methodological challenge was whether to change the issue focus in the post-2000 period. At the time I was writing the updated chapter 7, which considered the first Chen term, it appeared that both social welfare and political corruption had become far less salient and party competition was becoming concentrated solely on identity debates. Although welfare has declined in salience; it remains one of the top ten issues. In fact in the first Tsai administration after 2016, pension reform has been highly salient and controversial. However, the continued importance of the corruption issue was apparent within months of the book's publication, as the issue contributed to the DPP's disastrous election results in 2005. It also was a critical factor in the fall of the DPP in 2008 and Ma's second

190 Dafydd Fell

term fall in popularity. In short, all three of the three issue areas remain at the top of Taiwan's election agenda.

Overall, though, the issue agenda has changed sufficiently that if a new version of *Party Politics in Taiwan* were to be written for the post-2005 period it would need to have chapters on the political economy of cross-Strait relations, greater attention to topics such as the debate over social justice, constitutional reform, environmental politics and gender politics.

Revisiting the *How?*

As I mentioned in the book reviews section, my moderate differentiation argument needed to be reconsidered in the advent of post-2004 trends in party change. Although public opinion perceived polarisation in the first Chen term, this was not actually supported by the election campaign data. There was growing hostility in the party system but not yet genuine policy polarisation. However, there was a clear trend of polarisation in the second term, particularly after the Lien Chan visit to China and Ma's assumption of the KMT chairmanship in 2005. A variety of evidence and studies make the case that there was a polarising trend in the final years of the DPP era (Fell 2011b). Moreover both the small parties and large parties were moving away from the centre and public opinion. So the question is, was the second Chen term an anomaly or a trend-setting period for the subsequent post-2008 period? If the latter, then my moderate differentiation argument would no longer be applicable for understanding current Taiwanese party politics.

The picture in the post-2008 period is mixed. Although voters do not perceive any major shift in the polarised state of the party system, my subsequent election communication analysis and studies such as Hughes (2014) do show a degree of change. The DPP has clearly attempted to move away from the image of being an anti-China and radical pro-independence Taiwanese nationalist party. In a pattern similar to the 1990s, it has moved closer to the softer Taiwanese independence appeals and shifted towards other issue appeals. This was seen in its acceptance of many of the post-2008 agreements with China such as ECFA. Nevertheless, it tended to initially oppose most of these agreements and then later grudgingly came to accept them. Following the DPP's second presidential defeat in 2012 it was under pressure to adjust its China policy. It did moderate further in the run up to 2016, but there are still limits to change and essentially its position remains close to the 1999 Taiwan Future Resolution.

As for the smaller parties, there has been continuity, particularly in the case of the TSU and NP. With the DPP trying to look more moderate on China relations, the TSU has dominated the anti-integration appeals. While the TSU remained at its original location, the NP has actually moved further to the right. On national identity spectrum we can regard the party at a point towards the far right between the CCP and the KMT.

The more interesting case in terms of change has been the KMT. In the 2008 elections Ma had tried to use broad inclusive identity appeals with significant use of

Party Politics in Taiwan revisited   **191**

Taiwanese identity compared to the style employed by his predecessor Lien Chan. However, after coming to power, the KMT not only brought closer economic integration with China through a range of agreements, it also increasingly appeared to be returning to its former Chinese nationalist ideology. The KMT–CCP dialogue, the role of former KMT chair people in cross-Strait relations, together with the SEF-ARATS negotiations gave the impression that the KMT was close politically to the PRC. There was a similar pattern in its handling of national identity questions both in government discourse and cultural policies, moving the party to the far right of the national identity spectrum (Hughes 2014). This has led some observers to talk about a clear resinification project.

One other area featuring a major shift has been the topic of political corruption. This had been a DPP owned issue since the early 1990s and even at the time the book was published this remained an issue favouring the DPP. However, the string of DPP linked corruption scandals that first emerged in autumn of 2005, culminating in the 2006 Red Shirt movement led to the reversal of ownership. From 2005 the KMT made heavy use of this 'DPP equals political corruption and economic recession' argument for the remainder of the second DPP term. Even as late as the 2012 elections the KMT was reminding voters of the DPP's corruption record (Fell and Chen 2014). However, in Ma's second term a series of KMT corruption cases caused ownership to switch back to the DPP. In other words, the corruption issue has remained salient but issue ownership has been much less stable than in the 1990s.

Although social welfare has been less salient in the post-2000 period, the pattern seen in *Party Politics in Taiwan* has generally continued. In other words, the parties continued to converge and while existing welfare schemes have been protected from retrenchment, new schemes have been introduced. For instance in 2007 the universal pension's bill was passed and came into effect in 2008. As had been the case in 1997 (Wong 2004), an attempt was made to reform the UNHI system in 2010 but the eventual outcome was the so called *second generation UNHI* that in effect left the existing system intact. Although this remains an issue seen as more favourable for the DPP, the party image gap in policy between the two has narrowed significantly. Nevertheless, the heated debates over pensions reforms affecting traditionally pro-KMT occupational groups in the first Tsai Ing-wen presidency reveal how the parties remain distinct on welfare.

Why?

I have continued to employ the Harmel and Janda (1994) framework since *Party Politics in Taiwan* was published. For instance I have used it to explain patterns of candidate selection in the main parties (Fell, 2006), as once again changes in inner party balance of power following electoral setbacks were critical in explaining change in selection methods for both the KMT in 2000 and DPP after 2008. It has also remained the foundation of much of my analysis of party positional change for both the KMT and DPP since 2000. I have argued for instance that as the DPP became further dominated by ideological leadership it became more extreme in the second Chen term and election setbacks became less important (Fell 2011b, 2014a). However, the 2008 setback and the rise of Tsai Ing-wen (蔡英文) to party leadership, together with a new post-Chen factional balance, contributed to the more moderate DPP approach to national identity and China relations and its attempt to reach out on a broader set of issues. Nevertheless factional balance of power has limited Tsai's room for manoeuvre towards the centre.

At least initially the framework worked well for the KMT as it attempted to learn the lessons of defeats in first 2000 and then 2004 and the new factional leadership power structure explains much of the changes first under Lien and then post 2005 Ma led KMT. I have argued that to an extent Lien learnt the wrong lessons from 2000, while Ma was better at learning the lessons of 2004 and we saw this in his successful 2008 campaign (Fell 2008). However changes in the case of the KMT since 2008 offer a number of challenges to my original framework.

First, if we take Ma as an election-oriented politician and on the back of his historic election success in 2008, the framework would expect he should take a centre to centre right approach on national identity and China relations, particularly in his run up to the re-election bid of 2012. However, as we discussed in the previous section he moved the party further to the right.

Second, with hindsight I underestimated the importance of international variables. In *Party Politics in Taiwan* I tried to operationalise the impact of external forces such as China and the United States as intervening variables. In other words, I argued they would exert pressure on parties via public opinion in elections. For instance, the 1995–1996 cross-Strait crisis served to push the KMT and the DPP towards the centre because public opinion would oppose too radical policies that risked a Chinese attack but also required parties not be too weak on standing up to Chinese threats. However the growing economic integration with China and post the 2005 KMT–CCP relationship has meant that the China factor has changed the equation. In recent elections the Taishang have tried to play a more active role in supporting the KMT and this was particularly apparent in the 2012 campaign. However, the much closer relationship between the KMT and CCP has clearly had a growing shaping effect on the KMT and this was apparent in the meeting between KMT Chair Eric Chu and Xi Jinping in 2015. Another area that I neglected was the US effect. Clearly the United States has also played a growing role in trying to avoid cross-Strait tensions by trying to moderate the DPP. This was apparent in the DPP era, in the run up to the 2012 election and again in the sensitivity to the 2015 Tsai visit to the United States.

A third challenge is the question of whether what was supposedly an election-oriented leader or faction can change labels. In *Party Politics in Taiwan* I had categorised Chen Shui-bian as an election-oriented moderate politician; however, by 2006 he was widely regarded as a radical. To a certain extent we have seen a similar pattern in the case of Ma. Despite the fact that Taiwan's public opinion has continued to shift towards the centre left, Ma tried to move his party and government in the opposite direction while he was president.

To what extent does the Harmel and Janda (1994) explanatory framework still work for understanding the small parties? Clearly all three (NP, PFP and TSU) remain highly dominated by a single party leader. In the case of the NP, for instance, since 2001 Yu Mu-ming (郁慕明) has been the NP chairman, and in terms of identity he has taken a very consistent pro-unification Chinese nationalist line. Poor elections results have had no moderating effect and as the framework would predict, elections have not really improved since. However, as I have looked at the smaller parties in greater depth, I have trialled a number of alternative explanatory frameworks that were developed for explaining the impact of small parties in western European party systems (Fell 2005b, Fell 2006, Fell 2014b).

Reassessing the *So what?*

Let me now return to the *So what?* element of *Party Politics in Taiwan*. Despite the more cautious line I have taken in assessing the state of Taiwan's democracy since 2005 I still remain generally supportive of many of the positive conclusions I reached on Taiwan's democracy. First, there are no signs that the importance of issues has declined in Taiwanese elections. Moreover, though, as I discussed in the book reviews section the moderate differentiation argument was challenged in the advent of the polarisation of the second Chen term, the last few national elections have shown voters have a genuine choice with differentiated parties. Voters have rich information to make informed choices on policies. Moreover, public opinion and election results continue to constrain radical politics. We have seen how the DPP had tried to react to its defeats in 2008 by moderating. In the aftermath of its disastrous defeats in 2016 it is clear the KMT will need to move closer to public opinion to remain competitive. As should be expected, new challenges have emerged in the party system that I did not envisage originally. One is the dissatisfaction with mainstream parties and widespread hope for real alternatives beyond DPP/KMT splinter parties. This led me to devote much attention to Taiwan's Green Party, the subject hopefully of my next single authored book. Although it had looked possible that the Taiwan Green Party would make a national breakthrough in 2016, instead it was a much younger party, the New Power Party, that made the breakthrough. This is highly significant, as this is the first non-splinter party to enter parliament. It will be interesting to see how such third force parties will affect the political process.

The widespread distrust with political parties has led me to give greater attention to Taiwan's social movements over the last decade. This was a topic that I neglected in *Party Politics in Taiwan*, but that has grown in importance since the book came out. Mass protests such as the 2006 Red Shirts and 2014 Sunflower Movement were defining moments of the final years of both the Chen and Ma. In 2017 I edited a book titled *Taiwan's Social Movements under Ma Ying-jeou* that attempted to capture the new role that civil society plays in Taiwan's politics (Fell 2017). However, even here I have not entirely abandoned my original party focus, as much of my work remains centred on the social movement–political party relationship.

194 Dafydd Fell

I am also cautiously positive when it comes to earlier conclusions on the relationship between election campaigning and tangible benefits to Taiwanese society. Democracy has continued to drive Taiwan's move from an unequal welfare system to a more universal one. This was seen in the eventual introduction of the universal pensions bill and also the maintenance of the UNHI system after a second attempt to reform the system in 2010. Tsai's pledge to reform the pensions system during the 2016 campaign meant she could not sweep the issue under the carpet after coming to office. Voters have grown less tolerant of political corruption and continue to punish parties for perceived corruption. We saw this in the 2005 and 2008 elections, and political corruption was a major factor in the KMT's declining popularity after 2012.

On the issue of national identity, the partisan divergence does raise questions to my description of a tacit consensus. The polarising patterns we saw in the Chen and Ma second terms suggest that parties have not been responsive enough to public opinion. The cooperation between the KMT and CCP against the DPP does seem to have an effect on the ability of public opinion to shape KMT positions. However, again I would argue that it is important that issues such as China relations and Tongdu are debated in the elections. To an extent voters did punish the DPP for extremism in 2008, and even in 2012 the DPP's failure to persuade voters it was ready to handle China relations contributed to its failure to return to power. Similarly, voters punished the KMT (as well as the NP and Chinese Unification Promotion Party) for taking positions too close to the CCP's in the 2016 elections.

Lastly, I have continued to make the case for the issue formula for election success. In other words, the key is to offer a moderate stance on national identity (and China ties) plus a broad range of issues that are seen as salient to voters. Thus, for instance, when the KMT came to power in 2008 it did so with an inclusive identity appeal, a China policy vision, a mix of anti-corruption, as well as social and economic proposals. In 2012 the DPP's Tsai did try to offer a more moderate image on China and identity, compared with Chen, and stressed social justice, but I argued that her secondary appeals were not substantive enough, and on China not yet persuasive enough, to attract sufficient numbers of swing voters to switch sides (Fell and Chen 2014).

Conclusion

Rereading *Party Politics in Taiwan* over ten years after the initial publication reveals the book's strengths and weaknesses. Naturally the book works best as a record of the 1990s patterns of party platform change. Many of the subsequent political developments since 2004 have raised challenges to a number of my conclusions. However, with some slight revision much of the *How?*, *Why?* and *So what?* of the book are still highly relevant to today's Taiwan. If I were to write a new version examining party change in the post-2004 era there would actually be a huge degree of overlap in the framework, issues and arguments with the first book. Naturally over the last decade I have found myself moving towards a range of elements of party politics that I did not address in the book, such as candidate selection, party system change, small parties, party switching and party mergers. I have thus tried through my subsequent work to offer a broader understanding of Taiwan's party politics. However, I still remain in the shadow of *Party Politics in Taiwan*, I have my life sentence to serve. I am already planning my next election advertising data collection and using these ads to plot another round of patterns of party platform change. Similarly, though I became more reserved in my evaluation of the state of Taiwanese democracy, in my writings since 2014 I have found myself concluding that Taiwanese democracy remains in robust health. For instance, the second edition of *Government and Politics in Taiwan* (Fell 2018) is much more optimistic than the first edition published in 2011 (Fell 2011a).

Notes

1 I used *United Daily News, China Times* and *Liberty Times* as the three most popular newspapers and, since I was based in Kaohsiung, I used the Kaohsiung editions of these papers.
2 On a practical level the university's kindergarten played a key role as they looked after my young son during the daytime.

References

Benoit, Kenneth and Michael Laver. 2006. *Party Policy in Modern Democracies*. London: Routledge.
Budge, Ian, Hans-Dieter Klingemann, Andrea Volkens, Judith Bara and Eric Tannenbaum (eds) 2001. *Mapping Policy Preferences: Parties, Electors and Governments: 1945–1998*. Oxford: Oxford University Press.
Cheng, Tzu-leong. 1992. Jingxuan wenxuan celue: Guanggao, chuanbo yu zhengzhi xingxiao (Campaign Propaganda Strategy: Advertising, Broadcasting and Political Marketing). Taipei: Yuanliu.
Cheng, Tzu-leong. 1995. Jingxuan guanggao: Lilun, celue, yanjiu anli (Campaign Advertising: Theory, Strategy and Case Studies). Taipei: Chungcheng.
Chu, Yun-han. 2006. 'Review of Party Politics in Taiwan'. *China Quarterly* 185, 189–190.
Fell, Dafydd. 2005a. *Party Politics in Taiwan: Party Change and the Democratic Evolution of Taiwan*. London: Routledge.
Fell, Dafydd. 2005b. 'Success and Failure of New Parties in Taiwan'. *China: An International Journal* 3(2), 212–239.
Fell, Dafydd. 2006a. 'Democratization of Candidate Selection in Taiwanese Political Parties'. *Journal of Electoral Studies* 13(2), 167–198.
Fell, Dafydd. 2006b. 'The Rise and Decline of the New Party: Ideology, Resources and the Political Opportunity Structure'. *East Asia* 23(1), 47–67.
Fell, Dafydd. 2008. 'Party Competition in Taiwan: Towards a New Party System?' In Steven Goldstein and Julian Chang (eds), *Presidential Politics in Taiwan: The Administration of Chen Shui-bian*. Norwalk: Eastgate, 49–84.
Fell, Dafydd. 2010. 'Taiwan's Democracy: Towards a Liberal Democracy or Authoritarianism?' *Journal of Current Chinese Affairs*, 39(2), 187–201.
Fell, Dafydd. 2011a. *Government and Politics in Taiwan* (1st edn). London: Routledge.

Fell, Dafydd. 2011b. 'Polarization of Party Competition in the DPP Era'. In Robert Ash, John Garver and Penny Prime (eds), *Taiwan's Democracy: Economic and Political Challenges*. London: Routledge, 75–98.

Fell, Dafydd. 2014a. 'Taiwan's Party System in the Ma Ying-jeou Era'. In Jean-Pierre Cabestan and Jacques deLisle (eds), *Political Changes in Taiwan under Ma Ying-jeou*. London: Routledge, 37–59.

Fell, Dafydd. 2014b. 'Measuring and Explaining the Electoral Fortunes of Small Parties in Taiwan's Party Politics'. *Issues and Studies. An International Quarterly on China, Taiwan, and East Asian Affairs* 50(1), 153–188.

Fell, Dafydd (ed.). 2017. *Taiwan's Social Movements under Ma Ying-jeou: From the Wild Strawberries to the Sunflowers*. London: Routledge.

Fell, Dafydd. 2018. *Government and Politics in Taiwan* (2nd edn). London: Routledge.

Fell, Dafydd and Chen, I-hsin Charles. 2014. 'Lessons of Defeat and Success: Taiwan's 2012 Elections in Comparative Perspective'. *Journal of Current Chinese Affairs*, 43(3), 13–43.

Fell, Dafydd and Isabelle Cheng. 2009. 'Testing the Market Orientated Model of Political Parties in a Non-western Context: The Case of Taiwan'. In Jennifer Lees-Marshment, Chris Rudd and Jesper Strömbäck (eds), *Global Political Marketing*. London and New York: Routledge, 175–188.

Harmel, Robert and Kenneth Janda. 1994. 'An Integrated Theory of Party Goals and Party Change'. *Journal of Theoretical Politics* 6(3), 259–287.

Heidenheimer, Arnold. 2002. 'Perspectives on Perceptions of Corruption'. In Arnold Heidenheimer and Michael Johnston (eds), *Political Corruption: Concepts and Contexts*, 3rd edn. New Jersey: Transaction Press, 141–154.

Hughes, Christopher. 2014. 'Revisiting Identity Politics under Ma Ying-jeou'. In Jean-Pierre Cabestan and Jacques deLisle (eds), *Political Changes in Taiwan under Ma Ying-jeou*. London: Routledge, 100–119.

Lees-Marshment, Jennifer, Chris Rudd and, Jesper Strömbäck (eds). 2009. *Global Political Marketing*. London and New York: Routledge.

Liu, Tsung-wei. 2002. 'The Effects of Electoral Laws on Party Competition in Taiwan. 1989–1998'. PhD Dissertation, University of Essex.

Petrocik, John. 2003–2004. 'Issue Ownership and Presidential Campaigning, 1952–2000'. *Political Science Quarterly* 118(4), 599–626.

Rigger, Shelley. 1999. *Politics in Taiwan: Voting for Democracy*. London: Routledge.

Rigger, Shelley. 2006. 'Review of *Party Politics in Taiwan*'. *China Review* 6(2), 174–176.

Rubinstein, Murray. 2006. 'Review of *Party Politics in Taiwan*'. *Pacific Affairs* 79(1), 114–115.

Sullivan, Jonathan. 2008. 'Campaign Advertising and Democracy in Taiwan', *The China Quarterly* 196, 900–911.

Sullivan, Jonathan. 2009. 'Campaign Advertising in Taiwanese Presidential Elections'. *Journal of Contemporary China* 18(61), 675–688.

Wong, Joseph. 2004. *Healthy Democracies: Welfare Politics in Taiwan and South Korea*. London: Cornell University Press.

12

WRITING TAIWANESE

Then and now, how, why and who?

Henning Klöter

Pathways to written Taiwanese

My initial interest in written Taiwanese (*Taiyu*) resulted from coincidence and curiosity. It was pure coincidence that first brought me to Taiwan in 1996, as an exchange student at National Taiwan University, where I took a seminar course in sociolinguistics at the Graduate Institute of Linguistics. One of the course readings was Huang Shuanfan's (黃宣範) seminal study on language, society and ethnic consciousness in Taiwan (Huang 1993), one chapter of which is a comparison of the national language movement after 1949 with the Japanese language movement. This chapter briefly touches on the nativist literature debate, i.e. the first attempts by the young intellectuals Ng Sek-hui 黃石輝 (1900–1945) and Koeh Chhiu-seng 郭秋生 (1904–1980) to create a nativist Taiwanese language literature (Huang 1993: 93–94). When reading these paragraphs, some questions immediately came to my mind. As a graduate in sinology, I had been aware of the fact that the oldest documents written in Southern Min dialects dated back to the Ming dynasty. In other words, when Ng, Koeh and other writers debated the question as to how particular Taiwanese words should be written, closely related Southern Min dialects already had a written history of more than 400 years. Thus, in a certain respect, the debate of the 1930s seemed like a re-invention of the wheel. This aspect, however, was left unmentioned both in the young intellectuals' debate on nativist literature and in Huang's study. Why was it not mentioned? When I was first thinking about this question, I was not aware that in ideological terms I was skating on thin ice.

My first stay in Taiwan happened to coincide with a time of controversial debates regarding the status of local languages vis-à-vis Mandarin as the national standard language. Not surprisingly, one issue in these debates was the question whether and how Taiwanese should be written. Many different proposals were devised and promoted by local language revivalist groups. Did this amount to yet another re-invention of the wheel? A more pressing question that initially came to my mind was clearly along the lines of philological sinology: *How* was Southern Min written during the Ming dynasty, *how* was Taiwanese written during the 1930s, and *how* was it written in the late 1990s? Which characters were used to render certain Southern Min and/or Taiwanese expressions? A first perusal of the materials at the Fu Ssu-Nien Library at the Academia Sinica revealed that my curiosity could only be satisfied through a broader-based project. This is the brief version of the story behind my PhD thesis simply entitled 'Written Taiwanese', defended at Leiden University in 2003 and published, with minor revisions, under the same title in 2005 (Klöter 2005).

As indicated above, at the initial stage of my research, philological curiosity prevailed over sociolinguistic interest. I hoped to provide as accurate a description as possible of how Taiwanese was written in the past and present. Such a description would serve as a key to understanding historical and present-day Taiwanese texts, be they written in Chinese characters or the Roman alphabet. It turned out that the answers would be quite complex from a linguistic perspective. Despite this complexity, it soon became clear that I was only looking at one side of the coin, fully ignoring another crucial question: why? To give a simple example, linguistic description can satisfactorily explain how the spelling 'chhù' of the Taiwanese word for 'home' relates to the pronunciation of the word in the spoken language. Similar explanations can be provided for the spelling 'chu^3' standing for the same word. Since there is a certain degree of arbitrariness in the use of letters and diacritics matching certain sounds, even the most accurate linguistic description would be unable to explain which of these two versions is better or more appropriate. But then, on the other hand, debates on written Taiwanese often foreground value judgments by declaring that a certain script, character, letter or letter combination or diacritic is 'inappropriate', 'wrong', 'to be rejected', etc. In the absence of a standard, different conceptions of right and wrong writing resulted in a plethora of spelling schemes, using Chinese characters, different transcription systems based on the Roman alphabet or a mixture of both. Interestingly, however, whereas it was not a major problem to find these schemes, it turned out to be quite difficult to find a justification of the advantages of one particular scheme in published form. Thus, if I wanted to find out *why* a certain scheme was supposedly 'better' than another, my only option was to find and ask the people behind the script. Therefore the question 'why?' consequently led to the question 'who?'. Fortunately, many of the dictionaries, prose collections, newsletters, etc. that I had in front of me contained contact details, and setting up interviews was not much of a problem. Anecdotally, the only minor obstacle was a misunderstanding that sometimes cropped up when first calling my prospective interviewees. My Mandarin self-introduction as a PhD student from a university in the Netherlands (Hélán) was occasionally misheard as Hénán, a province in mainland China. In one case, this misunderstanding led to a prompt rejection of my request, which was fortunately withdrawn once the misunderstanding was resolved. This and other similar reactions alerted me to the political sensitivity of my project.

My attempt to unfold the ideological dimensions of written Taiwanese therefore resulted in a series of semi-structured interviews, which will be explained presently. These interviews greatly contributed to my understanding of the heterogeneities of written Taiwanese at the beginning of the early twenty-first century. In short, the book *Written Taiwanese* (Klöter 2005) is an attempt to find answers to the questions 'how?', 'why?' and 'who?'.

A short history of written Taiwanese

As mentioned above, when I first arrived in Taiwan, I had just received a Master's degree in sinology from Leiden University. By foregrounding historical developments, using philological methodology, and looking at literary texts and dictionaries as the most obvious manifestations of writing, the concept of my dissertation was very much in line with my previous sinological training. Combined with the aforementioned three questions, this approach resulted in five chapters. The first chapter is a general introduction to Taiwan's language situation, complemented by a brief linguistic description of Taiwanese phonology, lexicon and a few peculiarities in the field of syntax.

The remainder of the book follows a strict chronological order, starting with the earliest extant sources written in Southern Min dialects, including printed editions of regional stage plays, songbooks and rhyme books of the seventeenth and eighteenth centuries as well as bilingual Southern Min–Spanish dictionaries written by anonymous Western missionaries and their Chinese tutors compiled during the same period. The briefest version of my answer to the question 'how?' would be: in many ways. As a matter of fact, in these earliest sources, most of the 'words which are typically Mǐn' (Norman 1988: 232) do not have standardised spellings, which results in a high degree of heterogeneity in terms of character use. At the same time, it was shown that due to early cultural contacts with Western missionaries, alphabetic writing of Southern Min has a history of more than 400 years. Why was Southern Min written in those early days? Mostly for the use of actors, singers, preachers and other performers. In other words, the written texts were not meant to be disseminated to readers; rather, they fulfilled auxiliary functions in performative situations of spoken language use.

The third chapter traces the history of written Taiwanese into the nineteenth century, when alphabetic writing (how?) promoted by Western missionaries (who?) reached unprecedented dimensions. By the end of the nineteenth century, Southern Min written in the Roman alphabet was widely read in Amoy mission circles, and it had crossed the Taiwan Strait to become the medium of the first printed newspaper in the history of Taiwan, the Tâi-oân-hú-siâⁿ Kàu-hōe-pò (*Taiwan Prefecture City Church News*), issued by the Presbyterian Church.

The fourth chapter looks at written Taiwanese in the historical context of the Japanese colonial period when the writing of Taiwanese became the object of both

200 Henning Klöter

governmental and non-governmental language planning (who?). The Japanese colonial government compiled a number of readers and dictionaries aimed at easing communication between colonial administrators and the local population during the first years of colonial rule. Written Taiwanese in these publications is a mixture of Chinese characters and Japanese *kana* (how?) for the indication of pronunciation. Non-governmental language planning during the Japanese colonial period marks an important turning point in the history of written Taiwanese. For the first time in Taiwan's history, it is possible to provide a combined answer to my three guiding questions: Literary journals of that period afford ample evidence of proposals by aforementioned language activists like Ng Sek-hui and Koeh Chhiu-seng (who?) as to *how* to write Taiwanese, combined with political statements of *why* it should be written. In its ideological dimensions, the writing of Taiwanese was connected to the rise of anti-Japanese sentiments and, closely linked to this, the growth of a Taiwanese national identity.

The fifth chapter jumps to the period of my research, i.e. the transition to the twenty-first century. When I conducted my research in Taiwan, the claim that there was a Taiwanese language on an equal footing with Mandarin and different from any linguistic variety spoken in China seemed to be widespread. In common language use, it had become utterly normal to speak of a Taiwanese language widely referred to as Taiyu (Tâi-gí or Tâi-gú in Taiwanese). Conducting research on written Taiwanese in the contemporary period allowed me to utilise the advantage of meeting the answers to my 'who' question in person. Concretely, between February 2000 and July 2001, I conducted a series of interviews with language activists and interviewed 16 people who were, in the widest sense, engaged in writing Taiwanese: literary writers, editors, language teachers, lexicographers, academics, etc. (for an overview, see Klöter 2005: 305–307; some five years earlier, transcripts of similar interviews with ten people had been published by a group of Taiwanese students, cf. Iunn 1995). The interviews were not intended to cover the current state of affairs in its entirety or to capture examples representing a general trend or even a possible outcome of the process of standardisation. My main intention was simply to get a better understanding of the social backgrounds, ideological motivations and activities of the 'people behind the scripts' (Klöter 2003). At that time, written Taiwanese was promoted by various language revivalist groups in all major cities. Until now, no study has assessed the dominance of a certain mode of writing in statistical terms, for example by comparing the numbers of active members of different revivalist groups, the number of publications in different scripts, etc.

During my research in Taiwan, it was, however, quite obvious that advocates of an alphabetic orthography were most active and attracted the largest audience. Since the establishment and spread of alphabetic writing in Taiwan was closely bound to activities of the Presbyterian Church, the alphabetic orthography widely used by language groups in southern Taiwan is known as Church Romanization (*Jiaohui luomazi* 教會羅馬字). In *Written Taiwanese*, I briefly introduce two groups, the *Ko-hiong tai-gi lo-ma-ji gian-sip-hoe* (Kaohsiung Seminar for Church

Romanization) and the *Tai-oan lo-ma-ji hiap-hoe* (Association of Taiwanese Romanization), both of which were founded by a local physician. The former was a rather loose, seminar-like group supported by some 600 people, mostly local schoolteachers, interested in the cultivation of Taiwanese and Church Romanization. The latter was formally registered with the Interior Ministry in 2001. It comprised about 200 members from Taiwan and abroad. Among the members were scholars, politicians, journalists, teachers and priests of the Presbyterian Church. The main argument in favour of alphabetic writing was its 'non-Chineseness' and its historical rootedness. As regards the former, the promotion of Taiwanese written with the Roman alphabet deliberately aimed at an ideological demarcation of Taiwanese from Mandarin. As one of the members of a local reading group explained during an interview, Chinese characters insult and damage Taiwan (cf. Klöter 2005: 219). The adequacy of alphabetic writing was, in other words, a 'negative adequacy': it was considered more adequate because it was not the Chinese script. In the general context of ideological de-sinification, it was not surprising that local language groups promoting alphabetic writing were quite successful in attracting members of different professional backgrounds.

The five chapters are appended by lists of Southern Min/Taiwanese expressions, ranging from an^3-$cuann^2$ 'how, why' to toh^4 'which', and their written representation in selected sources from the past four centuries. If I had to sum up the insight gained from these lists in one word, it would be heterogeneity. Heterogeneity applies with regard not only to the use of different characters, but also to the use of different scripts in general, such as Chinese characters, the Roman alphabet and Japanese *kana*. In order to distinguish more clearly between the different facets of heterogeneity, I applied the terms digraphia and diorthographia, which were first used by Petr Zima with reference to the existence of two scripts for the Hausa language. According to Zima, digraphia refers to the co-existence of 'two types of written form of one language ... based upon the usage of two distinct graphical systems (scripts) by the respective language community' (Zima 1974: 58). Diorthographia, on the other hand, is defined as the co-existence of '[t]wo types of written form of a particular language ... using the same script, but they are based upon the usage of two distinct orthographies by the same language community' (ibid.). Since the publication of Zima (1974), the term digraphia has been applied in several case studies where it is mainly applied to two situations, viz. (a) the co-existence of two writing systems for the same language, (b) the change of writing systems for a language (Grivelet 2001: 3). As regards written Taiwanese, the term digraphia turns out to be too limited if we want to capture the degree of orthographic heterogeneity. Obviously, as mentioned above, there are more than two writing systems used to write Taiwanese. Within different scripts, there are various ways to render the same expression. In *Written Taiwanese*, I therefore proposed the term 'polygraphia' to account for the existence of more than two scripts for writing the same language (2005: 37ff.).[1]

In very brief terms, the history of written Taiwanese is a history of polygraphia and polyorthographia, the concrete manifestations of which can only be

202   Henning Klöter

understood in the context of what is identified by the questions how, who, and why. In the conclusion of *Written Taiwanese*, I therefore argue

> that the complexities involved in the examination of sources require a complementary approach. Only descriptions of the ways in which various scripts render the Taiwanese language legible enable us to approach the contents of Táiyǔ literature and lexicography. On the other hand, answers to questions on the diversity of written Taiwanese lie outside the realm of grapheme-morpheme relations. Instead, they are to be sought in the changing ideological patterns which have emerged from Taiwan's tumultuous past.
>
> *(Klöter 2005: 251)*

Written Taiwanese – then and now

The book edition of my dissertation was published in 2005 and reviewed in four international journals (Alleton 2005, Heylen 2007, Lien 2006, Mair 2006). The reviews are all favourable and only identify minor points of criticism. To give one example, my aforementioned argument about the distinction of texts written for individual (silent) reading and texts written for recitation aloud has important implications for the analysis of polygraphia. The neglect of this important argument in *Written Taiwanese* was pointed out by Lien (2006: 145). When looking at the reviews, however, it becomes evident that all reviewers have a similar academic background to my own, i.e. sinology combined with linguistics or vice versa. The reviews therefore helped me to reflect on specific details and arguments within the boundaries of my original framework, but not to question the framework as such. The remainder of this chapter will therefore be devoted to a reappraisal of my previous research on written Taiwanese by identifying new or modified analytical approaches to the subject matter. This reappraisal inevitably leads to the question whether and how the situation of written Taiwanese has changed since I collected my data some 20 years ago.

In general terms, my reappraisal of some of the ideas and arguments set out in *Written Taiwanese* was the attempt to develop a stronger comparative perspective. This attempt greatly benefited from the unfolding of Taiwan Studies in Europe at the beginning of the twenty-first century. Regular interdisciplinary dialogue with academics specialising in neighbouring fields of Taiwan Studies, such as history, literature, politics, society or media, helped me in placing my own research in a comparative perspective within Taiwan Studies. This resulted in articles on language planning before and after the change of government in 2000 (Klöter 2006), language ideologies during the Japanese colonial period and after 1945 (Klöter 2009), language regimes (Klöter 2010), language ideologies in Taiwanese TV advertisements (Klöter 2012a, 2012b) and ideological diversity behind the nativist literature debate of the 1930s (Klöter 2012c). Outside Taiwan Studies, new developments in the fields of sociolinguistics and language planning helped me to deepen my understanding of two of my three guiding questions: who and why? To be sure, in *Written Taiwanese*, I had been able to identify individuals who can be

Writing Taiwanese. Then and now, how, why and who? **203**

associated with past or present attempts to write Taiwanese. New publications in the fields of language attitudes, language ideologies (for example, linguistic purism and language secessionism), historical sociolinguistics and orthography studies have shown that a comparative perspective with examples from outside Taiwan can contribute to a better understanding of these individuals and their sociolinguistic agenda. Thus, in the sections that follow, I expand on my previous research by linking it to definitions, examples and explanations in recent sociolinguistic publications.

Why? – Writing, ideologies, and language activism

Promoting a script for an unwritten language is closely linked with language attitudes and the ideologies behind them. Attitudes and ideologies are mutually dependent. As Garret points out, '[w]ithin sociolinguistics and language attitudes, language ideology has come to the fore as a politically more sensitive backdrop to investigations of language variation and language change and the values placed on linguistic alternatives' (Garrett 2010: 34). He specifies the link between language attitude and language ideology by applying it to the legitimisation of standard languages. He writes that

> [s]tandard languages are given legitimacy and prestige over non-standard alternatives. Speakers tend to confer prestige on language varieties that are seen as those of higher social classes. Some legitimacy is also achieved through the writing of histories of languages, which can be seen largely as codifications of the standard language, legitimising it, in part, through supplying it with 'continuous unbroken history' (Milroy 2007: 138). Against such a backdrop, then, language attitudes can be viewed as being influenced by powerful ideological positions.
>
> *(Garrett 2010: 34)*

The same argumentation can be applied to non-standard languages or language varieties, especially if their status is contested. In the case of Taiwanese during the Japanese colonial period and today, legitimisation is *attempted* legitimisation of an aspired status as a response to linguistic marginalisation. Such attempts to give legitimacy and prestige to non-standard alternatives have different forms, writing language histories – or at least some kind of historical account – being one of them. Much more emphasis, however, lies on attempts to create a written standard for languages which, due to a lack of standardisation, do not possess an established form of written expression. In theories of language planning or language management, such attempts are known as 'graphization', i.e. the 'provision of writing systems for unwritten languages' (Cooper 1989: 126). Emphasising the linguistic and technological dimensions of writing, traditional orthography studies view orthography 'as a technology for 'reducing a language to writing'' (Sebba 2000: 926, referring to Lepsius 1855 and Pike 1947). As Sebba (2012: 1) points out, for some linguists 'developing a writing system was to be viewed mainly as a technical matter, a matter of assigning "one letter, and one letter only for each phoneme" in the words of Kenneth Pike (1938: 87)'. However, as Sebba and many others have rightly argued, this traditional view disregards the ideological dimensions behind script selection and orthography debates. In the words of Sebba, we should reject 'the idea that writing systems and orthographies are socially neutral technologies' (Sebb 2012: 9). In a similar vein, Schieffelin and Doucet write that

> the creation of supposedly arbitrary sound/sign (signifier/signified) relationships that constitute an orthography always involves choices based on someone's idea of what is important. This process of representing the sounds of language in written form is thus an activity deeply grounded in frameworks of value.
>
> *(Schieffelin and Doucet 1998: 285)*

The ideological dimensions behind writing become more evident when we compare this linguistic understanding of writing with an ethnographic understanding. In a much quoted article, James Clifford equated writing with 'the making of texts' (Clifford 1986: 2) and hence as a mode of production 'that is always caught up in the invention, not the representation of cultures' (ibid.).[2] It is at this precise juncture that the two meanings of *write* – 'production, invention' and 'representation of language with a script' – interact. The identification of a language – its 'production' or 'invention' – coalesces with the ideological re-evaluation of existing varieties previously regarded as dialects. The re-evaluation is in turn closely linked to attempts to establish a written norm for the language. Written languages generally enjoy higher prestige than unwritten languages. As Coulmas aptly writes,

> Writing always meant distinction, and consequently language groups since antiquity have vied to attain written status for their languages. A written language used for government, law, schooling and cult is at the same time an instrument and symbol of dominance.
>
> *(Coulmas 2005: 206)*

Both the creation of a written standard for a hitherto unwritten language and the change of a script typically occur within processes of cultural and ideological reorientation. For example, analysing the promotion of written Corsican, Jaffe writes that Corsican 'texts "proved" that Corsican met conventional and dominant criteria of "languageness": that it had internal unity and structure, and was clearly differentiated from other linguistic codes' (Jaffe 1999: 41). In the light of the previous arguments, the writing of Taiwanese is more than just searching Chinese characters for Taiwanese morphemes (cf. Cheng 1978). It is about the attribution of 'languageness' to what, until the Japanese colonial period, was perceived as distinct Southern Min dialects spoken in Taiwan. Significantly, according to Hsiau, it was primarily because of the confrontation between the colonialized and the colonizer that categories such as 'Taiwanese people' and 'Taiwanese language' were created

(Hsiau 2000: 4). In other words, writing Taiwanese is about the invention of a Taiwanese language and its status within the linguistic hierarchy of Taiwan.

In short, writing Taiwanese in a linguistic sense – the (attempted) establishment of a standard orthography – cannot be separated from writing in the sense of 'production': the production or invention of a Taiwanese language, the proof of its 'languageness'. In the case of Taiwanese, this 'invention' or the identification of Taiwanese as an independent language leads to the question to what extent can it be distinguished from other varieties – a process which is known, mostly in the Spanish context, as language secessionism ('secesionismo lingüístico', cf. *inter alia* Agulló Calatayud 2011). Since the mutual unintelligibility of regional Sinitic varieties has been pointed out in various publications, it would thus not take much effort to define Taiwanese 'languageness' vis-à-vis Mandarin, Cantonese or Shanghainese. The case is more complicated, however, if Taiwanese needs to be seceded from its related Southern Min dialects in mainland China and Southeast Asia. Put in other words, what makes Taiwanese different from Amoy, the Southern Min spoken in the city of Xiamen? How can one justify the secession of Taiwanese from other Southern Min varieties? Compare the following two claims. The Ethnologue database writes: 'Amoy and Taiwanese are easily mutually intelligible' (Simons and Fennig 2018). According to Lí Khîn-hōaⁿ, a linguist at National Taiwan Normal University, 'Amoy and Taiwanese appear to be two different languages' (Li 2003: 65). From a linguistic perspective, it would indeed be unproblematic to identify a high degree of mutual intelligibility between Amoy and Taiwanese. On this basis, we could support the first claim and reject the latter as an ideological construct. But this would be to oversimplify matters, since it would imply that the identification of a language is purely based on linguistic criteria. Following Chambers and Trudgill's (1998: 4) argument that 'paradoxically enough, a "language" is not a particularly linguistic notion at all', we should not deny the importance of language ideology and, by implication, the relevance of non-linguistic factors when it comes to language secessionism. The linguistic map of the world as we know it today abounds with glossonyms that are the results of ideology-driven social movements, be they secessionism or processes of nation building. In this respect, the claim that there is a Taiwanese language is by no means exceptional.

It is only a short step from the expression of attitudes or beliefs about language to language management. To quote Spolsky (2009: 4): 'beliefs that are most significant to language policy and management are the values or statuses assigned to named languages, varieties, and features'. Language planning involves the question of agency (who?). In sociolinguistics, the issue of language attitudes and their expression in language planning by members of particular social groups has received attention in the context of linguistic purism. As Langer and Nesse (2012: 616) write:

> Traditionally, we identify members of the educated elites as the key players in puristic efforts, although in modern times these are only very rarely people

with an academic training in linguistics ... but in previous centuries, being a grammarian typically coincided with being a translator, a poet or writer, and a lexicographer. The emergence of linguistic purism in most European languages is causally linked to the desire to make one's vernacular language into a standard variety. In the seventeenth century several societies concerned with language emerged in many European countries, whose aim was to promote the use of vernacular languages. The foundation of such societies, whose members were typically drawn from the aristocracy and bourgeoisie, was prompted by an aversion to the use of foreign languages in educated discourse.

Instead of following the specific notion of purism, I look at expressions of language perception in general terms, and the articulation of language perception by particular individuals in particular social contexts. Individual responses to language policies dominated by Japanese or Mandarin arguably have much in common with language purism in European contexts some 300 years earlier. They are linked to a perceived weakness and to ideals of standardisation, and they are expressed by people with an interest in language, but not by linguists. Referring to Europe in the seventeenth century, Langer and Nesse (2012: 616) write:

> At a time when linguistic variation was seen to be a sign of chaotic weakness, in contrast to the much more uniform model languages of Latin and Greek, a further ambition was to provide a standardized language with a uniform grammar, an ideal pronunciation, and a pure lexicon. Language scholars, either as part of such societies or independently, pursued these aims by engaging in metalinguistic discussions and publications.

Here I am not concerned with language scholars in the narrow sense, but rather in a broad sense with language activists, i.e. 'individuals or groups who, through various means, actively defend their right to venerate and freely use their languages in multiple, often public domains' (Combs and Penfield 2012: 462). Language attitudes developed 'as a reaction to larger, state-imposed efforts to suppress or discourage the use of non-dominant languages' (ibid.). In sociolinguistic literature, non-governmental groups or individuals have been identified as one group of agents of language planning. Spolsky (2009: 204), for example, writes that '[l]anguage activists are significant participants in language management. They constitute individuals and groups whose ideology is clearest in support of the maintenance or revival or spread of a threatened target language'. Lacking institutional backing, the measures taken by non-governmental activists are typically less promising than those of government institutions. As Cooper (1989: 183) writes: 'Language planning may be initiated at any level of a social hierarchy, but it is unlikely to succeed unless it is embraced and promoted by elites and counterelites.' Edwards has a more pessimistic stance when he draws a clear line between 'effective areas of language planning' and planning by 'non-dominant groups': 'I write "effective" here because, as noted, many individuals and non-dominant groups are

Writing Taiwanese. Then and now, how, why and who? **207**

also in planning exercises: their status, however, means that most of their management efforts are tenuous or ephemeral' (Edwards 2012: 429, original emphasis).

Who? – Dentists and other 'folk linguists'

The aforementioned promotion of alphabetic writing for its 'non-Chineseness'
nicely exemplifies the force of language ideology behind language planning, be it
governmental or non-governmental. In the case of written Taiwanese, it has to be
emphasised that the demand for political independence is not necessarily con-
comitant with de-Sinification as an ideological *leitmotif* behind orthography design.
In *Written Taiwanese* (Klöter 2005: 200–206), I introduce the example of the
novelist, publisher, ex-political activist and self-taught philologist Yang Qingchu
(Iûⁿ Chheng-chhiok, 1940–). A former worker at an oil refinery in the southern
port of Kaohsiung, Yang was imprisoned for political activism after the Kaohsiung
Incident in 1979.[3] After his release in 1983, he embarked upon philological
research on the etymology of Taiwanese expressions and Taiwanese character
readings. What at first sight may seem a radical break from story writing was in fact
a consistent attempt to solve a practical problem that Yang had encountered during
his early years as a writer. The lack of a satisfactory reference work for Taiwanese
in the 1970s had prevented him from enriching his works by writing in pure Taiwanese. In order to fill this gap, Yang privately hired six research assistants and
retired to the rooms of his new publishing house in Taipei. His efforts led to the
compilation of a bilingual Mandarin–Taiwanese dictionary and a corresponding
Taiwanese–Mandarin volume (Yang 1992, 1998). A 15-volume Taiwanese textbook series (Yang 1999) was published just one year after the latest edition of the
dictionary. This series serves the dual purpose of exemplifying Yang's orthography
and reviving the Taiwanese reading tradition of Chinese classics.

Yang Qingchu is not an individual case. Like him, quite a few compilers of
Taiwanese dictionaries operate individually, i.e. outside a network of language
activists. They qualify as what Albury (2014: 85–86) has dubbed 'folk linguists':

> unlike official language policy makers and planners who have presumably
> attained a level of linguistic training that qualifies them to carry out their
> duties, these individuals, families and communities are in the vast majority of
> cases neither linguists nor employed in a professionally linguistic capacity.
> Their inexpert status in linguistics, however, does not prevent them from
> drawing on their folk knowledge and beliefs about language to carry out, and
> even design language policy. They routinely decide how, when and where to
> use language and, in effect, solve language problems. These inexpert linguists
> are by default folk linguists of language policy.

When presenting the results of my research on written Taiwanese, I was more than
once criticised for including Taiwan's folk linguists. The core of the critique shall
be explained by comparing the following two scenarios. Scenario 1: A retired

dentist devises a Taiwanese script in his dusty, abandoned office. He uses this script in teaching manuals and a voluminous dictionary comprising 1,528 pages. The dictionary makes its way to the shelves of a few bookstores, but the script is never ever used in any Taiwanese text except those written by the dentist himself. Scenario 2 is represented by groups promoting alphabetic writing sketched above. In scenario 1 we encounter individual language planners without an efficient network that would enable them to disseminate their 'aspired standards' much beyond the boundaries of their working environment. Due to their professional backgrounds, their approaches to written Taiwanese cannot be legitimised by academic authority. At the same time, there are quite large revivalist groups in terms of number of participants, which are successful in regional networking and cooperating with local education authorities. These groups are promoting a script that, due to its long history of usage in Taiwan, does not require legitimisation on the grounds of academic authority. Why, then, bother with the former and not focus on the latter? To do so would imply that language activism is only worthy of scholarly attention if it has a chance of success. This approach would be too narrow, since only an examination of a broader spectrum of agendas in the field of language planning aptly reflects the full spectrum of language ideologies and language attitudes at a certain time. To be sure, the question of representativeness should not be evaded. We can also assume that the aforementioned dentist will in all likelihood not succeed in becoming the founding father of the first Taiwanese standard orthography. Yet his contributions are still meaningful in sociolinguistic terms. His textbooks and dictionaries were written in response to a perceived lacuna and as an act of attempted legitimisation of a language that is 'unwritten' in two senses: lack of standard orthography and recognition as a language.

Writing Taiwanese today: Between Holopedia and Taiwanese literacy?

From the perspective of language planning, a question that suggests itself is whether written Taiwanese would ever be standardised. Some 20 years ago, the prospects were dim, which led me to 'claim that idiosyncrasies in the written representation of Taiwanese are here to stay' (Klöter 2005: 252). At the same time, I had become aware of the fact that 'students of written Taiwanese are at times hard pressed to keep apace with developments' (Klöter 2005: 251). This now leads to the question whether developments towards the standardisation of written Taiwanese have taken place during the 15 years since I completed my book manuscript. This question will be addressed in the final section of this chapter.

When I conducted my first research on written Taiwanese in the late 1990s, the digital revolution was in full swing. Although it was clearly foreseeable that the digitalisation of reading and writing would create various new spaces of representation for written forms, appropriate research methods had not been developed systematically. Since it would be beyond the scope of this chapter to trace the development of digitally written Taiwanese over the past 20 years, I shall limit myself to the example of the multilingual online encyclopaedia Wikipedia. Although it is banned in the PRC, the Chinese language edition has reached the top category of more than one million articles. 'Chinese' here refers to modern written Chinese, including articles in traditional and simplified characters. Significantly, the second strongest Sinitic language, comprising more than 200,000 articles, is identified as Bân-lâm-gú/Hō-ló-oē, which includes Taiwanese.[4] Even more importantly, since the overwhelming majority of articles are written entirely in the Roman alphabet, the Bân-lâm-gú Wikipedia (also known as Holopedia) is the only Sinitic Wikipedia with virtually no Chinese characters. Obviously, this seems to confirm my previous impression that advocates of an alphabetic Taiwanese orthography have been most active in spreading their aspired standard. Figure 12.1 shows the beginning of the entry 'Republic of China' on Holopedia.

To be sure, the successful occupation of one virtual space is not the same as standardisation. It is, however, an interesting example of the possible effectiveness of individual agency in language planning (for a discussion of individual agency, I refer to Zhao and Baldauf 2012). Yet as pointed above, however effective this initiative may be, it will not lead to standardisation without the support of governmental language planning. This in turn leads to the question whether the Taiwanese government, during the past 20 years, has applied a new policy to promote and protect regional languages in general and to standardise written Taiwanese in particular. At the beginning of the twenty-first century, the Ministry of Education was very reluctant when it came to the standardisation of written Taiwanese and related language planning measures. For example, a draft language equality bill

FIGURE 12.1 The entry 'Tiong-hoâ Bîn-kok' ('Republic of China') in the Holopedia

210 Henning Klöter

(*yuyan pingdeng fa*) did not become law. At the time when this chapter was written, a similar plan had been released by the DPP government. According to the press release, the draft bill 'guarantees the right of citizens to use any of Taiwan's national languages and establishes the equality of all languages and cultures' (Executive Yuan 2018). At this point, it is too early to assess the possible impact of the planned law.

In the field of written Taiwanese, prospects for standardisation were rather bleak when I conducted my fieldwork in 1999/2000. A research project aimed at compiling a list of recommended character spellings for frequently used Taiwanese expressions, initiated in the late 1990s, was discontinued. In 2012, however, the Ministry of Education released an online dictionary of frequently used Taiwanese expressions (MOE 2012) and one for the Hakka language. In his preface, then Minister of Education Cheng Jei-cheng 鄭瑞城 writes that 'the dictionary is without doubt a milestone for the promotion of local language education and the teaching of Southern Min' (Cheng 2008). It needs to be emphasised, however, that this is not the same as the prescription of a written standard. In order to test the status of the MOE dictionary, it would be necessary to find out to what extent the recommended character spellings are actually used in teaching manuals and other Taiwanese texts. Against the background of the introduction of 'mother tongue education' as a compulsory subject in primary schools in 2001, Taiwanese textbooks and their role in teaching are of crucial importance. However, due to a lack of empirical research, the sustainability of the measures taken in the field of Taiwanese language education cannot be ascertained.

If we take the Holopedia not only as a sign of the vitality of alphabetically written Taiwanese, it turns out that today, like 20 years ago, governmental and non-governmental language planners still do not pull together, in terms of both intensity and substance.

It has to be emphasised that individual non-governmental agency in language planning cannot be limited to the Holopedia community. More robust conclusions about the nature of governmental and non-governmental interaction in language planning would require a thorough update of the research I conducted some 20 years ago. Ideally, such an update would be coupled with a broader perspective and modified research questions. Most importantly, the question 'who?' requires critical rethinking. In *Written Taiwanese* and subsequent publications, I have reduced this question to the issue of agency in language planning. What has largely been neglected, however, is the question 'by whom', referring to the receiving end of language planning or, more specifically, to the readers of written Taiwanese texts. In the light of the mother tongue education programme initiated some 20 years ago, the following questions deserve systematic inquiry: What are the didactic objectives of mother tongue education? Is mother tongue literacy part of the programme? What textbooks are currently used? Are these textbooks standardised in terms of orthography? To what extent has mother tongue education influenced the language competence and the language attitudes of students?

In brief, I conclude by arguing that future research needs to go beyond written texts and should look at texts in their contexts of usage. Only such a contextualised

Writing Taiwanese. Then and now, how, why and who? 211

FIGURE 12.2 A Taiwanese campaign ad
Source: Picture taken by the author in Wulai 烏來 on 12 December 2007.

approach will allow for a better understanding of the vitality of Taiwanese, both spoken and written. Another neglected area of research on written Taiwanese is known as 'linguistic landscapes' (LL). To quote Shohamy and Gorter (2009: 1):

> It is the attention to language in the environment, words and images displayed and exposed in public spaces, that is the center of attention in this rapidly growing area referred to as *linguistic landscape* (LL). While language is used by people, spoken and heard, it is also re-presented and displayed; at times for functional reasons, at others for symbolic purposes.

For previous research on LL, I refer to the studies by Melissa Curtin (2007, 2009). Although she briefly touches on questions of regional languages and LL, sociolinguistic questions relating to 'Taiwanese on the wall' deserve more attention in future research. An example of a Taiwanese LL is shown in Figure 12.2.

Notes

1 When first using the word, I was not aware that a similar term 'polygraphy' had been coined almost 50 years earlier, referring to a 'Slavonic-Latin symbiosis' on medieval documents (Vucinich 1958: 543; see also Bunčić 2016). Similarly, Haarmann uses 'polygraphism' to describe 'the simultaneous use of several writing systems in a speech community' (Haarmann 2006: 2406).

212 Henning Klöter

Haarmann's example is the use of three scripts (Kanji, Hiragana, Katakana) for the writing of Japanese, which he considers 'a rather exceptional case' (ibid.).
2 This paragraph is based on Klöter (2009).
3 The remainder of this paragraph is based on Klöter (2005: 200f.).
4 In Taiwan, the glossnym Hō-ló-oē is used frequently alongside Tâi-gí and Tâi-gú.

References

Agulló Calatayud, Víctor. 2011. 'Análisis de la realidad sociolingüística del valenciano'. *Papers: Revista de Sociologia* 96(2), 501–514.

Albury, Nathan. 2014. 'Introducing the Folk Linguistics of Language Policy'. *International Journal of Language Studies*, 8(3), 85–106.

Alleton, Viviane. 2005. 'Comptes rendus: Henning Klöter, Written Taiwanese'. *Études chinoises* xxiv, 611–614.

Bunčić, Daniel. 2016. 'History of Theoretical Research on Biscriptality'. In Daniel Bunčić et al. (eds), *Biscriptality: A Sociolinguistic Typology*. Heidelberg: Universitätsverlag Winter, 27–50.

Chambers, Jack K. and Peter Trudgill. 1998. *Dialectology*. Cambridge: Cambridge University Press.

Cheng, Jei-cheng 鄭瑞城. 2008. 'Bùzhǎng xù 部長序' [Minister's preface]. Online at http://twblg.dict.edu.tw/holodict_new/index.html

Cheng, Robert, L. 1978. 'Taiwanese Morphemes in Search of Chinese Characters'. *Journal of Chinese Linguistics* 6(2), 306–314.

Clifford, James. 1986. 'Introduction: Partial Truths'. In James Clifford and George E. Marcus, eds, *Writing Culture*. Berkeley, Los Angeles: University of California Press, 1–26.

Combs, Mary Carol and Susan D. Penfield. 2012. 'Language Activism and Language Policy'. In Bernard Spolsky (ed.), *The Cambridge Handbook of Language Policy*. Cambridge: Cambridge University Press, 461–474.

Cooper, Robert L. 1989. *Language Planning and Social Change*. Cambridge: Cambridge University Press.

Coulmas, Florian. 2005. *Sociolinguistics: The Study of Speakers' Choices*. Cambridge: Cambridge University Press.

Curtin, Melissa. 2007. *Language Ideologies on Display: Local, Regional and (Trans)National Identities in Taipei's Linguistic Landscapes*. PhD dissertation, University of New Mexico, Albuquerque.

Curtin, Melissa. 2009. 'Languages on Display: Indexical Signs, Identities and the Linguistic Landscape of Taiwan'. In Elana Shohamy and Durk Gorter (eds), *Linguistic Landscape: Expanding the Scenery*. New York: Routledge, 221–237.

Edwards, John. 2012. 'Language Management Agencies'. In Bernard Spolsky (ed.), *The Cambridge Handbook of Language Policy*. Cambridge: Cambridge University Press, 418–436.

Executive Yuan, Department of Information Services. 2018. 'Executive Yuan approves Draft National Language Law'. Press release, online via https://english.ey.gov.tw.

Garrett, Peter. 2010. *Attitudes to Language*. Cambridge: Cambridge University Press.

Grivelet, Stéphane. 2001. 'Introduction'. *International Journal of the Sociology of Language* 150, 1–10.

Haarmann, Harald. 2006. 'Language Planning: Graphization and the Development of Writing Systems'. In Ulrich Ammon, et al. (eds), *Sociolinguistics: An International Handbook of the Science of Language and Society*, vol. 3. Berlin: de Gruyter, 2402–2420.

Heylen, Ann. 2007. 'Written Taiwanese: Henning Klöter'. *Journal of Multilingual and Multicultural Development* 28(5), 418–419.

Hsiau, A-chin. 2000. *Contemporary Taiwanese Cultural Nationalism*. London: Routledge.

Huang, Shuanfan [Huang Xuanfân 黃宣範]. 1993. *Yuyan, shehui yu zuqun yishi: Taiwan yuyan shehuixue de yanjiu* 語言、社會與族群意識: 台灣語言社會學的研究 [Language, society and ethnic identity: A sociolinguistic study on Taiwan]. Taipei: Crane.

Iunn, Ungian 楊允言 (ed.) 1995. *Tâi-gú chit-tiâu-loo*台與這條路. Taipei: Taili chubanshe 台笠出版社.

Jaffe, Alexandra. 1999. 'Locating Power: Corsican Translators and their Critics'. In Jan Blommaert (ed.), *Language Ideological Debates*. Berlin: De Gruyter Mouton, 39–66.

Klöter, Henning. 2003. 'Writing Taiwanese: The People behind the Scripts'. In Christina Neder and Ines Susanne Schilling (eds), *Transformation! Innovation? Perspectives on Taiwan Culture*. Wiesbaden: Harrassowitz, 45–63.

Klöter, Henning. 2005. *Written Taiwanese*. Wiesbaden: Harassowitz.

Klöter, Henning. 2006. 'Mandarin Remains More Equal: Changes and Continuities in Taiwan's Language Policy'. In Dafydd Fell, Henning Klöter and Bi-yu Chang (eds), *What Has Changed? Taiwan before and after the Change in Ruling Parties*. Wiesbaden: Harrassowitz, 207–223.

Klöter, Henning. 2009. 'Re-writing Language in Taiwan'. In Fang-long Shih, Stuart Thompson and Paul-François Tremlett (eds), *Re-writing Culture in Taiwan*. London: Routledge, 102–122.

Klöter, Henning. 2010. Taiwan ni okeru gengo hensei no hensen: Ideorogī to kōka 台湾における言語編制の変遷——イデオロギーと効果 [Language regimes in Taiwan: Ideologies and effects], transl. by Fujita Misa 藤田美佐. Patrick Heinrich and Matsuo Shin 松尾慎 (eds), Higashi Ajia ni okeru gengo fukkō: Chūgoku, Taiwan, Okinawa wo shōten ni 東アジアにおける言語復興中国　台湾　沖縄を焦点に [Language revitalization in East Asia: Focus on China, Taiwan, and Okinawa]. Tokyo: Sangensha 三元社, 63–84.

Klöter, Henning. 2012a. 'Brokers beyond Babel: Language Choice, Ideology and Identity in Taiwanese TV Advertisements'. In Chang, Bi-yu and Henning Klöter (eds), *Imaging and Imagining Taiwan: Identity Representation and Cultural Politics*. Wiesbaden: Harrasssowitz, 89–104.

Klöter, Henning. 2012b. Hok-khi la oder hundertjährige Destillerie? Genuss und Sprachwahl in der taiwanischen Fernsehwerbung. In Cornelia Schindelin*et al.* (eds), *Sprache und Genuss: Festschrift für Peter Kupfer*. Frankfurt/Main: Peter Lang, 89–106.

Klöter, Henning. 2012c. 'Taiwan Literature and the Negotiation of Language from Below: Huang Shihui and His Ideological Convictions'. *Studia Orientalia Slovaca* 11(1), 65–77.

Langer, Nils and Agnete Nesse. 2012. 'Linguistic Purism'. In Juan M. Hernández-Campoy and Juan Camilo Conde-Silvestre (eds), *The Handbook of Historical Sociolinguistics*. Chichester and Malden, MA: Wiley-Blackwell, 607–625.

Lepsius, Richard. 1855. *Standard Alphabet for Reducing Unwritten Languages and Foreign Graphic Systems to a Uniform Orthography in European Letters*. London: Seeleys.

Li, Chin-An. 2003. *Taiwanese Lexical Change and Variation*. Taipei: Zhenping Qiye.

Lien, Chin-fa. 2006. 'Comptes rendus: Klöter Henning, Written Taiwanese'. *Cahiers de Linguistique Asie Orientale* 35(1), 141–148.

Mair, Victor H. 2006. 'Review of Written Taiwanese by Henning Klöter'. *Journal of Chinese Linguistics* 34(1), 155–163.

MOE [ROC Ministry of Education]. 2012. *Taiwan Minnanyu changyongci cidian* 臺灣閩南語常用詞辭典 [A Dictionary of frequently used Taiwan Southern Min expressions]. Online version: http://twblg.dict.edu.tw/holodict_new/index.htm.

Milroy, James. 2007. 'The Ideology of Standard Language'. In Carmen Llamas, Louise Mullany and Peter Stockwell (eds), *The Routledge Companion to Sociolinguistics*. London: Routledge, 133–139.

Norman, Jerry. 1988. *Chinese*. Cambridge: Cambridge University Press.

Pike, Kenneth L. 1938. 'Practical Suggestions toward a Common Orthography for Indian Languages of Mexico for Education of the Natives within Their Own Tongues'. *Investigaciones Lingüísticas* 2, 422–427.

Pike, Kenneth L. 1947. *Phonemics: A Technique for Reducing Languages to Writing*. Ann Arbor: University of Michigan Press.

Schieffelin, Bambi B. and Rachelle Charlier Doucet. 1998. 'The 'Real' Haitian Creole: Ideologies, Metalinguistics, and Orthographic Choice'. In Bambi B. Schieffelin, Kathryn A. Woolard and Paul V. Kroskrity (eds), *Language Ideologies: Practice and Theory*. Oxford: Oxford University Press, 285–316.

Sebba, Mark. 2000. 'Orthography and Ideology: Issues in Sranan Spelling'. *Linguistics* 38/5, 925–948.

Sebba, Mark. 2012. 'Orthography as Social Action: Scripts, Spelling, Identity and Power'. In Alexandra Jaffe *et al.* (eds), *Orthography as Social Action: Scripts, Spelling, Identity and Power*. Berlin: Mouton de Gruyter, 1–19.

Simons, Gary F. and Charles D. Fennig (eds). 2018. *Chinese, Min Nan. Ethnologue: Languages of the World*, 21st edn. Dallas, Texas: SIL International. Online version: https://www.ethnologue.com/language/nan

Spolsky, Bernard. 2009. *Language Management*. Cambridge: Cambridge University Press.

Vucinich, Wayne. 1958. 'Review: Istoriski časopis: Organ istoriskog instituta SAN'. *Speculum: A Journal of Medieval Studies* 33(4), 541–550.

Yang, Qingchu. 1992. *Guo-Tai shuangyu cidian* 國台雙語辭典' [A Mandarin-Taiwanese bilingual dictionary]. Kaohsiung: Dunli Chubanshe.

Yang, Qingchu. 1998. *Tai-Hua shuangyu cidian* 台華雙語辭典 [A Taiwanese-Mandarin bilingual dictionary]. Kaohsiung: Dunli Chubanshe.

Yang, Qingchu. 1999. *Iunn Ching-chiok Tai-gi cu-im tok-pun* 楊青矗台語注音讀本 [Textbooks with Taiwanese transcriptions by Yang Qingchu]. 15 vls. Kaohsiung: Dunli Chubanshe.

Zhao, Shouhui and Richard B. Baldauf. 2012. 'Individual Agency in Language Planning: Chinese Script Reform as a Case Study'. *Language Problems and Language Planning* 36(1), 1–24.

Zima, Petr. 1974. 'Digraphia: The Case of Hausa'. *Linguistics* 124, 57–69.

13

DEPOLITICIZING A STRUCTURALLY POLITICIZED SOCIETY

The importance of responsible political agency

Mikael Mattlin

Introduction

My first book *Politicized Society: The Long Shadow of Taiwan's One-Party Legacy*, published by NIAS Press (Mattlin 2011), was the outcome of a long period of intensely studying Taiwan's politics. I had first gone to Taiwan in the autumn of 1998 for three months to gather material for my Master's thesis. Intrigued by this experience, and sensing that I had only scratched the surface of understanding Taiwanese politics, I embarked on a long doctoral project revolving around the concept of *politicization*. Methodologically, I was inspired by the ethnographic methods used by political anthropologists, and coupled this with grounded theory as a general research strategy. I relied on a broad array of more specific research methods and data sources. Much of my insight into Taiwanese politics derived from numerous interviews and close observation of Taiwanese politics during several field research stints between 1998 and 2006.

I finally finished my doctorate in 2008 at the University of Helsinki. The book *Politicized Society* is broadly based on the dissertation, although thoroughly re-written. In the book, I argued that Taiwan's society had become structurally politicized due to a confluence of several structural factors related to the legacy of the Kuomintang (KMT) party's long one-party rule on the island. This structural origin of Taiwan's intense politicization was particularly evident during the eight years of Democratic Progressive Party (DPP) rule from 2000 to 2008. The DPP's somewhat accidental victory in the 2000 presidential election ushered in a political showdown that was waged in subsequent elections, in the legislature as well as in the streets through political mass mobilisation, as the new government tried to dismantle the bases of the KMT's previous power and the old political elite fought back. As Dan Slater put it in a superb review article: vertical and horizontal accountability came into conflict (Slater 2013). It is this pivotal time period in

216 Mikael Mattlin

Taiwan's political development, from 2000 to 2008, and these sequences of events that I took a scholarly interest in and that my book mainly deals with.

My interest was particularly piqued by the fact that politicization appeared to be such a prevalent and permeating feature of Taiwanese society at the time of the power transition and the years that followed. Yet, there were practically no studies available of politicization as a comprehensive societal phenomenon – what I termed structural politicization. Even today, there is little literature available in English that discusses politicization as an encompassing, society-wide phenomenon. However, some studies have been produced on several more specific instances of politicization of various sectors of society, such as the media, the financial industry or some specific issue (e.g. Li 2005; Rich 2005),[1] and many other scholars note politicization in passing (see e.g. Clark and Tan 2010: 115–120; Chang et al. 2011: 602).

I recently produced a second, revised and expanded edition of the book,[2] for which I conducted a new round of elite and expert interviews in Taipei. This provided me with an excellent opportunity to return to, and reassess, my original argument in light of subsequent events, new research and received critique. This chapter has three aims. First, I engage with the feedback that I received on the first edition of the book, primarily in the form of book reviews, but also feedback received during conferences and seminars. Second, I re-evaluate my argument in light of subsequent events, both in Taiwan and elsewhere. Finally, I debate what it would take to alleviate Taiwan's structural politicization, drawing some insight from the political trajectory of my native Finland. But before this, I shall briefly summarise the gist of the argument of my book's first edition, especially for the benefit of those readers who may be unfamiliar with it.

The gist of the argument[3]

I argued that political transitions are seldom painless. In political systems that democratise without prior experience with democracy, transitions tend to be both long and turbulent. The great challenge to the long-term viability of Taiwan's democratic experiment, in my view, was to break out from the plight of structural politicization that was eating at the foundations of its representative democracy. I therefore endeavoured to explain what it was that generated this intense politicization. My book illuminated the structural origins of Taiwan's intense politicization, focusing more on informal political structures than on formal political institutions.

Many other scholars had argued that the semi-presidential constitutional arrangements adopted in Taiwan promote political gridlock, or that the electoral system was deeply flawed and gave rise to factionalism. I did not directly dispute these assertions. Institutional features such as semi-presidentialism, the SNTV election system and a partisan media certainly contribute to politicization. Instead, I argued that focusing exclusively on institutional flaws is inadequate. My argument was that the fundamental reasons for the intense politicization of Taiwanese society lay deeper in the structures of Taiwanese society and politics, and that institutional arrangements mainly exacerbated the problem.

In some ways my study re-affirmed several general observations of earlier studies on politicization, e.g. the relevance of underlying social or political cleavages, the crucial role of early party competition and the nature of the state. However, my book systematically developed what was at the time a surprisingly unresearched area of the study of politicization, namely the empirical study of intensely politicized societies. I maintained that Taiwan's intense politicization stemmed from five structural features:

1. an incremental political transition and related political cleavage (the one-party-state legacy);
2. a semi-presidential constitution that enabled a power split between two political teams;
3. Taiwan's geopolitical *tornness* that I described as *asymmetric integration*;
4. strong vested interests, a.k.a. the patronage state;
5. a social structure that facilitates political mobilisation that I called *nested pyramid structures*.

My argument further went that, taken separately, these five factors might not necessarily result in intense politicization, and there is some empirical evidence from other countries to suggest that many of these features can appear in isolation without structural politicization resulting. However, in conjunction with each other they can produce an explosive mix. Instead it was in the interplay of these factors, so I argued, that we needed to look at in order to grasp the roots of Taiwan's structural politicization.

Taiwan's political transformation has been noteworthy because – rather than making an abrupt break with its authoritarian past – democracy had developed in an evolutionary manner from within a one-party state, with that 'one party' still largely intact and powerful. There was no radical disjuncture with the past. Blood did not flow on the streets. The process was hailed as a model for others to emulate. However, my argument, in essence, was that it was precisely some of the things that initially made Taiwan's political transformation such a success story that contributed to later problems. While Taiwan certainly managed to pull through an initially smooth political transition, the unfinished nature of this transition (Rigger 2004) made it more protracted, with adverse consequences, such as political gridlock. The intense politicization of society brought about a decrease in social trust, a lack of trust in political institutions and a loss of faith in representative democracy.

While the KMT built an elaborate system of rule where the party-state's reach into society was broad, the apparent democratisation of the political system disguised a considerable amount of inertia in underlying political and social structures, deriving from the old one-party system, including latent nostalgia for the authoritarian past (see Mattlin 2011; Chang and Chu 2007; Chang et al. 2011). At the time of the power transition in 2000, many of the structures underpinning this

218 Mikael Mattlin

system, such as permeating mobilisation networks and massive party assets were still largely intact. Chang et al. (2011: 602) have summarised well the circumstances and challenges prevailing at the time:

> a number of residual authoritarian elements were preserved and incorporated into the new regime, leaving a series of challenges for the new democracy to face as it slogged along the road towards consolidation. The first issue was the politicization of the military and security apparatus. Second, the new competitive party system retained the established patterns of ubiquitous presence of partisan politics in all organized sectors of the society (including the civil service, mass media, academia, religious groups, secondary associations, and unions), all-encompassing social mobilization in electoral contests, and a monopoly by political parties in elite recruitment and organizing the political process. The opposition parties (there were several besides the DPP) aimed to curtail the reach of the dominant party, but they themselves were forced to try to become mirror images of the KMT in order to compete with it.

Under these circumstances, the constitutional reality of a semi-presidential system ushered in a *cohabitation* situation where a reformist president and cabinet became locked in long-term battle with an obstructionist legislature protecting vital material and even existential interests, although for the opposite reason than in the French system (Chang et al. 2011: 615).

Despite the long trend of localisation in the KMT since the 1970s, the party never entirely localised. In fact, for more than a decade the trend was in the opposite direction, with mainlanders (外省人) regaining control of the party leadership upon Ma Ying-jeou's ascendancy to power. The question of the KMT's future is inextricably tied to the fate of the Republic of China (ROC), somewhat similarly to how the Honecker regime's fate was tied to that of the German Democratic Republic. In the party-elite's self-conception, the party's 'right to rule' partly stems from the ROC, which is a major reason why they have been adamant about retaining the symbolic trappings of the ROC state. The party has, for example, resisted efforts to rewrite the constitution, as opposed to amending it. Senior party politicians and cadres have repeatedly stressed that the KMT will not abandon the Republic of China, the state founded by the party. In short, the ROC state is the political framework that provides the *raison d'etre* for the KMT party.

The social system built by the KMT on Taiwan did not comprise a universal welfare state like those used in northern Europe. Instead, and until fairly recently, the party-state chose to provide discretionary benefits to parts of the population. This was a system that was highly beneficial to some, with others receiving little, if anything. A substantial part of the population was linked to the KMT party-state through party membership and party-affiliated associations, government employment, local factions or elected and appointed positions – if not directly, then as a family member to someone else who was. However, large sections of the population remained outside of the institutions of the party-state. They received little

Politicized Society revisited   **219**

from it, had little at stake in it, and as a consequence often developed a deep antagonism towards it.

The state's legacy of granting privileges, favours and benefits was not discontinued by political liberalisation. Only belatedly were there efforts to build a semblance of a welfare system. Importantly, in Taiwan, the indirect consequences of building a universal welfare state imply the loss of privileges for some. The patronage systems, sanctioned by the party–state, created powerful vested interests in various segments of the population, and powerful resentment at such privileges in other segments.[4] The continuity of patronage arrangements after power transition was a key difference to Mexico, a state that otherwise shared several of the traits of Taiwan. In Mexico, the PRI's one-party dominance crumbled as the ruling party lost its ability to use the state for political patronage (Greene 2007). The KMT was more successful in holding on to its patronage assets.

The stakes in the political game were further raised by the geopolitical situation of Taiwan. Existing in international limbo, without widely recognised statehood, the frictions caused by the asymmetric integration with Mainland China, especially the pull of ever-deepening economic integration, gave a great sense of urgency to those who wished to make a clearer political break with the Mainland before it was too late. However, the close economic integration between Taiwan and the Mainland also made formalising the political break through a declaration of independence highly risky. Instead, the political conflict over Taiwan's status gravitated towards a highly politicized perennial squabble over symbolic nationness and, consequently, about the legacy of the ROC state. Since symbolic nationness is also an issue that has much relevance for ordinary people, mass political mobilisation has tended to revolve around the symbols of Taiwaneseness and Chineseness.

Given this structural background, any political issue that was likely to shift the power balance between the two political camps, either directly or by affecting the resources at the disposal of either side, developed into a political conflict and often a stalemate due to the president and cabinet representing the pan-greens, while the pan-blues held a majority in the legislature. Being neither clearly a presidential nor a parliamentary system, the system is inherently prone to severe political gridlock, as happened after 2000, when both sides frequently blocked or overturned each other's proposals and initiatives.

However, my argument, and one of the main contributions of the book, was that institutional arrangements were not the root cause of Taiwan's intense politicization. In the absence of the clear and venomous political cleavage, the same arrangements might not be problematic at all, as France has earlier shown. Rather it was the intense partisan bifurcation, deriving from the enduring one-party legacy that made the institutional arrangements problematic.

Engaging with the critics

The first edition of the book enjoyed a good number of reviews. Traditional book reviews have appeared in many of the leading China and Asia studies journals.[5]

220   Mikael Mattlin

The book has also been reviewed or noted in newspapers, academic blogs and magazines, e.g. in *The Diplomat* and in the *Taipei Times*. *Politicized Society* also managed to break through the area studies barrier by being included in an extensive review article by Dan Slater in *World Politics* (Slater 2013). The book reviews have been overwhelmingly positive, several of them even laudatory, with one notable exception: the book review in *China Review International* by Bruce Jacobs (2012a), who did not seem to like the overall argument that I made in the book, which led to a debate between us in the CRI.

I will not dwell any further on the positive things said about the book, but rather seek here to engage with my critics, especially with regard to the criticism that I consider to be valid and/or particularly important for the book's argument. I will first address briefly smaller issues, and then move on to more serious challenges to the argument.

One of the points raised by Murray Rubinstein was the relatively little space that I gave to the role of the United States in backing Taiwan after the war and serving as a watchdog on its politics, thereby pushing for opening up of the political system (Rubinstein 2014: 259–260). This criticism is fair, and partly reflects the fact that I am a European scholar. In fact, I state at the beginning of the book that I am trying to look at Taiwan's political system with a European parliamentary system as the implicit point of comparison, as opposed to comparing it with the American political system, which has been more common and which I find is in many ways problematic.[6] Nevertheless, I think Rubinstein is correct in that I probably neglected the U.S. factor a bit too much in the first edition. I have sought to remedy this in the second edition by adding text on how and when the United States sought to steer Taiwan in the desired direction.

A similar criticism is that raised by Jacobs – that I did not pay sufficient attention to the role of the *dangwai* movement in preparing the ground for the first opposition party, the DPP, to emerge. While I did note the *dangwai*'s role, Jacobs is right in that I probably did not give it the weight that it deserved in the first edition – and certainly not nearly as much as Jacobs himself did in his own book that appeared one year later (Jacobs 2012b). Again, for the second edition I have sought to remedy this.

A third minor point is that some astute observers of Taiwanese politics considered my assessment of the state of Taiwan's politics to be on the bleak side, and perhaps a bit too much so. When I presented the book at the ERCCT (Tübingen University), Gunter Schubert mentioned that the main thing that he would somewhat disagree with is the overly pessimistic-sounding ending to the book. Similarly, in a recent review of the Taiwan studies field, Shelley Rigger put my book in the category of more pessimistic assessments of Taiwan's democratic development (Rigger 2018). Partly this probably reflects the timing of the text. I wrote up the bulk of the first edition in 2008–2010, when many people in Taiwan had become quite disillusioned with the way politics had turned out. Still, I never intended to convey a message of doom and gloom. In fact, I tried to strike a fine balance between not neglecting the many real and unsettled issues in Taiwan's

Politicized Society revisited **221**

political transformation, while still taking the cautiously optimistic view that over time these issues can be worked out.[7]

The second edition ends on a somewhat more optimistic note. Seven years later, it seems that many of the legacy problems in Taiwan's political system, which have promoted Taiwan's structural politicization, are in the process of being gradually resolved. Purely on its own terms, Taiwan's political development does not appear particularly worrisome, certainly not in comparison with many other Third Wave or unstable democracies. The one factor that looms large over this development, however, is the augmenting political and military pressure from Beijing that is largely outside of Taiwan's control.

Among the theoretically more serious criticism that the first edition of *Politicized Society* encountered, I consider the following three points:

1. Is politicization in Taiwan also a mass or mostly an elite phenomenon?
2. Does the book over-emphasise structural factors to the detriment of political agency?
3. Is there any point in comparing Taiwan's political transformation to Mainland China, i.e. are the lessons portable?

The first of these points was raised by Wang Hung-chung in his *Issues & Studies* book review. Wang argued that his own research on roll-call votes supports the argument that Taiwan's elite has become increasingly politicized, as there had been a dramatic increase in votes along partisan lines in Taiwan's legislature (Wang 2011). However, Wang was more sceptical towards my contention that politicization had turned into a society-wide phenomenon in the early 2000s. As evidence, Wang presented survey data comparing Taiwan with the United States in 2008, which did not support the idea that the Taiwanese public was particularly politicized compared with the United States. Basing the counter-argument of survey data from the year 2008 is somewhat problematic, as that was around the time of the backlash against the overly politicized preceding decade. Many ordinary Taiwanese were then fed up and disillusioned with politics and returned the KMT to power. After many exhausting years of incessant political mobilisation and battling, there was little appetite for more political mass action.

However, Wang's criticism touches a nerve, since it always seemed to me that the means that typically are used to capture the general public's engagement in politics are poor at explaining the phenomenon of politicization as I understand it. So, while voter turnout in Taiwan's first couple of presidential elections might appear high to an American observer, they are nothing spectacular from a European perspective. Similarly, traditional politicization measures, such as the importance of the state in the economy, or the size of public expenditure as a share of GDP (Akkerman et al. 2004; Heidar and Saglie 2003; Kostadinova 2003; Putnam 2000), pale in comparison with many European states. And finally, while the KMT in its heyday showed an impressively large party membership, the DPP's membership, even as a ruling party, has not been particularly large.

222 Mikael Mattlin

In short, I grappled for years with the question of how to explain this discrepancy. Part of the explanation lay in the sheer intensity of engagement among that segment of the general population that was politically engaged. I explained this in the second edition by giving the examples of voter turnouts in national elections for Sweden and the United States in 2016 and asking which country would look more politicized by the measure of voter turnout? (Mattlin 2018: 299–301) Sweden would, hands down, look like it is the country where people are more engaged in politics. Yet, most people would probably today intuitively agree that the general public in the United States in 2016 was way more politicized, and this is because my definition for politicization is more closely aligned with the lay understanding of the term instead of the conventional political science ways of operationalising the concept. I had defined structural politicization as 'a tendency towards concurrent polarization and political divisiveness over a number of issues and in a variety of institutions in a society'.

The second major criticism, the agency issue, was broached by Bruce Jacobs at the 2015 World Congress on Taiwan Studies in London University, if I recall correctly, specifically with regard to the crucial role played by Lee Teng-hui in Taiwan's democratisation. Indirectly, Malte Philipp Kaeding also made this point in his book review, as he mentioned that reading a publication on political agency in Taiwan as a companion to *Politicized Society* would give readers a very comprehensive picture of Taiwan's political development (Kaeding 2013).

The structure vs agency problem is of course a perennial one. The debate – very big in late 1990s sociology and international relations – is one of those probably unsolvable chicken-or-egg discussions, to which constructivist Alexander Wendt has given one of the most persuasive accounts (Wendt 2010). Under any actual historical circumstances, there will be both structural factors at play, as well as scope for human agency. Marx famously said 'Men [sic] make their own history, but they do not make it as they please; they do not make it under self-selected circumstances, but under circumstances existing already, given and transmitted from the past' (Marx 1852). Or as Wendt would say: 'Structure confronts actors as an objective social fact that constrains and enables action in systematic ways, and as such should generate distinct patterns' (Wendt 2010: 184).

As Wendt makes clear, 'structural theorising' and 'process theorising' answer different questions. For purposes of analysis, we often need to bracket one, in order to focus on the other (Wendt 2010: 186). In the first edition, I opted to put my focus clearly on the structural side of the argument. I emphasised how the way that the KMT party-state had been structured, as well as how various political-cultural practices, which had been established already under the authoritarian era, still greatly shape and condition politics in Taiwan. This then was an argument emphasising the inertia in old structures and practices that means a transition towards genuine democracy is inevitably a very protracted, uncertain and arduous process. I did not claim that the book's argument was the complete and exhaustive story of Taiwan's political developments. On the contrary, I chose to emphasise a particular lens and angle in order to bring the argument out more clearly.

Politicized Society revisited **223**

I do recognise the important role that human agency plays, especially at so-called 'critical junctures' (Mahoney 2000). In the second edition, I highlighted this by counterfactual thought experiments involving three such critical junctures. First, the decisions by president Chiang Ching-kuo during 1986–1988 to allow the opposition party to establish itself and move towards limited political liberalisation. Second, the KMT split around the 2000 presidential elections that handed the victory to the DPP for the first time, and allegedly was fomented by outgoing president Lee Teng-hui. Finally, the KMT's choice of Ma Ying-jeou as party saviour and presidential candidate in 2007–2008. What role did human agency play in these sequences of events and could the trajectory of Taiwan's political development conceivably have taken a different turn? I concluded that of these three events, the 2000 party split was the one 'fork in the road' where the KMT's fortunes could have turned out very differently. So at least at this historical juncture human agency (Lee Teng-hui) may have played a critically important role (Mattlin 2018: 326–334).

Finally, the third major issue has been raised directly or implicitly in different ways by Steve Tsang, Bruce Jacobs and Dan Slater, as well as in the review in the *Taipei Times*. When I presented the book at Nottingham University in 2011, Steve Tsang asked from the audience why we would have any reason to think that the CPC in Mainland China would look towards Taiwan for lessons in political transformation? Dan Slater – in his foreword to the second edition of the book – also gently nudged me towards considering the lessons from Taiwan's political transformation also for other polities beyond Mainland China (Slater 2018). Bruce Jacobs' criticism was more fundamental. Jacobs apparently did not like at all my exhortation that we should not forget about the origin of 'Chinese' political parties and some political practices in the turbulent political struggles in Mainland China in the first half of the twentieth century that were carried over to Taiwan (Jacobs 2012a).

Of all the criticism raised towards my book's argument, I believe this one is the toughest nut to crack, and the one towards which I am also now uncertain. Until the 2012 CPC Party Congress, it was not unreasonable to envision that the CPC might one day follow in the footsteps of the KMT and allow, at first limited and cautious, political liberalisation, and later perhaps even more if the initial steps proved workable. There were some signs, although admittedly faint, that the leadership was contemplating and experimenting with ever so slight moves towards at least a more relaxed authoritarian system (soft authoritarianism). Even so, I knew that drawing the links explicitly between the KMT's past trajectory to the hypothetical future trajectory of the CPC was a bold one.

However, events after 2012 have made me doubt this. My claim essentially rested on the fact that the KMT had been structurally dominant in the Taiwanese political system in the mid-1980s, and thereby could 'afford' to liberalise, with relative confidence, that it could continue to dominate politics after liberalisation as well on the back of its vastly superior position and resources. What I apparently miscalculated is how unsure the CPC leadership is that it could maintain its leadership and social stability following such moves towards even gradual

224 Mikael Mattlin

liberalisation. Today, it seems that even the slightest sign of people not falling in line with the 'core' of the party is considered a major security problem to be dealt with both swiftly and harshly. Consequently, while history has a way of surprising us, and I hesitate to say that it will never happen, I no longer consider incremental political liberalisation a likely scenario for Mainland China.

The argument's robustness in light of subsequent events

All in all, the issues raised by the reviewers have not – save for the last point – caused me to fundamentally rethink my argument. In most cases, they were largely about matters of emphasis. However, events in Taiwanese and world politics over the past eight years have done more to alter my thinking on some aspects of my argument.

The future is notoriously difficult to predict. One might add that it is equally hazardous to extrapolate the future from the way things look under the prevailing circumstances. In retrospect, it is clear that some of the confident statements that I made in the first edition were influenced by how things looked at the time of writing. The broader point here is the difficulty of making political science predictions about the long-term implications of rapidly unfolding political events. Former Chinese Premier Zhou Enlai was suitably cautious when asked about the implications of the Paris student demonstrations a few years later, as he responded that it was still too early to tell.

In this vein, I would like to highlight three areas especially, where I have revisited my argument with a critical gaze. First, the notion of the Taiwanese political party as a 'nested pyramid structure (NPS)'. This description was one of the earliest completed parts of my overall argument. According to the NPS model, individual politicians and their personal networks combine forces to form larger agglomerates of dyadic support networks (factions), which then form yet larger agglomerates of factions (i.e. parties). I developed this idea during field work in 2000–2003, and the idea first appeared in a *China Quarterly* article (Mattlin 2004). The sketch of how political support is built and a political party is structured is, of course, a simplified abstraction. It bears some similarity to how Niall Ferguson in his recent book depicted an 'idealised hierarchical network' (Ferguson 2017: 39–40). Actual politics is often much messier and there are always going to be exceptions to the basic picture.[8]

I still believe that the abstraction is useful for thinking about the differences between various kinds of support (e.g. local factions vs ideological base supporters), and the particularistic and dyadic nature of political support. However, when it comes to the fragility of political support in such a structure, that I had postulated, I have had to do some rethinking. In retrospect, the early 2000s stands out as a period of particularly intense party realignment following the KMT's first loss of power. While there was conjecture of the DPP splitting after its 2008 defeat (and even some party insiders saw the situation as bleak), and the KMT splitting again after 2016, with the brief ascension of conservative Hong Xiuzhu to party leader, by and large major parties have been able to hold together.

Politicized Society revisited **225**

In other words, even if the Taiwanese political party is typically built up in the way that I claimed, it is not quite as fragile a structure as it seemed at the time. Furthermore, the last few years have demonstrated that even supposedly entrenched party systems in established European democracies are perhaps less stable than commonly perceived. While few European countries have experienced the kind of wholesale collapse of the old parties that Italy went through in the 1990s, the rapidity with which new parties and political movements have emerged and challenged established parties across Europe has been astonishing. The list would include *Syriza* (Greece), the *Five Star Movement* (Italy), the *True Finns* (Finland), *Alternativ für Deutschland* (Germany), *Podemos* (Spain) and *En Marche!* (France).

Second, the DPP's second coming to power has amply shown how crucially important it is to have a parliamentary majority to effect changes to the political structures. Although I did debate this extensively already in the first edition, and built an entire sub-chapter around it, it has still been somewhat surprising to observe how rapidly the DPP-in-majority has been able to deal with some of the legacy problems of the party-state that for so long eluded the party in minority. For example, the issues of party assets and transitional justice, the political party law and pension reforms have all moved forward through legislative action. Granted, many of these issues will still be haggled about for years, and there will at times be heated protests from those set to lose out from the reforms, but today I would put even more emphasis on having a legislative majority. This actually is a modestly encouraging sign for the health of Taiwan's politics. Despite a lot of extra-legislative political action by all major parties, challenges to election outcomes and legislative obstruction, at the end of the day the major parties have still respected the utmost boundaries set by the constitution and election outcomes by not resorting to widespread political violence in defiance of these.

Finally, many developments outside of Taiwan since 2011 have put developments in Taiwanese politics in sharper comparative relief. The populist features exhibited by the DPP during Chen Shui-bian's presidency, that at the time often appeared irresponsible, today look almost quaint compared with the excesses of populistic politicians in Europe and the United States. While there were several somewhat concerning or unhealthy features in Taiwanese politics in the early 2000s, ranging from vote-buying and local factional influence to the misuse of referenda for partisan campaigns and excessive mobilisation of parts of the electorate, these now pale in comparison with the derailment of many other Third Wave and less established democracies. Thailand has still not returned to civilian rule following the military's latest coup in 2014. Turkey and Russia have gone wholesale autocratic, and much of Eastern Europe is sliding back into populist authoritarianism, with only Hungary being furthest along on a road that Poland, the Czech Republic and Slovakia also seem to be embarking on.

Today, Taiwan's democratic transition looks remarkably successful and its democratic system relatively healthy, certainly in comparison with other East Asian or Third Wave democracies. Just to mention a few points, Taiwan's Freedom

226 Mikael Mattlin

House score is the second highest in Asia after Japan (Freedom House 2018) and its press freedom is the most advanced in all of Asia (IPI Press Freedom Index 2018).

What would it take to alleviate structural politicization?

This section debates what – building on my book's argument – it would take to alleviate the structural circumstances that gave rise to the strong politicization of Taiwanese society during the DPP period. Essentially, this requires that the argument is turned around. In other words, the factors that have driven politicization in society should change, or lose their relevance over time. Since all of the factors are essentially structural in nature (with the partial exception of political institutions) it would be unrealistic to expect quick changes to any of them. However, over a period of several years – say two presidential terms – one can expect to observe some changes in them.

It is reasonable to expect society's politicization to lessen as time goes by. After all, a heightened level of politicization is not a natural state of affairs in a representative democracy. Almond and Verba (1963) already argued that politics is not the main concern of most people most of the time, and this in many ways is a healthy thing. If ordinary people spend much of their time actively engaged in politics or are *too* interested in politics, all sorts of political instability and conflict often follow in due course; in the worst case, even resulting in civil war.

My native Finland is a good example. Observing the very tranquil politics and society in Finland today, it is hard to imagine that for most of the first six decades of its independent history, Finland was plagued by extremely divisive politics and perennial political instability. In fact, the country started out with a vicious civil war, complete with internment camps, just weeks after proclaiming independence. In the space of a few bloody months, around 1 per cent of the entire population succumbed to violence, disease and starvation, rivalling the civil war in Bosnia in the 1990s.

As late as in the 1970s, politics still permeated many corners of Finnish society. Many organisations and associations, from media to sports clubs, were strongly politicized, people actively took political sides and flaunted their 'political colours' (or tried to hide them in workplaces), political debate was active from universities to factories,[9] political circumstances locked one large party (the National Coalition Party, *Kokoomus*) semi-permanently out of government, and governments were short-lived, with an average life-span of just one year, as opposed to a four-year election cycle.[10] Yet, just two decades later, people in Finland were generally rather disinterested in politics, voting participation rates had fallen rapidly and party membership even more. Most of the media had turned non-partisan. Successive governments managed to encompass as many as six political parties, representing the breadth of the political spectrum, and still sit out the entire four-year term, without major political crises.

In one generation, Finland had thus moved from a situation of permeating politicization and high political instability to a rather depoliticized and politically stable society. In other words, it had joined the political mainstream of relatively stable Western democracies, where political depoliticization and general lack of voter enthusiasm had been the norm for some time (Putnam 2000; Akkerman et al. 2004; Heidar and Saglie 2003; Kostadinova 2003). However, the populist wave now sweeping over Europe questions whether this seeming stability in European polities was only a temporary state of affairs – a side-product of the long Post-War economic boom.

While the circumstances of Finland's political transformation are not entirely comparable to those of Taiwan, there are some interesting similarities. For example, Finland used to have a semi-presidential system with a strongman president (Urho Kekkonen). Later, the political system moved towards a parliamentary system, partly through a constitutional reform in 2000, partly through successive presidents progressively 'disarming' the presidency of its excessive powers through a conscious exercise in restraint. In the Post-War period, Finland also built up a comprehensive social welfare system (Finland had been a laggard among the Nordic countries) that really came to its fruition only after the 1970s. Finally, the torn nature of Finland's difficult Post-War international position dramatically changed during 1989–1991. Before this, Finland had tried to maintain a difficult balancing act of self-proclaimed neutrality between the Eastern and Western blocs. Being obliged by Post-War treaties and deep-seated political realism to pay close attention to Moscow's political sensitivities – a phenomenon that was pejoratively described as Finlandisation (Forsberg and Pesu 2016) – Finland was until 1989 in a grey area, not entirely part of the West, but also not a member of the Soviet bloc.

In the case of Taiwan, the first of the factors that I identified as driving politicization (the one-party-state legacy) is the most fundamental of them all and concerns the very nature of Taiwan's political transition. We would have to engage in counterfactual argumentation in order to think of another trajectory that Taiwan's political transformation conceivably could have taken. Where we could expect to see changes over time is in the related political cleavage running through society. That is, do we have evidence of an amelioration of the pan-blue/pan-green line of division that at its worst ran through, not only political institutions, but also many of the civic institutions of society? This could be taken as a re-statement of the old arguments by S. M. Lipset and Stein Rokkan of cross-cutting cleavages (ethnic, linguistic, religious, political etc.) promoting political stability, while coinciding cleavages have the opposite effect (Lipset 1960; Rokkan 1967).

The second factor of a semi-presidential constitution that enabled a power split between two political teams is the one institutional factor that I incorporated into my more deeply structural explanation. The difference between institutional and structural in this context is that institutional arrangements can, at least in theory, be changed rather quickly by the political actors involved (in practice it may, of course, be far more difficult), whereas structural factors are more deeply embedded in society or its international context and can therefore not be changed at will. During Chen Shui-bian's rule, Taiwan clearly had an unsuitable constitutional set-up for the political circumstances that Taiwanese society found itself in.

The third factor is Taiwan's geopolitical 'tornness', which I termed asymmetric integration. In other words, the tricky situation of managing very deep economic dependence on Mainland China with a desire to keep some political distance. This essentially was my re-statement of the so-called (re)unification vs independence debate. I argued that while both of these extremes were unlikely to be attained, and in fact undesired by the majority of society, the issue was more of *how much political distance* Taiwan should maintain from Mainland China. The issue has repeatedly manifested itself in vicious squabbles over symbolic nationness. During the DPP's rule, the ruling party, for example, attempted to change the names of state-owned companies and various landmarks, while the KMT started its rule by again changing back these names. The multiple referenda arranged in conjunction with the recent 9-in-1 local elections again saw an attempt to play on these national symbols, as one of the referendum questions (that voters rejected) asked voters whether they wished for Taiwanese sportsmen and women to compete in international sports events under the name Taiwan.

On the surface, changing the structural circumstances Taiwan finds itself in is the one factor that Taiwanese politicians seemingly have the least ability to affect. However, this is only partially true. It is certainly the case that Taiwanese politicians can only exercise limited influence on Taiwanese business investment in Mainland China, and even less on how leaders in Beijing perceived their 'core interests' (核心利益), of which Taiwan is one. However, the issue is not so much about actual *de jure* independence or formal (re)unification, but rather about disputes related to symbolic nationness. How these symbols are activated, mobilised and stirred up is something over which politicians and political parties, in particular, have much more latitude, and thereby also agency and responsibility.

The fourth factor was that of strong vested interests, aka the patronage state. Here, ameliorating structural politicization would require, on the one hand, that the perceived special benefits for some sections of society (e.g. pensions for government employees that because of generous interest rates could even exceed work time salaries) were dismantled, while at the same time a more universal welfare state was erected. From the vantage point of ameliorating society's structural politicization, the objective would be to build a sense and confidence among the general population that the state is there for everyone and not just for some privileged and politically connected people.

Finally, the last factor that I perceived as being closely associated with fostering intense politicization was a social structure that facilitated political mobilisation. This built on my field observation that one of the fundamental features of politically relevant social structures in Taiwan is the importance of vertical personal relationships. When local elections were introduced in Taiwan in the late 1940s and early 1950s, political loyalties were built on pre-existing social networks, rather than, for example, on ideology, on party identification or on media image. This tradition became firmly entrenched in the way elections were fought. The mobilisation of particularistic ties, e.g. through local factions and vote buying in election campaigning, became crucial, while both Taiwanese politicians and voters tended

Politicized Society revisited **229**

to be rather opportunistic about their party loyalties. The way that election campaigns were fought was then already partly established prior to political liberalisation and it retains many features from a one-party authoritarian context.

These strong particularistic social networks can constitute an effective means of political mobilisation, and Taiwanese politicians and political parties also frequently draw on such networks and partisan civic organisations. This has in the past promoted the intense politicization of society and gives an impression of strong political participation. In their political battles, political parties' tools of choice have been mobilisation through reliance on such social networks – the nested pyramid structures that make up parties – and mass mobilisation for political action with a view to 'bringing out the political forces' and displaying strength (造勢 *zaoshi*).[11] Both of the main political parties have honed these mobilisation tactics, although earlier the DPP was more adept at mobilising for street action (demonstrations, protests and mass rallies), while the KMT employed its social networks to deliver the vote on election say. Later, both parties emulated the other one's success in mass mobilisation for rallies and votes.

Intriguingly, the passionate participation of parts of the population coexists with increasing political disappointment and apathy among those who are not actively participating (Lee 2011; Wang 2011). Incumbency provides significant material benefits. Widespread opportunism and relatively low party loyalty further raise the stakes for politicians. Political support in Taiwan can be fickle and potential losses for politicians substantial. When the political situation remains relatively evenly divided, political opportunists within the two major political blocks often switch to whichever side appears to offer better prospects. This puts the onus on politicians, especially leading politicians, not to put these social structures in the service of partisan politics to the extent that they come to undermine political and social trust, as well as trust in democracy itself.

Concluding remarks

Samuel Huntington famously argued that a transition to democracy would not be complete until power had changed hands twice in a peaceful and orderly manner; once from the old ruling party to a new ruling party and the second time back to the old rulers, i.e. the so-called double turnover test (Huntington 1991: 266–267). By this token, Taiwan's democracy was consolidated in 2008, when the KMT returned to power, which ended a period of democratic careening, similar to, but in some important ways different from, Thailand (Slater 2013). However, as my argument has been that the problems of Taiwan's democracy run deeper than just the political institutional setting of elections and constitutions, my own test for Taiwan's democracy is stricter. For me, the real litmus test would come if and when the KMT lost power for a second time, as the first time the opposition party was not able to break the KMT's structural hold on power.

More than two years have now passed since the KMT's second loss of power, and one can say that it looks as if Taiwan's political system will pass the litmus test. Gone are many of the more problematic aspects of Taiwanese politics, such as

230 Mikael Mattlin

ruling party-organised mass demonstrations and instrumentally used partisan referenda, as well as the excessive manipulation of national symbols for partisan ends. Instead, the DPP has focused more on achieving its desired political and social transformations through the Legislative Yuan and other institutional means. In other words, politics has increasingly confined itself to that sphere of society where it belongs, rather than spilling over into other spheres. Taiwanese society is gradually becoming depoliticized.

Visible signs of politicization subsided post-2008 for several reasons, one of which was people's general sense of *ennui* after several years of intense political fighting. Latent structural politicization cannot be overcome overnight, as it has created its own political culture that thrives on, and continuously re-enacts confrontational politics (Mattlin 2018: 26–27). Culture – as Wendt cogently reminds us – is a self-fulfilling prophecy. Culture does not preclude change, but it does tend towards homeostasis and relative stability. This suggests that Taiwan's overly politicized society can be transcended over time. There is always scope for contestation in culture, there are often internal contradictions between different cultural logics, and agents are never perfectly socialised (Wendt 2010: 186–189). What the previous section points to is that leading politicians and other influential actors (e.g. prominent journalists and scholars) have an important responsibility in not purposefully playing on and playing up political divisions, thereby activating society's latent politicization potential. For democratic competition to work well despite partisan bifurcation, responsible political agency is a central prerequisite. In a politicized society, politicization is akin to a daily referendum, to borrow the famous expression by Ernest Renan. This is one referendum that could do with a lower turnout.

Democratic consolidation requires not only a shared normative commitment, but also a behavioural commitment by all sectors of society to the democratic system (Linz and Stepan 1997: 14–33). On this count, many of the key political players flunked the test during the first period of DPP rule. As Chang et al. (2011: 615) put it, 'they paid only lip service to civility, compromise, tolerance, due process, and rule of law, all essential elements in making a liberal democracy work'. So far things look a bit better during the DPP's second time in power. However, it must be stressed that learning civility in democratic politics is a long process, which can also go into reverse. Norbert Elias famously argued that exercising self-restraint is the essence of civilisation (Elias 1982). Later, Wendt also gave self-restraint a prominent role when explaining how relationships between states can be transformed and collective identity built (Wendt 2010: 357–363). Recently, we have gotten ample evidence that political civility and self-restraint can also be lost, even in established democracies, if it is not protected by its guardians, i.e. by leading politicians. Responsible political agency is today in short supply globally.

Acknowledgements

The author would like to thank Dafydd Fell for constructive comments on the first draft of this chapter, as well the audience at the 2nd World Congress of Taiwan

Studies in London SOAS, June 2015, for good comments on the presentation based on the first draft.

Notes

1 Earlier, the concept had been used (usually in passing) by a few studies on other countries, but in a narrower meaning, related mainly to politicization of the civil service.
2 *Politicized Society: Taiwan's Struggle with Its One-Party Past* (Copenhagen: NIAS Press, 2018).
3 This section is based especially on the final chapter of the first edition of *Politicized Society* (Mattlin 2011).
4 Lipset has stated that '[t]he greater the importance of the central state as a source of prestige and advantage, the less likely it is that those in power – or the forces of opposition – will accept rules of the game that institutionalise party conflict and could result in the turnover of those in office' (Lipset 1994: 4).
5 Reviews have appeared in, among others, *The China Quarterly, The China Journal, China Information, The Journal of Asian Studies, China Review International, Issues & Studies* (a double-book review) and the *Taiwan Journal of East Asian Studies* (17-page review).
6 Another notable American scholar, Thomas Gold, agreed that the comparison with the U.S. system is 'a fundamentally misguided approach' (Gold 2013).
7 As a side-note, the first book cover suggestion for the first edition was rather dramatic, with a pitch-black background, a fish-shell pattern and a cracking font. I immediately rejected this cover suggestion because it did not convey the fine balance that I wished to strike with my book.
8 Political scientist Nathan Batto stressed the point that Taiwan's political networks are, in his view, somewhat more fluid than the nested pyramid structure model lets on. Discussion in Taipei, 3 January 2017.
9 It even happened that students were expelled from school for having the 'wrong' party affiliation.
10 In political science books on European politics, Finland used to be placed in the same bracket as Italy and Belgium, with perennially unstable governments.
11 Already the very early *dangwai* candidates made extensive use of social networks, based on kinship, friendship and community faction, in order to build political support (Chao and Myers 2000: 402).

References

Akkerman, Tjitske*et al.*2004. 'The Interactive State: Democratisation from Above?' *Political Studies* 52, 82–95.
Almond, Gabriel and Sidney Verba. 1963. *The Civic Culture. Political Attitudes and Democracy in Five Nations.* Princeton: Princeton University Press.
Chang, Yu-tzung, Yun-han Chu and Min-hua Huang. 2011. 'Procedural Quality Only? Taiwanese Democracy Reconsidered'. *International Political Science Review* 32(5), 598–619.
Chang, Yu-tzung and Yun-han Chu. 2007. 'Traditionalism, Political Learning and Conceptions of Democracy in East Asia'. Working paper series, 39. Asian Barometer Project Office Taipei.
Chao, Linda and Ramon H. Myers. 2000. 'How Elections Promoted Democracy in Taiwan under Martial Law'. *The China Quarterly* 162, 387–409.
Clark, Cal and Alexander C. Tan. 2010. 'Taiwan Enters the 21st Century: A Rude Awakening to the Costs of Success'. In Lee Wei-Chin (ed), *Taiwan's Politics in the 21st Century: Changes and Challenges.* Hackensack, NJ: World Scientific.

232 Mikael Mattlin

Elias, Norbert. 1982. *The Civilizing Process*. New York: Pantheon.
Ferguson, Niall. 2017. *The Square and the Tower. Networks, Hierarchies and the Struggle for Global Power*. London: Allen Lane.
Forsberg, Tuomas and Matti Pesu. 2016. 'The "Finlandisation" of Finland: The Ideal Type, the Historical Model and Lessons Learnt'. *Diplomacy & Statecraft* 27(3), 473–495.
Freedom House. 2018. 'Freedom in the World 2018. Table of Country Scores'. https://freedomhouse.org/report/freedom-world-2018-table-country-scores
Gold, Thomas B. 2013. 'Book Review of Politicized Society: The Long Shadow of Taiwan's One-Party Legacy'. *The Journal of Asian Studies* 72(1), 187–188.
Greene, Kenneth F. 2007. *Why Dominant Parties Lose: Mexico's Democratization in Comparative Perspective*. New York: Cambridge University Press.
Heidar, K. and Saglie, J. 2003. 'A Decline of Linkage? Intra-party Participation in Norway, 1991–2000'. *European Journal of Political Research* 42, 761–786.
Huntington, Samuel P. 1991 *The Third Wave. Democratization in the Late Twentieth Century*. Norman, OK: University of Oklahoma Press.
IPI Press Freedom Index. 2018. World Press Freedom Index. https://rsf.org/en/ranking/2018
Jacobs, J.Bruce. 2012a. 'Review'. *China Review International* 19(3), 367–375.
Jacobs, J.Bruce. 2012b. *Democratizing Taiwan*. Leiden: Brill.
Kaeding, Malte Philipp. 2013. 'Book review of Politicized Society: The Politicized Society: The Long Shadow of Taiwan's One-Party Legacy'. *The China Journal* 69, 209–212.
Kostadinova, Tatiana. 2003. 'Voter Turnout Dynamics in Post-Communist Europe'. *European Journal of Political Research* 42, 741–759.
Lee, Jyun-yi. 2011. 'The Specter of the Past: Explaining Politicization in Taiwan'. *Issues & Studies* 47(4), 178–181.
Li, Chenghong. 2005. 'Two-Level Games, Issue Politicization and the Disarray of Taiwan Cross-Strait Policy after The 2000 Presidential Election'. *East Asia* 22(3), 41–62.
Linz, Juan and Stepan, Alfred. 1997. 'Toward Consolidated Democracies'. In Larry Diamond *et al.* (eds), *Consolidating the Third Wave Democracies. Themes and Perspectives*. Baltimore, MD: The Johns Hopkins University Press, pp. 14–33.
Lipset, Seymour Martin. 1960. *Political Man: The Social Bases of Politics*. New York: Doubleday and Company.
Lipset, Seymour Martin. 1994. 'The Social Requisites of Democracy Revisited: 1993 Presidential Address'. *American Sociological Review* 59(1), 1–22.
Mahoney, James. 2000. 'Path Dependence in Historical Sociology'. *Theory and Society* 29(4), 507–548.
Marx, Karl. 1852. 'The Eighteenth Brumaire of Louis Bonaparte'. Available at: www.marxists.org/archive/marx/works/1852/18th-brumaire/ch01.htm
Mattlin, Mikael. 2004. 'Nested Pyramid Structures: Political Parties in Taiwanese Elections'. *The China Quarterly* 180, 1021–1039.
Mattlin, Mikael. 2011. *Politicized Society: The Long Shadow of Taiwan's One-Party Legacy*. Copenhagen: NIAS Press.
Mattlin, Mikael. 2018. *Politicized Society: Taiwan's Struggle With its One-Party Past*, 2nd edn. Copenhagen: NIAS Press.
Putnam, Robert D. 2000. *Bowling Alone: The Collapse and Revival of American Community*. New York: Simon & Schuster.
Rich, Timothy S. 2005. 'Taiwan in Crisis: The Politicization of SARS and Chen Shuibian's Re-election'. *Graduate Journal of Asia-Pacific Studies* 3(1), 67–75.

Rigger, Shelley. 2004. 'The Unfinished Business of Taiwan's Democratization'. In Nancy Bernkopf Tucker (ed.), *Dangerous Strait: The U.S.-Taiwan-China Crisis*. New York: Columbia University Press, pp. 16–43.

Rigger, Shelley. 2018. 'Studies on Taiwan's Democracy and Democratisation'. *International Journal of Taiwan Studies*, 1(1), 141–160.

Rokkan, Stein. 1967. *Geography, Religion, and Social Class: Crosscutting Cleavages in Norwegian Politics*. New York: Free Press.

Rubinstein, Murray A. 2014. 'Book Review of Politicized Society: The Long Shadow of Taiwan's One-Party Legacy'. *Taiwan Journal of East Asian Studies*, 11(1), 253–269.

Slater, Dan. 2018. 'Portable Feasts: The Timeless Value of Case Studies like *Politicized Society*'. Foreword to *Politicized Society. Taiwan's Struggle With its One-Party Past*. Copenhagen: NIAS Press, xi–xvi.

Slater, Dan. 2013. 'Democratic Careening'. *World Politics* 65(4), 729–763.

Wang, Hung-chung. 2011. 'Is Taiwanese Society Intensely Politicized?' *Issues & Studies* 47(4), 182–185.

Wendt, Alexander. 2010. *Social Theory of International Politics*, 13th edn. Cambridge: Cambridge University Press.

INDEX

Note: Illustrations are indicated by page numbers in *italics*.

Abbott, Diane 48
*Alternative Chinese Opera in
  the Age of Globalization* (Lei) 173
Anarchical Society, The (Bull) 68–69
Anderson, Benedict 66
Andrade, Tonio 126, 135n29
Australian Journal of Chinese Affairs, The
  19–20

Beijing massacre 5, 53–55, 64, 114
Belden, Jack 49
Betting on Biotech (Wong) 10
Bianco, Lucien 50
Bilateral links between civil society and
  democracy 27–28
Blacklist Workshop 171
BNHI *see* Bureau of National
  Health Insurance (BNHI)
book reviews 8–9
Bosco, Joe 81
Bourdieu, Pierre 44
Boyer, Christine 107n8
Brazil 147
Brown, Melissa J. 9, 11, 112–132
Bull, Hedley 68–70
Bureau of National Health Insurance
  (BNHI) 144, 147, 156
Burma 54

Carlson, Ellsworth 35
Carroll, Peter 167–168

Carter, Jimmy 40
Chan, Lien 53, 183, 190
Cheek, Timothy 124, 126
Chen, Rou-Lan 128
Chen Chu 83–84, 105
Chen Fang-ming 185
Cheng Jei-cheng 210
Cheng Tzu-leong 180
Cheng Ying-chen 39
Chen Ming-chang 171
Chen Ming-tong 82
Chen Sheng 171
Chen Shui-bian 118, 171, 175,
  185, 192, 225, 227
Chen Wen-chien 185
Chen Yi 83
Chiang Ching-kuo 35–36, 38–39,
  64, 78, 223
Chiang Kai-shek 34–35, 64, 77–78
Chile 147–148
China: civil society organisations in 26–27;
  Cultural Revolution in 36, 164;
  diplomatic recognition of, by US 51;
  Hong Kong and 56; imperialism and 122;
  political distance with 228; reunification
  with 57–58, 76–78, 83, 121, 125,
  183–185, 193–194, 228; threat of 58
*China and the Question of Taiwan: Documents
  and Analysis* (Chiu) 65
China Journal, The 19–20
China Tribune (magazine) 18

Index **235**

Chinese Cultural Renaissance 164
Chinese identity 37, 39, 44, 67–68, 70, 83, 87, 123, 128–129, 134n18, 134n20, 165–166, 183–184, 207, 219
Chinese Nationalism in the Global Era (Hughes) 10
Chinese Studies 1
Chiu Hungdah 65
Chuang, Ya-Chung 129
Chuang Ying-chang 132n6
Chu Yun-han 187–188
civil society 18–19, 21, 26–30
civil society organisations (CSOs) 26–27
Clark, Cal 124
Clifford, James 204
Clough, Ralph 51
Cohen, Judah 168
Comparative Economic Transformations (Wu) 142
conference organisations 1
Confucian China and Its Modern Fate (Levenson) 63
consumption inequality 153
Contending Approaches to the Political Economy of Taiwan (Winckler and Greenhalgh, eds) 41
Corbyn, Jeremy 48
corruption 182–183
cosmopolitanism 130–132
Cradock, Percy 53
CSOs *see* civil society organisations (CSOs)
Cuba 54
Cultural Revolution 36, 164
Czech Republic 225

Dawley, Evan N. 124
democracy 27–30; welfare and 145–147
Democratic Progressive Party (DPP) 23–28, 42, 56–58, 68, 76–78, 82–85, 87n3, 91, 144, 149, 151, 175, 180–186, 189–193, 215, 220–221, 224–226, 229–230
Democratization in China and Taiwan: The Adaptability of Leninist Parties (Dickson) 86
Deng Xiaoping 54–55, 63, 112
Dependent Development (Evans) 40
Dickson, Bruce 86
Dikötter, Frank 50
diplomatic recognition 55–56
Dirlik, Arif 129
doctoral dissertations 6–7
Dreyer, June 72

Eighteen Lords Temple 104
elections 8, 22–23, 27, 45, 57, 64, 68, 72–73, 76, 78–83, 86, 87n3, 123, 146,

171, 175, 176n5, 179–195, 215–216, 221–223, 228–229
Embedded Autonomy (Evans) 142
Environmental movements 24–25
environmental sociology 16–17
Evans, Peter 40, 142

family 94, 97–99, 105–106
farmers' movement 21–22
Feldman, Marc 127
Fell, Dafydd 8–10, 132n1, 162, 178–195
feminism 103; *see also* gender; women
Fenno, Richard 80–81
Fifty Years of Peking Opera in Taiwan (Wang) 169
Finland 226–227
Fligstein, Neil 44
folk linguists 207–208
Fong, Shiaw-chian 124
Formosa Betrayed (Kerr) 65
From Opposition to Power: Taiwan's Democratic Progressive Party (Rigger) 81
Fukuyama, Francis 54

Gates, Hill 38, 96–98
Gellner, Ernest 66
gender: and intersectionality 105–106; labour and 96–106; in post-industrial Taiwan 106–107; Taiwan in literature of 93–96
Gini coefficient 145, 149, 152–153
Gladney, Dru 79
global industrialisation 93–96
Gold, Thomas B. 2, 10, 34–45, 65
Governing the Market (Wade) 142
Government and Politics in Taiwan (Fell) 9–10
growth 148–150
Guy, Nancy 4, 8, 10, 160–176, *163–164, 170*

Haggard, Stephan 79, 142, 148
Halperin, Rhoda 127
Han 115–117, 119, 124
Harrell, Steve 123, 127
Hau Pei-tsun 185
HCIP *see* Health Care Improvement Program (HCIP)
Health Care Improvement Program (HCIP) 156
Healthy Democracies and Welfare Politics in Taiwan (Wong) 3, 141–157
Hershatter, Gail 127
Holliday, Ian 143
Homei 92–96, 107n3
Hong, Keelung 123

236 Index

Hong Kong 56
Hsiao, Hsin-Huang Michael 8–9, 15–31
Hsieh Chi-ta 186
Hsieh Tung-min 98
Hsu Hsin-liang 39, 68, 185
Hsu Ying-chun 168
Huang, Shuanfan 197
Huang Chun-ming 39
Hughes, Christopher 8–10, 63–74
Hungary 225
Huntington, Samuel 43
Hu Yaobang 52, 63–64

identity, national 66–67, 70, 78, 87, 117,
   119–121, 123–124, 128, 130, 180,
   182–184; *See also* Chinese identity;
   Taiwanese identity
industrialisation 93–96
inequality 152–153
International Journal of Taiwan Studies 2, 10
intersectionality 105–106
*In the Name of Harmony and Prosperity: Labor
   and Gender Politics in Taiwan's Economic
   Restructuring* (Lee) 3, 91–107
Island China (Clough) 51
Is Taiwan Chinese? (Brown) 9, 11, 112–132

Jacobs, Bruce 220, 223
Jacoby, Annalee 49
Japan 148, 226
Johnson, Chalmers 43

Kafalas, Philip 123
Kaohsiung Association for the Promotion of
   Women's Rights (KAPWR) 101,
   103, 105
Kao Hui-lan 168–169, *170*
Kaufman, Robert 148
Kedourie, Elie 63, 66
Kekkonen, Urho 227
Kerr, George 65
kinship 97–99
Kissinger, Henry 36
Klöter, Henning 4, 11, 197–211
Koeh Chhiu-seng 197, 200
Koo, Vivien Huai-chun 174
Koo Chen-fu 78, 174
Korea 28
Kung, H. H. 34
Kuomintang (KMT) 9, 18, 21–28, 37–39,
   41, 43–45, 48–50, 53, 57, 64, 66–67, 70,
   73, 76–78, 80, 82–84, 86, 98, 144–149,
   151, 162–168, 173–175, 180–184, 186,
   190–191, 193–194, 215, 217–219, 221,
   223–224, 229

labour: foreign 96–97; gender and 96–106;
   migrant 96–97; in post-industrial
   Taiwan 106–107
labour movement 21
Lamounier, Bolivar 80
language: and folk linguists 207–208; policy
   11; Taiwanese 4, 197–211, *211*
Laos 54
Lee, Anru 3, 91–107
Lee Ching-hua 186
Lee Teng-hui 64–65, 67–68, 71, 76–77,
   184–185, 223
Lei, Daphne 173
Leifer, Michael 72
Levenson, Joseph 63, 69
Levine, Sheila 122
Leys, Simon 69
Li, Yitan 129
Liao, Ping-Hui 129
Li Kuo-ting 39
Lin Feng-yi 168
linguistic landscapes 211, *211*
Lin Hwai-min 39
Lin Shengxiang 171
Lipset, S. M. 227
Living Rooms as Factories 98–99
Long, Simon 3, 48–59
Long March generation 56
Long March to Power, The (Harrison) 50
Lo Wen-chia 185

Magic of Beverly Sills, The (Guy) 10, 170
Mahoney, James 151
Mao Zedong 37, 67
Mattlin, Mikael 4, 8–9, 215–231
Mayall, James 65, 68
Ma Ying-jeou 55, 175, 183, 218
Ma Yuqi 161, 169
memorialisation 103–105
Memorial Park for Women Laborers
   99–106
Merwin, Douglas 42
Metzger, Thomas 134n18
Mexico 147, 219
Miao 118–119, 134n15
middle class 27–30, 92
migrant labour 96–97
minjien social force 18
minjien society 18
Minogue, Kenneth 63, 66
MITI and the Japanese Miracle (Johnson) 43
*Mobile Horizons: Dynamics across the Taiwan
   Strait* (Yeh) 83
Murray, Stephen 123
Myers, Ramon 134n18

Index   237

Nachman, Lev 10
National Coalition Party (Finland) 226
National Health Insurance (NHI) 143–144, 146, 150–151, 155–156
national identity 66–67, 70, 78, 87, 117, 119–121, 123–124, 128, 130, 180, 182–184
Nationalism and International Society (Mayall) 68
Nationalist Party *see* Kuomintang (KMT)
National Unification Council 76
National Unification Guidelines 76, 185
nativist literature 39
New Party (NP) 180, 184, 189–190, 193
New Tide Faction 185
Ng Sek-hui 197, 200
NHI *see* National Health Insurance (NHI)
Nixon, Richard 35–36
North Korea 54
NP *see* New Party (NP)

Oberlin College 34–35
Ooi, Su-Mei 124
Origins of the Chinese Revolution, The (Bianco) 50

Pang, Cecilia 167–168
Pan Inghai 114–115, 127
Parsons, Talcott 36–37
parties, political 4, 11, 25, 27, 29, 39, 51, 66, 68, 86–87, 146, 149, 152, 154–155, 178–186, 188–195, 218, 223–226, 228–229; *See also specific parties*
Party Politics in Taiwan (Fell) 9, 178–195
Pathways From the Periphery (Haggard) 142
Peck, Graham 49
Peking Opera and Politics in Taiwan (Guy) 4, 160–176, *163–164, 170*
Peng, Ito 150
Peng Ming-min 67, 73, 185
People First Party (PFP) 189
PFP *see* People First Party (PFP)
PhD 4–7, 10, 15, 36, 64–65, 72, 79, 161, 178–179, 186–188, 198
Philippines 54
Pierson, Paul 151
Pike, Kenneth 204
Poland 225
Political Change in Taiwan (Cheng and Haggard, eds.) 20
Politicized Society: The Long Shadow of Taiwan's One-Party Legacy (Mattlin) 4, 215–231

Politics in Taiwan: Voting for Democracy Revisited (Rigger) 3, 75–87
Prmi 130

Qi Rushan 164

Remaking Taiwan: Society and the State since the End of Martial Law (Gold) 44
reviews, book 8–9
Rigger, Shelley 1, 3, 5, 8, 10, 65, 75–87, 187–188, 220
Rokkan, Stein 227
Rubinstein, Murray 187, 220
Rueda, David 155
Russia 225

Schram, Stuart 64
Schubert, Gunter 220
Senkaku Islands 36
Sharpe, M.E. 42
Shen Xingyi 124–125, 135n23
Shih, Chih-yu 124
Sills, Beverly 10, 172
Silvio, Teri 172, 176n1
Skocpol, Theda 37–38
Slater, Dan 10, 146, 220, 223
Slovakia 225
Smith, Anthony 65–66
Snow, Edgar 49, 67
SOAS University of London 1
social movements 19–21, 26
social science theories 7–8
social welfare 21, 23–24, 34, 142–144, 148–152, 154, 180–183, 186, 189, 191, 227
Social Welfare Movements in Taiwan (Hsiao and Lind, eds.) 24–25
South Korea 28, 54–56, 142, 144–147
Soviet Union 54
State and Society in the Taiwan Miracle (Gold) 2, 34–45, 65
state-society relations 20–27
subsequent research 9–11
Sullivan, Jonathan 2
Sutton, Don 127

TAHR *see* Taiwan Association for Human Rights (TAHR)
Taiwan and Chinese Nationalism: Identity and Status in International Society (Hughes) 3, 63–74
Taiwan Association for Human Rights (TAHR) 84

238 Index

Taiwan: China's Last Frontier (Long) 3, 48–59
Taiwanese identity 43, 45, 65, 68, 83, 101, 113, 117–118, 120, 123–124, 128, 130, 134n18, 183–184, 191, 219
Taiwanese language 197–211, *211*
Taiwan's Consumers' Movement: Theory and Practice (Hsiao et al) 16
Taiwan's Emerging Social Movements (Hsu and Sung, eds.) 19
Taiwan's Future Trends (Hsiao) 17
"Taiwan Society at the Fin de Siecle" (Gold) 43
Taiwan Solidarity Union (TSU) 75–76, 189–190
Taiwan's Social Problems (Yang and Yeh, eds) 16
Taiyu *see* Taiwanese language
Tan, Hwee-San 167
Tan, Shzr Ee 168
Taste of Freedom, A (Peng) 67
Taylor, Jay 50
Teng, Emma 128
Thailand 225
Thelen, Kathleen 151
Tiananmen *see* Beijing massacre
Tiaoyutai Islands 36
Treasure Island 92–93
Tripartite links of middle class, civil society and democracy 29–30
Trump, Donald 58–59
Tsai Ing-wen 58–59, 77, 192
Tsang, Steve 223
Tseng, Chiu-yu 127
TSU *see* Taiwan Solidarity Union (TSU)
Tujia 118–120, 130
Tunghai University 35
Turkey 225
Twenty-five Ladies' Tomb 100–101, 104

University of Texas at Austin 1
urban non-homeowners protest movement 23

Vietnam 54
Vogel, Ezra 36

Wachman, Alan 65, 124
Wade, Robert 142
Wakeman, Fred 122–123
Wang, Fu-chang 124
Wang An-ch'i 169, 172
Wang Chen-ho 39
Wang Daohan 78
Wang Hung-chung 221
Wang To 39
wealth inequality 152–153
We Have Only One Taiwan: Anti-Pollution, Eco-Conservation, and Environmental Movements (Hsiao) 16–17
welfare: political parties and 181–182; *see also* social welfare
welfare state 142–147
Weller, Rob 127
Wendt, Alexander 222, 230
White, Theodore 49
Why Taiwan Matters (Rigger) 10, 83
Wolf, Arthur 123, 127, 132n6
women 94–95, 99–106, 131
Wong, Joseph 3, 8–10, 141–157
Writing Taiwanese (Klöter) 4, 11, 197–211
Wu, Yu-Shan 142

Xi Jinping 55, 58, 112, 132n2

Yahuda, Michael 65
Yang Ch'ing-ch'u 39
Yang Qingchu 207
Yao Li-ming 185
Yeh, Wen-hsin 83
Ye Shenglan 160
Yinger, Milton 36
Yugoslavia 68

Zhang Huimei 171
Zhou Enlai 119, 134n16, 224
Zhu Toupi 171
Zima, Petr 201